Adrenaline Adventures: Dream it. Read it. Do it!

A Guide to
Cool Personal Challenges,
Fun Competitive Dates, and Ways to Bond With
Your Child in a Weekend

By
Fran Capo

1663 LIBERTY DRIVE, SUITE 200
BLOOMINGTON, INDIANA 47403
(800) 839-8640
www.authorhouse.com

© 2004 Fran Capo
All Rights Reserved.

No part of this book may be reproduced, stored in a retrieval system, or transmitted by any means without the written permission of the author.

First published by AuthorHouse 06/25/04

ISBN: 1-4184-6417-1 (sc)

Library of Congress Control Number: 2004093585

Printed in the United States of America
Bloomington, Indiana

This book is printed on acid-free paper.

Cover Design by Steve Heiden
Heidenstudio.com

What Readers Are Saying about *Adrenaline Adventures*:

"Fran's new book is a *motivator*. The challenges that she describes in these fantastic stories give you the adrenaline rush to actually go out and do them. As a career United States Marine at the highest enlisted rank of Master Gunnery Sergeant (equivalent to Sergeant Major), I've faced many challenges in my life including service in Desert Storm, Somalia, and many places throughout the world. Fran's wonderful sense of humor and keen writing skills bring a special brilliance shining a light on the life- enhancing value of challenging yourself to the greatest degree. Having read many of Fran's works before, I already had high expectations. I was *NOT DISAPPOINTED*. Buckle up your seatbelt , this book takes you on a roller coaster ride through the greatest adventures that a modern day person can even imagine."

Ted Isaacson
Master Gunnery Sergeant
United States Marine Corps

"As the Guinness Book World Record holder for the most world Records, I am always looking for new things to challenge my mind, spirit, and body. I love exploring the world for new places to break records, and new records to try for the fun of it and to prove that nothing is impossible. Fran Capo's book, *Adrenaline Adventures*, has that same spirit, and the best thing is she tells it in a funny way. I'm inspired to go out and try some of the adventures that I didn't know about. Fran tells it in a way that makes people feel they are living the experience and then motivates them to reach inside themselves, put fear aside, and just do it."

Ashrita Furman,
Guinness Book's World's Most Versatile Man
He has set 82 Guinness world records

Dedication

To my wonderful mom, Rose, who always stopped whatever she was doing to hear about my thoughts, dreams, and challenges. You were always there for me no matter what I chose to do. And above all, it was you who taught me that nothing is impossible,
and obviously every chance I get, I set out to prove you right.
Thanks Mom ☺ I love you.

Table of Contents

What Readers Are Saying about **Adrenaline Adventures**: v
Dedication vii
Author's Note and disclaimer xiii
Introduction xix
HOW TO USE THIS BOOK xxv
A WORD ABOUT THE MILD TO WILD METER xxvii

Chapter 1 "Call out the Saint Bernard"
          Downhill Skiing 1

Chapter 2 "Okay, I'll jump. Just don't push."
          Static Line Skydiving 13

Chapter 3 "Getting High Before Class"
          Flying Lessons in a Cessna 23

Chapter 4 "Full of Hot Air"
          Hot Air Ballooning 33

Chapter 5 "A Plunge into Dark Waters"
          Night Diving 43

Chapter 6 "If you hit a wall - climb over it"
          Rock Climbing and Rappelling 53

Chapter 7 "Crawling a Mile Below"
          Spelunking 63

Chapter 8 "A Rubber Band!"
          Bungee Cord Jumping 73

Chapter 9 "Smokin' Tootsies"
          Walking on Hot Coals 81

Chapter 10 "A Crater Full of Adventure"
          Biking Down a Volcano 93

Chapter 11 "A Bird's Eye View of Paradise"
          Parasailing 103

Chapter 12 "Look Ma No Engine."
   Soaring in a Sailplane 111

Chapter 13 "Thar She Blows"
   Whale Watching 121

Chapter 14 "Riding the Big Kahuna"
   Surfing 135

Chapter 15 "Where's Rudolph When You Need Him?"
   Dogsledding in Alaska 143

Chapter 16 "Swim with the Sharks"
   Scuba Diving with Sharks 151

Chapter 17 "You Don't Need a Cell Phone or High
   Heels to Climb a Mountain"
   Rock Scrambling 161

Chapter 18 "On Top of the World"
   A journey on a Ultralight 171

Chapter 19 "The Doorless Chopper"
   Learning to Fly a Helicopter 181

Chapter 20 "Niagara - Not Just for Lovers"
   Jet Boat Ride 189

Chapter 21 "I Ain't Afraid of No Ghost"
   Ghost Sighting 195

Chapter 22 "She Flies Through the Air...."
   Learning the Trapeze 205

Chapter 23 "Is that an Alligator I see?"
   Everglades Airboat Ride 215

Chapter 24 "Whatever you do, don't roll me"
   Kayaking 225

Chapter 25 "Rafting the Magnificent Canyon"
   Whitewater Rafting 235

Chapter 26 "Running into the New Year"
   New Year's Eve Midnight Run 245

Chapter 27 "A Silent Adventure"
   Snorkeling With Manatees 255

Chapter 28 "I'll Get You, Red Baron!"
   Fighter Pilot For a Day 267

Chapter 29 "At the Speed of Luge"
   Winter Luge 277

Chapter 30 "Just Call Me Maria Andretti"
   Racecar Driving 289

Chapter 31 "To the Top in the Land of Oz"
   Bridge Climb 299

Chapter 32 "Just How Long is This Borough Anyway?"
   Running a Marathon 309

Chapter 33 "Don't Forget to Put on Your Back-up Lights"
   Backward Race 331

Chapter 34 "This Ain't No Stationary Bike!"
   Bike New York..341

Chapter 35 "Everything You Always Wanted to Know about
   Survival But Didn't Know Who to Ask"
   Survival School...357

Chapter 36 "There's Still Gold and Ghosts in Them Thar Hills"
   Panning for Gold...383

Chapter 37 "A Dolphin Adventure and Other Marine
   Encounters of the Best Kind"
   Swimming with Dolphins 399

Chapter 38 "Zorro for the Day"
   Fencing 411

Chapter 39 "The Hidden World of Akumal"
   Cavern Diving...423

Chapter 40 "A Hot Weekend of Glass"
   Glassblowing..443

Chapter 41 "Horses and mules and jeeps ... oh my"
   A Western Spirit Adventure 459

xi

Chapter 42 "A Leap of Faith"
    Tandem Skydiving 477

Chapter 43 "Leader of the Pack"
    Learning to Ride a Motorcycle 495

Chapter 44 "Who You Calling a Blimp?"
    Blimp Ride..513

Chapter 45 "Skydiving without the Splat Factor"
    Simulation Skydive..529

Chapter 46 "That's Just Bull!"
    Riding a Mechanical Bull 537

Chapter 47 "Sleeping with the Fish"
    Sleeping at an Aquarium..545

Chapter 48 "Becoming a Polar Bear"
    Doing the Polar Bear Plunge....................................557

Chapter 49 "An Inward Adrenaline Rush"
    Floatation Tank 571

Chapter 50 "This Ain't Coney Island!"
    Two World Record Rides..583

FINAL NOTE 595

Check out Fran Capo's other books....................................597

Look for Fran's upcoming books...599

Author's Note and disclaimer

The author assumes no liability for accidents happening to, or injuries sustained by, readers who engage in activities described in this book. These are risky adventures. Use common sense, take only calculated risks, and make sure the outfit you are doing the adventure with has experience and a good safety record.

Thank you, thank you, thank you!

- To my adorable son, Spencer, who not only joins me on many of these wonderful adventures, but also understands my endless hours of writing about them so others can go out and enjoy them as well. As our friend Anna used to say about Spencer, "That kid's going to grow up to me a mattress salesmen, just so he can get some rest!"

- To my wonderful, fiancé Steve, who in the beginning, when he was trying to impress me in the courting stage, went on many of these adventures with me and paid for them to boot! These days he picks and chooses and has no problem with me taking others along for the ride; in fact, he even suggests that I take ex-boyfriends on some of them. Now that's one special guy. Either that or he is trying to get rid of me. ☺

- To my fantastic editor, Charlene. Thank you. This is our fourth book together. You not only make me look like I know where all my commas and quotes go, but you offer support and invaluable advice. I am going to hold you to your word that we will do an adventure together one day. (Oh and one disclaimer: if you see any mistakes in grammar, punctuation, or spelling, they are all mine. Sometimes Charlene offered advice and I stubbornly said, "No, I need to say it this way, even if it's grammatically incorrect. (You know us comics, rather go for the laugh than the grammar.)

- To my patient mom, Rose who sat with me for twelve hours picking out pictures for the book.

- To Steve Heiden, my creative cover guy. Thanks for doing another awesome job. And thank you for all your support and confidence in all my projects, even if you do think I'm nuts. You still have to come out to a comedy show one of these days.

- To all the instructors on these many adventures who have safely led my friends, family, and me on awesome trips—Thanks! Thanks for your knowledge, expertise, and for a fantastic time. You gave me something to write about.

- To Dan Heise at AuthorHouse who worked with me to get this book out on the fast track. You have been supportive and great to work with since my last book, *Almost a Wise Guy*. You were always on top of things, and because of you and your team, we were able to meet the deadline. And remember: no bald, fat gerbils, alligators, or cats were harmed in the making of this book.

- To Brian and Steven of the Steven Style Group, thanks once again for a dynamite media campaign. We did 231 radio shows in one month last time, let's see if we can set a new world record.

- To Charles Higgens, Alex Marine and Dale Preston at AuthorHouse, thank you so much for your expertise on the formatting of this book. You made it look great.

- To Eric Kendall and the production team at AuthorHouse, thanks for working so fast and efficiently.

- Thanks to all of my friends, Viv, Malcolm, Heidi, Keith, Martha, Alan, Lisa, Dee and J.M., and Todd who went on these adventures with me.

- Thanks to my friends, Ted, Ashrita, Ali, Nancy, Donna, Noami, Pam, Janette, and Barry for being so supportive of my work.

- Thanks to Jamie Davis for being a good sport and keeping up with your dad's crazy fiancée and trying out new things. I'll get you to run marathons without fancy sneakers yet!

- To all the EFT staff, thanks for not panicking when I take your boss out on yet another adventure.

- Thanks to Dr. Forim for always getting me better just before I have to do one of these adventures, and his wife Miriam for all her in-house publicity on my books.

- Thanks to Michael Johnson, Robert McCormack, Herb, Celestina, Carmel and Joan - my team at AuthorHouse, my wonderful publisher, for believing in me so much that they sponsored, in part, my adventure to climb Kilimanjaro which will be featured in *Adrenaline Adventures Two*. When you guys say you are with an author every step of the journey, you really mean it!

- Thanks to my other sponsor, Snickers Marathon Energy bars, who with their delicious bar kept my son, Spencer and I powered to the top of Kilimanjaro!

- To the Big Kahuna in the clouds. Thanks for always keeping me safe on all these adventures.

- If there is anyone I left out, you will just have to join me on a future adventure so you can get your name in print.

Introduction

"**Never be afraid to try something new.
Remember that amateurs built the Ark.
Professionals built the Titanic."**
—**Author Unknown**

When I was a kid, my mom, Rose, gave me three pieces of philosophy to live by: 1) Have a positive attitude. 2) Nothing's impossible. 3) Try new things.

My dad, Frank, (Or Frankie Crooks to those of you who read *Almost a Wise Guy*) added his two cents by teaching me to laugh at things and not to take life so seriously. So between the two of them, I would try something new, and if it didn't work, I'd learn to laugh at it later. I don't think either of them realized what a comedic daredevil they were creating.

My parents didn't just casually hand out these philosophies.

They had me live them. My dad, as you will read in the motorcycle chapter, had me riding on the front of his motorcycle at the tender age of two, and he would take me down to the Hudson River to throw rocks in. (Trust me, they were rocks, nothing else.)

At the age of four we were shooting fireworks off the roof of our Greenwich Village apartment. (Hey, I was a kid. I didn't know it was illegal. I just knew it was fun, and if we saw a cop, I was told to keep quiet.)

We moved to Jamaica, Queens, when I was five, and my mom had a field day. We lived behind Goose Pond Park. So, naturally, I was climbing trees and hoping fences, and my mom didn't seem to mind. Some of her friends said that I was a tomboy. My mom told them to mind their own business, that I was just being a healthy kid.

As was my mom's philosophy, she thought the best way to know what you wanted in life was to try a bit of everything, and then you could decide with an educated judgement. So my mom introduced me to karate (where my sister and I were the only girls allowed to spar with the boys, while my dad placed bets on us); ballet (where I was not a pillar of grace but at least I saw what I looked like in a tutu); transcendental yoga (where I wanted to trade in my mantra for a newer one); and the Ouija board (where my mom tried to bless the board with holy water after *The Exorcist* came out). My mom gave me a sense of wonder and a desire to explore the world.

It was at the age of twelve, though, that I really started to get creative. I remember coming home from the circus one day and convincing my sister, Sharon, to sit on my shoulders as I rode my bike in circles in front of our house. I don't know who was braver—her or me! All I remember is my mom looking out the window and yelling, "Watch out for the cars!" My dad was probably off somewhere placing bets on how long it would take us to fall.

The adrenaline bug could hit me at any time, and any little thing could spark an interest to try something. Watching a Bob Hope movie in which he was fencing made me join the high school fencing team. Watching *The Wizard of Oz* made me try hot air ballooning, and reading a phone bill made me try the luge. (You are going to have to read the chapter to understand that last one.)

In college I upped the ante when I went skydiving with my friend Sheldon. I think at that point my mom started to worry a bit, but instead of telling me to not try the adventures, she just insisted on coming along, saying a prayer, and being the camera person with the hopes that if had it on film I wouldn't have the desire to do it again.

As I got older, the search for more adventures continued. And that's where I ran into a problem. I loved sharing these adventures and not all my friends, especially my girlfriends, were willing to do the so called "crazy" things I liked to do. My one adventurous female friend, Vivian Kalman, who introduced me to the world of scuba diving and was always ready to hop a park fence, moved away. So I decided to unleash my thrill seeking passions on the unsuspecting men in the dating world. Before long, I'd made a spirit of adventure and competitiveness, along with a good sense of humor, an absolute requirement for my men. I married two men, and I think I wore them out. I have a very high energy for life, and I tend to be (okay, I'm really) competitive, but always with a playful spirit.

To me, whether it's a casual date or a lifetime mate, you really learn a lot about the other person and bond with them (or at least test the strength of the glue) when you take on a challenge together.

You're bound to look at each other a whole lot differently when you see them handling a ten-foot shark in water rather than a one-foot loaf of bread in a supermarket. The way I see it, boredom breeds contempt. Playful competition and a spirit to try new things keeps the romance alive. You're more likely to get into an argument going to Blockbuster for the millionth time than if you're bungee jumping with them, and your energies are concentrating on not hitting the ground at one hundred miles per hour, so the local police don't have to draw a chalk line.

Some say I have a death wish, but they're wrong. I have a *LIFE* wish! I don't want life to pass me by. And it's not just boyfriends and ex-husbands who are victims of my life wish. My son, Spencer (who at this writing is fifteen), is often the happy participant in many of these adventures too. He has already gone dog sledding, surfing, soaring, spelunking, diving, swimming with dolphins and manatees, and the list goes on ... you should see his scrapbook.

In fact, he has done so many adventures that I have often had teachers of his call the house and tell me my son has a very vivid imagination. When I ask about what, they say, "Oh, he said you were crawling around on your stomach with hundreds of bats in a cave, and he also said he felt moss on the back of a manatee." When I tell them this is true, they are usually speechless. Then they say, "Ms. Capo, you do realize this is not the typical stuff a child is introduced to."

"Yeah, well, who wants a typical life?!"

And I don't plan to stop soon either. As a matter of fact, we are climbing Kilimanjaro together shortly after this book comes out. I do think I should add one thing, though—my son does not just blindly go on these adventures. He does put his foot down on occasion. Take for example the time I tried to sign up as a contestant for a TV show that was going to train people to be astronauts, and the winner would get to travel to the Russian Space Station, MIR. To me it was the ultimate challenge, outer space. When I told Spencer, he said, "Ma, I've put up with all your adventures. I draw the line when you leave the planet."

Lucky for Spencer, the MIR was brought down in March of 2001 and is lying on the ocean floor. So for now, it looks like my adventures will keep me earthbound. Oh well, there's still plenty to do here. Spencer and I just signed up for a forty-two-mile bike race through the five New York boroughs.

And now this brings me to why I wrote this book and how you the reader can benefit from it.

I like to read to find out about new adventures. Over the years, many of the adventure books I've read were either dedicated to just one "extreme" sport, which is good for the fanatic or expert, or covered a variety of adventures but listed the same ones over and over again: canoeing, kayaking, hiking, diving, biking, etc. I started wondering, "Where's a book that covers the really cool extreme sports and adventures that you don't have to train for three months, don't have to be an expert at, and don't have to spend a million bucks on the equipment? Where are the adventures you can try once, feel the thrill, and then move on to the next adrenaline rush?" There was a void, and I decided to fill it.

So I wrote down all of my adventures. Some are really exciting, some are expensive, some are cheap, and all are told with humor. Soon I'd collected a series of short stories of my (mostly) one-time adventures, and I began to publish the articles in magazines such as *Caribbean Travel and Life, Latitudes,* and on various Internet sites like www.travelnewsletter.com and www.uniquetravelstories.com. People started writing me, and I began to realize just how many people love these kinds of adventures. So I put fifty of them into one book, and you are now holding that book in your hands.

But of course the search doesn't stop here. I'm already planning my next several adventures.

The bottom line is this. I'm not crazy or nuts for doing these things, although some may say otherwise. At most, I'm told I'm a real character. But to me, life is to live, not to watch. There is so much to explore in the world that it doesn't make sense to limit yourself to doing the same things over and over again, unless you really like them. That's like going to a buffet table and only trying one dish!

Exploring life with passion and enthusiasm and sharing the thrills with mates, family, and friends has great payoffs. You build your self-esteem and find a renewed vigor for life. Your kids think you're pretty cool (even if the teachers think you're crazy). You can get a good back rub from your mate (that is, if you're both not too exhausted), and you'll stay in shape. Life becomes exciting and filled with great memories. After all, you don't want your biggest claim to adventure to be the day you had a tooth pulled without Novocain.

Remember, I'm not an expert at any of these things myself. I'm just someone who was curious enough to give each one a try, and look for the humor in them at the same time. I'm also a single mom who believes that the best way to show kids that nothing is impossible is by being a living example. Walk your talk. These adventures are not just for the young.

My mom and dad had mottoes, and now I will tell you mine. "Fear Nothing—And if you do, do it anyway!" Challenge your mind, your body, and your spirit. God gave us this life. I hope when I finally meet Him, I can proudly tell him I used up everything he gave me.

Okay, enough said. You are about to read about my life through my adventures. I hope you will try these adventures yourself. If you have the urge, do it. Don't wait. You don't want to be ninety-years-old and sitting in a rocking chair saying, "If only I had tried …." Get out there, enjoy, and create a life of adrenaline adventures!

And don't forget to take pictures!

Create a great life!
Fran

HOW TO USE THIS BOOK

Actually it's pretty simple. Since each chapter is self-contained (meaning you don't have to read the previous chapter to get the benefits of the one you want), you can use this book in several ways.

- You can read the entire book, cover to cover, and find out about all the cool adventures and then decide a) which ones you want to try immediately, b) that you are tired from just reading what I did and are happy to get your thrill from that, or c) that you are going to do at least one of these adventures yourself someday but are not quite sure when.

- You can go right to the adventures you've always wanted to try and read the chapters then a) procrastinate another five years, or b) use the at-a-glance information to finally experience the adventure for yourself.

- If you are short on time, you can read only the adventures at a glance, which are the summaries of the adventures found at the end of each chapter, and then decide what chapters you want to read entirely.

- You can read only the motivational quotes, rewrite them, and hang them in your bathroom as thoughts to ponder.

- You can read the whole book, try every single adventure yourself, and live life to the fullest.

A WORD ABOUT THE MILD TO WILD METER

The mild to wild meter is very subjective. If it was up to me, only adventures with the intensity of bungee jumping, diving with sharks, and combat air flying would be considered a level 5. But after speaking to my editor and several of my friends, I agreed that not everything has to be at that high a level to be a 5.

For example, if someone is scared of heights, a hot air balloon ride or going in a blimp can be pretty intense. On the same note, if someone is claustrophobic and they go spelunking, that could be a level 5 plus to them.

Therefore, I've tried to gauge an adventure with the idea that most people want a rush, or they wouldn't be reading this book, but at the same time, they might not react to these adventures the same way I did, and their adrenaline levels might change as they try more adventures and get used to taking risks.

The bottom line is that everything new to me is a rush. I just love exploring life, and my heart beats wildly with each new experience. I hope some of these adventures will thrill you in the same way.

The meter is merely a guideline. You know what scares you and what doesn't. The best way to know is to try something for yourself, and then you can always adjust your own meter. Enjoy!

"If you want to do something you find a way-
If you don't you find an excuse."
-Todd Williams

Chapter 1
"Call out the Saint Bernard"
Downhill Skiing

I found my first adventure pal in the third grade. I had just transferred to a new elementary school, PS 131 in Queens and on my very first day there I met Vivian, or Viv as I called her. We became best friends.

Viv and I were tomboys; more accurately, we were girls who liked to do the same things boys did and had the same amount of confidence. While most girls were taught not to climb the fence because they might get hurt, Viv and I not only climbed it but felt we could do it faster than our male counterparts and would often tease them when we did.

Maybe it was the competitive nature of our mutual astrological sign of Leo the Lion that gave us the confidence, or maybe it was just that we had parents who taught us nothing was impossible. Either way, no nook or cranny was left unexplored when we were together.

Our love for adventure was twofold. Not only did we like it, but we found out at an early age, (yes our devious little minds in the third grade were working overtime) that one of the best ways to really get to know the boys was to play sports with them. Through our growing years, we played soccer, baseball, rode the highest roller coasters, went inside "haunted houses," had bike racing contests, climbed fences, built club houses, and even invited the boys to sleep over at Vivian's aunt's farm to ride horses bareback. Unfortunately her aunt didn't think that was a good idea. So instead we talked about boys and continued to do our adventures.

Our first real adrenaline adventure that required money was downhill skiing. Neither of us had tried it so when our high school, Jamaica High, announced a one-day trip to Hunter Mountain, located in upstate New York, we jumped at the opportunity. We filled out the necessary trip consent forms, had our moms pay the fee and we were on our way.

After a very loud bus ride, we arrived at the snow-covered mountain. We were given our prepaid lift tickets and then had to get geared up. If you have never been to a ski resort then getting the equipment itself is an adventure. First you have to fill out a form with all your vital information, including your height and weight. At any age, no girl likes to give out that information. After the forms are filled out, you begin to wait on various lines.

The first line is for ski boots. You give your size to the attendant and then you are given these Herman Munster type boots to try on. If these beauties fit, you move onto the skis section. Then the fun really begins—you get to tell your weight to a complete stranger. There's no getting around it because they have to adjust the skis to work with your weight. You can try to whisper it, but the person next to you, usually a guy, suddenly develops supersonic hearing, and then your weight might as well be broadcast all over the six o'clock news along with the announcement that they are looking for Shamu the whale.

Guys for some reason don't seem to have a problem with their weight being announced publicly, as long as they can see their shoes, even if it's with the aid of a hand held mirror, they feel just fine. Anyway, having survived the weight ordeal, we got our skis— two long wooden planks on which we were expected to balance ourselves while sliding down a very long, slick hill. Of course, Viv and I couldn't wait to try them out.

With equipment ready, we proceeded to find a locker to store our street shoes and our other accessories that were not needed while swishing down the slopes. As Viv and I quickly found out, the lockers are like parking meters, they take quarters—every time you need to get into them. So Viv and I had to scrounge around for some change. I vowed next time to come with those little metal change-makers like the vendors have at baseball stadiums.

After storing our streetwear, we were ready to don our ski clothes, which in this case consisted of a pair of jeans, some layered shirts and a ski jacket. Since we didn't know if we were going to like this sport or not, we figured we'd save the $250 bucks on the snowbunny outfit and matching garb for next time. We put on goggles (hoping they would make us look a little like we knew what we were doing), hats (fifty percent of body heat is lost through the head, so you definitely want a hat), gloves (fingers and toes are particularly subject to frostbite) and these pullover turtle neck scarves that could also be pulled up to cover your mouth while your zooming down the hill if need be.

The first challenge for any beginning skier is getting used to walking in those monstrous ski boots. But once you get the knack, you can get this nice clomping rhythm going and can easily walk up the stairs, out of the lodge and mosey on over to your ski instructor.

The package price included a half-hour introductory lesson so we took advantage of it—no machismo here. In our ski class there were about ten fellow students from Jamaica High. The instructor, Gene, took an overall assessment to see if any of us were ringers. None of us were. We were all virgin skiers ready to fall on our butts in the name of adventure. Luckily we were on fairly level ground. After all they don't start you on Mt. Everest your first time out.

Our handsome instructor, (which is always a nice bonus for the girls), began the lesson, "Okay guys and gals since none of you has ever skied before we are going to start by finding your balance. I want you to stand in your boots so that the pressure from the tongue of the boot feels equally distributed from shin to calf. Most of your weight should be felt between the heel and the arch of the foot. Now can you all feel that?"

We all shifted around and nodded. Gene continued, "Good. Now you are going to discover how to walk skiing style. All you have to do is alternate sliding one ski in front of the other." We all tried it, looking rather spastic. It seemed we were putting an awful lot of effort into moving a few lousy inches. Eventually we all managed to form some semblance of a line. Since the lesson was only a half hour lesson Gene moved on to the next skill.

"Okay gang, now we are going to walk up the bunny hill just a little bit so we can later get a feel of what it is like to go down. I want you to walk up sideways, and keep your shoulders and hands facing down the hill. This way you won't slide down the hill while you are trying to go up. Make sense?" Seemed logical enough. Of course, theory is always easier than reality.

After a few minutes he told us we have gone far enough. I looked down, I think I had moved about a foot and Viv was just a few inches ahead of me.

Gene continued, "Okay, get in a line. Now with small steps I want you to point your skis downhill, while putting your weight on your poles. One by one I want you to stand on parallel skis, with knees bent and lean slightly forward with your weight on the poles. Then when I point to you, just lift your poles off the snow and go!"

The moment of truth was here. I was first in line, meaning I had the added pressure of being the guinea pig. Luckily I went down without much of a problem. Actually it seemed like I went kind of slow, but for now it was okay. Viv came next and did fine. We watched the others, and then we all repeated the exercise. On the third try Gene had us inching our way up almost half the bunny slope.

Now we were ready to learn to control our speed. He told us, "Okay guys you're doing great." (Like if we really sucked he would say it.) He explained the maneuver called a "gliding wedge" aka snowplough. You put your feet in a V-shaped position by sliding both ends of the backs of your skis out an equal distance while keeping the front of your skis—the ski tips—together. It almost looks like you are sitting over a toilet but trying not to touch the seat. The reason for this ridiculous looking position is because this V shape creates resistance as you go downhill and slows you down. A common exercise is to gradually make the wedge wider (and hopefully not fall on your ass) as you ski straight down the hill. Eventually you come to a stop. This is the real beginner stuff, because I've never seen an Olympic skier come down a mountain at eighty miles per hour like this.

Twenty minutes into the lesson we had learned balance, how to go up the hill, go down the hill, and how to control our speed to some degree. Seeing as you can't very well just go straight down the side of the mountain because you'll gain too much speed and wind up leaving an outline of your figure in the side of the lodge like a cartoon character, the next step is to learn how to turn.

Gene showed us how to use the wedge, turn and stop technique. He explained it in a very basic manner. "You might not believe this, but you can turn without any actual twisting, turning or leaning of your body in the direction you want to go. All you have to do to turn is simply apply very subtle pressure to your left ski, while gliding straight downhill in your wedge formation. It is absolutely critical that you apply this pressure while keeping your body still". It sounded more complicated than it was. I wanted him to draw a diagram in the snow.

We practiced the one knee turning method a couple of times and then we were ready for some serious dance moves. We combined the wedge turns. By linking the turns instead of coming to a complete stop, a new turn is initiated before you lose all the momentum. The result, you zigzag happily and slowly down the hill.

I noticed I was able to remember the procedure better when I sang the "Hokey Pokey" to myself. "You put your left knee in, you put your left knee out, you put your right knee in." I didn't risk the part where you shake it all about.

The final thing Gene taught us was how to get up in the likely event that we should fall. This advice was priceless and the hardest to follow. Of course, Gene made it sound like a piece of cake, "Okay guys, you've done great. All that is left is for you to sit on your butts." That was an easy step to follow. He sat down, we sat down.

He continued, "Now, turn yourself and your skis sideways to the hill. Place both poles on the uphill side. Lean into the mountain and simply pick yourselves up." Yeah right. It is easier to lean downhill,

Adrenaline Adventures

but that of course causes you to go rolling down the hill like a snowball. Gene demonstrated this procedure and was on his feet in a matter of seconds.

Viv and I tried this getting up method. We looked like a bunch of weebles. We'd get up one side and fall over the other. And if we really spaced out and weren't careful, our skis started pointing downhill the second we stood up, and then we'd start sliding downhill. I decided the easiest way to avoid having to practice this maneuver was to just make sure I didn't fall. (Yeah right. Why don't I just promise to never eat cheesecake again while I was at it.) Gene watched us all practice our final moves and then bid us farewell.

Now that the lesson was over Viv and I decided to practice our new found skills on the bunny hill. After a few times down the hill we felt pretty confident, so we moved it up a notch and went up to the towrope.

For those of you who have never been skiing, the towrope is just what the name implies. It's a rope that you hold onto and it gently tows you up the slightly inclined bunny hill. We were instructed by the tow rope operator that if we fell we should simply let go of the rope and move out of the way.

Falling is embarrassing. Everyone behind you getting towed can see you're the one uncoordinated fool who can't hold onto a rope going up a hill at a ten-degree angle. It seems far better to have your face dragged up the side of the hill than to let go. Luckily the learning curve is quick and by the end of the day, riding the towrope will be easy.

After a few times going up and coming down, Viv and I ran into some of the boys from our school. They were the class nerds, and they were skiing with ease. They seem to take a perverse pleasure in the fact that we were still on the bunny hill. These nerds convinced us that we should be going on the chair lift up to the bigger hills. They grinned and chuckled as they said it. Viv and I looked at each other—"If those wimps could do it, so could we." Never mind that they had been skiing several times before and that they were math geniuses and probably knew the angle of the slope divided by the rate of speed and could calculate the best rate and angle of descent.

Fran Capo

We were woman and we wanted them to hear us two Leos roar. Besides, the bunny hill was getting boring.

So up the chair lift we went. If you have never been in a chair lift, it's a cool experience. First you have to wait on a line as the chairs swing around attached to a pulley on the top. They come at intervals of about every twenty seconds. So as soon as the car in front of you is loaded with people you have to quickly stand by a yellow line and aim your butt toward the oncoming seat. The seat swoops you up, and you put the safety bar down. Then you are lifted up over the hill. It's usually a gorgeous and peaceful ride, especially after new fallen snow. Your ski-clad feet dangle or you can rest them on a foot bar. Most chair lift rides last three to five minutes.

About one hundred feet before you need to depart from your seat, there are signs instructing you to lift the safety bar and keep your ski tips up while getting off the chair lift.

We watched the people in the chair in front of us get off the lift. Seemed easy enough. Viv and I lifted the bar, pushed ourselves off the seat, had our ski tips up, held hands and clumsily made our way down the exit ramp.

We looked at each other. "Okay, that wasn't so bad, now what?" We turned around and looked down the real mountain–the mountain we had to ski down. It looked a lot higher from the top. Viv and I were tempted to go back down the mountain, but we found out there were no round-trip tickets on the lift chair.

Determined to conquer this challenge, but not totally confident in our skills, we decided we needed to come up with our own speed control method. We settled on the ever-popular tree-to-tree method. We figured if we skied that way, we really wouldn't build up too much speed. Of course, we didn't calculate the pain of slamming into a tree and stopping on impact.

We both aimed toward the first tree…success! We went to the second tree. Again, success. Just when we thought we had found a new safe way to ski, we aimed at the third tree at the same exact time and … BOOM! We did not have the nerds with us to do the correct mathematical calculations that would have enabled us to avoid banging our foreheads together. We both went down. Viv had a tiny spot of blood on her forehead. Out of nowhere, a S.W.A.T.

team with a Saint Bernard dog came with a medical emergency sled. They picked Viv up, put her on the sled, and merrily headed down the mountain. Viv laughed and waved. "See you at the lodge."

I yelled out to the medical emergency team, "What about me?"

"You look fine!" they yelled back."

"But I can't ski!" It was too late. They were gone.

So there I was alone on the hill. Well, there were actually other people there as well, but they weren't my friends. I saw a sign for a black diamond hill. I figured, "Hey, I like diamonds". Then someone told me that the black diamond hills are the toughest around. They told me the easiest hills were marked with a green triangle. I wanted to do one better and immediately started looking for a picture of a girl walking down the mountain. No such luck.

I decided I was tired of walking. So I started to try what I learned in class. I slowly applied pressure from knee to knee. It began to work. But at one point I built up too much speed and got a tad nervous. I decided to take my skis off and walk down the hill. People from the chair lift were laughing at me. At least I thought I heard laughing.

I hooked up with Viv about twenty minutes later. She was sitting in front of the fireplace in the lodge sipping a hot chocolate. She said "Fran that was the coolest ride down. You should have come!"

"I wanted to Viv, but the Saint Bernard Express left without me. I think we need to rethink that tree-to-tree method".

We decided to pull one of the instructors over to the side and get some pointers. We picked the cutest instructor to ask for help. (Hey, if we were going to play damsel in distress why not go for Prince Charming. You guys know you would do the very same thing.) After a few additional pointers, we were determined to conquer the hill. Now we were determined to go down the hill because *we* wanted to, not just because some nerds challenged us.

Once again we went up in the chair lift. We lifted the safety bar at the precise time. We got off the chair without a hitch. At the top we decided that we would make gigantic S-turns and go as slow as we felt comfortable.

We headed down the hill, this time avoiding all trees. At first it felt like a lot of work. But on the positive side I felt I was building up my thigh muscles. I knew my legs were a bit tense because I didn't want to ski out of control.

When Viv and I made it down the hill, we had a great feeling of accomplishment. We continued on that hill for the next few hours. Soon we were relaxing into the "ski" position and even building up a little speed. It felt awesome.

By the end of the day we were tired but really proud of ourselves for not giving up. We liked the feeling of power and speed that you can get while skiing. We met the boys that had told us to go to the top of the hill in the first place. They were laughing. "So did you girls make it down the hill okay?" They started elbowing each other.

"Actually we made it down fine". I said. Viv and I hoped they hadn't witnessed our little tree incident. The boys were obviously disappointed that we hadn't broken a limb.

At just that moment, Gene our first instructor happened to walk by. He nodded to us. "I saw you girls up on the hill. Nice job!" He gave us the thumbs up. The timing couldn't have been more perfect. The boys walked away mumbling to themselves, their plan foiled. Viv and I laughed. We had found a new sport, had a great time, overcome a minor setback, and proved, once again, that we could be just as good as the boys.

Adrenaline Adventures

Chapter 1
Adventure at a Glance - Dare to Do it   Mild to Wild Scale: 2
Title: Downhill Skiing
Children allowed: Yes.
Age requirement: Four and up, with parent consent.
Length of trip: Half-day to full day.
Where to try this adventure: Any ski resort. This author recommends:
Hunter Mountain, Route 23A Southside, Hunter, New York
Main phone: 518-263-3800 Toll free: 888-Hu-nterMtn.
www.HunterMtn.com Or visit your local ski area. Go to web and type in the word ski resorts.
Best time of year to go: Winter
Approximate cost: $40 to $100 per day, including gear rentals and lift tickets. Toddlers and those over 60 ski free.
Reservations necessary: No
Fitness requirements: Must be in good health.
Personal gear required: Warm clothes preferably ones that wick away (take sweat away from your body). Most resorts have a place where you can rent skis poles and boots.
What NOT to bring: Cotton clothing, expensive jewelry, cell phones and radios.
Photo opportunities: Yes

Notes: If the resort offers lessons, definitely sign up for them. Most websites will tell you; directions, nearby lodging, package deals and tell you how many lifts and trails the resort has. Midweek is cheaper than weekends.

Cool trivia: A man by the name of Ron Cram made a commitment to ski non-stop no matter the month. His downhill record for skiing holds at ninety-one straight weeks. He holds other records as well.

"Do or don't do - there is no try."
- Yoda, Star Wars

Chapter 2
"Okay, I'll jump. Just don't push."
Static Line Skydiving

While sitting in my college math class studying the Pythagorean Theorem and thinking how useless this knowledge was, my mind started to drift. I missed my adventure pal Viv who had moved out-of-state for college. I felt the need for an adventure and in her honor I had to choose a suitable substitute. My close pal at the time was a guy named Shelly Jacobowitz, he has since changed his name and become a highly decorated police lieutenant.

Shelly and I were good students, but we also did our share of joking around in class. One day I leaned over and whispered to Shelly, "Hey Shelly, let's come up with a wild adventure idea. The wildest idea we come up with, we have to do." Neither of us was into drugs or breaking the law, so we knew we were safe. Or were we?

Into the arena ideas were tossed. We settled on Shelly's idea of parachuting. My mom thought we were nuts. Shelly didn't bother to tell his parents.

We found a skydiving place in Lakewood, New Jersey. The cost was $150, which included a three-hour training class and the jump.

Adrenaline Adventures

We were both excited and a bit nervous, though neither of us showed it.

The class started early in the morning, so we left our homes at dawn. My mom decided to come and watch. She said she wanted to take pictures so I would have it on film and never feel the need to capture this moment again. I knew that was only part of the reason. My mom was mainly coming because of the protective mother instinct that says, "If I'm around, somehow I can prevent imminent danger from happening to my child." Yeah, right! If I went splat, she'd have to pick me up with a spatula just like anyone else. Now there's a pleasant thought.

Along on our sojourn was a guy we called Nervous Rob. Rob was the quirky boyfriend of a mutual friend Dorothy. Dorothy had also wanted to jump, but Rob had decided that he needed to check out the situation for her first. The whole ride up, all we heard was his questions, "You sure you want to do this? This is dangerous. What if you get hurt? Did you check out how many people get killed or maimed from this?" My mom was ready to stick duct tape on his mouth and give him a tranquilizer.

As we pulled into the parachuting place, we saw a guy being carried out on a stretcher.(How's that for adding to your nerves?) Shelly and I looked at each other and laughed. We always did that. He had this devilish chuckle like the cartoon dog Smedley. Rob looked rather smug, and my mom was waiting for us to say something intelligent.

So I complied. "Well, they say that one out of every hundred or so might get hurt. There's the one. Now we don't have to worry." That wasn't exactly the quote my mother was looking for. But let's face it, Shelly and I might not be math majors but we knew the odds were in our favor.

We paid our money, and then we were sent to classroom instruction. My mom and Rob waited outside. The instructor, Tim talked about safety and the speed of acceleration. "The distance fallen per second up to terminal velocity is sixteen feet for every one second. In other words, pretty damn fast. Today you have chosen to do static line. You will be dropped from an altitude of 2,500 feet, about twice the height of the World Trade Center. You will be given a parachute and a reserve chute. One end of the static line will be attached to your main chute; the other end will be attached to the plane ... hopefully." He chuckled.

I turned to Shelly. "Is it my imagination or is this guy getting some perverse pleasure in watching us squirm?" Before Shelly could respond, Tim continued his instruction describing the famous spread-eagle position – a position in which all your limbs are spread wide a part. (And a position that we would have to stay in during the decent—which seemed to be fine with all the men in the room.)

After a few more hours of instruction and constant reminders of the danger, we were given a release form to sign.

The form was the standard thrill-seeker release form. "You agree of your own free will to put your ass on the line. You trust us enough to give us your money to do it. But hey, if it doesn't work out, don't come running to us." As if we could! Like anxious lemmings, we signed.

Next came the simulated practices. We were all fitted in white overalls and sent off to the backyard where we were supplied with helmets. Our outdoor instructor, Charlie, had us climb onto a wooden platform that was about six feet high and kind of looked like the type of platform prisoners would stand on before being hung. Once on the platform, we were instructed to go to the edge, turn, put our hands on our helmets, and jump off the platform—backward. We were told to roll as soon as we hit the ground.

It was a little scary at first, but Charlie explained that accidents happened mainly because of two reasons, one of which was that people don't roll as soon as they hit the ground and therefore their parachute remains open. The open parachute naturally catches the wind and then drags their sorry butts across the ground at a very rapid speed. The other reason for accidents was that people often forget to look off toward the horizon as they landed, and instead looked straight down. If they look straight down, it looks as if the ground is coming up too fast. Instinct then kicks in and makes them lift their legs up. If they do this, they miscalculate when they will touch down. Further, their legs are in the wrong position to land, and they can break a leg, or two. (Not bad if you're in the Soprano family business, but not good for parachuting.) Anyway, this is what happened to our friend who was in the stretcher as we came in.

Charlie added, "There is also the slight chance that accidents will happen because the chute gets tangled or just doesn't open. That's a lot more messy." There was that sadistic instructor twist again. Shelly let out a Smedley laugh.

We practiced emergency procedures in case the main chute didn't open. To do this we had to punch the reserve chute, which was stuffed in a little bag and attached around the front of our waists. Then we had to pretend to scoop the chute away from our bodies so that when it deployed, it wouldn't tangle with our main chute. We repeatedly practiced these drills on the ground for forty-five minutes, the idea being that if you do them long enough, you'll remember the procedures and hopefully use them when falling towards the earth like Newton's apple.

Then the moment of truth (or craziness) came. We were given our harnesses and parachutes. We boarded the fourteen-seat Cessna airplane ... which was missing one little element—seats! We were told to sit on the floor in between each other's legs. Cozy. My mom meanwhile was popping her head inside the plane and snapping pictures with the camera as if she worked for the *Discovery Channel*. Rob was shaking.

When we were airborne, we were given our final instructions. "Remember, on the count of one, sit in the doorway of the plane. At the count of two, lean out as far as you can in the arch spread eagle position. At the count of three, jump. And don't make me count again or I'll push ya." He smiled then added, "Oh yes, and to amuse ourselves, we always pack one faulty chute. It's like Russian roulette." There was that satanic sense of humor again. I think jumping from the plane would have been enough of an adrenaline adventure without Charlie and his gang of closet comedians.

He continued, "Remember to count ... arch 1,000, arch 2,000, arch 3,000. If you get to 7,000 and you are still falling too fast, time to use the reserve. Stay calm. We will be in radio contact with you at all times. When you feel your chute open, reach for the toggles to steer. Any questions?"

Fran Capo

I felt like a dumbfounded deer with headlights shining in my face.

I was second in line. The first girl got ready to jump. They attached the static line. The count came, she jumped, and I heard "Bang!"

"What was that?" I asked.

Charlie smiled and said, "We lost one."

Shelly laughed. Sure, he could laugh, he wasn't next. I knew the instructor was kidding but needed reassurance. I looked at him with my eyes begging for another answer. The instructor reassured me, "It's the static line hitting the plane. Now get ready to jump."

At every juncture in life, there comes a point of no return—a point when you know that you have already decided to do something and it's time to take action. At that point, you know you have to go ahead with your decision no matter how scared you are. I was at that point—ready to take my literal leap of faith.

"One." I put my legs out the door. "Two." I arched my back in the doorway. "Three." I jumped without hesitation. I free-fell for about ten feet—the length of the static line—and then I felt a slight upward lift. It was my parachute. My beautiful, white, round parachute. I felt the cool breeze against my face. It was like a dream.

It was then I realized I probably should be counting. How many seconds had passed? Should I start at arch two thousand instead? Ahhh! What am I saying; the chute is already open. I reached up for my toggles to turn the parachute left and right. I heard a tiny voice come over the radio that was attached to the parachute harness. A radio that was there so in case you panicked the instructors on the ground could talk you down. "Nice jump. Doing great. Turn left. Easy girl ... nice ... now just enjoy the view. Easy ... easy ... coming in for a landing."

I saw my mom taking pictures. I smiled. Then I saw a guy stuck in a tree with his parachute. Not good. I wanted to signal my mom to take a picture of him, but decided against it. Then I spotted the target, a big red dot that I was supposed to land on. I looked off toward the horizon. Within seconds, I felt my feet touch the ground, and I immediately rolled and ran around the chute. I felt fantastic and hugged my mom.

Adrenaline Adventures

I quickly got out of the target zone and looked skyward. I saw Shelly coming in for a perfect landing. We gave each other the high five. It was exhilarating and over way too fast, kind of like a Haagen Dazs ice cream on a hot summer day.

My mom was relieved and seemed confident that I would never skydive again, since it was captured on film. Rob practically fainted and kept telling us how lucky we were to be safe.

After all the jumpers finished we received our "FIRST JUMP" certificates. The instructor signed our parachuting logbooks and made an entry for memory's sake: "Jump 1 - 8/22/78 - Lakewood, NJ - static line – 2,500 feet - 3 second delay." He signed his name and added a special message to my logbook: "Pretty jump, just like the jumper." I smiled.

Shelly and I drove home thinking math class would never be the same again.

Fran Capo

Chapter 2
Adventure at a Glance - Dare to Do it   Mild to Wild Scale: 5
Title: Static Line Skydiving
Children allowed: No
Age requirement: Must be 18 years old.
Length of trip: Half-day but be prepared to stay a full day depending on how many times you choose to jump.
Where to try this adventure: Skys the Limit.
1-800-335-Jump
website: www.skysthelimit.net. They are open seven days a week and are located just fifty miles from New York City, in northern New Jersey at 248 Stickles Pond Road in Newton, New Jersey. There are many skydiving places located around the country, check the Internet or your local yellow pages for a place in your state.
Best time of year to go: Summer, spring and fall (although some hard core jumpers do it all year round.)
Approximate cost: $150 - $250 per jump
Reservations necessary: Strongly recommended.
Fitness requirements: Must be in good health and preferably weigh under 250 pounds. Do not drink alcoholic beverages with twenty-four hours.
Personal gear required: None
What to bring: Comfortable clothes, sneakers and valid ID.
What NOT to bring: Sandals or boots.
Photo opportunities: Yes

Notes: The place I went skydiving in Lakewood, New Jersey has since closed. There are many places around the country that offer skydiving, check the Internet or you local operator for listings.

Cool trivia: People had been parachuting from airplanes in the U.S. since 1912. Capt. Albert Berry was the first to do a plane jump on March 1st, 1912. "Tiny" Broadrick was the first woman to jump from an airplane in 1913. She had done so many times before from balloons. There were plenty of sport parachutists after WWII.

"Hold fast to dreams,
for if dreams die,
life is a broken-winged bird
that cannot fly"
–Langston Hughes

Chapter 3
"Getting High Before Class"
Flying Lessons in a Cessna

With my first airborne adventure (skydiving) successfully completed I was ready to take to the skies again. This time, I decided to try flying lessons. Shelly wasn't interested, so I had to look elsewhere for a partner.

At that time, I knew this really cool older kid named David who was into motorcycles and adventure. David had a slight crush on me and would do things to annoy me. One time my mom, my step-dad, myself and David were in the car coming back from a daytrip. David and I fell asleep in the back of the car, and from that day on he insisted on telling everyone we had slept together, just to see me turn red and make my Italian blood boil. It was especially annoying because I was still a virgin in college (which was a self-imposed venture onto itself) and I was waiting till I got married, and everyone knew it.

But as annoying as he was, my thrill for adventure took over. I loved to ride on his motorcycle and so naturally when I wanted to take flying lessons, he was a perfect candidate to be my adventure partner.

Neither of us had ever flown a plane, but we were willing to learn.

We called around and found out that there was a flight school at Islip MacArthur Airport in Long Island. I was starting a new semester in college and the soonest time they had available was on a Tuesday morning at six o'clock. I quickly calculated that if we got up early, drove out there from my house, took an hour-long class, and drove back, I could make it to my 9:20 accounting class on time.

The next Tuesday David picked me up at four in the morning. We drove out to the flight school, paid our forty-five dollars each (which was pretty steep for a college student at the time), and were set up with separate instructors. My guy was named Richard, a good-looking man with a friendly disposition.

After filling out a few forms, we walked to where the small planes were parked. We would learn to fly a Cessna' 152 plane, a two-seater. This was my first time in a small plane, never mind flying one. I was excited.

The first thing we did was an inspection of the plane, inside and out. We climbed inside and turned on the master switch. We checked the quantity of fuel. We turned off the master switch. We checked the ignition switch and made sure the throttle was closed. Richard had a pre-flight checklist, an inspection that he said every pilot follows. Next we went over to one of the wings and unscrewed the gas cap and looked inside to see how much fuel was there. Richard explained we had to do a visual fuel check as well as a fuel gauge check to make sure everything was okay. I was all for that—I mean its not like you can stop at a gas station at 5,000 feet.

We had this little tube that we took underneath the wing. We checked the sump (that's the low point where fuel can be drained and inspected) on each side. We drained some fuel into the tube and then checked for water and sediment in the fuel. We looked at the fuel vents to see if they were open, then checked the landing gear. Just like a used car salesman we checked the plane's tires. I kicked it once to feel like I was helping. We also checked the brakes. Next we visually inspected the wings, making sure there were no nicks, or birds stuck in them. Although, I think that would have been pretty obvious.

Next on the list was checking the ailerons (the movable part of the wing near the tip that is responsible for making turns); they appeared to move without a problem. We removed the control locks. We then moved to the back of the plane and checked the movement of the rudder. We checked for oil leaks, loose wires, fittings, and the motor mounts, which looked like screws holding the plane together. Finally we checked the air intake and exhaust system. It was a lot to remember, but nothing that a good checklist and some Gingko Bilboa couldn't solve.

With everything up to par on the outside, we were ready to get back inside the plane, where another whole of things had to be checked: fuel selector on, mixture-rich, carb heat-on, seatbelts fastened, flight instruments checked and set ... and on and on. There was so much to look at I was convinced that I was going to have to take a memory course just to fly this thing.

Finally we were ready to get approval for take off. With our headphones on so we could communicate with each other, Richard called the tower, gave some fancy pilot lingo to clear his taxiing off the runway, and was told where to go to taxi. The engine sounded like a loud lawnmower, and had this buzzing quality to it. The little plane moved down the runway, making turns and then finally was on the takeoff strip.

The plane built up speed, and soon we were airborne. I loved it. There's something about being shoulder to shoulder with the pilot that really makes you appreciate flying. Richard kept switching dials on the radio that corresponded to the information the tower was giving him. He was told at what altitude he had to fly, and what frequency to remain on. Since this was a first instruction, and not just a scenic tour, Richard began the lessons, "Today we are just going to do some basic turns and see how well you can keep this baby at the same altitude." We leveled off at 2000 feet and flew over the Long Island Sound, which was part of the north practice area. Richard explained, "You can control an airplane in three directions: pitch, roll and yaw. Forward and backward is pitch. To the left and right is roll, and twisting motion is yaw. Now hold the control column, which is like the steering wheel of a car, and pull back on the controls." I did as he'd instructed and the airplane's nose rose. When I pushed

Adrenaline Adventures

forward, the planes nose lowered. The plane was very sensitive to the movement of the control column so I had to make sure I didn't dive-bomb the plane.

Next he told me to turn the controls to the left, which caused the ailerons on both wings to make the plane turn left. Then I turned the plane to the right. I had to make sure I didn't apply any downward or upward pressure to the control column while I was turning the plane.

I turned the plane a few more times and started to feel comfortable with my piloting skills. I watched the artificial horizon gauge, which looked like a leveler tool with the green bubble inside; it let me know I was keeping the wings level with the horizon and not unknowingly doing some acrobatic stunts. Of course, it's important not to get fixed on the fake horizon and forget to look outside at the real horizon - which could be a problem since the fake horizon doesn't tell you if there's a REAL plane coming in your direction. So it's rather important to look out the window every now and then.

After a few turns Richard told me to go up to 2,500 feet and then level off.

It was cool making the plane rise into the sky. But for some reason, I was started to get that itch for an adrenaline rush. I voiced my desire to Richard. He smiled. "Okay, how about a power out stall?"

I had no clue what that was so I happily agreed. The next thing I knew he raised the nose of the plane until the engine cut off. That was freaky. However, as soon as he lowered the nose, the engine went back on. I actually enjoyed that. Richard didn't seem worried, so why should I? I guess I figured as I do with most adventures that a) the person does this for a living and wants to live another day to do it and b) this ain't the first time he's done this. Of course, Richard could have been a failed Kamikaze pilot and then I'd be out of luck.

But seeing as we recovered nicely from the stall we moved on. Knowing that the plane could do all these cool things, I wanted to know what it took to become a pilot. Richard told me, "There is a minimum of thirty hours of dual instruction, eight hours of ground instruction, and six hours of solo flight. But no one ever seems to do it in that time, usually takes more like a total of fifty hours".

"And this is for people over eighteen right?"

"Well, the age requirement is fourteen and up. You can solo at sixteen and get your license at seventeen."

"Really?" I was shocked. "I know kids at fourteen that I couldn't trust to walk a dog much less fly a plane, but then again I could say the same for a lot of adults."

We flew for a few more minutes and he said we were going to go in for a landing.

"Before we do can we do a loop or something?" I asked.

Richard laughed. "This isn't an acrobatic plane".

"Oh come on, there has got to be something this plane can do that would give us a rush."

He laughed and said, "Okay girl, hang on." Then he grabbed the column and did some kind of dive, spin and swirl. All I know was that my stomach felt like I was on a roller coaster and I loved it. It was over in a matter of seconds. He said, "I haven't done that in years." Then he winked.

I met David on the ground. We both had enjoyed our flights and decided at that moment we wanted to become pilots. We signed up for our next lesson and bought a logbook to record our first flight.

I was slightly late to my accounting class that morning. The professor, a very stiff guy, reprimanded me. "I will not tolerate lateness. What is your excuse?"

I proudly blurted out, "I was flying."

He looked me straight in the eyes with his pocket protector aimed in my direction. "Ms. Capo. Getting high is nothing to be proud of."

At that moment I realized what I had said. "What? You think I was doing drugs? I've never even smoked pot. I was flying a plane."

"Young lady, am I supposed to believe that?"

"Look, I can prove it to you. I pulled out my logbook."

He glanced over it with a look of disdain. "Keep your feet on the ground in my classroom and your head out of the clouds." Then he turned to the blackboard and continued his lesson, feeling that he had squashed my spirit.

I took 6.5 hours of flight lessons after that, and then two things happened. I lost my ride and my wallet. David got sent away to college, and I ran out of money. I took two lessons after David left, but I couldn't keep it up. I vowed one day to return to the sport.

Adrenaline Adventures

Twenty years later, a writing friend of mine, Clayton Davis sent me an autographed copy of a book he wrote called *So you Want to be a Pilot*. It re-sparked my interest. I looked up my old flight school. It no longer existed; in its place was Mid Island Air Service Inc., a family-run business that had been training pilots since 1946. I explained to the flight manager, Jim that I had taken a few lessons, but it had been a while and I needed a refresher course. He assigned me an instructor, gave me the directions to the school, and we set up a date. I was instructed to call the flight school the day before to check weather conditions. Ah yes, I remembered that. The old adrenaline feeling started to come back.

Driving to the airport brought back memories of college days. This time, however, I could see the road clearly since I didn't have to get up at the crack of dawn to take the lesson.

I walked into the fight school and met my instructor, Nettsie Carr. A woman! This was fantastic! In the time I had taken lessons before and in all the years that I had met pilots, I had never met a female pilot—they were always men. Here was not only a female pilot, but an instructor as well. I was thrilled.

Once again after filling out some necessary forms, we walked to the plane, a Cessna 152. We did the pre-flight check with Nettsie explaining everything. Much of it came back to me.

Once the cockpit check was done, Nettsie started with the radios. But for some reason she explained in a way that made me finally understand all the numbers. She said, "We use the radio to check on different things. We check ATIS—which stands for Air Terminal Information Service—for the weather and airport conditions. We check in for clearance delivery. We check in with ground control for our taxi runway, and finally with the tower for take off and landings in the terminal area." Finally, after all these years, I got it.

She was an excellent instructor, pointing out things that she as a pilot was looking for. "Over there by the tower you will see the windsock that shows air direction."

Once we were on the runway, she got clearance for take off. "This is 15 Ralph Alpha Serra Whiskey requesting permission for take off."

The control tower repeated the plane's identification, which was 15RASW, and gave permission. Once the plane was in the air, Nettsie got clearance delivery for us to go over the north practice area, a place I had flown over several times in what seemed like a previous lifetime. The south practice area, she explained, was over the Atlantic Ocean.

We did the familiar banks and turns, leveling off and just keeping the plane at a certain altitude. I told Nettsie my biggest fear in flying was that I would get lost and not be able to find the airport. She pointed out landmarks and told me how to look for them. But then she laughed and said, "We all go through those fears. The tower will guide you in. You will get used to it." She had such an easy way about her that I felt I could learn in no time under her guidance.

The lesson was over quickly. I didn't ask for any daredevil spins— not because I still didn't have the adrenaline fever, but because I had a different appreciation this time around for flying. It was something to be respected, and over the years, I realized the rush came in mastering the art, rather than in pushing the plane to its limits— although I can't swear I'll never again do acrobatics in a plane.

Time stands still when you're in a plane. And the feeling of "getting high" was still as great. Nettsie signed my logbook, next to my old instructor's name.

Two decades later— a new chapter began.

Adrenaline Adventures

Chapter 3
Adventure at a Glance - Dare to Do it   Mild to Wild Scale: 3

Title: Flying Lessons in a Cessna
Children allowed: Age 14 and up
Age requirement: 16 to solo, 17 to get a pilot's license
Length of trip: Around 70 hours of practice is required to get a pilot's license.
Where to try this adventure: Mid Island Service Inc. at MacArthur Airport in Ronkonkoma, New York Check out their website at www.midislandair.com or call 631-588-5400
For those in other states, check any certified flight school in your area.
Best time of year: Year round. Check first for weather report before flying.
Approximate cost: $85 for introductory flight (Average cost for total flight training to get pilot's license $7537.00)
Reservations necessary: Yes
Requirements: Good health, good vision.
Fitness requirement: None
Personal gear required: None
What NOT to bring: Bad attitude
Photo opportunities: Yes, while someone else is flying the plane.

Notes: If you are going to do this, set aside the money so that you can finish the course, otherwise you have to keep starting and stopping.

Cool Trivia: On Oct. 14, 1947 the Bell XS-1 rocket plane became the first manned vehicle to break the sound barrier during level flight. It can go up to 700 mph. And to date the fastest, highest flying aircraft in the world is the North American X-15 A-2. It is a research aircraft, with a speed of 4,520 mph, and a ceiling range of 354,200 feet. It made its first flight in 1959.

"If the winds of fortune are temporarily blowing against you, remember that you can harness them and make them carry you toward your definite purpose, through the use of your imagination."
-Napolean Hill

Chapter 4
"Full of Hot Air"
Hot Air Ballooning

I had the airborne adrenaline bug. I'd jumped out of a plane and I'd flown one. I wanted to get up in the air again. My sister Sharon's birthday was coming up so I figured it would be a great opportunity to turn my next flight into a "family" venture. This time I choose hot air ballooning.

I convinced my boyfriend at the time, Manny; my friend Martha; and her sister, Techi, to come along with us. It was cheaper if we split the cost among five people. We found a ballooning outfit that flew in Connecticut. It turned out ballooning is done at either sunrise or sunset because that's when the wind is the calmest since the sun is low in the sky. We choose sunrise, which required getting our band of balloonists together at three in the morning. We followed the directions we'd be given to a farm field in Connecticut. At first we thought meeting in a farm field a bit odd, but we were told the cool thing about balloons is they don't' need an airport or runway. In fact, they don't even need a hanger or a tie down; they can take off and land practically anywhere, within reason of course—you don't' want land in the middle of the water, or in a bull corral.

Driving out to Connecticut we found ourselves playing beat-the-clock, racing to beat sunrise.

Thanks to Manny's superb driving skills (and an extra five miles over the speed limit) we arrived in time. We emptied our bladders in a port-a-potty (since there are no bathrooms in a hot air balloon) and were greeted by our pilot, Sam, and his crew. We introduced ourselves and moments later Sam said, "Well, no time to lose. Let's get started".

The crew took the balloon out of the pickup truck. As they unloaded, Sam explained what was happening, "A hot air balloon comes in three parts: The envelope (which is the colorful part of the balloon), the burner (which is where the fuel is), and the basket (which is usually made out of wicker and where the passengers ride)." As he said that, the crew laid the rainbow- colored envelope out in the field. The morning sun was starting to rise.

"How long will it take to inflate?" I asked.

"A good ground crew, which I have, can inflate and launch the balloon in about fifteen minutes. So we're doing fine." Sam motioned for Manny to help hold open the envelope while two of his other crew members worked with him. Then they took out the propane tanks and lit them with a striker, which is like the thing that welders use to light their torches. Sam told us that some balloons have built in electric igniters. But whether built-in or manual, once lit, an intensely hot, long flame shoots up from the burner into the balloon to fill it with hot air. The liquid propane is capable of heating large volumes of air quickly. A rope at the top of the balloon, called a crown line, was used to stabilize it during the inflation.

Once the balloon was filled, we were instructed to quickly get into the basket. We all obeyed, since we didn't want to be like Dorothy in *The Wizard of Oz*, left out of the wizard's balloon. The sun had just risen, so the timing was perfect.

Fran Capo

We all stood inside the basket. Sam sized us up and did quick calculations of who should be on what side of the balloon to even out the weights. You don't want to be the one lard ass who makes the balloon lean over to one side.

As we scrambled to our assigned positions, the balloon quietly rose above the trees and into the atmosphere. It was so peaceful. We watched birds fly by at the same altitude. Of course at that moment a bizarre visual crept into my head. "Just out of curiosity Sam, what happens if a nearsighted bird flies into one of these things?"

Sam laughed, "He'd probably bounce off it, like a giant trampoline. The fabric is much tougher than it appears. This balloon is made of a ripstop nylon, and some others use Polyester. This balloon could actually still keep on flying with a hole large enough for a man to go through, as long as the hole wasn't at the top of the envelope."

Manny asked, "These balloons are fireproof, right? Is it okay if I smoke?"

I gave him a dirty look. Sam answered casually, "Not advisable because of the possibility of propane fires or explosions from a leak, and the envelope could be damaged by a stray spark or hot ash. Even though the material is fire- resistant, similar to what racecar drivers and firemen wear, I'm sorry to say my friend, the answer is no."

Martha, who always liked joking around said, "Hey, how do you steer this thing?"

Sam laughed. "I know it looks as if I'm doing nothing but really a balloon floats with the wind."

"So we can wind up in Kansas?" Martha asked sarcastically.

"Possible, but not probable. First, I am a FAA certified licensed balloon pilot, so I do have some practice." He laughed then continued, "The main thing is, before you guys got here, I checked with the weather bureau to see which way the wind was blowing and made sure in my pre-flight planning that there were plenty of places to land downwind. Even though I don't know exactly where we will land, I do know it will be downwind. If you notice below us, my crew is in a chase car, following our every move so they can greet us after we land. Second, while I cannot steer the balloon I can control its altitude. The air is in layers, and the different layers may be moving in different directions. So I simply move the balloon up and

Adrenaline Adventures

down using the burner to find a layer of air that allows the balloon to change direction. We want to keep it downwind, since we can't fly upwind or crosswind."

Sam's spiel was interrupted by a rooster crowing. We looked down and saw some farm people waving at us.

I noticed we were the only balloon in sight. "Are there any other balloons around here, or do we have the skies to ourselves?"

"Well, there are over 3,500 balloons, and another 1,000 or so in other countries in existence, but apparently they are not in this part of the state today."

I looked over to see if my sister was enjoying the ride. She was smiling and just enjoying the breeze, like a puppy with its head out the window. (No insult intended – just a mere comparison.)

As always when things are too calm and relaxed my adrenaline desire kicked in. "Is there any way to make this balloon go faster?"

Everyone looked at me as if to say, "Capo, can't you relax just once?"

But Sam was nice and answered, "I'm afraid that once a balloon is buoyant, it moves with the air mass in which it floats. It doesn't go faster, or slower or in a different direction. But I tell you what I'm going to do. You see that water down there?" We all nodded. "I will touch the bottom of the balloon to that water."

I was ecstatic ... now we talking! Everyone else gripped onto the basket's sides. The basket slowly lowered, then brushed against the water. About an inch of water came into the bottom of the basket. Our shoes got slightly wet, but I loved it. We watched the water drip out of the bottom as we ascended again. That was really all I needed — a dip in the adrenaline pool.

Stirred out of her blissful state, my sister asked, "Could this balloon go over a mountain?" I eagerly awaited the answer ... go Sharon ...this was getting good!

Sam answered, "Actually it can, but it can present some problems. Balloons work on a simple principle, hot air, which is lighter rises, cold air, which is heavier, sinks. We fly at sunrise and sunset to avoid turbulent air which is caused by the difference in temperature in the clouds, over water, etc. Since the sun heats the earth unevenly, it controls the wind. In the mountains, the wind varies too much, plus there are not that many great places to land, and it's hard to get the balloon out later. "

"So then balloons can't fly at night?" Techi chimed in.

"Actually they can but visibility isn't good so we don't' like too."

"I heard the balloons at one point were used during wars?"

"Yes, during the Civil War, World War I and World War II, hot air balloons were used as tools of warfare, for transportation surveying and as a means of communication."

"See and we just thought it was a big colorful toy!"

"Today balloons are used primarily for two purposes, sport or scientific research. Sport balloons mostly use hot air like this one. Scientific balloons generally use hydrogen, helium, methane, or ammonia."

"Geez, puts a whole new light on these balloons."

Almost an hour had passed and our flight was coming to an end. The ever- faithful chase vehicle was still below us. Sam talked to his crew on occasion with the radio that was in the balloon. For the next ten minutes we all stared out in silence. It was extremely peaceful. And the weird part was, you couldn't even detect the balloon was moving.

Except for the occasional blasts of air from the burners controlling our altitude, all you could hear were the noises of the countryside stirring below and getting ready for another day. The smell of freshly cut grass filled our noses. We could see for hundreds of miles on this beautifully clear day.

When it was time to land, Sam allowed the air to cool by lowering the heat. The balloon became heavier than the air and we slowly descended. I was glad he didn't do it too quickly or we'd have dropped like an elevator with a broken shaft line.

Sam radioed the crew who had already obtained permission from the land owner for us to land. Then he let out a drop line so that the ground crew could pull us to an exact spot.

Like a soft floating feather we touched the ground. The crew held tight to the ropes as we got out. Within minutes they had packed the balloon back into the chase vehicle. The final touch was a bottle of champagne that was included in the flight cost to toast to my sister's birthday and our adventure.

Adrenaline Adventures

With balloon packed and toasts made, the chase vehicle drove us back to the launch site where we said our thank you's and got in our car. We drove away with another adventure under our belts and another day to explore.

Fran Capo

Chapter 4
Adventure at a glance - Dare to Do it   Mild to Wild Scale: 2
Title: Hot Air Ballooning
Children allowed: Yes, with parents
Age requirement: Three and up
Length of trip: An hour at dawn or at dusk
Where to try this adventure: For a list of balloon ride companies in the United States do to either baloonridesacrossamerica.com or http://www.launch.net/us_rides.html
Best time of year: Spring or fall.
Approximate cost: $175 per person, group rates offered.
Reservations necessary: Yes
Fitness requirements: None - but you do have to be able to climb into the balloon basket
Personal gear required: wear sneakers.
What NOT to bring: Baggage.
Photo opportunities: Yes

Notes: Some festivals like the annual Hot Air Balloon Festival at Solberg Airport, in Redington, New Jersey held during the summer in the month of July, offers balloon rides at a discount. The largest hot air balloon festival is the Albuquerque International Balloon Fiesta which is held each October in Albuquerque, New Mexico. This event was started in 1972 with just 13 balloons, today it has over one thousand.

At most of these festivals you can see famed publisher Malcolm Forbes specially shaped balloon collection. He has nine specialty balloons such one shaped like his chateau in France; a two hundred foot long balloon shaped like a Harley-Davidson motorcycle, and a bust of Beethoven bigger than the faces on Mount Rushmore.

Cool trivia: On September 19, 1783, a sheep, a duck, and a rooster become the first passengers in a hot air balloon launched by two brothers, Joseph and Ettienne Montgolfier, for a royal demonstration at the court of Louis XVI and Marie Antoinette.

"Columbus did not know where he was going. When he got back, he didn't know where he had been. And he did it all on borrowed money. There's hope for us all".
-From the book, *Do it!* by John-Roger and Peter McWilliams

Chapter 5
"A Plunge into Dark Waters"
Night Diving

When I was first certified as a scuba diver, I imagined it would be like swimming in a giant fish bowl with friendly dolphins and millions of brightly colored fish gliding next to with their gills glittering in the sun. I pictured my hair perfectly in place as I surfaced, like those James Bond girls, not covered with dangling seaweed like the creature from the Black Lagoon.

A diver must be certified by one of the two major diving certification outfits, commonly known as PADI or NAUI. Both require that you take a few hours of classroom instruction, generally spread out over a period of five weeks, which ends in a written test and a few hours of pool training which ends in a skills test, to make sure you will not blow your lungs out or get decompression sickness, commonly known as the bends.

Once you pass both tests you are ready to apply your knowledge and be tested in open water, meaning an ocean, lake or close facsimile.

Adrenaline Adventures

If you pass the three open water dives you are then given a temporary card, so you can dive until your permanent card comes in the mail. Sounds like a lot but usually this can all be accomplished within a month.

There is a lot of gear involved in scuba diving; mask; fins, snorkel, regulator, alternative pressure gauge, BCD(Buoyancy Control Device), weight belt, dive computer, compass, booties, a wetsuit if the water is too cold and of course an aluminum or steel tank filled with compressed air (not pure oxygen).

As soon as you hit the rough, smacking waves of the open water with all this gear, it's like the wakeup call in the movie Poltergeist, "We're heeere."

You need to take your temporary card with you to do your three required open water dives, which can be done anywhere in the world that is allowed to give you your certification card, or C-card as divers call it. I choose to do my first three dives in Bonaire, one of the ABC islands (Aruba, Bonaire and Curacao) islands off the coast of Venezuela.

I once again teamed up with my childhood adventure pal, Viv, who was already a fully certified diver. Viv, was the one who introduced me to the sport in the first place, in a muddy quarry in Texas. Although we were in murky water at the time, and I was buddy breathing off her spare hose called the octopus, she assured me that when you can see things in clear water, diving is much more pleasant. It's equivalent to meeting someone in a dark bar at night and then being shocked with what they look like in broad daylight. Trusting Viv's word, I decided to get certified.

We arrived in Bonaire and met our tall, blonde, tanned and somewhat spacey, dude type instructor named Diver Dave. He was very flirtatious, even though I was married at the time. Men never seem to see the ring, when a girl is in a bathing suit.

I had my first open water dive session right outside the hotel where we were staying. Viv dove nearby. Dave began by reminding me of the different types of water entries in scuba.

"Okay Fran, if you remember from your reading and pool sessions there are three main types of entries; the two from the boat where you can either do a giant stride entry, which looks like you are playing

Fran Capo

a water version of "Mother May I?" or the Jacques Cousteau-type entry where you roll backward off the boat into the water, or the third type, a beach entry. Right now we are going to do a beach entry. I know it's the hardest type, but you're a tough New Yorker, so I know you can handle it."

Dave and I stood on the beach ready to enter the water. Before we did, we did a buddy check to make sure our air was on, hoses were working and that our masks were clear. You want to defog your mask before you dive, or everything will look foggy. New masks have a protective film on them that you can clean off with toothpaste. You can clean a used mask with specially designed chemical drops or good old-fashioned spit—yes, you spit into your mask, wipe the saliva around with your finger, and then wash out the mask. (There's an appetizing thought). The saliva creates a film that doesn't let the mask fog.

As Dave and I walked into the water holding onto each other's shoulders for balance, he explained, "You don't want to wear your fins into the water unless you walk in backward, but that's pretty hard 'cause the waves will knock you over. If you fall over you'll feel like a beached turtle and I wouldn't want that to happen. So I want you to hold your fins in one hand and go in waist deep. Then we can hold onto each other and, one at a time, put our fins on." It sounded a hell of a lot easier than it was since the waves were smacking me in the face, and my mask was strangling me. Scuba is not a graceful sport.

Once we had our fins on, we submerged and went through the various drills; taking the mask off under water, putting it back on and clearing it, regulating buoyancy etc.

After five open water dives over the course of two days, I was certified. I was now the proud owner of a PADI c-card which meant I could dive without an instructor, but as a golden rule in diving, never without a buddy.

On the third day in Bonaire, Viv and I went in the water together. Bonaire is a scuba diver's paradise. There are shipwrecks, lots of fish, coral reefs and water so clear the visibility was about eighty feet. Since Viv was a scientist by profession and an experienced scuba diver, she pointed out all kinds fish to me. We saw moray eels,

Adrenaline Adventures

groupers, clown fish, and the resident steely-eyed barracuda with an overbite—all just thirty feet from shore. The barracuda, by the way,, is not a pleasant looking fish. The one we saw looked annoyed and acted like he was from New York.

I loved this new world and wanted to see more. There's something about getting a license that always makes me want to push it to the limit. When I got my driver's license I drove in Manhattan, on a major highway, and upstate all in my first day. I wanted the full experience. Getting my C-card was no different. The ink on the license wasn't even dry, no pun intended, when I decided Viv and I should take it a tad further. I wanted to dive at night. Viv had told me that night diving was an awesome experience, so I wanted to try it—now.

With scuba diving one of the things you have to watch for is that you don't build up too much nitrogen in your system. That's how people get the bends. There is a diving chart that a diver uses to calculate the buildup of nitrogen in his blood by calculating the depth of their dive and the time he spent down at a certain depth. You always want to do your deepest dive early in the day, spend some time on the water's surface to let the residual nitrogen get out of your system and then dive again later on, using your charts or computer to decide what depth and length dive is safe. Viv and I used the chart, figured out our time, and knew that we were safe for a night dive.

There is something ominous about plunging into dark waters at night. The thought of it scared and thrilled me. Like a burglar entering a house and wondering if the owner is waiting with a baseball bat, you are on guard. The same creatures are in the ocean at night, but it feels even more like you are invading their privacy than it does during the daytime. The nocturnal sea animals, like the octopus and lobster, crawl out at night and their sudden movements can cause your heart to skip a beat. Like all dark places the fear of the unknown lurks around every corner.

I told Diver Dave we wanted to do a night dive. He said he would come along even though technically we didn't need him. Better safe than sorry. Viv had done a few night dives, but was unfamiliar with these waters.

Fran Capo

The locals had observed Viv and I during the week, trying to pick up the American chicks. Most of them had been diving since they were two—I think they had built-in fins. They moved like mermaids, rather mermen, in the water.

Equipped with flashlights and scuba gear, we headed into the night waters from the beach. Diver Dave went in first. Viv and I held hands like two nervous schoolgirls going into a haunted house. The locals sat on a nearby pier and watched in amusement. When we were waist deep in the water, we put on our fins. Then we started to descend. I really had no idea what to expect.

I heard that fish sleep but was curious as to what position they slept in—fetal, spread out, spooned together? It's not like Charlie the Tuna actually gets in the little sardine bed like he does in the commercial.

As we leveled off at twenty feet, out of nowhere, came hundreds of fish. They started biting us. Was it something we said? I felt like I was in a bad sci-fi movie—The Attack of the Killer Groupers.

I looked at Viv in panic. Why were they attacking us? Do they hate Americans? In case you don't realize, you can't exactly talk under water. You can communicate through sign language, noises, or writing on a slate. But when you are being treated as appetizers for fish, you want a more immediate answer. I signaled for Viv to surface.

We popped our heads above the water only to hear the laughter of the locals. They were throwing bread from the pier right over our heads so the fish would bite near us. The fish must have had cataracts, however, because they were biting us instead of the bread. The locals thought this was hysterical.

Relieved that the fish weren't piranhas, we descended again.

We caught up to Diver Dave. He was teasing a moray eel. "Are these people around here nuts?" I thought. We watched as put his fingers next to the eel's mouth. And then—boom!—the eel bit his finger. Blood. I knew I heard the soundtrack from Jaws and wondered where exactly was that damn barracuda? They have a tendency to sneak up on you, especially with the blood dinner bell is ringing. Barracuda's are one of the fastest fish in the water. They also happen to be very territorial, which is just great since barracuda's don't have a doormat outside marking off their area.

Dave was unfazed. He laughed at our surprised expressions. I was amused by the sleeping fish who were just floating—not blinking their eyes or swimming—just floating. It reminded me of commuters on the subway in New York at five o'clock.

After a while you forgot I was in the water. The water was warm, and I felt like I was resting in a large bathtub. Of course, since I couldn't breathe normally, it was like a bathtub on another planet.

Diver Dave motioned for us to turn out our lights. The moonlight was bright enough to illuminate a faint pathway underwater. I kept turning around quickly to make sure nothing was sneaking up on us, like a shark with a head cold who had just caught a whiff of Dave's blood.

Dave moved his hands in the dark water and little fairy dust like particles sparkled. They were called bioluminescence—glow-in-the-dark microorganisms that illuminate with movement. They were pink, purple and yellow. It was like a scene out of a Disney movie. It was gorgeous. I felt like singing "We all live in a yellow submarine".

I was in a dreamlike state. I wasn't nervous anymore. It was odd knowing the vastness of the ocean and then thinking that any fish had access to me and I couldn't see them coming. I kept looking around trying to take it all in. From every nook and cranny I saw life. Lobsters scurried along on the sandy ocean floor, octopi hid in shallow crevices and seahorses, hung on to swaying plants.

After about forty-five minutes under the water we decided to surface. Actually it was the barracuda that gave us the signal. I was laughing (which is hard with a regulator in your mouth) while observing this cute little spunky Damsel fish about the size of a quarter, with the attitude of a rhinoceros. That little fish kept pecking at my mask as if to tell me to get away—when all of a sudden our barracuda friend popped into my vision. Like a tough big brother he seemed to be saying, "Ain't so funny anymore huh, pal?"

We ended the dive quickly, but we felt exhilarated. That night I could think of nothing else but our dive as I looked out on the dark ocean from the shore. Viv and I talked about how awesome life can be.

To think, I was in that huge ocean in the dark exploring the waters, not knowing, what laid just a few feet ahead of me. Sitting on the beach that night, I thought about life in general and how it's important to take those risks. We really never know what is ahead of us. We can plan all we want, we can try to make our lives "safe", but ultimately the coolest things sometimes come from just trusting and taking a plunge into the dark and exploring the unknown, and ultimately we always come out the wiser for the experience.

Adrenaline Adventures

Chapter 5
Adventure at a Glance - Dare to Do it   Mild to Wild Scale: 5
Title: Night Diving
Children allowed: No (although a child can be certified at age 12)
Length of trip: Half to full day, with up to three dives depending on depth.
Where to try this adventure: Look on the Internet for scuba diving instructors and locations. Popular dive sites include the Caribbean, the Great Barrier Reef in Australia, and Mexico.
Contact: PADI (www.padi.com) or NAUI (www.naui.com)
Best time of year to go: Spring, summer, and fall
Approximate cost: $50 for one tank dive, $90 for two tank dive. Night dives - $65, six day package about $450.00
Reservations necessary: Yes with scuba diving outfit. Once you are certified you can go offshore with dive club or buddy providing you have the proper equipment.
Requirements: Must be in good health and have a C-card.
Personal gear required: Mask, fins, snorkel, booties, BCD, regulator, octopus, wetsuit. As a side note, prescription masks are available if you wear glasses. You'll also want to bring a dive bag to carry all your equipment, a logbook to record your dive and of course a bathing suit.
What NOT to bring: Jewelry that might attract sharks or barracudas.
Photo opportunities: Yes, with underwater cameras.

Notes: If you haven't dived for a year or more, brush up on your skills with an instructor before attempting to go in the water. You have to wait twenty-four hours after you dive to fly in a plane.

Cool trivia: On January 4, 2004, his twelfth birthday, Charles Jessop, became the youngest diver in the English-speaking world to qualify as a Master Scuba Diver.

"The desk is a dangerous place from which to watch the world."
—Christopher W. Miller, Ph.D., Founder, Innovation Focus Inc.

Chapter 6
"If you hit a wall - climb over it"
Rock Climbing and Rappelling

In every walk of life there are obstacles or "walls" that we hit on the way to our dreams. Some are physical. Some are mental. Runners talk about hitting the wall. Writers talk about writer's block. In a job its called stagnation, in a marriage it's the seven-year itch, and in aging it's the midlife crisis. Walls are a part of our lives. We want to get over these walls, not crash into them.

I always like to take on physical challenges and transform them into building blocks for mental stimulation. What better way to get over the walls in your life, than to confront a real wall and climb it? Of course, you could always use dynamite and blow the wall to pieces, but I usually choose the more constructive and challenging route.

My pal, Viv had moved back east from Texas and was now living in Danville, Pennsylvania. We had both graduated from college. She was a full-fledged scientist and I was a standup comic. We were both

Adrenaline Adventures

working in the "real" world. She was exploring it, and I was making fun of it. We hadn't had an adventure together in years and figured we were due one. We decided to climb a wall.

Viv heard about an outfit named Quest, an outdoor club associated with Bloomsburg University in Pennsylvania. She said that Quest was modeled after the international Outward Bound programs and that it had a bunch of outdoor weekend adventure programs, such as rock climbing and rappelling, kayaking and wilderness trips in areas all over the United States.

Viv found the number, called Quest, and signed us up for the full-day rock-rappelling course. The cost was only forty-five dollars and all the climbing equipment was included: helmet, harness, ropes and climbing shoes—which looked like ballet slippers with rubber on them. All we needed was to bring was loose fitting pants or shorts. Since I didn't want to have to worry about scraping my knee or some guy below me looking up my shorts, I decided to wear long pants. Viv agreed.

The rock climb took place in a little town called Berwick on Route 11. The mountain that we were going to climb had a long Indian name, Mocanaqua. Which by the end of the day I decided to rename, Ma-can-I-cry?

Viv and I got to Berwick at 8:30 to sign in. There were the maximum twelve students in the class. There were three instructors. We students signed the standard release forms and then we were geared up.

Our lead instructor, Brian explained. "You will notice that some parts of this mountain wall look more difficult than others. The climbing system runs from 5.0 to 5.14. Anything after a 5.0 you need to use your hands to climb, and anything near 5.14 you have to be Spiderman."

Viv and I glanced over to an area not far from us. Some guys were practically climbing upside down.

Brian noticed Viv and I looking at each other with that tilted head dog look that says, "How the hell do they do that?" Brian read our minds. "Climbing like that is like climbing on a mirror with two pennies glued to it for finger holds. It all depends on the rock's angles and the paths leading straight up." Viv and I looked at each other again and shrugged. He laughed. "Don't worry girls. That's not happening for us today. Although you will get a chance to try out what a free climb would feel like on that boulder over there."

The whole class turned to look at the boulder. Even if we climbed to the top, it was only about a six-foot jump down. How hard could that be? Viv and I were ready for the challenge. The other class members seemed to have the same feeling.

Brian decided to let us all have a crack at the practice boulder. To demonstrate, he scrambled up the boulder like a spider. I volunteered to go next into his web. I got about two feet off the ground and I was already in a position where I couldn't find a foothold. The rock jutted out, so my body was almost parallel with the ground. I lost my grip and fell. I tried again, determined and somewhat embarrassed. Again I fell. Viv was up next. I could see her fingers turning red as she gripped hard to hang on. She fell too. After all of the students were sufficiently humiliated, we realized climbing was not going to be as easy as the experts make it look.

Brian chuckled, "Don't worry, no beginner gets that rock. You guys will be climbing on a wall that is a 5.4 and considered easy. The key thing to remember in climbing is that it requires three points of contact at all times. Two hands and a foot, two feet and a hand…you get the picture."

He continued, "My staff and myself will put anchors in the wall as we climb, and you guys will simply follow the anchor system up. We will teach you how to belie, and once you get to the top we will show you how to rappel down. The main thing is to remember is climbing equals intense concentration. You need to focus and not give up. Use any little nook to propel yourself further up the cliff. And please trust your partner. Trust that he or she has you tight enough and isn't annoyed at anything you might have said or done earlier." He smiled.

I turned to Viv. "This might not be the best sport for husbands and wives to perform together."

With the explanations over for now, we were instructed to wait at the bottom of the mountain until they set things up. Brian and his team began by chalking their hands so they could get a good grip on the rope. Brian had his fancy toe shoes on, his harness, ropes, nuts,

Adrenaline Adventures

cams and carabineers—the metal clips that the rope feeds through. He secured himself in his harness and handed his partner, Rick, the other end of the rope. We all watched intently. Rick fed Brian the rope as he needed it in a kind of pulley fashion. He pushed it up with his front hand whenever there was slack and used his back hand to grip the rope behind him and keep it steady. And just for safety purposes Rick was also tied to a tree to root himself, in the awful event that Brian might fall. If he did fall

at least Rick wouldn't go flying in the air, where in the middle the twain would meet.

As Brian climbed, Rick belied him. To belie is simply to keep the rope tight so that if the climber falls he won't go crashing down—but not so tight as to impair his future breeding process.

Brian ascended, slowly placing pegs in the rocks to anchor him to a point where he stopped. Every several feet he would place another anchor. Our necks got stiff from looking straight up, but it was a small price to pay for making sure he did the job right, thus protecting all us.

When he got to the top of the mountain wall he yelled, "Off belie!" Brian unhitched the rope, pulled it up, did some fancy tying at the top and then rapidly rappelled himself down. I sure hoped he was paying attention in knot tying class.

Now it was time to for us students to take a crack at it. Brian reminded us that if a rock fell loose as we climbed it was our obligation to yell, "Rock!" so our team member below wouldn't get pelted in the head.

We were divided into teams. Viv, myself and this girl named Sandra were hooked up.

Viv and I were athletic and anxious to scramble up the rocks. Sandra seemed a little leery, but game. After we were harnessed up we decided that Viv would go first, then me, then Sandra. We were attached to one another with a rope system. By today's standards, it was an antiquated system. The breaking device was yourself, which has since changed. Good thing because it was rough on your body. As one person climbed to a certain point they would then secure themselves against a rock. The next person would then ascend putting all the pressure on the rope attached to the person above. If the person below let go, your body had to absorb the pressure—big time!

Viv chalked her hands then looked for her first foot and hand holds. Once she found it, she started up the mountain face. If I spotted a foot or hand holds as she climbed, I would tell her things like, "Viv to the right. Wait there's one up a little to the left, near your hand." Viv made it to the first resting place, and then it was my turn.

The cliff felt cool. I saw the handholds Viv had used and followed a similar path. At times I used rocks that seemed the size of peas to propel myself up farther. I realized the intense concentration it took, and that rock climbing is a great teaching device for life in general. It shows you how to look at everything in front of you as a way to go up and toward your goal. It was either that or camp out in a vertical position all night long.

I used every part of my body: elbows, knees ... I'd even have used my teeth if I'd had to. I didn't want to fall. It was a pride issue. I also wanted to impress the teacher and myself. I pretended I was in the movie *Cliffhanger*. No way I was letting go.

There were a couple of times that I thought I had reached a dead end. But then I stepped over to the left or right a few inches and saw a tiny window of opportunity. As I climbed, face pressed against the rock wall, I didn't realize how far up I was. At one point Brian, who had been watching me ascend, yelled, "Smile, Fran. Stop and look around." I stopped. For the first time, I noticed I was above the trees! I was about sixty feet up. It's amazing how far step-by-step can take you. I got to Viv and we hugged each other. Now it was Sandra's turn to go up.

I leaned against the rock with the rope around my waist. Viv was behind me taking in the slack of the rope as Sandra climbed. Sandra was a robust girl. I'm not saying I'm some kind of Barbie Doll, but the girl was big. I gave her credit for trying this. She was doing nicely the first twenty feet, then for some reason, she tensed up and panicked because she couldn't find another foot hold. She kept saying, "I can't find one, I can't find one."

Viv and I tightened our grip on the rope. "Just look around. You'll find it." Viv yelled.

Adrenaline Adventures

Sandra was frozen. She lost her confidence and gave up. She screamed in frustration and then just let go. Great, my luck I would get some girl that didn't understand Newton's Law. Here was a big girl dangling from a rope that was wrapped around my waist. When she went in the direction of gravity, the rope around my waist tightened my stomach to a size that even Scarlett O'Hara would have been proud of.

It was at this point that I wanted to rename the mountain, "Ma-can-I-cry?" because that's what I wanted to do. I was in a lot of pain.

Barely breathing, and holding the rope as tight as we could, Viv and I convinced Sandra to stop dangling and hold onto the rocks again. Actually we said something more like, "If you don't grab hold, we are going to have to let go and you will go crashing down. So grab the rope!" With that dose of reality she grabbed onto the wall—so much for female bonding.

Once I could breathe again, I talked her up the mountain, then proceeded to smack her. (Well, not really, but I sure as hell wanted to.) Sore ribs left me not thrilled with the experience, although with the harnesses they have today, that never would have happened.

After she made it up to where we were, we regained our composure and gave her a pep talk. We had to—we still had to climb farther and make our final ascent to where Brian and the rest of the students were gleefully waiting. With her assurance that she would not panic, we all pulled as a team and climbed to the top.

It felt great to make it to the top—all ninety feet. The view from up there was spectacular. We could see above the trees and across pastures beyond. It was quite an accomplishment. We congratulated Sandra for not giving up.

Now came part two, the rappel and decent. We really had to rely on our partners and the umbilical cord of rope, our life line. Brian began his instructions. "You have to put your body perpendicular to the cliff, and then kind of bounce down to the next section of rock. Just like in the movies only there is no stunt double. As you back down over the rock you will get nervous at first when you see no rock below you to put your feet on. Just trust the rope and your partner. Who's first?"

Fran Capo

Knowing Sandra's track record, we decided to be the last group down. One by one each student descended.

When our turns came, I backed down over the cliff first. If you don't look down and just stare at your feet, it's not too bad. But once you see that there are no footholds and you just have to bounce off the rocks, it gets a bit scary. After the first mini rappel you quickly learn you are not going to come splashing down, so you get a little braver. My second bounce was bigger and the rappel faster. At one point I got a little over-confident and wound up crashing into the mountain. That quickly put things in perspective.

Standing at the bottom, I felt great. My arms were trembling a little from the adrenaline rush. Viv and I were like proud little kids. We could see Sandra still standing at the top of the cliff. She decided not to take the plunge even though we all cheered her on. She walked down the mountain and met us an hour later. As we waited for her to catch up with the rest of the group, Viv and I looked up at the wall. I said, "We did it. Whadda'ya think, Viv, Mount Everest next?"

"Fran, I said I'd climb the wall, not the whole mountain!" Then she laughed.

"At least not today anyway."

Yup, just like Scarlett O'Hara once said, "Tomorrow's another day!"

Adrenaline Adventures

Chapter 6
Adventure at a Glance: Dare to Do it   Mild to Wild scale: 3
Title: Rock Climbing and Rappelling
Children allowed: Yes, but children under 12 must be accompanied by a parent
Age requirement: 13 and up.
Length of trip: From one day to a month.
Where to try this adventure: Contact Quest to find locations: http://orgs.bloomu.edu/quest or call (570)389-2100
Quest Program at Bloomsburg University of Pennsylvania
Bloomsburg, Pa. 17815
Best time of year to go: Spring, summer, and fall—and winter if you ice climb .
Approximate cost: $45 a day for the rock climbing.
Reservations necessary: Yes
Requirements: Just show up. List of equipment sent to you via online for longer trips.
Fitness requirement: Good physical fitness.
Personal gear required: Loose clothes.
What NOT to bring: Jewelry, rings, cell phones, radios.
Photo opportunities: Yes

Note:
- The director in charge of Quest is Roy Smith. Roy is a mountain guide on five continents –leader of two National Geographic expeditions in the Arctic and Africa and a corporate trainer. He is the man to use in the United States if you need an expert. After speaking with him I decided I am going to climb Kilimanjaro with Ron's buddy, Corbet Bishop– but that story is for *Adrenaline Adventures II*.

Cool trivia: The fastest climber in America is a woman, Lyn Hill. (That's an appropriate last name!) She is the only person who has climbed the 3,000-vertical-foot Nose on El Capitan in Yosemite National Park with no artificial aids in under twenty-four hours.

"In a moment of decision, the best thing you can do is the right thing to do. The worst thing you can do is nothing."
---Theodore Roosevelt

Chapter 7
"Crawling a Mile Below"
Spelunking

When I first heard the word "spelunking," I thought it was the name of a Russian satellite missile satired on "Saturday Night Live." Either that or it was the sound of a painful belly flop. Little did I know, it was the sport of crawling on your stomach in pitch black, dark, damp fifty-five degree caves, often a mile below the surface of the ground. Enticing? To me it was just another challenge yet to explore.

Okay, let me get this straight right up front. This is not the picnic walk through caves like Howe Caverns where you are holding onto railings, nice bright lights are hanging from the ceiling, and educated tour guides are explaining all about stalagmites and stalactites.

This is the hard-core type cave—the type where you are equipped with helmets with attachable flashlights, backup lights, kneepads, and where your clothes get so dirty that you could be the poster child for a Tide commercial. In this type of spelunking you crawl through tight spaces that make you think your Jenny Craig diet is

Adrenaline Adventures

not shedding the pounds that it should be. Some of these caves have water waist deep in places and require a wetsuit. Most of these caves have bats; some have snakes and other creatures from the Black Lagoon. Got the picture?

First I had to locate other strange humans involved in this activity. So I did some research and found out there are groups called "Grottos" in some of the states and all over the world. I located a New York Grotto officially called Met Grotto and got in touch with their head crawler, Chris, and arrange to go on a beginner spelunking trip at a place called Pompies Cave in Newburgh, in upstate New York. Chris gave me a checklist of things to bring: a change of clothes, hat, gloves, kneepads, extra batteries, flashlight, knapsack, bottled water, and garbage bags to put my dirty clothes in after the adventure. I was psyched.

I decided to bring a very athletic friend, Keith, along with me, to share in the fun. Keith and I took the two-hour drive up together. We rendezvoused with the rest of the spelunkers at six in the morning near the cave. We were the first to arrive so we started putting on our layer of clothes.

Since had been told this was a wet cave, so we had brought our scuba diving wetsuits and booties. We didn't know exactly what to expect.

Within twenty minutes, our crew of six had arrived. Keith and I were the newbies. I noticed there were no other women. I guess crawling around getting muddy is not a favorite feminine pastime. We were a motley looking crew in our "I wouldn't be caught dead at a Laundromat with these old' clothes on" attire.

Chris introduced everyone. People sat by the open trunks of their cars getting dressed and just chatting. After another twenty minutes, Chris pulled out a map of the cave and we all gathered by the hood of his car to look at it. He pointed to the high and low points of the cave, showed us the entrance point, and identified an emergency exit point that could be used if necessary. He said the cave wasn't that long—about eight hundred feet—but that it would still take a good three hours to go through it.

I asked if he knew how long the longest cave was, and he said, " Kazumura—Olaa Cave System, which is actually a lava tube in

Fran Capo

Hawaii is 3,614 feet—the longest cave in the United States, and in fact the word is the Mammoth Cave System, in Kentucky it's 346,010 miles long."

"Man, that would take us years to crawl!"

Chris laughed. "Well, let's start with this one." Since Keith and I were new, he told us a couple of spelunking pointers. "Remember three points of contact at all times. There are going to be some places in the cave where we will climb up or down one at a time. When you are climbing if a rock falls yell 'rock' so the person below will know. Don't start climbing till the person above you yells 'clear'. This is an easy cave. If you get cold, let us know immediately. The last thing we want is hypothermia setting in."

Ahhh, that was something I hadn't thought of. Too late, I was already there. I felt the pressure wheel tighten, because I was the only woman. I didn't want to wimp out and perpetrate the myth of the weak female.

We walked about a quarter of a mile and then stopped by this four-foot-by three-foot opening in the ground. There was a locked metal gate over the opening. The lock was the type used on high school gym lockers; it was meant to protect the cave from unauthorized persons. Honestly, if the gate wasn't there and you just happened to be wandering in the woods and stumbled across this opening, you would think it was a large pothole, not the beginning of an underground passageway that winds for about a mile in the earth.

Chris unlocked the gate and hid the lock. Before we descended in he said, "We all need to respect the caves. They have been here long before us, and we want others to be able to enjoy them. You will see several cave formations, and the main two are stalagmites, a type of speleothem which grows upward from a surface, and stalactites which grows downward. An easy way to remember the difference is the 'g' in stalagmite stands for 'ground' and the 'c' in stalactite stands for 'ceiling.' These two cave formations are formed when water containing dissolved minerals, frequently calcite, but there are other types that I won't go into, are deposited on the same spot over thousands or millions of years. We ask that you please don't touch these formations. They may seem just like rocks but they are growing. And if you touch them, they stop growing in that area because the dirt or oil from your skin prevents water from reaching the growing formation. Enough touches and the formation will die. We don't want that, so please be careful. Okay, let's go in."

One by one we descended down a wooden ladder. At the bottom of the ladder we had to call 'clear' and then get on our hands and knees and begin to crawl for about fifty feet. The ground is cold but not wet ... yet. My heart was beating faster for some reason I found it very exciting, not knowing what laid ahead.

At the end of the fifty-foot stretch we reached an area that we could stand in, hunched, for the next few yards. At this point we could see no light from the outside and it was dark except for the shining of our helmet lights. We crawled a bit farther and then we came to this dead end ... water. All of our flashlights shined their beacons on the muddy water ahead.

Now the fun begins. "Follow Me!" yelled Chris. I looked at Keith. We both shrugged. We felt a weird mixture of excitement and tenseness. I think I watched too many Outer Limits episodes as a kid. I kept picturing a seaweed-draped hand shooting up out of the water and grabbing my arm or leg.

Since I was the shortest of the bunch, I had the honor of being the first to submerge emerged chest deep in the water. I felt the mucky ground sucking my feet.

The waterway passage was only about a five-minute walk, but in those five minutes I came up with a bunch of sci-fi scenarios. What if one of us stepped into a bottomless pit in the water and sunk down and wound up in middle earth? What if there were miniature cave dwellers beings who were hiding in the water and waiting to take us hostage for invading their home? What if we found Jimmy Hoffa?

Eventually we were back to crawling, and then walking around hunched. Finally we were able to walk upright again. I felt like I was reenacting the stages of evolution. Soon we were back on our knees and came to a fork in the cave. Where is Rand McNally when you need him? I hoped Chris had the map with him, 'cause quite frankly when I had looked at the cave map earlier, I didn't know how the hell to read it.

Without hesitation Chris took the right fork. As soon as he did the cave ceiling lowered drastically. We crawled on our stomachs, inching our way forward. I could hear the sounds of labored breathing. It sounded like the killer's breathing in those movies where the killer chases a girl (always some stupid girl in high heels.

My helmet, which was a bit too large, kept sliding over my eyes. I just keep crawling even though the helmet kept banging on the ceiling.

At one point when we were crawling on our knees, Chris stopped. He pointed out a cluster of slightly frosted beings in a crevice—it was a family of hibernating bats. He told us not to shine our flashlights on them because then their body temperature would heat up and they would think it was time to come out of hibernation and they could die. So we shined the lights in their general vicinity to get a quick look. It was fascinating to be only inches from about seven tiny bats. They had this white, thin layer of frost on their two-inch bodies. It was like they were frozen in time. I know most people don't' think of bats as cuddly, but they really did look cute there all snuggled together. Of course, that's my personal opinion.

Finally, after about forty-five minutes of contorting my body in every conceivable position, we came to the end of the cave. We were able to sit up.

We stopped for a water break. I didn't want to drink too much since I didn't think bathroom facilities were plentiful down there, and I didn't have the male advantage.

Chris asked us all to turn off our helmet lights and hand held flashlights and just sit in total darkness and listen to the sounds of the cave. We did. It was weird at first. Then I placed my hand right in front of my face and couldn't see it. I sensed it, but couldn't see it. I imagined how scary it would be to be stuck in a cave and trying to find your way out. After about a minute we turned our lights back on.

Then came the moment of decision. Chris said, "Well, these are the choices. Straight above us is an opening. We can crawl up through there and be above ground in about ten minutes, but it's a tight space. Or we can crawl back through the cave. Let's decide who wants to do what."

It was unanimous; we'd crawl straight up. Great, only one problem. Chris tried to go up and he couldn't fit. Then Al, the other

Adrenaline Adventures

leader tried and couldn't fit. The other two guys tried. No luck. This was not looking good. My friend Keith tried. He is tall, muscular, and agile. He fit easily. He crawled up out of sight and. Chris looked at me. "Look, if you want to go up and follow him it's easy. You will see which way to go. We will go back out the way we came. We can yell to you from above. It will only take us twenty minutes to get out. If you start in ten minutes, in about another ten minutes you'll be able to hear us calling to you.

Keith shimmied back down to be with me. We waited in total darkness as the others left. I started to think this was a bad B-movie plot with two idiot characters—us—waiting for our impending doom.

I told Keith to go first so I could follow his lead. He climbed up, and I could see him wiggling. He yelled, "Clear!" I started up. I got up about ten feet and then my hips got stuck. I tried to suck in my stomach, but I could do nothing to reduce the size of my hipbones. I started to panic but tried to sound casual when I said, "Ah, Keith, I think I'm stuck."

I tried to pry myself out, but the more I did, the tighter I felt the rocks squeezing me. I knew if I tried to go farther up, I'm definitely be wedged in. Keith was already beyond my view. I heard the guys yelling from above ground

I yelled back up to Keith, "I am going back down." Keith yelled that he was at the top. He encouraged me to try again. I was in the cave alone. I tried once again, and once again my hips got stuck in the same spot. I was really embarrassed. Five foot two, 121 pounds, and my hips were too big!

A decision was made above ground. The pros would come back through the cave to get me. They told me to sit tight. I sat and waited. It was too quiet. I knew I was safe, but I felt impatient. I remembered the way out of the area and decided I'd meet the pros halfway. Slowly I started to crawl out.

It is really felt like an adventure. It really felt like an adventure. I no longer was scared, but excited. I knew they were coming to get me, but I got to experience being in a pitch-black cave all alone. Knowing that above me were five people who would rescue me if need be, made me feel secure.

Fran Capo

I made it back to the waist-deep water. It became a game for me. I wanted to meet the pros as close to the opening as possible.

I got to the fork. Oh man, which way? I remembered a comment Chris had made on the way in, "Hug the wall." I kept one hand on the wall as I crawled. I ended up meeting them almost three-quarters of the way back. They were impressed. I was impressed with myself—minus the hip embarrassment

We surfaced totally covered in mud. I snapped pictures to archive the event. I knew this was one for the books as far as challenging myself, with a trip into utter darkness ... alone.

Adrenaline Adventures

Chapter 7
Adventure at a glance - Dare to Do it!   Mild to Wild Scale: 3
Title: Spelunking
Children allowed: Yes, but ages 10 to 18 need a parental waiver.
Length of trip: One day
Where to try this adventure: Check with your local Grotto or go to Met Grotto's website: http://www.galaxy.net/~trbarton/met/
The Met Grotto is the home for cavers in the metropolitan New York City area, with members from New York, New Jersey, Connecticut, Pennsylvania, West Virginia and beyond.
Best time of year: Offered all year long.
Approximate cost: Free to minimal.
Reservations necessary: Yes
Requirements: Can't be claustrophobic or afraid of the dark. Should be in good health.
Children allowed: Ten and up, needs waiver from Parent.
Fitness requirement: Reasonable good shape, flexible
Personal gear required: Loose-fitting clothes that you don't mind getting dirty, helmet with light, kneepads, gloves, water bottle, fanny pack, change of clothes and a garbage bag to put dirty clothes in.
What NOT to bring: Anything of value. Whatever you bring WILL get muddy and could get lost. Hide your car keys outside the cave or bring a duplicate set.
Photo opportunities: Extremely limited by light.

Notes: Expect to get TOTALLY muddy.

Cool Trivia: Caves have been used for a variety of purposes: refrigerated food storage during pioneer times, saltpeter mining and weapons storage during the 1800s, speakeasies and hideouts for moonshine stills during Prohibition, and dance halls during World War II. According to the Tennessee Cave Survey (TCS), Tennessee currently has more discovered caves than any other state at over 8,400.

"Courage is not the absence of fear, but rather the judgment that something else is more important than fear."
– Ambrose Redmoon

Chapter 8
"A Rubber Band!"
Bungee Cord Jumping

By now you can tell I get a thrill out of trying something that pushes me to my limits of fear. Granted I wouldn't want to be in a traffic jam behind a group of Hell's Angels with my horn stuck, but calculated risks, I get pleasure out of.

Life is too short to do the same things over and over again. You wouldn't eat pizza every night no matter how much you loved it (unless maybe your family owned a pizzeria). With this in mind I decided it was time to take the plunge, a 220-foot plunge ... and bungee jump. I found out that a local hot air balloon festival was offering a chance to bungee jump out of one of their hot air balloons. The flyer read, "Defy Gravity." I liked it already. I liked the idea of bungee jumping out of a balloon instead of off a bridge, which I

Adrenaline Adventures

always thought seemed a tad suicidal. I asked my friend Keith to come along for the jump; no fun taking the plunge alone.

The bungee jump was only offered in the wee hours of the morning, so once again I had to get up at seven, and we left before sunrise. I always feel like a fugitive when I leave my house that early with bags in tow.

We arrived at the place and were sectioned off in an area of our own. There were twenty other daring souls. A hot air balloon was set up and tethered to a post—a very strong post. A registration table was to our right. We had to sign release forms. The standard "you will not hold us responsible for anything because you agreed to do this nutty thing in the first place, without a gun to your head" form. And once again, I signed. Although, I had no doubt if a limb came off, I would head over to the nearest lawyer, slam my severed limb onto his desk and say, "Hey pal, can you give me a hand?" Okay corny, but it fits.

The next step, which is the reason why many women don't bungee jump, was to be weighed in. Yes, they weigh you on a public scale with large numbers. Then they yell out your weight to be recorded on your chart.

Now as embarrassing as that is, face it, bungee jumping is not the place you want to lie about your weight. Imagine you go plummeting to the ground and snap the cord, then they have to draw a nice white chalk line around your dead body—"Shouldn't have lied about that extra five pounds, babe."

After they yelled out all our weights, they took the humiliation one step further. They lined us up in weight order—the heaviest going first. I always like going first to get these things over with; plus I am like a little kid excited and can't wait my turn. But in this case, being the only woman on this jump, I was the lightest, thank goodness.

I asked the instructor, Sal, why we had to be weighed.

"Weight is a safety matter that is taken very seriously. A jumper's weight determines the number of cords to be used. We have a limit of 250 pounds."

"Man how embarrassing would that be if someone just ate a hotdog and is one pound over the limit."

Sal just smiled as if to say, "Don't be a wise guy."

Once we were all lined up, Sal began to explain in detail how it was going to work. "When it's your turn I want you to walk over to the balloon, and climb in. Then the balloon will rise to 220 feet and be then stop at that height by the tethered rope. At that point you simply climb out of the balloon and onto the jumping platform that is attached to the balloon. Then listen to our backwards count. When we say, 'one,' you jump. The main thing to remember is, whatever you do, DON'T GRAB ONTO THE BUNGEE ROPE. You will get a nasty burn and peel the skin off your hands, plus it makes for a rougher ride. Just relax and go with the flow. It will be over before you know it."

The first guy walked up to the hot air balloon. Up it went. The guy climbed out of the balloon, and after a count of five, he jumped. So far so good, but then he did exactly what he wasn't supposed to do, he grabbed the rope. He got knocked around pretty bad, and his hands got a nasty rope burn. The second guy did the same thing.

I turned to the Sal, "What's up with that?"

He laughed. "As long as I've been here, the men never listen to the instructions. They think they are macho and can grab onto the ropes and control it. But after one time doing that they quickly learn. The more relaxed you are the better it is."

To kill time and not think about my leap, I asked Sal, "How did bungee cord jumping start anyway? Did someone have a bad suicide attempt or what?"

Sal answered, "Bungee jumping originated in Pentecost Island in the New Hebrides, where a local tribe of natives performed their manhood-rites by jumping off a twenty-five-meter-high bamboo tower with a stiff vine like stem of liana tied to their feet."

"Jeez, I guess it's better than circumcision –that is unless you hit the ground."

"Yeah, well the way we do it, it's safe. The modern bungee jumps originated in New Zealand in the late eighties. But instead of a vine, they used a rubber rope."

"And then what, it just caught on?"

Adrenaline Adventures

"No, there was this New Zealand guy, A.J. Hackett. He jumped off the Eiffel Tower in Paris. The jump was shown on TV all over the world, and then it spread all over Europe and then came here."

It was now my friend Keith's turn. Up he went, and down he came, a bit stiff so he banged into the rope a few times. I made a mental note to definitely not touch the rope.

Now it was my turn. The harness was placed up through my legs and around my waist. I liked this better than the kiwi jump, which is the type where they place it around your ankles. That would have been too intense. What happens if I had slippery socks or my feet just slipped out? I liked it around my waist much better. With harness secure, the bungee cord was attached. I saw them adjust the bungee and asked why.

"The bungee is calculated for weight, that's why we try to keep all the same weight groups together, so we only have to adjust it down a bit each time."

I stepped inside the hot air balloon and up it rose ... 220 feet. Once again when it reached the full length of the tethered rope it stopped. I looked over the side of the balloon. Two hundred and twenty feet seems a lot higher from the air. The instructor smiled. "Climb out." Good thing he didn't say "Get out" or I would have felt like I was dealing with a Bugsy Malone gangster type in some B rated flick.

I stepped outside the balloon and onto a tiny platform. The instructor said,

"Now remember, relax."

"Relax! Skid marks are going to be left in the air."

He said, "If you relax, the rubber band won't break."

"The rubber band? What's holding me to the balloon ... a staple?" All of a sudden I wasn't feeling too comfortable.

But then I heard the countdown from the onlookers and fellow jumpers below. "Five ... four ... three ... two ... one ... jump!"

With that I closed my eyes, leaned forward, and fell. It's an odd feeling just falling like that. You feel like you are falling into the abyss, not knowing at exactly what point you will be yanked back up like a rag doll. I kept my eyes closed on the first descent because I didn't want to see the ground rushing up at me.

Fran Capo

I resisted all temptation to grab onto the rope. But the thought did cross my mind. It's the only solid thing up there, and you want to grab it like it is your umbilical cord.

You seem to fall forever ... Gravity takes you down ... and you go down ... but then you come back up ... think ...."Holy cannoli! "

You've reached the full length of the bungee and you become a human yo-yo. The grounds close, the ground's far, the ground's ... ahhhh too close! Now, it's far ... the birds are upside down, which way is up? All the time I'm thinking, "Relax, Capo, just relax. Relax ... relax ... RELAX!" I stayed so relaxed, I was limp. My hair was dangling down as the bungee cord came to a stop. I just lay there like a rag doll. Someone from below yelled, "I think she had a heart attack." So I lay there longer for a more dramatic effect. It cracked me up. The whole thing was over in twenty-eight seconds.

After they realized I wasn't unconscious, the balloon lowered me to the ground. I stood up, unharnessed myself and walked over to Keith. We high fived each other, then hugged. It was a fantastic rush.

Of course, what adventure would be complete without being able to purchase a video so you can prove to yourself and your friends, just how insane you were. The great thing about the tape is, you have forever immortalized your actions and never have to do "that" again! And why would you? There are always more adventures.

Adrenaline Adventures

Chapter 8
Adventure at a Glance - Dare to Do it   Mild to Wild Scale: 5

Title: Bungee Cord Jumping
Age requirement: Preferably 18 and over, but kids can jump with a parental consent form.
Length of trip: Half day
Where to try this adventure: There are bungee jumping companies all over the world. Visit http://www.bungeezone.com/clubs/ to find a location near you. Also check out http://www.bungee.com to see all the types of jumps you can do.
Call 503-520-0303 for more information.
Best time of year: Summer, fall, and spring.
Approximate cost: From $45 to $100 per jump.
Reservations necessary: Yes
Requirements: None
Fitness requirement: Good health, weigh no more than 250 pounds.
Personal gear required: None
What NOT to bring: Tight clothes
Photo opportunities: Yes

Notes: Don't go on a full stomach.

Cool trivia:
- The DSC (Dangerous Sports Club) kicked off this "sport" when they jumped off the Clifton suspension bridge in England on April Fool's Day in 1977. They promptly were arrested for this. A story about the jump hit the world press the next day. But it wasn't until the nineties that it became popular in England after the New Zealanders made it a commercial sport.
- The highest bungee jump, according to the Guinness Book of World Records, was performed by Curtis Rivers from the UK. He bungee jumped from a hot air balloon at 15,200 feet over Puertollano, Spain, on May 5, 2002.

"The greatest pleasure in life is doing what people say you cannot do."
--Walter Bagehot

Chapter 9
"Smokin' Tootsies"
Walking on Hot Coals

For some crazy reason, several years ago I decided to walk on fire. Not knowing exactly how this would improve my resume, or where I could use this skill other than at a family barbeque where they'd run out of room on the dance floor and I could hop up on the Hibachi and do the Macarena, I still had a burning desire to do it.

I had read about fire walking and had always wondered how those guru mystics were able to do it without searing their feet. Then, one day in the mail a possible answer to my question came. I received an Anthony Robbins Fire Walking Seminar flyer. The flyer explained that fire walking was a metaphor for "unlimited power." It said that if you can master your communication skills, beliefs and physiology, then you will be truly successful. The fire walk was a tangible way for you to conquer what holds you back by taking a quantum leap in your life through the fire walk. It went on to explain that with the fire walk you literally condition your mind and body to consistently react with power and focus in any situation. The seminar was three days or you could opt to just do the one day fire walk. I decided my life was pretty successful, but that I wanted to give the fire walk a shot. Of course, what better way to bond with a family member than to attempt a feat so great together? So I asked my mom, and in true Capo style, she said "Yes."

I told a few of my friends that I was going to walk on hot coals, and as usual they thought I was crazy. They thought that my mom was even crazier, but they forgot that my mother is the one who raised me with the mantra that nothing is impossible.

Some friends offered to set up a barbeque grill in their backyard and save me the cash. Many had their own theories about how fire walking was possible. Some considered it a parlor trick with smoke and mirrors. The more scientifically minded friends said that people could do it because of water vapor or the Leidenfrost Effect (an effect named after the man who first described the water vapor theory). Supposedly Leindenfrost said that the moisture on the sole

Adrenaline Adventures

of a person's foot creates a vapor barrier that prevents the foot from actually making contact with the coals and getting burned. Kind of like when you lick your finger and put out a match. However, a physicist by the name of Jearl Walker tried to prove Leidenfrost's theory. He thought it was impossible to get burned while fire walking, so he tried it and got severely injured … and, as they say, his theory went up in smoke.

Another friend told me about the Conductivity Theory. This theory basically says that coal is a poor conductor of heat and that's why a fire walker is able to walk on it regardless of temperature. Apparently the Discovery Channel wanted to see if this theory was correct. They did a show on this theory where they had physicist Bernard Leikind visit a place called the Fire Walking Institute of Research and Education (F.I.R.E.) which was run by the father of fire walking, Tolly Burkan, the same guy who taught Anthony Robbins how to do it.

The show had the physicist strap two sirloin steaks to his feet and then walk across a bed of coals. Then he showed the steaks to the camera, and they were uncharred. Then the physicist placed a metal grill in the coals and, when the grill was glowing red hot, he placed the same steaks on the grill and the metal instantly seared the meat. The physicist grinned like a Cheshire cat, feeling he had proved that a mental state had nothing to do with fire walking. He concluded his segment by saying that it would be impossible for humans to walk on his red hot grill without any kind of injury.

Well, apparently the people at the Fire Walking Institute wanted to show him otherwise, so several of them walked on his red hot grill. Apparently the grill was so hot that the metal was soft and bent upon the weight of the firewalkers, but not one of the fire walkers got so much as a blister. The physicist was baffled. The Fire Walkers Institute has the grill with the molded footprints on display as a souvenir to show that the Conductivity Theory was disproved.

With naysayers in the wings I felt it was time for me to conduct my own personal fire walking experiment, with my mother in tow.

The day was March 23, 1991. The place, a hotel in Philadelphia. The time 7 p.m. About 1,400 eager feet of all ages, shapes, and sizes gathered in a large ballroom, ready to learn the secret to charcoal feet.

For the first few hours Anthony (a.k.a. Tony) talked in his very passionate way about awakening the giant within. He explained that you have to challenge yourself to go beyond where you have gone before. In short, you have to find the guru within you. I was willing to look; I just hoped he didn't look like Yoda.

Tony talked about how fear stops people. He said, "The key is to learn to control and harness your fear, not to get rid of it. Once you can ride it like a bucking bronc, you take action."

To prove that the coals were real, and to inspire us further, he marched all seven hundred of us in a double file to a parking lot two blocks away. There in the empty lot were about one hundred rows of burning red coals. Each row was about twelve feet long. I asked one of the nearby assistants what was under the coals, and she said, "Incense cedar or white birch is generally what we use. It produces the best coal beds. Other woods would either reduce themselves to ash too quickly and you guys wouldn't get a nice hot coal effect—either that or it would produce sharp-edges on the coals. Some woods leak sap and gum that can stick to a person's foot. So we stick with these." Good thing, because the last thing I would want is my foot sticking to the coal. The thought alone is painful.

Individually we walked over to the red-hot briquettes and felt the wave of heat rise in our faces. I could actually feel the heat on my eyeballs. To really drive home the point, we were told the coals glow at the temperature that turns steel into a molten river. A hot stove is only 675 degrees; these coals were 2000 degrees! Or to put it another way ... OWWWW!

I remembered reading that human flesh even momentarily exposed to 1,200- degree heat can sustain a third-degree burn to the epidermis and dermis layers of the skin. Basically at that temperature the coals should, by all logical science, char the entire thickness of skin to a blackened carbon residue. We were about to learn something that even physicists can't explain.

After our encounter with the burning reality, we all marched back to the hotel to begin our three-and-a-half-hour fire walk mental training. We were excited, nervous, and, to some degree, fearful.

Adrenaline Adventures

When everyone was back in their seats, methodically Tony began to dispel our fears and explain our inner processes. I was used to challenges like bungee jumping and swimming with sharks, but somehow bare feet on hot coals seemed different. It defied logic. So I listened very carefully. My mom seemed quite at ease. She reminded me that my state of mind was the most important tool to control. She was calm, Tony was calm, so I figured all I had to do was just learn the technique. Besides, if thousands before me had done it, so could I.

The first technique Tony taught us was Neuro Linguistics Programming (NLP). NLP's working premise comes from a long line of psycho-scientists like Maslow and Erickson. Basically it's the belief that words (linguistics) program beliefs. Beliefs affect the physiology. Physiology controls the nervous system and your mental state. You combine and control the two through trigger points and you have winning results.

We were told to remember an event in our lives that made us feel unstoppable, like winning a law case, graduating college, getting a job we really wanted, or simply falling in love—a time of peak performance. Once we remembered the event we were told to imagine it in detail. Tony wanted us to not only to remember but also relive how we felt when we felt unstoppable. He said it was important to feel the same surge of energy and elation in our bodies that we felt at the time of the original event. Once we had the feeling and the image in our minds, we were instructed to touch a target place on our bodies. (Keep it clean, folks.)

Most people touched their shoulders, elbows, and necks. This was to set the NLP trigger link. The principle is to not only think but also feel the positive thoughts and keep touching your chosen body part, creating a link between your thoughts and your nervous system. You associate the two. So whenever you touch your trigger point, you feel successful. He stressed that the key is feeling, not just thinking successful.

The next step was for us to visualize walking on the hot coals. But get this—to get over our fears we had to picture the worst case scenario happening to us. Tony told us to picture our worst fears about walking on the hot coals. He told us to picture our feet smoking or burning to a crisp or even that we only had burnt chicken bone legs left. Whatever we were afraid was going to happen to us we were to picture in detail. He gave us a few minutes to form an image. I imagined my feet sticking to the hot coals because they accidentally used the wrong wood and me screaming because I couldn't get off the coals.

Once we got ourselves worked up and faced our greatest fears of being burnt he continued. "Now that you all have those images in your minds, I want you to take that image and make it into a cartoon. Play with the image—distort it, mold it, stretch it as if it were on Silly Putty. Then take that and shrink it down to nothing. Squish it, and make it disappear."

The purpose was to take the way you looked at the fear and distort the image into something unrecognizable and even laughable. Slowly but surely as each person played with the image, laughter filled the room, dispelling all tension. I sneaked a peek at my mom, and she was smiling as if the whole thing was a cake walk.

Tony moved onto the topic of controlling our inner dialogue or voice. You know the voice—the internal voice that tells you how you are going to fail, or get hurt, or that you are stupid for even trying this. The voice that says, "What am I freaking nuts walking over hot coals? If I was meant to be barbecued, I'd be a hot dog."

We were instructed to block out that inner voice by repeating the words "Cool Moss" to ourselves nonstop while we walked across the coals. The theory is if you have something to chant, you don't have time to hear your inner voice and sabotage yourself with your fearful thoughts. Tony explained how even one moment of doubt during the walk can cause you to burn yourself. I started chanting on the spot ... I wanted my mind to become imbedded with the thought that I could do this.

Then Tony went into the importance of body language and how it sends signals to the brain. He started with eye placement. He pointed out that when you are depressed you generally look down at the ground. But when you are confident you look up. We were instructed to look up, over and beyond the hot coals to our goal at the end—the sidewalk. Looking up would send a message to our brains that we were confident.

Continuing on the subject of physiology, we were told it was extremely important to WALK, not run, over the coals. We were to walk over the coals at a normal and direct pace. Is there a normal walking pace over hot coals? I made a mental note to check the Road Runner's Manual on that one.

Above all, he said, "Once you have committed to doing it, under no circumstances stop. Just go for your goal. It's like this with the hot coals and anything else in life. Commit!"

Finally we were told to use a technique that many Olympic athletes do. We were told visualize the whole walk from start to finish and imagine ourselves at the end having completed the walk successfully. To help program our minds we were given the affirmation, "My mind will do whatever it takes to protect my body." After an hour of this final drilling we were ready and willing soldiers. There was literally a feeling of electricity in the room as we all lined up once again to go to the parking lot. But this time it was real not a dress rehearsal.

We walked laughing and joking along the way. Once in the lot we separated and formed lines behind the hot smoldering coals. We took off our shoes as we approached the coals. The lines moved steady and relatively fast. Cheers were heard as each person completed their walk. I couldn't wait to go. I just wanted to be at the other end of the coals.

There was an assistant coach standing at the beginning of each line. I went first and my mom was right behind me. As I got up to the beginning of the row of red hot coals, I was given my final set of instructions.

"Okay remember, touch your trigger point. Feel empowered. Look up, say 'cool moss' and begin walking. GO!"

The training must have worked because without hesitation I began the slow walk across the twelve-foot bed of fire. I had absolute faith in myself. I felt nothing burning. It was so weird. I was like in a trance. My eyes were focused at the end of the coals where all the cheering people stood. All I could remember was the words, "Cool moss, cool moss, cool moss". I was in a heightened state. There was no time or room for negative thoughts to enter, and because of that, my mind did whatever it had to, to protect my body.

Fran Capo

I only became aware of my feet when the assistant at the other side of the coals doused my feet down with a water hose to put out any smoldering pieces that had been caught between my toes. I turned around just in time to see my mom's feet being doused as well. She was smiling. How many moms are that cool? People continued to cheer one another's successes.

It was amazing. I started to think maybe it was a trick, and maybe the coals were no longer hot. I went back to see, and they still had that red, glaring, menacing glow. Then all of a sudden I became aware that my feet hurt on the pebbles in the parking lot. How the hell can the pebbles hurt more than burning coals? Simple, I wasn't in the state anymore. My body now felt everything.

Out of the seven hundred people who walked across the hot coals that day, three chickened out, and one got blisters. The rest were fine. Pretty amazing stats. We all went back to the hotel/training room to celebrate our newfound power. It gave me a touch of what it would feel like to be invincible.

The purpose of fire walking as Tony mentioned in his flyer, is not to become a proficient fire walker, but to use it as a metaphor to break through fears and challenges in life. Hell, if you can walk across fire, think of how easy cold sales calls will become! If you do something outrageous like this, you have changed what you believed once to be your limits.

Look, if you never walk on fire, that's fine. But at least once in your life challenge yourself beyond what you think are your physical and mental limitations and then celebrate the powerful results.

I saw the shift in my way of thinking that same evening. While driving back to New York, I was so mentally elated and feeling so powerful that when I saw a car coming at me the wrong way on a one-way street I didn't panic. I swerved and avoided a head-on collision but was unable to totally get out of the way in time. His car hit mine. Luckily, no one was hurt.

I got out and saw there was no damage to either car. I told the guy to be more careful and cheerfully drove home. Normally I would have been ranting and raving at the guy, and shaken by the event. But I saw the event for what it was ... an accident in which no one got hurt—even though it was careless on the part of the other driver.

Adrenaline Adventures

I realized then that with any event in life, it's not what happens, but how you react to what happens, that makes the difference. And the great thing is, you can control your reactions at any time by simply choosing to do so.

Honestly, I was shocked at how calm I was. I couldn't believe I didn't panic, get angry, or even feel in the slightest that it had ruined my evening. Now THAT, for a New Yorker, is something beyond belief.

Fran Capo

Chapter 9
Adventure at a Glance - Dare to Do it!   Mild to Wild: 5
Title: Walking on Hot Coals
Children allowed: The youngest participant has been four, the oldest eighty-nine. In some seminars they allow children with written permission from a parent.
Length of trip: One Day
Where to try this adventure: Tony Robbins offers this program around the world. Website: www.anthonyrobbinsdc.com
Best time of year: Limited to when the seminar is offered.
Approximate cost: $495 - $695 for a one-day class depending on location.
Reservations necessary: Yes
Requirements: None
Fitness requirement: None
Personal gear required: None
What NOT to bring: Doubt and fear
Photo opportunities: Not usually –the snapping of cameras can get people out of the mental state needed to walk over the coals.

Note: There are other NLP practitioners and F.I.R.E.–certified instructors who offer fire walking. Tolly Burkan has a program to certify those interested in teaching it. Tolly's program has taught more than two million people worldwide to fire walk. Fire walking seminars are now offered on six continents. For more information go to http://www.firewalking.com or call 800-218-0055.

Cool trivia: The longest coal bed on record was 167 feet long. However, a number of people have walked a 40-foot coal bed, back and forth, without leaving the coals, 13 times: accomplishing a 520-foot fire walk.

The origins of fire walking are unknown. What is known is that it predates written history. A Hawaiian named Kahuna walked across lava flows. Vikings walked on red-hot steel chains. Native Americans, Fijians, and a number of Christian saints were also said to have fire walked.

"Enthusiasm is the soul's electricity"
--Wally Amos

Chapter 10
"A Crater Full of Adventure"
Biking Down a Volcano

My first husband, Pat and I both liked physical activity. Every morning while he jogged I would roller skate beside him. We had taken scuba diving lessons, ballroom dancing lessons, and yes, even tap dancing lessons together—now that's a brave man. So it was only natural that when we chose our romantic honeymoon spot in Maui, we planned into it some adventure.

One of our outings was a bike ride down a 10,023-foot dormant volcano, called the Haleakala Crater. It would have been nicer if the volcano was dead rather than dormant, but hey, you go with the flow, and hopefully in this case it would not be a lava flow. The Hawaiians boasted this volcano as the eighth wonder of the world with the world's fastest ascent from sea level. If going up were quick, I decided going down would be a breeze.

The brochure listed three options: a sunrise, day, or midday tour. Included in all tours was a custom, single-speed cruiser bike

Adrenaline Adventures

with mountain drum brakes, featuring a wide saddle seat, a helmet, windbreaker jackets and pants, and insulated gloves. Also included was round-trip transportation from the hotel or condo.

The tour was open to everyone except beginners, children under twelve, pregnant woman, and scuba divers who had dove within the previous twenty-four-hour period. The scuba regulation was because of the residual nitrogen that builds up in a diver's system when he dives. A diver can't do a drastic change in altitude within that time frame or he will get the Bends. Usually as a diver you think of the difference in altitude when flying in an airplane, but this volcano was so high, it would be the equivalent of being in a small puddle jumper craft.

Seeing as we met all the requirements, we made reservations for the sunrise tour. The locals told us that the sunrise was gorgeous from Haleakala Crater and that around ten o'clock the clouds started rolling in and completely obscured any great views. So sunrise it was. However, this was a honeymoon and there was one big drawback … we had to get up at one in the morning since they would pick us up at two A.M. at our hotel. We decided to do what any logical newlywed couple would do—pull an all-nighter.

Following the reservation clerk's suggestion we dressed in layers. We were told it was cold at the top and that when you are zooming down the mountain, it gets even colder. We also donned our sneakers and sunglasses, two requirements for the tour.

At two A.M., the tour van pulled up to our hotel. Loaded on top were thirteen bikes. Inside were eight sleepy passengers. We made our way around to the other hotels to pick up the remaining bikers and then headed for the volcano.

In an effort to wake us up, the tour guide started to give us some facts about the volcano. "Aloha. Today you are going to visit one of the most exotic places in Hawaii, Haleakala Crater. Haleakala literally means "House of the Sun" and you will see why when you see the sunrise. The crater is actually a deep pit at the top of a dormant volcano that many years ago formed the island of Maui. The pit was formed by erosion, but it looks like a crater so we call it one.

The crater has a circumference of twenty-one miles, and for those of you from New York, you could easily fit the island of Manhattan into it, to give you an idea. The crater is a United States National Park and is run by the National Park Rangers. We will travel up the 10,023 feet by van, eat a continental breakfast, watch the sunrise and then be geared up and bike down. We will ride through the towns of Kula, Makawao, Haiku, and Paia. We will pass volcanic ruins, forests, farms and many kinds of flowers.

We have one flower up here called the Silversword Plant. This volcano is the only place in the world it grows. We will point it out to you along the way.

After your morning exercise, you will be escorted back to the vans, and then you can sleep your way back to your hotel."

By the time her speech was over we were at the top of the mountain. I could already feel the cold mountain air seeping into the van. Pat was still asleep—apparently this all-nighter thing wasn't his bag.

The van pulled into the dark parking lot. We all got out and could barely see anything. It was cold and a little hard to breathe. I mentioned this to the tour guide. She said, "Up here at the summit there is about twenty-percent less oxygen. You'll get used to it after your body acclimates for a few minutes. Walk around; take it slow."

There were several crewmembers. Some were setting up an area for breakfast, others were taking the bikes down, and others were getting us to sign releases and handing out gear. Everyone mingled around the food area munching on fresh fruits and breads.

We were all then instructed to look toward the crater. Light was starting to show on the horizon. There was this morning midst that gave the crater a surreal look, like we were on the moon. We were higher than everything else on Maui, the air was thin, and it was very quiet, which all added to the effect.

We watched in silence, waiting for the sun's grand entrance, waiting for the proverbial curtain to go up.

We kept looking in that direction and then suddenly as if all the lights in a Broadway theater were flicked on, the sun made its fantastic entrance. It came up and over the crater wall. It was shining at us with its full intensity as if to say, "Lucy I'm home!" We all oohhed and ahhed and then clapped at nature's beauty.

Soon the whole area was filled with light. After a few minutes another tour guide, John, gathered us and gave us some safety instructions. "We are going to go down in a single file, with the slowest biker in front so that no one is left behind."

I looked around, trying to figure out which one in our group was going to be that party pooper. The guide continued, "There are cars and vans that will be driving up the same narrow winding road you will be going down, so be alert and stay to the side. Remember to use both front and rear brakes when braking. We don't want anyone going over head first. There will also be bikers coming up the hill, so watch out for them also."

I turned to Pat and said, "What biker in his right mind would come up this mountain?"

"One that desperately wants to get away from his new wife and her crazy ideas?"

"Be careful, I might just have to push you over the edge of the crater ... by accident, of course."

The tour guide broke us up. "Now, now you two honeymooners."

"We're just practicing for marital bliss," Pat said and laughed.

Since the tour guide had no idea who the faster riders were he decided to stick all the women in front. A bit sexist, but for now I was game. I was placed second from the front. A forty-three-year-old lady in a Hawaiian shirt and big white-framed sunglasses was first. She looked like she hadn't been on a bike in years. I nicknamed her Matilda.

We all slowly left the parking lot and started down the hill. The grade on the hill was steep, and it was easy to build up speed—you know, the old gravity rule. The bikes went fast, and we had to negotiate S-shaped turns. At first it took some getting used to since we didn't know what lay ahead. But within minutes it seemed the group had it together.

There was a tour guide in front, one in the middle, and one in the back. The van was in the rear following us down or ready to pick up any downed bikers.

Fran Capo

I noticed that whenever we picked up a nice pace, Matilda dear would slam on her brakes, nearly causing a fatal domino-effect accident. She did this several times.

We stopped along the way a few times as the guide pointed out things to us. On one of the stops I suggested that Matilda could ease on the brakes, slow it down, not try to stop on a dime. She smiled, but it seemed as if she was one of the creatures that may have come out of the morning midst—she was in the proverbial fog.

As we started up again, she was fine, but then she would trail back from the lead tour guide. It's not like I'm a speed racer when it comes to biking down a volcano, but I would have liked to have gone down the hill faster than a kid on a tricycle. For a moment I wondered how fast Matilda would move her butt if the volcano erupted and lava was flowing down, burning the rubber off her bike's tires. I wanted to say something to the guide, but I didn't want to sound like a whiney tourist.

I mentioned it to Pat and he said to just ride on her tail a bit and see if I could nudge her forward. It seemed like a good plan. Now I was set.

But just like when your tooth stops hurting when you go to the dentist, Matilda on the next few runs seemed to go a bit faster, no speed demon, but I could live with it. The problem was solved. Now I could enjoy the scenery and get my adrenaline rush at the same time.

The bike ride down was gorgeous. There was a clean country smell in the air, and as promised, we passed forests and farms. It was cold but not unbearable.

As we had been warned, the road was very windy and we were sharing it with cars, so at times it did get a bit harrowing. Since we were mainly coasting, we did get a chance to stop and look around at the flora and fauna. (Notice that everybody always puts those two words together?)

Anyway, just when I thought everything was coasting along nicely, Matilda decided to go slower, even slower than before. How that was possible I'm not sure.

Well, we were only about halfway down so I asked Matilda if we could switch places. She refused. Now I was not a happy camper.

Adrenaline Adventures

So I decided to try a new strategy. I would let her get far ahead and then I would speed up and catch up to her. I did this a few times so I could at least get the sensation of zooming down the volcano with the wind in my hair. It was a good thing I had glasses on because the cold air made my eyes water. But I loved it.

I was happily zooming along, twisting with the S and U turns, when Matilda decided she would stop short in the road, no warning, no pulling over, no loud horns ... nada to tell me she was stopping. I almost crashed into her, and everyone behind me had to stop short as well. This woman was a hazard on the road. Now I was angry. "Listen, didn't anyone ever tell you to pull over to the side if you are going to stop? These are blind curves. You could have caused a thirteen-bike pile up!"

She just shrugged. "Hey, I needed to stop. I didn't have time to think of you guys behind me. Just go slower."

"Look, lady, any slower and we are going to be going backward up the hill. Come on, we all want to have fun. When's the last time you've been on a bike?"

"I'm an expert. I ride almost every day!"

"How is this possible? No offense, but I saw snails passing you."

"Hey, I'm first and you have to go at MY speed."

"Oh really? Okay." I smiled, got back on my bike, and made a hand motion as if to say, "Go ahead, my dear."

She smiled, thinking she had won.

Now it was time to put Pat's plan into effect.

Matilda got on her bike and kept breaking. I could feel her evil grin. So I rode on her tail. She yelled for me to back off, but I wouldn't. So she rode faster. I kept up. And she rode even faster. So the woman could move if she wanted to. Then she sped up so fast that I was impressed. As she did she took her eyes off the rode and turned around to give me the finger.

As she did she miscalculated the turn and tried to brake. She flew headfirst over the handlebars and landed in a bush. At first when I saw her go I was shocked. I mean, I didn't like her, but I didn't want her to get killed. But then when I saw her just lying in that bush and saw her white glasses cockeyed and heard her cursing up a storm, I just laughed.

The tour guides stopped, picked her up and she was fine. She was put in the van for the duration of the ride. Call me evil, but I did get a sense of satisfaction out of it.

Now I was in the lead and was able to enjoy the rest of the ride down. As we got closer to the bottom, we could smell the aroma of pineapples from the farms below. At the bottom we saw a caravan of vans coming up, getting ready for the next tour's ride.

We were all given certificates stating we had biked down the crater. Despite my little run-in with Matilda, it was awesome and a great way to start the day. It was only ten o'clock and we were done with our adventure. We had biked thirty-eight miles!

As we got in the van, Pat came over to me and whispered, "I said, nudge her on, not push her over the cliff!" He smiled.

"Hey, if she hadn't decided to flip me the bird, she'd still be sitting pretty on her bike. Just proves never take your eyes off the road."

"Yeah, and it just proves to me once again that no one can know what to expect when they are dealing with Capo."

"I'll take that as a compliment."

"It was meant as one," he said. "So what's next on the agenda?"

"How do you feel about parasailing, a catamaran evening cruise and wreck dives?"

"They all sound good to me."

"Good, they are all ready booked ... maybe this marriage won't be so bad after all."

"Well, at the very least we know it will be filled with adventure."

Adrenaline Adventures

Chapter 10
Adventure at a Glance - Dare to Do it   Mild to Wild Scale: 2

Title: Biking Down a Volcano
Children allowed: Yes. Riders must be 12 years old and meet the height requirement of 4' 10" (with some outfits requiring a height of at least 5 feet).
Length of trip: Half day
Where to try this adventure: Haleakala Crater National Park www.haleakala.national-park.com
Best time of year: Year-round in Maui
Approximate cost: $76 - $116 per person plus tax.
Reservations necessary: Yes, only 13 riders per tour are allowed
Requirements: Have to know how to ride a bike
Fitness requirement: Must be able to bike ride 38 miles. PLEASE, NO BEGINNERS OR PREGNANT WOMEN.
Personal gear required: Must wear sunglasses or prescription glasses and closed toe shoes. Wear layers.
What NOT to bring: Pocketbooks and big bags
Photo opportunities: Yes

Notes: There are three bike tours options. The sunrise journey picks you up at the hotel around two A.M. and includes breakfast so it costs about $20 more. The day journey picks you up around seven A.M., and the midday journey picks you up around nine A.M. A scuba diver must wait twenty-four hours after a dive before going up the crater.

Cool trivia: The Apollo astronauts trained at Mount Haleakala.

"Always depend on the calm knowledge that you can be master of anything that may happen to you."
—Norman Vincent Peale

Chapter 11
"A Bird's Eye View of Paradise"
Parasailing

With seven glorious days of honeymoon adventures to explore in Maui, parasailing was next on our list. My new husband, Pat, and I had just finished biking down a volcano, and we were ready to sit back and fly in the wind like a kite. Neither of us had ever parasailed, so it was fun to try another new adventure together.

Parasailing is readily available at almost any beach resort in the world. It doesn't require a reservation, and it only takes up about twenty minutes of your time, the willingness to zoom up into the air, and about fifty bucks apiece.

There are three methods of parasailing that are currently offered to tourists around the world. They are the beach, the platform, and

Adrenaline Adventures

the winch-boat method. The winch-boat method is the most popular and by far the most widely accepted and safest.

But just for the sake of clarity let me explain all three so you can decide. In the beach method, you start by standing on an exotic beach (duh!). While on the beach, clad in your finest bikini, you are strapped into a harness, which is attached to a parasail canopy, which in turn is connected to a towboat via a rope.

In the beach method the parasailor has to do some work. He or she is instructed on how to steer the parasail canopy left or right by pulling on the left or right rear risers on the parasail. Once you have located these steering devices you are ready for your adventure. The beach crew signals the boat driver to power up and tighten the towrope, which in turn inflates the parasail canopy.

You are instructed to step, walk or run forward towards the boat. This you must do or you will be jerked forward from a standing position and possibly get whiplash, which is never a good thing. The boat then speeds up, and hopefully the two of you coordinate, and you go flying into the air. Once you are airborne the boat controls the speed. The boat travels into the wind and is constantly adjusting to keep you at a constant height. After all, you don't want to be swooping up and down like a dive-bomber. When the ten minutes is up, the boat driver positions the parasailer over the beach and reduces speed and hopefully the parasailor lands on the beach. I say "hopefully" because if a good wind comes along you could be thrust back over the water and make a splash landing. So be prepared. The problem with this method is it can be extremely dangerous, and is not recommended for even the most experienced parasailor, because aside from a complete water survival training course in emergency landing, if something goes wrong, there is very little you can do. You would be stranded out there with a giant canopy and harness on you in the middle of the water, making it rather difficult to swim. Okay, now that I've scared you away from that technique let me tell you about numbers two and three.

I have tried both. The platform method is number two. I tried that while on my honeymoon with Pat. At the time this was the parasail de jour. So we went with the flow and enjoyed it. To sign up, Pat and I simply walked out to the beach at our hotel, talked to the local parasailing outfit, and within minutes we were on a speed boat heading out toward a wooden platform that was floating in the water about one thousand feet from shore.

We were the only two on the boat at the time so it added to our sense of adventure. There were two options, a four-hundred-foot towrope, which gave a seven-minute ride, or an eight-hundred-foot towrope, which gave a ten-minute ride. We opted for the eight-hundred-footer. Hey, if you are going to fly high, why not go the full length?

Pat decided he would go first. Once the boat reached the floating platform Pat and the instructor got out and stood on the giant red dot centered in the middle—a perfect target for birds flying from above. The instructor strapped him in the harness, which looked like a giant baby diaper. As with the beach harness, the parasail canopy is connected to the towboat via a rope. Once he was secured Pat was told to go to one end of the platform. The guy signaled the boat driver. The towboat and platform begin moving forward inflating the canopy. This is a tricky maneuver since you have to steady yourself a bit as you are on this giant floating piece of wood for a few moments. It was kind of like a being on giant surfboard. (Some platforms are motorized which makes it easier, but this one wasn't).

As the towboat and platform move faster, you rise toward the heavens. Pat let out a big, "Yee haw!" I was slightly embarrassed but who the heck was going to hear, the fish?

I snapped pictures as Pat was blowing in the wind and being whipped around the sky. Over the beach he flew and then back over the ocean like a wayward kite. I heard tiny yelping sounds along the way. He's a very verbal guy.

Ten minutes passed quickly, and then he was ready to come in for a landing. The expression on his face and position of his body was priceless. His mouth was in a giant O shape and he had his arms and legs fully extended, like a giant old-fashioned baby doll with rigid arms. He later told me it looked like the guys were going to miss the platform and he was trying to brace himself. However, he came to a perfect landing back on the platform.

It was my turn. I was now on the platform, diapered up and ready to be thrust skyward. The initial lift is the scariest part since you are

Adrenaline Adventures

not quite sure when it's going to happen. When you first lift off, your feet are pretty close to the water, so you think if they slack at all on the rope you might fall in. But soon you are lifting, lifting, lifting and everything below looks like ants.

I'm not scared of heights so I totally enjoyed sailing around the sky. I do have to say, though, that eight hundred feet looks a lot higher from above than from below. When I was watching Pat, it didn't seem he was that high, but now that I was the flying in the air, I felt the full effect.

I had my camera with me and was snapping bird's eye view pictures. I thought it was going to be more of rush sensation, but once airborne I got a pretty smooth ride, and since I was at the full distance of the rope, I didn't feel the sensation of speed, but more that I was being tugged slightly. It's the closest thing to being a kite, with the powerboat driver being the string master.

The coolest thing was when a bird went by and I felt as if I could reach out and touch him. Okay, it actually wasn't that cool, because he startled me and for a moment I thought he was going to puncture a hole in the canopy. He looked angry, and I thought that maybe this was some psychotic bird that thinks he owns the sky and is willing to battle me for his turf. But the bird just aimed at me and then at the last minute swooped skyward. What a showoff! I think I heard him snicker.

I was getting used being airborne when I started being lowered back to the platform. The weird thing is not having any control in the landing. There were no toggles for me to tug on. If the boat driver miscalculated I was going to be dunked, there was no way around it. So I just hoped that the guy had his eyesight checked recently.

Just as I thought the driver had 20/20 and we were going to make a landing, the driver picked up speed and I was airborne again.

I yelled down, "What happened?"

Pat yelled back, "You would have missed the platform."

"Okay, that's not good. Take two." I looked up and saw the same bird laughing at me. He flew off to tell his friends.

The boat circled around and once again I was lowered. This time I landed right on the giant red dot. I felt as if I scored a ten in the Olympics. I steadied myself on the platform and was soon unharnessed. Pat and I hugged, it was an awesome ten minutes and we'd have great pictures for the scrapbook.

It wasn't until ten years later, long after I was divorced from Pat (Yes, adventures are not guarantees that a couple will stay together), that I took our son, Spencer, who was then nine, parasailing while on a trip to Mexico. By this time parasailing had evolved into highly safe form.

They were now using a third method, winch-boats. Winch-boats are used ninety percent of the time today in parasailing. In the winch-boat method, you have two choices: the rigid chair or the body harness. In both options you take off and land back on the boat itself. There is no standing on a beach or wooden floating platform. The boat is equipped with a parasail inflation system, and a hydraulic winch (hence the name) is powered by the main drive engine located at the rear of the boat.

You take off and then after ten minutes you are reeled in like the catch of the day.

Since Spencer was only nine at the time, we chose the rigid chair option—the lazy man's way to parasail. With this method, you are seated in a partially reclined floating chair that has a bar and no straps. The chair is attached to the parasail canopy, which is connected to the towrope, which is connected to the hydraulic winch, which is obviously mounted on the boat.

The canopy is inflated by hand, the boat accelerates, you feel the boat slide out from underneath you, and then you and your lawn chair are airborne. You view the scenery, and sit back and relax. All you need is a nice, cool lemonade to make it perfect. Within ten minutes you are back on the boat. Spencer and I both enjoyed it, but we agreed it wasn't too exciting. It felt too safe.

In all honesty the harness is so much better. You get the sensation of flying with nothing holding you. Your feet dangle below. You get to skim the surface of the water on the way up and down. If you are looking to get a rush, do the harness method; if you are looking to just get a bird's eye view but need something to hang onto, do the chair method.

Either way, it's a ten-minute ride that you should try at least once in your life.

Adrenaline Adventures

Chapter 11

<u>Adventure at a Glance - Dare to Do it   Mild to Wild Scale: 2</u>
Title: Parasailing
Children allowed: Yes, but there is a weight limit
Age requirement: None, but must be with parent if under 18
Length of trip: Seven to ten minutes depending on length of rope
Where to try this adventure: Almost any beach resort around the world
Best time of year: Parasailing is available on Maui from May 15 to December 14. There is no parasailing during whale season. In Mexico the times are more flexible.
Approximate cost: $44 - $48 for 400-foot line/$50-$55 for 800-foot line
Reservations necessary: Yes
Fitness requirements: If you are riding alone, you must weigh at least 120 pounds. If doing a tandem flight, your combined weights must not exceed 350 pounds.
Personal gear required: Bathing suit
What NOT to bring: A fear of heights

Photo opportunities: Yes

Notes: The winch-boat method is the safest to do.

Cool trivia: Mark McCulloh made the first working prototype of the winch-boat and tested it in 1974. He patented the idea on October 26, 1976. However, it took a while to work out the kinks. There were several winch-boat accidents, one which was publicly recorded in 1977 during a media event at Sunset Beach at Treasure Island, Florida. But Mark did not give up. He worked at perfecting the winch-boat, and in the mid eighties it was released commercially and is now the standard that most parasailing operators use today.

"It's alright to have butterflies in your stomach, just get them to fly in formation."
- Dr. Rob Gilbert

Chapter 12
"Look Ma No Engine."
Soaring in a Sailplane

Since I had already tried several methods of air travel, from small Cessnas to hot air ballooning to parasailing, I thought it was time to try the sport of motorless flight, which is interchangeably called soaring or gliding. Actually it didn't take much forethought on my part. I was in South Carolina with my first husband, Pat, visiting his parents. We happened to drive by this little airfield, and I saw a sign for an introductory soaring ride. I asked him to pull over so we could find out the deal.

I walked inside this little office and spoke to the man in charge. He said, "We can have you up in the air in the next fifteen minutes, if you like."

I was thrilled.

"How long is the ride and how much will it cost me?" I asked.

"I can give you a half hour ride for sixty-five bucks."

"You got a deal. Hold on, I just gotta talk to my husband."

I ran out to the car to tell Pat. He didn't think it was safe so he decided to stay on the ground for this one. I asked if he minded

Adrenaline Adventures

waiting the half hour and he said, "Look, once you get something in your head, I know you are going to bug me 'til you do it. So let's get it over with now."

I jumped up and down like a little kid. "Thanks!"

I love when that type of stuff happens in life. You see something and then you can immediately do it ... instant gratification, some call it. I call it, having a dream and pursing it immediately. I guess its all semantics.

I ran back inside. "Okay, I'm ready."

The man smiled. "The name's Hank. That there is my glider. Let's go!"

While walking out to the plane I told Hank that my husband didn't think this was a safe thing to do. Hank said, "Soaring is one of the safest forms of aviation. It has an excellent safety record. Driving to the airport can be a lot more risky than your flight today." Hank noted my accent. "Where you from?"

"New York."

"New Yawk...hell, this soaring is a lot safer than living in New Yawk."

'Well, I think he was worried because there wasn't any engine. So what if we are up there and the wind quits?"

"As long as there is air and gravity we can glide safely. See we are going to be flying in what they call a sailplane or glider. The wings on this baby are long and graceful. The glider has a glide ratio of 20:1"

"Okay, what does that mean in English?"

"Means for every foot that the glider goes down, it travels twenty feet forward. See typically the sailplane will descend about one hundred to three hundred feet every minute. But we are going to use the air currents, and we can stay up for long periods of time. It's not unusual to stay up for five or six hours, if you like. And the best thing is we don't have to worry about running out of gas, or the engine dying on us. The sailplanes use solar power, and they are designed to be safe and fast."

By now we were at the sailplane. Hank lifted the glass hood and told me to hop in. It was a two-seater glider. I sat in the front, (which I thought was odd) and he sat in the back.

"Don't you need to be up front to steer this thing and see where we are going?"

"Nope I've got dual steering back here. And if you want I can let you fly it a little too."

"That would be fantastic. Okay so how are we going to get this thing off the ground if we have no engine?"

"Well, we could shoot us into the air with a bungee."

"That sounds more like something you'd do with a spitball and rubber band. You're kidding me, right?"

"Nope. One of the methods, actually the oldest method of launch, is having the glider perched on top of a ridge with a rubberized rope attached to a tow hook. Then a bunch of burly guys go running down hill on each side of the nose and hurl the glider into the air stream near the face of the ridge."

"Well seeing as I don't see a team of runners and no cliff, I gather we are not doing that method today."

"Good guess, but it sure would make a good story to tell back in New Yawk."

"That's for sure. So how are we going to get up?"

"Well there is also the winch method whereby a wire is attached to a powerful engine that heaves the glider two thousand feet into the air … but we ain't doing that method either."

I could tell Hank was having fun messing with my head. What he didn't know, though, was those methods actually sounded like fun to me.

"There's even talk about a self-launching motor with a fold away engine, but that's a few years away from now."

That sounded like the Jetsons space stuff to me. I pictured Hank pulling out a briefcase and putting the engine away in it after we launched.

I saw a small plane in front of us, but since we had come from around the back side of the glider, I hadn't noticed that the glider was attached to it with a towrope.

"Okay," Hank said. "Enough talk … you ready to go on the ride of your life?"

"Ready."

Adrenaline Adventures

With that Hank gave a signal and the towplane started down the runway. The plane went up and we tagged along. It was awesome. I could hear the sound of the towplane's engine, it was loud like a swarm of a million bees.

Then, when we reached about 3,500 feet, Hank pulled a lever and I saw the towrope drop off. All of a sudden it was quiet and we were gliding in the air.

At first it felt odd without the sound of the engine. But then, as we swooped in the air, it was nice not to have any mechanical sounds.

The view out the window of the glider was gorgeous. Unlike in a commercial aircraft, we had a full panoramic view since the top of the plane was made out of glass also. We weren't constricted to looking outside just the front windshield.

The plane was descending and then all of a sudden we were making circles and climbing higher and higher. I knew the theory of air currents but I wanted to know exactly what was going on, so I asked Hank how he did that.

"Gliders use the theory of lift to gain altitude and stay aloft. As pilots we are trained to be looking for three forms of energy. The most common form is called thermals. Thermals are columns of warm air that rises. Once you get in a thermal you make tight circles so you stay in the lift until you feel you are at a high enough altitude to fly cross country to another thermal."

"So it's only these thermal things that can do it?"

"No, there are two other sources. There's ridge lift, which is created by wind that flows up the windward side of a ridge or mountain. So you take that and ride it up the side of the mountain. There is also wave lift. This happens on the leeward side of the mountain when a strong wind blows perpendicular to a mountain. The wind is forced upward and you can get altitudes clear over thirty thousand feet on a good day."

I was totally enjoying the ride when Hank said, "You seem like a girl who likes adventure. Wanna go for a spin?"

"Absolutely!" I love the feeling I get when my stomach drops because of the strong G forces, plus I had done a spin in a Cessna so I figured I was prepared. Well, I wasn't! Hank put the glider into a spin and the whole world turned. I hadn't counted on the added affect that a clear top with total viewing would have on my stomach. Seeing the entire panorama spin, as opposed to just a front view changed the whole perspective. It was awesome, but a bit scary ... I held tight to the plane laughing as we spun. For one brief second I wondered if Hank had secured the roof of this thing on tight. I sure didn't want to be doing my own personal rendition of ejector seats.

After we came out of the spin I had a whole new respect for these gliders.

"That was fantastic! How long does it take to learn to fly one?"

"That depends on how fast you learn. You have to pass a written exam and several flight instructions before you can solo. A person as young as twelve can train, but you have to be fourteen to be able to solo."

"Do you want to fly it a bit?"

"I'd love to." With that, I took the controls. I watched how little effort it took to get the plane to cooperate. Hank led me to a thermal. I still didn't understand how he could see where they were, but he assured me it comes with practice. I, of course, was trying to figure out a way to have these thermals color coated ... it would make things a whole lot easier.

Once we were in the thermal, Hank told me to keep the glider circling. This was a bit harder. I did a few circles but pulled out of the thermal too early and we lost some ground.

It was getting time to head back, and Hank took over the controls. We glided toward the airport and I saw our car off in the distance. As Pat saw us, he waved. The plane touched down ever so lightly.

I got out and shook Hank's hand. I knew that I would once again try this adventure, and I did, nine years later when I was no longer married to Pat. I took our son, Spencer, up in a glider. Spencer's first comment was, "Ma, if we were meant to fly, God would have given us wings."

"He did give us wings, Spencer, and they are called gliders. And if imitation is the highest form of flattery, then God would be pleased since we are imitating the flight of his magnificent eagles and hawks."

Spencer rolled his eyes. "Okay, Mom."

Adrenaline Adventures

I was never fond of kids rolling their eyes so I felt he needed a lesson. I winked at the pilot and motioned for him to roll the plane. He did.

"Figured I'd help you out with that eye rolling."

Spencer's eyes were wide and staring straight ahead. Now I rolled my eyes.

"You weren't scared, were you?" I laughed.

"Scared? That was cool. Let's do it again!" And with that my son's view on aviation was forever changed and he never rolled his eyes at me again.

Fran Capo

Chapter 12
Adventure at a Glance - Dare to Do it   Mild to Wild Scale: 3
Title: Soaring in a Sailplane
Children allowed: Yes, children of any age can ride.
Age requirement: You can begin training at 12 but must be 14 to solo.
Length of trip: They have 20, 30, and 40-minute flights.
Where to try this adventure: The Soaring Society of America's Web site: www.ssa.org will give tons of soaring information. Also a company called Soaring Sports specializes in all types of sky adventures. Website www.soaringsports.com or 1-800-226-1116.
Best time of year: Seven days a week, year round, hours vary according to season.
Approximate cost: Soaring Sports has rides for $171 per person for a half hour anywhere in the continental U.S. They also have one place in Long Island where two people can ride for $192 for fifteen minutes.
Reservations necessary: Most of the time, but you can catch them at a slow time and just walk right in.
Fitness requirements: Be in good health
Personal gear required: None
What NOT to bring: Fear of heights.
Photo opportunities: Yes

Notes: I found my first soaring adventure by noticing a sign at a local airfield. I don't remember the name of that airfield since it was long ago. The pilot charged me his own rate because he owned the aircraft and because there was no middleman. Today there are many places that you can go to try this adventure. Just ask around at your local airfield and ride with someone you feel comfortable with.

Cool trivia: The world altitude record in a glider is more than 49,000 feet. The world distance record currently stands at slightly more than 2,000 kilometers, or 1,250 miles.

"Man's mind, once stretched by a new idea, never regains its original dimensions."
– Oliver Wendell Holmes, Jr.

Chapter 13
"Thar She Blows"
Whale Watching

The great thing about whale watching is that you can do it from almost anywhere in the world. More than forty countries conduct whale watching tours. But whenever you are dealing with sightings of wild mammals the outcome is unpredictable, unless you're at an aquarium. However, if you follow the migration charts, your odds of catching a glimpse of Shamu are a lot better, give or take a few days. Face it, animals don't have a timecard that they have to punch. One lazy bloke may just decide to take his sweet time before swimming to the other side of the continent. After all, these whales do have a few tons to lug along it's not like they can just opt for carry on baggage.

The interesting thing is although migratory whales move north and south in both the Northern and Southern hemispheres; in general the northern populations do not meet their southern counterparts. Maybe it is some kind of whale civil war with the equator acting as a natural barrier to the larger whales, who carry too much blubber for tropical waters— nothing a good exercise program couldn't fix!

I have been whale watching four times in my life; twice at the tip of eastern Long Island in Montauk in the Atlantic, where fin, minke, and humpback whales can be spotted; once in the Pacific Ocean on a trip to Hawaii, off the gorgeous island of Maui; and once

Adrenaline Adventures

at Gloucester, Massachusetts off of Cape Ann, where the film *The Perfect Storm* was shot.

The first whale watching trip turned out to be a bust with the whales staying submerged and just out of sight. Had we been in a submarine, it would have been great, but since we weren't, it was more of an exercise in boating.

The second time in Montauk was the first real adventure I took my son, Spencer on—he was only two. We saw a few sprouts of water bursting up (called blows) and a humpback mother whale and her calf that decided to peek up long enough to pose for a Kodak moment.

The fourth trip, in Gloucester, Massachusetts, was a decent trip but not of the caliber of the good whale watching story I'm about to tell.

It was the third whale watching expedition that was the whale watching adventure of adventures. The one that took place when I was hired by a company named Bellcore, to fly to Maui to do an impostor routine posing as a high tech executive giving them the spiel on a few new sales tactics for their latest product. An imposter routine, by the way, is not me posing as Frank Abagnale, Jr. (of *Catch Me if You Can* fame) but really just a way for a company to break up five grueling days of seminars with comic relief. It's one big put on, with one of the company's top dogs in on the secret. I couldn't wait to go.

On my flight over, I happened to be sitting in first-class (a nice perk of corporate travel) next to this guy named Jeff from Merrill Lynch. Turns out he was going to the same hotel as I was, the Grand Wailea Resort Hotel & Spa. He took my business card and said he would see if his company would be interested in hiring me as an impostor, too. Jeff agreed to introduce me to his boss during the trip. Networking happens in the strangest of places.

The Merrill Lynch gathering was for salespeople that had made the "millionaire club." They were getting a lot of perks on this trip—A LOT! Jeff said if I wanted to, I could join them later in the week on their whale watching expedition. Sounded good to me. We agreed to coordinate our schedules after we checked in.

Fran Capo

The first things I noticed at the Grand Wailea hotel were the unique architecture, and the statues of fat women. This I liked— made me look like Kate Moss. The place was gorgeous with several pools, world-class gardens, paintings by famous artists, a chapel, and spa.

After I checked into my room, I glanced out the balcony window, which overlooked the ocean. I could see tiny mists on the surface of the ocean. I looked closer and realized I was seeing whales spouting! I couldn't wait until I could be on the water frolicking with the whales. But for now it was business.

I checked in with Roy, the Bellcore guy who set this all up. I was scheduled to do my impostor speech in four hours. I went back to my room and rehearsed. Four hours flew by, and before I knew it, I was up in front of the Bellcore group performing. By the end of my twenty-minute spiel, with me fading in and out of my fast talking, bogus exercises, and ridiculous charts, the employees realized I was a hired imposter and everyone got a good laugh. With my job done, the time was mine to explore Maui and get up close with Moby Dick.

I went down to the hotel dive shop and arranged for two dives.

The next morning, on my first dive, the dive master asked me if I wanted to use an underwater scooter since the current was rough. I had never done this before, so I was game. I felt like a character out of the *Johnny Quest* cartoons as I zoomed around the ocean floor with my newfound toy. Unfortunately, the sound of the propellers kept the whales away.

On the second dive I opted to try to see these gentle giants up close and personal. The dive master, Charlie, took me outside of our resort area to a rocky-shored dive spot where we had to do a land entry.

I asked Charlie if we would see whales. He said he couldn't guarantee, but we would definitely hear them. He said, "Male humpbacks have long, complex patterns which are repeated and can sound like songs. If you listen carefully the song will go on sometimes six to eighteen minutes."

"That's longer than a hit single!" I said.

He laughed. "Hey, these whales don't fool around with their music. They introduce new songs all the time." (Apparently whales

Adrenaline Adventures

can only stand a playlist so long, too.) "The cool thing", he said, "is some scientists have found that whatever song was popular at the end of a previous breeding season, they'd return with the following winter."

"Now that's a long time on the charts!" I commented. "Maybe there's a Frank Sinatra of whales."

"Maybe," he replied, "but how they do it is a mystery since they don't have vocal chords."

"Maybe they're lip synching." I added. And with that we donned our masks, put the regulators in our mouths and submerged.

As soon as we got in the water, I could hear the singing of the whales. They sounded like actual songs. It wasn't a tune I knew, but I could hum it. It was wonderful yet a little eerie at the same time.

Since sound carries far underwater I couldn't tell which direction it was coming from, nor could I spot these giant mammals. Charlie said divers rarely see whales because the bubbles that divers make are interpreted as an aggressive sound to a whale—a sound of a fish wanting to fight. He told me I'd have a much better chance seeing whales while kayaking, because it's quiet. He said the whales will actually poke a giant eye out of the water and come right up to the kayak to check you out.

Since I had never kayaked before I started thinking, that's all fine and good, but what if I get a clumsy whale who comes to close the kayak and knocks it over? Then I'd be upside down in the water drowning because I didn't know how to do that roll thing and get back up. I'd be getting a good underwater view but probably turning blue in the process.

So once again I would have to wait to see these behemoths of the ocean until I rendezvoused with Jeff. In the meantime, I occupied myself looking at giant sea turtles and schools of fish with the muzak of the whales in the background.

The next morning, I woke up at 8:15. Since it was a magnificent day, and I didn't have to meet Jeff for the whale watching until noon, I decided to take a walk along the beach. I walked for three and a half hours and got lost on the way back. Okay so I'm not a candidate to write a Fodor guide.

Fran Capo

I walked fifteen minutes past my hotel. I didn't know if I would make it back in time for the whale watching, so I started to run. I caught sight of Jeff in the lobby. He motioned to me to hurry up. "You're late. If you want to come you have to come right now, just the way you are." Great. I was sweaty, and didn't have my camera, sunscreen, or money. But I wasn't going to miss the free whale watching. I could always go later and pay, but why?

So I boarded the air-conditioned bus that was going to take us to the boat. Luckily bagged lunches were handed out. Jeff had a camera, and he promised he would send me copies of whatever pictures he took.

We boarded the boat that had been reserved especially for the Merrill Lynch crew. The captain and a naturalist, Brett, who was going to give us the lowdown on whales, greeted us. He began by welcoming us aboard then gave us the usual where to find the life jackets in case of emergency speech and then was on to the good stuff, an explanation of the whales, some of which, hopefully, we were about to see.

Since it was mid-March, we were at the tail-end of the whale-watching season in Maui, which runs from mid-December through mid-April. The whales migrate 3,500 miles from Alaska, where they spend the summer months feeding, to the warm waters of Hawaii where they mate and have their calves.

Sometimes whales known as "aunts" even help with the birthing process by biting off the umbilical cord of the mother. Now that's true friendship.

With much more knowledge than the memorized facts I got out of the hotel brochure, Brett began. "Whale watching as a commercial activity began in 1955 in North America along the southern California coast. Today, whale watching is carried on in the waters of some forty countries, plus Antarctica." (I knew that!)

"Cetaceans, which includes whales, dolphins, and porpoises, are the world's largest living animals. They are not fish but air-breathing warm-blooded mammals that nurse their young. There are seventy-eight species of cetaceans, which range in size from the one hundred-foot-long blue whale to the five-foot-long harbor porpoise. To put it

Adrenaline Adventures

in better perspective, you could fit a car inside the mouth of a blue whale and a dog could run along some of its blood vessels."

Everyone oohh-ed and ahh-ed. Comparisons like that always make the reality of something hit home.

After seeing the captive audience's reaction, Brett continued. "There are two types of whales: toothed and baleen. Toothed whales include the sperm, killer, and beaked whales, porpoises, and dolphins. They mainly feed on fish and squid. Killer whales, that's the kind that Free Willy was, also feed on small marine mammals and other whales."

At this point I asked, "Was Moby Dick a killer whale?"

He smiled. "No, Moby was a sperm whale."

"A sperm whale! Then what the hell was he so angry about?"

Everyone laughed. Jeff looked nervous. Apparently he didn't appreciate my interrupting the guide.

Brett continued, "The other type of whales are baleen. The baleen whales are toothless." Obviously a full set of teeth is not an important factor in attracting a mate in the whale world. Although, maybe that's why they don't form long-term bonds. The missing teeth factor gets to them after a while. Brett said, "Instead of teeth baleens have rigid strips of material similar to human fingernails, called baleen, that hang down from their upper jaws. They catch and eat plankton and small fish. Blue, gray, and humpback whales are baleen. Maui is the perfect place to see humpback whales in their natural breeding area."

Good, so if anybody falls overboard, they don't have to worry about being sucked inside the stomach of a humpback and taking up residency. But to make sure, I asked, "Well, how can you tell the difference between the two types of whales, just in case a killer one is lurking about and you don't want to wait till they open their mouths to find out?"

"Good question," Brett said. "Blowholes are the external opening to a whale's nasal passages, rather like our nostrils. In baleen whales, there are two blowholes side by side; in toothed whales, there is just one. Blowholes are situated on or near the top of the head, so before you fall in the water take a quick look and you'll know."

Fran Capo

Brett continued to talk while everyone was looking around to see if they could see signs of whales. The blow, which is the whale exhalation on the surface, was usually the first sign of the whale's presence. I know everyone was just itching to yell out, "Thar she blows."

But for now there was no activity, so Brett continued, "Don't worry, we'll see a whale if they're out there. The humpback whale is the fifth largest of the great whales. The calves weigh an average of 1.5 tons and are ten to sixteen feet in length. Males reach forty-two feet in length, while females are about forty-five feet. The humpbacks weight about eighty thousand pounds and live about thirty to forty years."

Wow, did they ever hear of Slim Fast?

Just then a shout came, "Off starboard at 3:00" Everyone rushed to that side of the boat. Sure enough there was that telltale blow, a burst of air and water vapor shooting out at speeds of up to 280 miles per hour, which can be seen as far away as three miles on a clear day.

We waited with bated breath to see where the creature would surface. We saw another blow, this time very close to the boat. We could smell the fishy scent emanating from the blow as the vapor dissipated. Skilled photographers stood back as they snapped their cameras, avoiding the oil content from the blow that can actually put a smear of oil on a camera lens if the photographer is too close.

Then, suddenly, as if the curtains went up and the lights came on, the whales decided it was show time.

Not one, but two, humpback whales decided to breach. (That's when they come fully out of the water.) It was amazing. I felt like I was watching a show at Disney, only this was real.

As soon as those two dove, and as if on cue, we spotted another whale doing a "pec slap." That's when they take their large pectoral fins and slam them against the water. It made a large "splat" sound, the kind of sound you make when you do a nice belly flop.

I looked at Jeff to see if he was snapping pictures. I couldn't believe he was just standing there holding onto the handrails claiming it was too rough to photograph. What! Too rough! We're on a boat that's stopped! We were gently swaying. What does he want Moses to part the sea so he can stand on solid ground to snap a shot? I don't mean to sound ungrateful, but this was a show of a lifetime and he was acting like a deer in the headlights.

I asked him nicely if I could take the pictures. But he got offended. "It's my camera. You don't know how to operate it." Apparently neither did he. What's to operate, you point and shoot! The guy was just holding onto the rail doing nothing! I couldn't believe this missed opportunity. A live nature show with God orchestrating and he's upset because the conditions aren't right.

Just then another two whales breached. We all watched in awe as they lunged their bodies fully out of the water and then fell on their backs with a tremendous splash. It was spectacular seeing these bus-sized creatures, leap out of the water as if jet propelled.

Apparently this pod of playful whales had just cut another hit record because they were in a great mood. And their repertoire of feats seemed endless. No wonder humpbacks are considered the most acrobatic of the species.

One did a tail slap, forcefully slapping its flukes (the end of the tail) on the water. Another one did a "head rise" or "spy hop", shooting straight up out of the water keeping its head just above the surface so you could see its eye. After a few seconds, it gently slipped back down, like butter on a hot pan, after it took a peek at whatever caught its curiosity.

I thought, wouldn't it be funny if we were the floating show to them, running back and forth on the boat, pointing and snapping cameras? Maybe they were under the water planning the next move. "Okay, Sheeba, you go on that side of the boat and come up and watch them run. Then at the same time I'll jump up. They won't know which way to turn." Then they high five each other with their pecs and carry out their little joke.

Either way, this whale display went on for almost thirty-five minutes. It was hard to keep track of where they were since they kept moving to all sides of the boat. Not that they are fast swimmers, they can get up to only about twenty miles per hour for short periods, but usually they stay within the three to six miles per hour range. Nothing the whale police would ticket on. Although one whale was spotted in both Mexico and Hawaii in the *same* winter, so you know he was cruising.

Brett commented that in all his years of whale watching he had *never* seen such an active display. He let us know emphatically that we were truly a lucky group.

I looked over again at Jeff. He was pale, not from seasickness but from fright. Still not one picture snapped. I was angry. I wanted to share this moment with Spencer and all my friends at home, via film.

The whales were winding down, and it seemed they were doing their closing number. I decided at that moment that I could sit there and be angry that that wimp didn't take any pictures or I could live in the moment.

I chose to savor the experience. I watched intensely and etched into my mind every detail. I looked at the whales' tails as they dove into the sparkling ocean shimmering from the hot Maui sun. I looked around and counted six whales surrounding the boat. I felt the warm sun beating on my arms as I stood on my bench in the boat. I looked around and saw that there was only ocean on all sides. I studied the people's happy faces and heard the snapping of cameras and the sounds of gleeful oohhs and awws from the crowd.

Absorbing everything put the experience into crystal clear perspective. I was here and this was now. Remember it. Be thankful that you got the chance to experience it.

I thought how truly magnificent it was to think that thousands of these creatures were swimming around beneath us, along with sharks, dolphins, and a whole sea of colorful creatures just hidden under the top blanket of water. How amazing it is to know what lies beneath.

After ten minutes of no activity, the captain signaled that the show was over. The engines of the boat started up, and we headed back to shore.

Despite my disappointment of not having any pictures to tell of the event, if it hadn't been for Jeff I wouldn't have been on that boat at that time in the first place. Maybe another boat would have had no whale activity. Maybe this was a lesson in living the moment and being there, and not doing it through the eyes of a camera lens.

Adrenaline Adventures

Maybe it was a lesson on depending on yourself and no one else. Who knows? Or maybe it was just a nervous guy with a good heart and an empty camera.

Later Jeff apologized, and true to his word he introduced me to the boss and we made plans for a future corporate gig. The last night when I did my stand-up routine for Bellcore, I used the whale watching event as material and everyone had a great time.

I did make arrangements with another guy on the boat that day to send me pictures, but they never came.

So all I have for you is this story, and the one picture from Montauk of the mother and her calf that my photographer friend, Malcolm Clarke took. Maybe that's better after all because if you want to experience the sensation of seeing the giants of the sea lunge out from the ocean depths ... you my friends, are going to have to get off your butts and onto a boat yourself and take the pictures.

Chapter 13
Adventure at a Glance - Dare to Do it   Mild to Wild Scale: 1
Title: Whale watching
Children allowed: Yes
Age requirement: None
Length of trip: One day
Where to try this adventure: Wherever whales are migrating
Best time of year: During whale migration season, usually spring and fall
Approximate cost: $35-$100 per trip
Reservations necessary: Yes
Requirements: Wear sneakers on the boat so you won't slip.
Fitness requirement: None
Personal gear required: Sunscreen, hat, camera
What NOT to bring: High-heeled shoes
Photo opportunities: Yes

Notes: Check http://www.whalewatchmaui.com for Maui whale watching trips. For a list of whale watching sites around the world, check out http://whale.wheelock.edu/whalenet-stuff/whalewatch.html

Cool trivia: Humpbacks swim tremendous distances during their migrations: up to 7,000 miles round-trip between their summer feeding areas of the North Pacific and their winter breeding grounds in Hawaii.

"Every oak tree started out as a couple of nuts
who stood their ground."
—Author unknown

Chapter 14
"Riding the Big Kahuna"
Surfing

Shortly after I took my son, Spencer, on his first whale watching adventure out in Long Island, I decided it was time for him to try another adventure. I returned to the island of Hawaii. This time we were guests of my childhood sweetheart and first boyfriend, Walter. He had tracked me down after a decade, was doing quite well, and invited my son and me over for a vacation. After establishing that this would be a family type vacation, I agreed to go.

Walter was an avid surfer and lifeguard. When we were dating, he spent his summers in Long Beach riding the waves and perfecting his craft. He was eager to show us a few tricks he'd picked up over the years.

Walter's living room was filled with seven brightly colored laminated surfboards, each one with its own hand-painted design. Walter said he was careful to keep them out of the sun so they wouldn't fade. There were pictures all over his wall of him riding gigantic waves.

Adrenaline Adventures

I couldn't wait to try surfing. Our first day in Hawaii we drove around Oahu, stopped at a beach, and went snorkeling to get Spencer familiar with the water.

The next morning we got up early, ate breakfast, and headed down to the beach, which was only a short distance from Walter's house. Walter had to go to work, so he left Spencer and me in the good care of several surfboard instructors. Spencer and I watched the surfers maneuvering in and out of the waves. They did it with such ease they made it look simple. Spencer was only four years old, but he already had my spirit of adventure and wanted to try it.

On the beach were a bunch of gorgeous Hawaiian surfboard instructors – male and female. I felt like I was on the set of *Baywatch* or better yet, *Hawaii 5-0*. We had a choice of either taking lessons or merely going for a ride. I asked one instructor, Louie, the difference. For a mere thirty-five dollars per person you could get a ride on a surfboard. He would take us out in about five feet of water, and we would ride the wave in with him on the board. The whole thing would be over in about ten minutes.

Or I could take surfboard instructions for an hour, a day, hell a month if my money held out. The instructors would go over rules and the etiquette of the sport, ocean safety, and awareness while in the water, the types of waves and different conditions, and of course how to control your surfboard. He said he would start on the beach teaching me how to stand up, then how to handle the board around waves. Then he would take me out no deeper than four feet so I wouldn't feel panicked. He said in the first lesson I would have plenty of opportunity to stand up and ride the waves.

He explained that there were long boards, short boards, and fun boards. I would start with a soft top beginner board—a board that would be safe and durable but give the performance of a hard board.

Since Spencer was a tad on the young side for lessons, I opted for the free ride. Louie nodded. "A ride it is, then. Come on little fellow." Louie had us do a practice on the beach. "I want you lie on the board and do a push up." I looked up at him since I wasn't sure I'd heard him right. He nodded. I did a push up. Spencer did his best to do one also.

Louie continued, "Once your arms are fully extended, I want you to pull both your knees toward your stomach and hop up on your feet. Yeah, right, just like that." I felt like I was in the Army doing a drill. I did what he asked, though, not wanting to look like a slouch. I was now upright with both feet parallel. He said that one foot had to be in front of the other for balance on the board. Then he threw some surfing lingo at me and asked me if I was regular or goofy. I had no clue what he was talking about. Turns out it was surfboarding talk for which way you position your feet. If you stand with your right foot forward you are regular, left you are goofy. I was a regular.

Louie had me practice the hop up a couple of times. Spencer, only having a mere two feet to go, got up quickly. Louie complimented us on a job well done and said, "When I tell you to get up, please do it as quickly as you can. Then we can ride the wave in. Timing is crucial."

Louie gave us each a life jacket, took the board, and we walked into the water about waist deep. I held Spencer in my arms, not that I'm a giant, but I am slightly over two feet.

When we were standing in relatively calm water, Louie instructed us to sit on the board, making sure that our weight was centered in the middle. At first it seemed that we were going to tip forward and in, but Louie balanced his weight on the back of the board as if we were on a seesaw.

After we were on, he slid up on the deck of the board and laid face down. He told us to scoot back towards him, so that the nose of the surfboard would rise and create a resistance. Once resistance was created we could start moving. Louie said the more resistance, the faster we would go. He began to paddle out to sea, alternately paddling his arms with his hands cupped. Paddling from shore looks simple, but when you are balancing your body with waves that are moving and breaking it takes skill. Add on top of that that you have a mom and kid on board and it takes some pretty fine maneuvering.

I asked what would happen if a big wave came at us, and he said, "We'd duck under it." I was hoping we wouldn't have to do that. One surfboard didn't seem big enough for the three of us.

Louie said that in a few seconds we would catch the first wave and to stand up when he signaled. He reminded me to grasp the sides

Adrenaline Adventures

of the board, also known as rails, and push up quickly. I nodded. I told Spencer to get ready and that if he fell in the water to relax, that I would get him right away. I also told him that he had a life jacket on and he would stay on top of the water. Spencer couldn't have cared less; he was eager and waiting.

I saw Louie study the small waves. As a wave approached, he turned the nose of the board toward the beach. He lay down and began paddling faster. All of a sudden I felt the wave lift the board. Louie said, "Lean forward ... now raise your chest ... ready ... hop up."

I quickly tried to push up, but fell in the water instead. Spencer was still on the board.

Man, standing on a surfboard is a whole lot easier when it's on solid ground. The waves lurched and laughed at my feeble attempts at balance.

Louie got me back on the board and once again we paddled out. A second time he gave the command, "Ready, set ... Stand!" Again I felt like a drunken sailor, trying to balance first on my left, then right foot ... then in. Spencer looked at me and said, "Mommy stay ON the board, not in the water."

"Ah yeah ... good point, Spencer. Don't you have a fish to catch or something?"

Once again, feeling somewhat of a wet rat, I climbed on the board. Spencer was getting amusement out of this and simply could not understand my lack of coordination.

Louie felt the need to give me more instruction. "Okay, I want you to grab the rails on the side and push up quickly. Then, as soon as you are up, extend your arms fully out and put your knees to your chest. Lean forward. I know it will go against your instincts, but trust me, if you lean forward it will add to the momentum of the ride. I will be controlling it from the back, so just keep yours and your son's feet firmly on the board. One foot in back ... one in front. You don't need to stand up completely, just keep your center of gravity, your stomach low. Think of it like a skateboard. And remember, don't look back at me, the board will follow your head and eyes, so if you look back you will fall. Just relax and focus. Are you ready?'"

Fran Capo

I was determined this time. Three's the charm, they say. When Louie gave his command I was able to get up and not fall. I grabbed Spencer's arms and put them out in front of him. We were able to ride a nice wave in. We did it one more time, and that time Spencer shouted, "Now we're cookin'!" Louie burst out laughing and so did I and we all fell in the water—but not before the on-land photographer caught a snapshot of us. It was great.

We thanked Louie, sat on the beach, ate lunch, and built sandcastles. Now, whenever we look out at the surfers, we can say, "Hey, I did that."

Adrenaline Adventures

Chapter 14
Adventure at a Glance - Dare to Do it   Mild to Wild Scale: 2
Title: Surfing
Children allowed: Yes
Age requirement: None
Length of trip: One-time ride or full-day lessons.
Where to try adventure: Anywhere in world where there is an ocean. You can start with California Surfing School at www.ca-surfing-school.com or Maui Surfing at www.mauisurf.com
Best time of year: Summer, but diehards surf year round.
Approximate cost: Free, with your own surfboard. $35 - $75 for a ride. Lessons cost a lot more and are given one on one.
Reservations necessary: Not usually
Requirements: None
Fitness requirement: None
Personal gear required: Bathing suit, possibly a wetsuit
What NOT to bring: Jewelry—it can get lost and the glitter attracts barracudas and sharks.
Photo opportunities: Yes

Note: At this level surfing is pretty tame. But when you ride the big waves in, I'm told this adventure can escalate to a level five on the mild to wild scale.

Cool trivia:
- Chris Carter began surfing at the age of 12. After he graduated college, he edited *Surfing Magazine* for 5 years. Today he is the creator and producer of *The X-Files*.
- Most surfers say the largest recorded ocean wave was the 112 footer that struck the USS *Ramapo* on February 7, 1933. But the *Guinness Book of World Records* credits an obscure Alaskan inlet with the world's biggest recorded seismic wave. This monster occurred on July 9, 1958 and was 1,720 feet high and hit the inlet at the speed of 100 miles per hour. No surfer dare rode it.

"What is the skilled approach of someone seriously interested in realizing his or her highest potential? Stated simply it is to keep the mind continuously in as happy and peaceful condition as possible."
—Lama Thubten Yeshe, *Introduction to Tantra*

Chapter 15
"Where's Rudolph When You Need Him?"
Dogsledding in Alaska

As both a standup comic and world record holder, I'm lucky in that I get asked to make people laugh and demonstrate my fast talking for them in different places around the world. If it's a really cool place (no pun intended), I bring my either son, my mother, my friends or my boyfriend.

I was thrilled when I got booked in Anchorage, Alaska, not once, but twice to do a week-long comedy gig. Once in the winter and once in the summer, so I got to experience the long days where the sun doesn't set until eleven and the long nights, where if you blink, you've missed the sun for that day.

The first gig I had was in the dead of winter, January 25 – February 1. I took my mom, Rose, and my son, Spencer, who was five at the time. After we settled into the condo that the comedy club had provided, I started to check out the local attractions.

Actually, that's the first thing I do whenever I go to a new place. I look for all the really cool things that I can't do anywhere else in the world. That first day in Alaska I saw a tiny ad for dogsled rides. I chose a mom and pop operation because I figured it would be less crowded and more personal. I spoke to the owner, Bert, who gave us directions to his place over the phone. Just getting to him was going to be an adventure since he was off the beaten trail.

We arrived at Bert's place, which was down a snow-covered dirt path and set back in the woods; he lived there with his wife and two kids, who helped take care of the fifteen dogs he owned. Each dog had his own little doghouse. It almost looked like a cul-de-sac of doghouses. One black-and-white husky apparently knew we were new to the area, and he stood on top of his house to check us out. Bert laughed. "That's Larry. He's the self-appointed watchdog, the nosiest one of the bunch, always has to check out what's happening." Larry barked as if to agree.

One by one, Bert unchained the dogs and introduced us to them. I felt like I was meeting Santa's reindeers. "This is Lance, Johnny, Brut, Samantha …

" I lost track after that.

"What kind of dogs are these?" I asked.

"All my dogs are either Alaskan malamutes or Siberian huskies. Some other operators use Eskimo dogs and Samoyeds. But almost any type of dog can be a sled dog."

"Any dog outside of lets say a poodle and a Chihuahua."

"Yeah, that would be accurate." He laughed.

"Hey, I'm a comic, wise cracks just slip out … sorry."

"No problem. Like I was saying mixed breeds like Siberians crossed with greyhounds make great combinations; you get the endurance from one breed and the speed from another."

Spencer and my mom petted the dogs. Spencer was getting a kick out of it, and every time a dog licked him, he laughed. The dogs seemed happy and eager to get hooked up to the sled.

"Man, these dogs are ready to work," I commented.

"For them, it's fun, its exercise. They know they get to go tromping in the woods. If fact, the dogs actually prefer cold, snowy days like today. They run faster and longer in the snow since the snow acts as a cushion and pads their feet while they run. Plus the cold keeps the dogs from getting overheated in their thick fur coats."

"Are we going to get a chance to mush our own sleds?"

"Unfortunately not on this run 'cause it's only an introductory ride. If we were doing a long trip over a few days or a week, then every client gets a chance to mush a team. But that's a whole different ballgame. Then you'd be set up with guides, dog teams, mushing equipment … the works. We'd show you how to harness the dogs, how to walk them, even how to clean their poop if you want."

"Ah … dog poop cleaning is not on my top ten list of things I gotta do, but thanks for offering."

"Okay, I hear you. Since there are three of you today, we are going to be using two sleds. Your mom and son can ride in one sled and you in another. Okay with you?"

"Sounds good to me."

"Good, let's get the dogs all hooked up. Spencer, why don't you come here and help me?" Bert let Spencer hold a harness, and it made my son feel like a big shot.

"The main equipment needed for dogsledding is a sled, dog harnesses, a gang line to connect all the dogs to each other and the sled, and on long trips you'd need sled gear bags for clothes, first aid kits, etc. Today we are going to use the service of five dogs per sled, two sets of two and a lead dog up front. If we were doing a big race like the Iditarod, we'd use a team of twelve."

Bert hooked up five dogs on both sleds. My sled was headed by the pure white dog named Sugar.

We were ready to go. Bert helped my mom lower herself onto the sled. She plopped down in the seat and started laughing, something she always does when something is awkward or clumsy. Spencer sat in between her legs. Bert covered them with a blanket. There was a place in the back of the sled seat for Bert to stand up on. From there he would command the team.

Bert explained that there were two types of sleds, the toboggan sled which is more of a work sled, and a basket sled, which we were

Adrenaline Adventures

using and which is faster, lighter and used for dogsled races. I got into my sled, and another musher got onto the back of my sled to drive the team.

Bert turned to us. "You guys ready?"

Spencer yelled, "Yes, sir!"

And with that Bert yelled, "Hike!"

"'Hike?' What happened to 'mush'?" I asked.

Bert laughed. "That's movie stuff. Mush is too soft a word to be a command word. We use the word 'hike' to get them moving. The main thing is to speak in a calm, firm voice. To the dogs, the musher is the lead dog. He takes his command from you, and you are part of the team, the leader of the pack. If you are hesitant or too soft-spoken, the dogs don't have any respect for you as a leader and will just do their own thing."

"Yeah the last thing you want is trouble in the ranks."

Bert then made a kind of kissing sound. With that, the dogs took off strong and fast. We whooshed through the countryside. I started having flashbacks to eighth grade when I had to read *The Call of the Wild* for school. I remembered thinking it would be fantastic to be on an adventure like that. And now here I was, mushing through the backwoods in Alaska. It was fantastic. This was only a small taste of dogsledding.

Up ahead we had to make a right turn, so Bert said the word, "Gee," and the dogs turned right. They had their own dog language. A left turn was signaled by the verbal command, "Haw", and when he wanted the dogs to slow down, Bert would just say, "Easy fellas."

The dogs seemed to have no problem zooming us around the countryside. A light snow was falling and all we could hear was the light thump of paws on the newly fallen snow. The land was gorgeous. At one point, we stopped to turn around and to take some photos. Bert said his command of "Easy" and we slowly came to a stop.

Spencer clapped his hands and yelled, "Nice doggies! Easy does it."

I was amazed at how well the dogs listened. Bert said, "Getting them started is no problem—it's getting them to stop that you usually have to work at. Once they start, they just want to run and run."

Fran Capo

We took some campy pictures while petting the dogs and just took in the surroundings. Larry was laying down and keeping his eyes on us. The other dogs seemed a bit antsy.

When Bert returned to the sled, with a tacit understanding, the dogs were up and ready. It reminded me of that dog commercial, "Lucky dog, lucky dog ... which way do we go ... which way do we go?"

With a "Hike!" and a kiss, the dogs were on their way. They seemed to know they were heading home and were doing double time. At one point, the sled seemed like it was on one leg as we sailed around a corner. I loved it. It felt so raw. It was an adrenaline rush of a different kind, the kind where you know you are experiencing something virtually unchanged from years past. Outside of the type of sleds used, I felt as if I were back in time travelling the way Eskimos of long ago did.

I looked back and saw that Mom and Spencer both had huge grins on their faces. That alone was worth the trip. We were back to Bert's house in twenty minutes. We got out of our sleds, petted the dogs a final time, and walked away having explored the backwoods of Alaska in a most unusual way.

Adrenaline Adventures

Chapter 15
Adventure at a Glance - Dare to Do it   Mild to Wild Scale: 1
Title: Dogsledding in Alaska
Children allowed: Yes
Length of trip: An hour (trips up to a week are available)
Where to try this adventure: There is some dogsledding done in the Pacific Northwest and Rocky Mountain states, but probably the best place to try it is Alaska. For more information, check out www.dogsledtours.com
Best time of year to go: Winter
Approximate cost: $50 per person for one hour
Reservations necessary: Yes
Fitness requirement: Stamina for the cold
Personal gear required: Warm clothes, gloves, hat, scarf
What NOT to bring: Unnecessary baggage—there is minimal space
Photo opportunities: Yes

Notes: I wasn't able to locate the original place I did my dogsledding adventure. You can call 1-888-300-MUSH or (705) 457-5281 or email info@winterdance.com or check the Internet to find a dogsledding location. Several outfits offer the same kind of trip.

Cool trivia: The Iditarod is the most famous and grueling dogsled race in the world. It takes place in Alaska, with the starting point in Anchorage and the ending point in Nome. The trail has 26 checkpoints, and although the distance is actually 1,151 miles, the traditional mileage and symbolic mileage for the race is stated as 1,049 miles (1,000 because the mileage always exceeds that and 49 because Alaska was the forty-ninth state to join the Union. The race leads teams of dogs (usually 16 dogs) over frozen tundra, through ice storms and blizzards, and across a sea of ice. In the history of Iditarod, only one original team of 16 dogs ever made it into Nome; usually they have to replace dogs that get sore or tired during the race. The 2004 winner, Mitch Seavey, made it into Nome with 8 dogs in 9 days, 12 hours, 20 minutes, and 22 seconds. He won $69,000.

"What would you attempt to do if you knew you could not fail?"
—Dr. Robert Schuller

Chapter 16
"Swim with the Sharks"
Scuba Diving with Sharks

This is not a chapter about vicious lawyers or cutthroat businessmen. This is about an actual swim with the sharks - TEN of them to be exact.

I wanted to challenge myself physically and mentally to face one of nature's greatest predators, in a controlled environment of course, and I could think of no greater challenge than to face these beady eyed, jagged toothed monsters head on.

The dive took place in Freeport, Bahamas with a company called UNEXSO. I had never encountered a shark in all my dives, so I figured the best way to do it safely, if that's possible, was to plan it.

Anticipation is a strange thing. It builds up an event so much that you can sweat just at the thought of it. And I was doing a lot of anticipating.

Adrenaline Adventures

On this particular adventure I once again teamed up with my childhood adventure pal, Viv, the one who got me into scuba diving in the first place.

My mother thought I was nuts but was behind me. We didn't tell Viv's mom until afterward for fear she might have a heart attack. We also brought along one of Viv's scientist friends, Susan. I wasn't nervous, but Viv and Sue were, and then I found out why. For some reason they received a brochure in the mail describing the sharks; I didn't. Viv called me a few nights before the dive.

"You sure you want to do this?"

"Sure, why not? They're probably just some nurse sharks. What could they be, two or three feet in length?"

"Try, eight to ten feet, and there are about ten of them. It's in the brochure."

"MMMMM ... never saw that bit of trivia."

The night before the dive I had nightmares of thousands of sharks heading toward me with their mouths wide open yelling "FEED ME!". Was this a precognition of things to come or just nerves? I passed it off as nerves.

The morning of the dive came too fast. At 10 a.m. the twelve divers scheduled on this adventure were shuffled into a briefing room. The first thing we were given was a release form—releasing UNEXSO legally if the sharks decided that the twelve divers looked like a buffet lunch and wanted a nibble. No less than three times during the briefing we were given the chance to change our minds. "Sharks are not trainable; they are wild and potentially dangerous," sneered the instructor. Tell me something I don't know!

"Our dives are constructed as safely as could be. We have one scuba diver who will be feeding the sharks, and three safety divers. Our feeder wears chain mail link gloves that are up to his shoulders. This is the same kind of gloves that butchers use to prevent chopping off their hands. A shark's teeth can penetrate the glove but they usually release it immediately because they don't like the feel of the steel in their mouths." Who tested this out?

The instructor continued, "Two safety divers will be located on each side of the feeder armed with four-foot sticks. Not electric prods or bang sticks—but plan old sticks. When a shark gets too aggressive our safety divers simply push the shark away." (Great, away from them and into us? How are we protected?)

Instructor Kreskin read my mind. "The other safety diver will be located behind you, the twelve guest divers. You guys will sit in a semi-circle directly in front of the feeder, so you can watch the action up close. There is a tank down there that you will put your backs against, so no shark can sneak up on you." I felt like I was in an old street gang and that our butts would be covered, but just in case I wanted to know what would happen if we had a rogue shark that didn't want to play nice.

"In the unlikely event of a shark attack, use anything in your possession, your camera, your fist, or your scuba console, and hit the shark in the eyes or gills. Those are his most sensitive areas to pain, not the nose as most people think. Make these repeated jabs quick and sharp. Sharks are predators and will follow through on an attack if they gain an advantage, so by jabbing him you make him unsure of his advantage, and you increase your chance to get away. Hitting a shark is not going to save you, but it lets the shark know you are not defenseless. Just remember to keep this in perspective; bees, wasps, and snakes are responsible for more fatalities each year than sharks, and for those living in the U.S. you are thirty times more likely to win the lottery or get hit by lightning than encounter a shark attack."

"Yeah, but a shark is much nastier to look at!" I said.

"True, but keep in mind that you are in a large group. Sharks aren't interested in crowds of people."

"Well, what if I get the one shark that was an entertainer in his previous life and not only likes crowds but thrives on them?"

"Chances are slim. We are going in the daytime when sharks are more lethargic. Shark attacks happen mostly during darkness or twilight hours when they are most active. At UNEXO we take all the precautions we can, which leads me to mention that if anyone has an open cut, or for the women if you are menstruating, we ask you to let us know now, or on the side; since sharks are drawn to blood we will have to ask you to bow out of the dive for today. We also ask that all jewelry be taken off since it reflects light and resembles the shine on fish scales which is attractive not only to sharks but barracudas, as well."

Adrenaline Adventures

The instructor glanced around and still saw some nervous faces. "Remember, as a diver you are safer than a surfer or even a swimmer for that matter. On the surface in wetsuits humans resemble a shark's favorite food—seals. When a shark sees a surfer on a surfboard, he basically sees an hors d'oeuvre sitting on a Ritz cracker. And when he sees a swimmer, the swimmer's moves resemble a floundering fish dying at the surface, another shark favorite since it's easy prey. So in actuality when you are sitting on the bottom in gear, you are a lot safer. Besides, the three most dangerous sharks are the great white shark, tiger shark, and bull shark ... none of which are we dealing with today, so please enjoy. We have a cameraman who will be recording the whole dive on video so you can prove to your friends at home how brave or nuts you are. Now let's go feed some sharks!"

"One last question, how long are we going to be down there?"

"We stay down for about forty-five minutes. We abort the dive when it is no longer safe. Just watch for our signal. When you see two thumbs up ... its time to get out of there as quickly, but calmly, as possible."

The boat ride out to Shark Junction only took ten minutes. It was close to shore, which I'm sure is very comforting for the beach swimmers to know.

One by one we jumped into the water. I expected the *Jaws* soundtrack to play at any second. As soon as I got in the water and started my decent I saw a shark come out of nowhere. I remembered they said to stay calm. Sharks whole bodies are like receptors and they can sense fear. So I casually swam over to the other divers. I would have whistled if I could, but the regulator was in my mouth. Besides, the last thing I wanted to do was get some shark angry because I was off key.

The action started out slowly. Within minutes, ten Caribbean reef sharks were circling around us, sometimes as close as five feet away. It felt eerie, but awesome at the same time. If you've never had a shark check you out it's quite an experience. They head straight toward you, and then at the last minute they turn like in a game of chicken. As they swim by you they give you a sideward glance with their steely eyes.

Fran Capo

    We had been told in the briefing that if they got too close to simply take both hands around our scuba gauge and lunge it toward them. Everyone was poised with gauges in hand. After a few minutes, shark and man got used to each other. We could sit back and enjoy the view.

    Their streamlined bodies glided through the water effortlessly. Soon we could tell the sharks apart. One shark had a rusted hook and the skeleton of a fish dangling from its mouth. Another one, obviously female with a baby shark swimming underneath, was the most aggressive. Another shark had two tiny pilot fish directly in front of his face, which seemed to anticipate the sharks every move. This seemed most annoying. Like a Sunday driver on the highway who slows down every time you try to speed up.

    After their initial curiosity the sharks were not the least bit interested in us, all they cared about was the free food in the feeders black container. My anxiety had subsided. It was amazing that just twenty short minutes before I was filled with fear. The fear of the unknown can be a powerful immobilizer, if you let it. I thought, "If I can do this, then everyday life should be easy."

    The sharks circled around the feeder and one at a time took turns being fed. Their cold steel eyes never blinked except when they bit on the food. Then a white film would cover their eyes as they bit, protecting their eyes from any morsels of food. Their mouths would distort into a P shape as they went to bite the fish.

    It was fascinating watching these beautiful creatures without being on the other side of the glass at the aquarium. I almost felt like reaching out and touching one of them and then realized it was not a Hallmark commercial.

    Viv, Sue and I inched up during the dive to get closer to the sharks. Everyone else had their backs against the tank, but us daredevils were a good five feet out there, front and center. You would think we were swimming with gold fish!

    Thirty- five minutes into the dive, it abruptly ended. A nine-foot, five-hundred pound female shark was getting too aggressive. She kept trying to rip the black food container out of the feeder's hand, even though she was pushed away with the sticks several times. It

Adrenaline Adventures

started to cause a ruckus with the other sharks—like a shopper with twenty-five items getting in the express lane at the supermarket.

At that point in the dive we received the two thumbs up from the feeder that meant the fat lady had sung. The show was over. We all slowly ascended towards the boat having experienced one of the most thrilling dives of our lives. Granted it wasn't the movie Jaws, but it was exciting.

So are you ready to go out and dive with sharks? If yes, that's great. If no, there are plenty more adventures. The point is, if you have a fear—break it. If you have a desire—do it. And if you have a dream—live it. For when you challenge yourself in life, you realize that it's the fear that paralyzes you and once you've conquered that, anything is possible.

Chapter 16
Adventure at a glance- Dare to do it!   Mild to Wild Scale: 5
Title: Scuba Diving with Sharks
Length of trip: One hour
Where to try this adventure: UNEXSO - Grand Bahama, 800-992-DIVE
Website: www.unexso.com
Best time of year: All year round
Approximate cost: $85 for one tank dive
Reservations necessary: YES! Call way in advance.
Requirements: Must be a certified scuba diver and have C-card
Children allowed: Yes, if scuba certified
Fitness requirement: None
Personal gear required: Mask, fins, and snorkel, but you can rent that equipment and the rest of the scuba gear at their dive shop.
What NOT to bring: Jewelry, spear guns
Photo opportunities: Yes

Note: UNEXSO also offers a four day intensive shark feeder program, where you can personally learn to handle and feed the sharks.

Cool trivia:
- The movie *Jaws* was based on an incident that actually happened in 1916 in New Jersey. One rogue great white shark, weighing in at three hundred and fifty pounds and measuring seven and a half feet in length, went on a killing spree over a twelve day period from July 1^s to July 12 killing four people and injuring one twelve-year-old boy. It was the first and only known case of a serial killer shark in the world. Most sharks do not attack humans. Great whites are now an endangered species due to their bad press, and the one psycho shark that was forever immortalized in the movie *Jaws*. (The full story is detailed in my book, "It Happened in New Jersey.")

"Success is not spontaneous combustion.
You must set yourself on fire."
--Reggie Leach

Chapter 17
"You Don't Need a Cell Phone or High Heels to Climb a Mountain" Rock Scrambling

To this day I can vividly remember the most peaceful moment I have spent on this planet. I was sixteen years old. I had just been driven up to a place called Mohonk Mountain House in New Paltz, New York. My mom and stepdad dropped me off, and I was supposed to meet my girl friend, Martha, and two of her friends. We were all splitting the cost of the room for the weekend. We hooked up hours later, but in the meantime I lay on the grass with not a worry in the world, and just took in all the beauty. I have never recaptured that solitary hour of total peace; I've come close ... but no cigar. Since then Mohonk has become one of my favorite places in the world. I've gone back almost every year, introducing new friends to the place and to the most adventurous spot at Mohonk, the Lemon Squeeze,

Adrenaline Adventures

which I will describe in detail later. For now, just know that I have always enjoyed my visits there and that many people have fallen in love with the place, and here's why.

Mohonk Mountain House is a sprawling Victorian castle that sits tucked away on 2,200 acres at the top of the Shawangunk Mountains. Its 280 rooms have a nineteenth-century atmosphere, featuring stone fireplaces, antique furniture, chandeliers, and polished wooden floors. It was built by Quaker twins, Albert and Alfred Smiley, in 1869. It's now a National Historic Landmark.

Mohonk House is at the northwest corner of Lake Mohonk, a sixty-foot-deep mountain lake that is half a mile long. Rock formations rise majestically above the water, and the natural surroundings remain virtually untouched from the days of its discovery.

The surrounding 6,400 acres known as Mohonk Preserve are complete with beautiful landscaping and 128 gazebos at varying points along the lush hills. Winding passageways lead safely into the woods, beautiful flower gardens with a rainbow of colors are sprinkled about, and many activities, from horseback riding to row boating to miniature golf, are available in this peaceful setting.

The tranquil atmosphere attracts many older people, and their theme weekends, from meditation to mysteries to wildlife photography, attract people of all interests.

Dinner at Mohonk requires formal attire, which is probably to keep out the riffraff. But if you forget a jacket, they'll give you a loaner. Who knows, maybe you'll be lucky and find a wallet in the pocket, which could offset the cost of the rooms since they are a bit on the pricey side. That's the reason I usually go as a day hiker; it's a less expensive option.

At the bottom of the mountain, you drive up to the gatekeeper, who will check to see if you have reservations. If not, you are known as a day hiker. You must arrive before two; if you arrive after two you must come back another day to see the Wizard. They only allow a certain amount of people on the mountain at a time.

Once you are given the go ahead, you are charged a minimal hiking fee and given a map and a day pass that entitles you to hike two miles up the hill to the Mohonk Mountain House? . There's a bus that can take you up for a few extra bucks, but that's for wimps. If you're gonna hike, do it all the way.

Once on Mohonk property, you can go on any of the many marked hiking trails that range from a mile-long walk to a rugged, dangerous climb. Each trail is marked, so you know what you're getting yourself into before you set foot on the path.

Of all my trips to Mohonk there is one that stands out in my mind, not because it was the most peaceful, but simply because I witnessed the most ridiculous things on that day.

On this particular trip, my son, Spencer, and my boyfriend, Steve, accompanied me. Spencer had been there many times before, but this was Steve's first time. It's kind of a ritual I put the guys I really like through, sort of a rite of passage. If they make it without complaining, then I upgrade them to other adventures.

It was a hot, sunny day, and the hike up to the mountain house was uneventful. A few spots were very muddy, but outside of that, it was just a regular hike following well-worn trails.

We stopped at the snack bar, an informal restaurant that is located on the way up to the mountain house, to replenish our water supply, grab a sandwich, and take care of nature the civilized way, since as day hikers we were not allowed in the Mohonk House.

As always, I was anxious to get to the "spot," my reason for coming. A few hundred feet from the Mohonk House is a small sign that indicates the beginning of a steep climb called The Labyrinth. The sign reads, "This is a rugged path. Participants must be in good health and physically fit. Terrain: Very rough." I love watching people's expressions as they read the sign.

Steve turned to me, "Capo what are you getting us into?"

I just laughed. "Nothing a big, strong man like you can't handle. Come on!"

Spencer and I smiled, knowing what lay ahead.

The trail is marked with red arrows painted on the rocks. It starts out pretty tame, a few small rocks to climb over and a few small wooden bridges to cross. But within five minutes you are climbing up narrow wooden ladders, crawling through spaces under big boulders, scaling giant rocks and squeezing through crevices in an upward direction (which would make sense since you are climbing UP a mountain). All

Adrenaline Adventures

this climbing is leads you to a destination, a cement tower 1,550 feet up on the top of a peak overlooking a gorgeous valley. What people won't do for a view!

The climb normally takes about an hour and a half at a steady pace. We had packed a lunch in our knapsacks and planned to stop on one of the gigantic rocks to eat it.

As we came to the place of the many fallen rocks (sounds like an old Indian name), we saw two small figures up ahead. As we got closer we saw that it was an elderly man and woman. The woman was clinging to the rock like a dress on stockings with no static guard. The man was in shorts and his pale legs were all scratched up. He was huffing and puffing like an asthmatic bagpipe player. They yelled, "Can you help us?"

We climbed over to them and could see the woman was petrified. She told us she was scared of heights. (So what was she doing a thousand feet up on a rough mountainside?) The man was resting on a rock and nursing his wounds. "We heard an eighty-four-year-old woman did this hike, so we figured we could too," he said. Yeah, well just because Moses climbed up Mount Sinai doesn't mean it's for everyone.

At this junction we were about thirty-five minutes into the climb. We asked what we thought was a logical question, "Why didn't you turn back?"

Amazingly they replied, "Because we thought it would get easier." EASIER! How is climbing farther up a steep mountain going to get easier? At the last two hundred feet an elevator is not going to miraculously appear. I felt bad for them; they looked like two lost mountain goats with amnesia.

We led them slowly to an area where there are easier, safer routes to the top of the mountain. The woman looked relieved to be on a solid path and not a bunch of fallen rocks. I saw her glance at her husband with that "I told you so look." The man's ego was bruised. He was obviously embarrassed and tired. He just wanted to thank us and get us out of hearing range for the blasting from his wife that he was about to get. I'm sure he'd paid for that mistake for a while.

Fran Capo

The three of us made our way off the path and back onto the fallen rock zone. We were nearing our destination, the climax of The Labyrinth, the "Lemon Squeeze."

At the Lemon Squeeze the mountain walls are less than an arm's width apart. (There should be a poundage limit or at least a girth requirement on this trail.) At this point we had to climb up three crooked wooden ladders that are wedged between the rock walls. Steve, who has a forty-two inch chest, looked at me—"You're not serious are you?"

"Hey, the worst that happens is you take off your shirt and squeeze through."

Spencer just said, "Mom!"

"I'm only kidding Spencer."

Steve smirked at me and scrambled up the first ladder.

The cool thing about this part of the climb is that you are guarded from the sun. It's like nature's air conditioning. Not to mention that the way the walls are set, it almost looks like a hideaway that Butch Cassidy and the Sundance Kid would have used.

Now the best part—after you get up the third ladder, there is a fifteen-foot-long crevice above you. The walls narrow even more. Your mission, should you decide to accept it, is to climb up and crawl out the top of the crevice to reach the plateau that leads you to the top of the mountain. This takes some finagling.

The best way to scale the crevice is to put your back against one wall and your feet against the other and inch your way up like a worm. Sometimes your hands and feet wind up awfully close to each other like in an intense game of Twister. You then have to look around and choose another resting area for your foot or hand, and continue to climb. You have to take off any knapsacks you're carrying to fit through. This works best in a team, one member goes up, and then the members below pass the knapsacks up and then crawl up themselves. We made it up unscathed.

After this you're pretty much home free. A few more quick rock scrambles and then you're on your way to the tower. Then, as if you haven't climbed enough, the tower has ten flights of cement stairs that take you to the top. At the top of the tower there is a door that leads you out onto a balcony. The balcony overlooks gorgeous mountains,

Adrenaline Adventures

valleys and lakes. You stand in awe, or, more honestly you stand to catch your breath, snap a picture and ready yourself for the descent.

There is an easy path down, the dirt road type of stuff that we stuck the elderly couple on, or you can go full scale and climb back down all the rocks that you just came up. Naturally, we, rather I, chose the rocks. This was in the early stages of our relationship, so Steve was still in the "I want to impress you"mode . So he acted as if he didn't mind the climb down.

We were all ready to climb back down the Lemon Squeeze when we were stopped by unexpected traffic—a second set, or rather group of ill-prepared climbers, a 150 strong! Okay, it was really a camel-paced group of fifteen, but they were so slow it seemed endless. This gang was attempting to make their way up the Lemon Squeeze. It was a sight to see.

Half the women were dressed in the latest matching workout clothes, and the other half looked they like had been beamed out of the Long Island Mall, complete with manicured nails, big hair, and heels! Yes, high heels! It was absurd. The men were no better with bad hairpieces askew, beepers dangling from their belts, and worn-out loafers. Obviously, this climb was a last-minute jaunt for this motley crew.

One attorney in the clan had his cell phone in hand. As he climbed, he was telling someone about how great it was to be away from the office and the mechanics of everyday life. What did he think his cell phone was? A homegrown eggplant?

Another lady must have passed her entire Christmas shopping through the crevice. Bag after bag spewed out of the cracks at the top. She was cursing up a storm. After an eternity, we saw her hands appear and smack down on the top rock. When she heaved herself up, her glasses were sideways and her flowered shirt was lifted which exposed her Buddha belly. Where's a camera when you need it?

A few in the bunch had to be coaxed out. One guy was the worst. He simply froze—stopped dead in the middle of the crevice wall and kept repeating an ancient defeat mantra, "How can I get out of this? How did I let them talk me into this? Why am I here? I'm stuck; I want my mommy."

Fran Capo

Finally I said, "Hey pal, maybe if you save your breath and take your foot off your hand, you can climb out of the damn hole."

He looked down, took his foot off his hand, and wheezed his way up and out of the Lemon Squeeze.

Before we scrambled down, we looked back and saw the bunch sprawled out on the rocks, panting and moaning. One woman was actually filing her nails! And as for the attorney, he was on the phone calling for a taxi. This entire procession of characters took more than forty-five minutes.

On the way down Spencer asked, "Why did that man want his mommy?"

"Cause he was scared."

"Why was he scared? I'm only a kid and I did it?"

"That's cause your mother trained you for these crazy adventures." Steve chimed in.

I smiled. "Spencer the thing in life is to try to be prepared, and plan for what lies ahead. You can do things spur of the moment, but you need to use common sense."

Two hours later we were down the mountain and back in our car. Spencer picked up a few lizards along the way, and Steve passed with flying colors, which, of course, meant he could move on to ice caving the next weekend.

The last we heard of the Long Island group was that they were found at the top of the tower trying to order margaritas through a carrier pidgin, and the old couple was still walking down the mountain mumbling, "But I'm only sixty-three."

The moral is twofold: One, Mohonk is a great place to go for a good workout and gorgeous view and two, even though fun should be your number one goal, think things through so that you can live another day to tell about your exploits ... without having to use expletives.

Adrenaline Adventures

Chapter 17
Adventure at a Glance - Dare to Do it   Mild to Wild Scale: 2
Title: Rock Scrambling
Children allowed: Yes, with parents. Although they recommend no one under age nine goes up The Labyrinth, so use your judgement.
Length of trip: A few hours to a whole day
Where to try this adventure: Mohonk Mountain House, 1000 Mountain Rest Road, New Paltz, New York 12561. For general info: 845-255-1000; reservations: 800-772-6646.
Web site at www.mohonk.com. You can also explore your local parks, resorts, and historic sites for adventurous hiking spots.
Best time of year to go: Spring, summer, and fall. The trails close where there is ice or heavy rain.
Approximate cost: Traditional room $215 – $428 per room, per night (Prices include 3 meals daily, two-night minimum stay on weekends.) $10 per person for a weekday hike pass
$15 per person for a weekend hike pass
Reservations necessary: Not for day hiking, but from May through September, they don't sell passes after 4:30 P.M., and from November until they close for the season, they don't sell passes after 2:00 P.M.
Fitness requirement: Be in good shape
Personal gear required: Sneakers, bottled water, knapsack
What NOT to bring: Tight clothes, luggage, high heels
Photo opportunities: Yes

Notes: There are 85 miles of hiking trails at Mohonk. You can try an easy trail first before attempting The Labyrinth.

Cool trivia: Andrew Carnegie and four presidents, Theodore Roosevelt, William Howard Taft, Rutherford B. Hayes, and Chester A. Arthur, all stayed at Mohonk.

"Losers visualize the penalties of failure. Winners visualize the rewards of success."
– Dr. Robert Gilbert

Chapter 18
"On Top of the World"
A journey on a Ultralight

This book is about going after your dream adventures but also having the sense to say "No" when it becomes too dangerous. I learned this lesson well during my ultralight experience.

Ultralights are hang gliders with engines. They were developed in the 1970s when some people who liked to hang glide felt that since the wind doesn't always cooperate, it would be nice to add engines to the gliders so they could have more control and be able to avoid colliding head on into a mountain. In 1982, the FAA implemented regulations for the craft and a new safe, affordable sport was born. Today there is an organization called the EAA (Experimental Aircraft Association) that administers ultralight self-regulation programs. The organization is made up of sport aviation enthusiasts dealing with all kinds of crafts, from ultralights, to home- built models, light planes, warbirds, vintage and aerobatic participants, and people who simply love aviation.

I recruited my son, Spencer, my friend, Edward, his eleven-year-old sister Liz, his business partner, Paul, Paul's son, Bret, and his girlfriend, Ruth.

Adrenaline Adventures

I found out about an ultralight place in Jackson, New Jersey, from someone on America Online, probably a disgruntled ex-boyfriend, but decided to check it out anyway. The cost was forty dollars for fifteen minutes, and we'd get a chance to fly the ultralight. (Hey for that money, it should fly itself and do my taxes.) Kids were allowed to ride, providing they were tall enough to be strapped in. A few tissues in Spencer's shoes would do it.

Just like hot air balloons, these babies only fly in the morning and evening because of the wind conditions. I think the pilots just want the time off to go fishing.

As a weird twist of fate, two weeks prior to us going, a journalist friend of mine from Jersey named Denise called. I told her about my ultralight plans. The dead silence followed by a gasp on the other line should have given me a hint. She told me that she had written about a person who had died in an ultralight accident at the same outfit two years ago. The cause of the trouble was bad weather. I promised we wouldn't fly if that was the case.

At 6:30 on Sunday morning we convened at my house for the journey. The caravan of cars headed toward Jackson, New Jersey. Paul said it was an adventure just trying to follow me on the highway.

We arrived at the Ultralight Flight Center at 8:30. We were all excited and were trying to decide who would go first. My hand shot up. I figured I should be the proverbial guinea pig, since it was my idea. Mainly I wanted to show the kids that I wasn't scared. I wasn't.

Vince, the owner, a short, pot-bellied man, greeted us gruffly. "It's very windy today. You are going to get bumped around a lot. Still want to go?" He gave that nod that a mechanic gives when he is about to tell you that the car you brought in for an oil change really needs a new engine.

"Absolutely," I said. "I didn't drive two hours to sit and watch."

Vince pulled out a release form. Even though I've signed a million of them, release forms always make me nervous. You are signing something written in microscopic legalize that only Clarence Darrow could figure out. Further, you are trusting your life to the people who hopefully know how to handle the thing you are about to do, and they want to take no responsibility. "Sign here." I signed as I always do. I do remember an attorney once telling me that you could really sue them if you had to, even if you did sign the release form. The instructor laughed. I laughed back. Instructors laughing never makes me feel easy. "We'll test it out with you. If it's too windy, the kids can't go." I agreed. It's okay for me to risk my life, but not my kids. Yeah, there's good logic. Leave Spencer as an orphan. But I had adventure and an adrenaline rush on the brain.

I handed Edward my 35mm camera and camcorder. My mom got me into the habit of getting all these adventures on tape so I could look back and see exactly what I really got myself into.

As always, I was psyched for the adventure. Vince walked me over to the ultralight and introduced me to the pilot, Burly. Did his mother actually name him that? Burly shook my hand, and I noticed he was missing three fingers on his right hand. Not a good sign. I decided now wasn't the time to ask if he lost them in an ultralight accident.

We climbed into the ultralight, which looked like a mini-plane with two seats, one behind the other. I felt like Orville Wright. We put on our headphones, took a few pictures, and were off on the gravel road they called a runway. My driveway was bigger.

The ultralight sounded like an angry fly at a clam bake. Within minutes we were airborne. I loved it. Burly started giving me the tour. "There's Great Adventures ... there's the beach ... oh yeah and over there is where the Hindenburg crashed." Thanks, I needed to know that.

I was curious about the craft I was in, so I started to ask Burly some questions. "So, how fast can this thing go?"

"An ultralight by FAA regulations must not go faster than sixty-three miles per hour, and it must not stall at speeds greater than twenty-eight miles per hour."

"How much does this thing weigh? I mean, is it ultra-light?"

"To be considered an ultralight it must not weigh more than 254 pounds."

"Wait a second, that seems less than you and me combined together."

"Nope, it's about even."

"Okay, that's a little frightening. How long can we stay up?"

"Well, this thing is not allowed to carry more than five gallons of gas. Remember this is not an airplane, doesn't need to be FAA registered, and you don't need a FAA license to fly it."

"You did have some kind of training, right?'

"Yes, of course, I took instructions, passed a test and now teach it myself."

Then, just as I was about to ask another question, Burly turned to me. "Okay, your turn to fly. Grab the stick in between your legs, and use the pedals at the same time to hold it steady."

I was tense but excited. It was a little awkward coordinating the movements at first. My knuckles were turning white trying to keep it balanced. But Burly gave me confidence. "You're doing great. Keep it steady … steady … good. You're doing fantastic. Wanna take her in?"

My throat tightened, but I was game. "Sure!"

"Okay, inch the stick forward and—"

Apparently I was rougher than I thought. I inched the stick forward, and the ultralight lunged down like a paper airplane ready to crash.

Burly grabbed the stick. "Time to take over." That was definitely a moment to be wearing a depends.

He glided us in safely. Next, Edward was up to bat. He flew around for fifteen minutes and came in safely.

Now it was Paul's turn. He didn't want to go. He said the more he watched us, the more nervous he got. Plus the wind was picking up.

We nudged him on, attributing his reluctance to fear, not common sense. We chanted, "GO, GO, GO!" After all, we were all on safe ground. He succumbed to our chant. Peer pressure does it every time.

Burly and Paul took off the runway with a very shaky start. The ultralight was swaying from left to right like a drunken sailor. A few moments later the ultralight righted and looked fine.

This was the third flight of the day, and it was getting pretty boring to watch. The real fun comes from experiencing it, or at least being able to see the expressions on the faces of your friends. At this point, they were too far out for us to see or hear anything.

Fran Capo

All of a sudden, we saw them coming back toward the runway. They were coming in for a landing ... sideways! Literally at a ninety-degree angle! Burly tried to compensate, and they flipped like a pancake to the other side. We didn't need to see Paul's face to know he was sporting a Don King hairdo and his pants probably needed a change. Just five feet off the ground, Burly righted the ultralight, and they headed straight up again. He had to swing around to come in for a landing. Unfortunately we were too busy staring in disbelief and missed the perfect Kodak moment and our chance to sell the tape to *America's Funniest Home Videos*.

Take two. This time they came in in perfect formation. The craft lightly touched down and came to a stop. Paul's face was as green as a seasick frog. He said he knew there was trouble when Burly said after a few minutes, "Do you think we should take it in?"

"Why is he asking me?" thought Paul. So he adamantly said "Good idea".

Burly smiled but was shaken. Paul was shaken but didn't smile. Ruth was shaking her head no. Edward and I were glad we went up when the wind was calm. The kids thought we were crazy. Burly said, "That was a close one; we never should have gone up in that wind." Ah, but they did. We all egged them on chanting, because we wanted all of us to get a ride and experience the fun, even though at that point we should have called it quits. Luck was on their side.

What is it that makes people push on in the face of danger? The thought of beating death? Or worse, the thought of riding home with a bunch of whiny kids in the car disappointed they didn't go on an adventure? The bottom line is you should always weigh the consequences of your actions. There is nothing wrong in saying, "No, not a good idea right now. There is always another day." Then again, there are times to push the envelope like with the case of Kerri Strug in the 1996 Olympics. She had trained for years for the Olympics but had broken her ankle shortly before. She decided to try for the medal anyway, and for the first time in history, due to her performance, the U.S. Women's Gymnastic Team won gold. Kerri pushed the envelope—it was a one time shot.

Adrenaline Adventures

An adventure like ultralights you can do on another day, you don't have to risk being splattered like a roach on the pavement and paying forty dollars for the pleasure.

So, would I go ultralight flying again? Absolutely, but only under the right conditions. That day, however, we decided to take the kids to Great Adventures. After all, there they could go on any ride they wanted to, and if they didn't want to go, they could just say "NO."

Fran Capo

Chapter 18
Adventure at a Glance - Dare to Do it   Mild to Wild **Scale: 4**
Title: Journey on an Ultralight
Children allowed: Yes, with parental consent. Generally ten and up.
Length of trip: Fifteen minutes to a full day.
Where to try this adventure: The place I went to in Jackson has since closed. If you got to EAA's Web site: http://www.eaa.org/ultralights/directory/lookup.html and enter your state, they will give you several instructors' names, phone numbers, and email addresses.
Best time of year: Spring, summer, fall
Approximate cost: $40 for fifteen-minute introductory ride
Reservations necessary: Yes
Requirements: None
Fitness requirement: None
Personal gear required: None
What NOT to bring: Tight clothes
Photo opportunities: Yes

Notes: Check weather conditions before you head out. Don't fly in strong winds.

Cool trivia: John Moody, from Brandon, Florida, is recognized in the industry as the "father of ultralight." On July 27, 1976, in a foot-launched McCulloch 101–powered Icarus II hang glider, John was the first to demonstrate ultralight aviation at the annual EAA fly-in convention in Oshkosh, Wisconsin. From that point forward, the world of ultralight aviation grew.

Try everything once.
Except incest and folk dancing."
—Sir Thomas Beecham

Chapter 19
"The Doorless Chopper"
Learning to Fly a Helicopter

After our ultralight experience, I thought Edward would be turned off to air travel. Oh contraire. He was now obsessed with it. What I didn't know was that he'd always had a secret desire to be a pilot. So when I told Edward about a three-hour evening seminar at the Learning Annex on how to fly a helicopter, culminating with actually flying one on a follow-up day, he jumped at the chance. Within minutes we were both signed up for the class via phone.

The class was held in Manhattan. We walked in at exactly seven P.M. There were only four other students. Apparently, flying helicopters is not as popular as talking to the dead or learning how to make floral arrangements. I, once again, was the only woman in the class.

Adrenaline Adventures

The instructor had a heavy accent. He spoke in a monotone voice. He started with a brief overview. "Helicopters have only been around for about eighty years, although the concept of the helicopter dates back to the late 1400s. They were first used extensively in the Korean War, and today they are used for a variety of things; to transport world leaders, fight forest fires, rescue people trapped in hard-to-reach places, transport critically wounded people and soldiers, for mail service, observation, aerial photography, fire suppression, and search missions. They are without question one of the most versatile vehicles in the world."

Then he went on automatic pilot, switched modes, showed a lot of charts, talked in detail about the mechanics, and quite frankly I kept nodding in and out, which was embarrassing because there wasn't anybody to hide behind. Edward, however, was fascinated. When the class was over, he walked up to the teacher and shook his hand so enthusiastically I thought it was going to come off.

The instructor then gave us our passes to take the introduction lesson out at MacArthur Airport in Long Island. I think he was a little leery to give me my pass since I kept falling asleep, but nonetheless I'd paid for it so he handed it over. Plus, I had Edward's notes to study.

We drove out to Long Island the following week to take our lesson. We were greeted by a flight instructor and told that we were each entitled to a half-hour private lesson. I opted to go first. Before we headed over to the helicopter, I was told never to walk behind a helicopter. I hadn't planned on it, but it was a nice reminder. Then I was asked if I wanted the chopper doors on or off. I had no idea that "off" was an option.

I asked him, "How do you normally fly?"

"With the doors off."

"Okay, then keep the doors off," I said nonchalantly.

"I only give you that option because some people feel more secure with the doors on."

"Understandably so, but I like the added fear factor."

"Okay then, off they stay. Do you remember the pre-briefing from your classroom session?"

"In all honesty, I fell asleep a lot so can you just do a brief review?"

"Sure. First, we are going to give this helicopter a pre-flight inspection, which I will lead you through." The instructor started to check the craft. As he did, he continued to talk. "We'll be on the ground for about six minutes with this, then we are up in the air for your first lesson."

I followed him around, watching him check the chopper.

"The main thing to remember is that in a helicopter, lift is obtained by one or more power-driven horizontal propellers called rotors. When the rotor spins, it creates torque, which makes the helicopter want to spin also. To compensate, the helicopter has a small rotor near the back that offsets that. On a twin-rotor helicopter, they spin in opposite directions and cancel each other out. The helicopter's speed is limited in that if the blades rotate too fast, they will produce a compressibility effect on the blade moving forward and the helicopter will stall."

"We don't want that."

"No. The main thing is to concentrate, since it's more complicated to fly than a regular fixed-wing craft. Okay, are you ready? Hop on board, strap yourself in, and we'll be on our way."

I hopped in, secured my belt very tight, and took one last look at the doors I was leaving behind. I was handed headsets to muffle the sound and to use to communicate with the pilot. I waved to Edward, who was salivating on the ground waiting for his turn.

There is a rush when you go up in a helicopter without any doors. It goes up fast and you can see the ground vanish. I laughed.

The instructor started explaining what he was doing. "This is the control lever at your side, also known as the collective control stick. It raises and lowers the helicopter while at the same time it controls the throttle. It is linked to the engine's power. When you move this up and down, it changes the pitch of the main rotors. If the pitch is increased, you get more power."

He let me try it, with his hands near the control. I dipped it a bit, but I felt secure knowing he was right there.

"Now, over here in front of you is another control lever called the cyclic control. This controls the helicopter going forward, backward, and side to side. It's almost like a joystick on a video game. You push it forward or backward and the nose goes up or down. If you move it right, the rotor tilts in that direction and the helicopter banks and rolls. You try it."

I tried making a slight left turn, then right turn. I loved how easily the helicopter cooperated. I then moved it forward and dipped it a bit too aggressively and he quickly pulled it up. "Okay, no kamikaze actions on this flight."

"Oops, sorry."

"Finally, let me show you one more thing for today. Look on the floor. Those are the tail rotor pedals. They control the pitch of the tail rotor. If you want to turn right, you push on the right pedal, which decreases the pitch of the tail rotor and turns the helicopter to the right. You do the same thing on the opposite side."

He was in charge of those foot pedals. We flew around a bit more, doing some more maneuvers. Then I asked him if he could just hover the craft.

"Sure. To do this we put the cyclic control in neutral. The rotor blades now have the same pitch throughout their cycle. The collective lever holds the helicopter suspended in space without moving in any direction."

There was something really cool about being in a manmade machine and not moving ... just hanging out in space.

"Hey, what happens if the engines conk out, can you still land this thing safely?"

"Yes, there is a condition called autorotation; without getting too technical, it is a free-wheeling unit that allows the blades to still spin, and with the momentum from the already spinning blades, I can do a controlled decent and find a safe place to land."

"So you're telling me with zero forward speed, and whether the engine is operating or not, you can still land this thing safely?"

"Exactly, and that's why I like the copters over the fixed-wing crafts."

I was feeling really confident now, almost tempted to tell him to turn the engines off just to test out the theory, but I figured having no doors was cool enough for my first helicopter adventure.

Fran Capo

The half-hour was up, and it was Edward's turn. I watched as he took off with a big smile on his face. A half-hour later he was down.

As we walked over to the car, he kissed me on the cheek. "Guess what?"

"What?"

"While you were up, I signed up for flying lessons. I decided that I am going to fulfill my dream and go after my pilot's license, after all. Flying this helicopter made me know this was the right decision."

"Very cool. When do you start?"

"Tomorrow. I plan to have my license in a few months. Wanna take the first ride?"

I thought for a moment about the safety of going up with a new pilot but didn't want to ruin his enthusiasm. "Sure thing, all I ask is that you keep the doors on."

"You got yourself a deal."

Six months later, I went up with Edward in a Cessna on an evening flight. We flew around Manhattan (this was pre 9/11). We flew close to the Statue of Liberty, and I thought,"Yup, land of the free, this is the greatest country in the world, where all dreams are possible!"

Adrenaline Adventures

Chapter 19

<u>Adventure at a Glance - Dare to Do it   Mild to Wild Scale: 3</u>
Title: Learning to Fly a Helicopter
Children allowed: Any age for a ride as long as they are accompanied by a parent
Age requirement: Can fly as young as ten with parental consent but must be 16 to solo, 17 to hold a license.
Length of trip: Lessons can be half an hour to an hour.
Where to try this adventure: In New York, Flight Training Inc. Telephone: 631-467-2232 www.flighttraininginc.com
2111 Smithtown Avenue. Ronkonkokma, NY 11779
For those outside New York, you can go to:
www.flightschoolsdirectory.com for a list of schools closest to you.
Best time of year: All year round, sunup to sundown, but pilots have to check weather conditions before flying.
Approximate cost: Introductory twenty minute flight - $87
Hourly rate - $197
Reservations necessary: Yes
Fitness requirements: You should be in good health. There is a weight limit on smaller craft. If you're too heavy, you will just learn on a bigger helicopter.
Personal gear required: None on introductory lessons.
What NOT to bring: Excessive baggage, hangover
Photo opportunities: Yes, but not while you're at the controls.

Notes: I went through a course at an adult ed school. Most flying instructions can be obtained directly from the flight school.

Cool trivia: The current world record for the highest flying helicopter is held by the Aerospatiale Lama. The SA315B Lama made its maiden flight on March 17, 1969. On June 21, 1972, pilot Jean Boulet reached an altitude of 12,442 meters, setting an outright world altitude record that remains unbeaten to this day.

"It's not what happens to people that's important. It's what they do about it."
— Author Unknown

Chapter 20
"Niagara - Not Just for Lovers"
Jet Boat Ride

I've been to Niagara Falls three times in my life and never with a husband or lover ... and I still enjoyed it. The first time was to sign autographs at the Guinness Museum on the Canadian side, and the second time was with a long- time friend, Kirk, and the third time was with my friend Dina and her daughter, Athena.

Dina mentioned that she wanted to join my son, Spencer, and me on one of our weekend adventures. I asked her if she was ready for the pace since we'd have to pack a lot in to one day. She was game.

Niagara Falls is a huge tourist attraction, and there are many things to do in the area. The falls are actually made up of several waterfalls. Horseshoe Falls is on the Canadian side and measures 167 feet tall and 2,500 feet wide. American Falls is a wee bit taller, measuring in at 176 feet but only 1,100 feet wide, and Bridal Veil Falls, near Luna Island, is the smallest of the three waterfalls. It resembles the train of a bridal veil, thus the name. (There will be a test.) Since I had previously seen most of the attractions in town, I was looking for something that I hadn't done yet. I found my adventure in a town just outside of the big tourist area.

We made hotel reservations and set off at three in the morning on Saturday so that everyone had a chance to have little shut-eye after school on Friday. The drive from New York City to Niagara Falls is about seven and a half hours (depending on if you want to break a land speed record or not).

We checked into our hotel at eleven, dropped our bags, and headed directly to our new found adventure, the Whirlpool Jet Boat Ride, the only thing we pre-booked on this trip. As planned, we met the tour guides at the rustic Riverside Inn in Lewiston, New York, not far from the falls.

There we were pre-briefed by this cute guide, Quinn (that always starts a trip out right). Quinn gave us background information: "At Niagara Falls the free falling water transforms into a mighty river which flows through a majestic river canyon. The force of the river

Adrenaline Adventures

causes world-famous rapids and the legendary Whirlpool, also known as St. David's Buried Gorge.

The whirlpool is accessible only by powerful jet boats. Today We are going to go to the edge of this swirling whirlpool on a one-hour, eighteen-mile jet boat ride that would reach speeds of up to seventy miles per hour. The climax of our ride will be getting soaked to the skin as we go through Devil's Hole, a class five rapid.

As you may know, rapids are rated by classes. Class one is mild. Class five is the legal limit of rapids that you can go on and not get killed. Class six is considered un-runnable. If you decide to do a class six, you better hope the boat has a black box, and you're sitting on it."

After the briefing we each were handed full-length rain suits, bright yellow ponchos, and life jackets. This was no vanity fair. We were also given the standard "donate your body parts to science" release forms. Dina and Athena exchanged worried looks as Spencer and I laughed. Face it, they don't give out release forms at croquet conventions. We were then lead to the jet boat.

The jet boat held forty-eight people; there were six rows that could hold eight people each. On our trip, there were only nine people, so we had plenty of room.

As I got on I asked how old the oldest passenger was.

"We had a ninety-two-year-old guy do this one year!"

"Very cool!"

Once everyone was seated, Quinn told us that he would go as slow or fast as we wanted but that we had to show enthusiasm. The boat took off slowly and before we were even out of the dock everyone was yelling "Go faster, *FASTER!!*"

The captain taunted us, "I can't hear you!"

Again all the passengers chanted, "FASTER! FASTER!" I looked over and noticed Dina and Athena were sitting white knuckled, gripping the railings on the boat.

The captain started speeding the boat and soon he was up to full throttle. Our confidence was building because we weren't getting that wet—YET. The boat bumped along the river, and then before we knew it, we were into the rapids, quickly going up in class. Soon we were getting splashed with big rushes of water. Spencer, who was a mere ten at the time, was laughing hysterically. Yes, like his mother—we laughed in the face of fear! Ha, ha, ha.

Then we spotted it, the Devil's Hole. The name was fitting. It looked like a bucking bronc of water. The waves were high and rough, and we were headed right toward them.

Quinn shouted, "Hold your arms out straight to brace yourselves. Hold tight onto the bars in front of you. On the count of five we're going in. Are you ready?"

We all shouted, "YES!"

Five ... four ... three ... two ... the jet boat headed full speed into the mouth of the Devil. There was no turning back now.

As if in a slow motion, action-packed movie, I saw a wall of freezing water about ten feet high engulf the boat. Then I felt it. It shocked my system. I put my hands on top of Spencer's to hold him securely. For a few seconds I wasn't sure when I was going to breathe again ... the wave of water seemed to keep coming and coming. Just when I thought I might need an oxygen mask, it was over. My hands were numb. Spence and I looked at each other in shock. I have to say it was pretty scary, so of course we went back for more—smiling all the way. Fear is always worse the first time around when you don't know what to expect; after the first time, we were ready for it.

Unfortunately, Athena did not share our enthusiasm. She moved to the back of the boat where the captain was, relatively dry. Dina laughed and cursed me out at the same time for bringing her on such a scary ride.

After three times through the Devil's Hole and feeling like a drowned rat, we returned to shore having experienced the rough rapids just a few miles north of the mighty falls.

We were soaked to the skin, we were exhilarated, and we knew we'd be back one day to do it again.

Adrenaline Adventures

Chapter 20
Adventure at a Glance - Dare to Do it   Mild to Wild Scale: 4
Title: Whirlpool Jet Boat Tour
Children allowed: Yes, six and up. Children under sixteen must be accompanied by a parent.
Length of trip: One hour, 18 miles
Where to try this adventure: Whirlpool Jet Boat Tours
PO box 1215–61 Melville Street, Niagara-on-the-lake,
Ontario LOS iJO
(905)468-4800 / (905) 468-7004
www.whirlpooljet.com or email: wjet@wjet.com
There are also jet boat tours available at other locations in the country like Columbia River Gorge, Hells Canyon, Wisconsin Dells, Lake Mead.
Best time of year: April – October
Approximate cost: $43 US adults / $37 US kids under 14.
Reservations necessary: Yes and must be paid in advance. Trips leave promptly at their scheduled time.
Fitness requirements: You cannot be pregnant or subject to heart, neck, or back problems.
Personal gear required: A change of clothes.
What NOT to bring: Loose glasses or anything that you don't want to get wet. Lockers are available for valuable items.
Photo opportunities: Yes and you can purchase a video as well.

Notes: You will get totally soaked no matter where you sit on the boat. The trip runs rain or shine.

Cool trivia: Captain Matthew Webb was the first man ever to swim the English Channel. He did it on August 24, 1875 in 21 hours and 45 minutes. In an effort to challenge himself further he attempted to swim the violent whirlpool rapids below Niagara Falls in 1882. He died during his attempt.

"The greatest discovery of my generation is that a human being can alter his life by altering his attitudes of mind."
– William James (1842-1910)

Chapter 21
"I Ain't Afraid of No Ghost"
Ghost Sighting

It started innocently enough. My son, Spencer, and I were reading stories out of a book called *The Ten Creepiest Places in America* by Allan Zullo. In it were tales of Area 51 in Nevada, Brown Mountain Ghost Lights seen in North Carolina, and America's Stonehenge in North Salem, New Hampshire. Then a story caught our eyes. It was about fifteen prankster ghosts who haunted the oldest continuously operated restaurant (since 1704) in the United States, the General Wayne Inn in Merion, Pennsylvania.

    According to The Ghost Research Society, local psychics, and the innkeeper, these ghosts, which included several Revolutionary War soldiers, barmaids, customers from the 1800s, a young girl, and a sea captain, had quite a sense of humor.

Adrenaline Adventures

They were known to fill the cash register with water, blow in customers' ears, shake glasses on shelves, and rearrange napkins, silverware, and glasses on preset tables. They would also play tricks on the owner's wife, making the calculators and adding machines add up the same set of numbers differently each time—my kind of ghosts.

Then an idea struck me. Why not go check this out with the family? Merion is pretty close to Philadelphia, and I often performed on weekends at a place called the Comedy Cabaret in Philly and stayed overnight. During the day, why not make a little excursion to Merion the next time I was booked? I told my plan to my then-husband, Bobby (husband number two), and son, Spencer.

At first, they looked at me like I had watched one too many episodes of *The Twilight Zone*. But shortly I convinced them that this would be a great adventure, and they were game.

I called the Inn and made lunch reservations. The way I saw it this was an historical adventure. After all, Ben Franklin and George Washington slept at the Inn (although dear George seems to have slept everywhere), and Edgar Allan Poe wrote several stanzas of his poem "The Raven" there. Although we probably wouldn't run into those characters, we might be lucky enough to have an encounter with some other dudes of the past.

Eager, we arrived there around 2:30 P.M. on a Saturday afternoon. We pulled up to a gray building with light brown shingles on the top. A sign that hung prominently on the top half of the building and was done up in old English lettering let us know we were at the right place. It simply read "General Wayne Inn." I don't know what I was expecting, but the place didn't look haunted to me.

As we walked in, the bar was to our left. Then it clicked. "Spencer remember in the story? This is the bar where supposedly one evening after the restaurant had closed the owner, Bart Johnson, was sitting on a stool relaxing with two remaining elderly women customers. They were having coffee and talking when all of a sudden a cannonball about the size of tennis ball dropped from the ceiling. The three were said to watch in amazement as it rolled toward them. When Johnson went to pick it up, it disappeared. No holes were found in the ceiling,

Fran Capo

and the three of them swore this story was true and repeated the story to that television show, *America's Unsolved Mysteries*.

Bobby just laughed at my enthusiasm.

A host came up and escorted us to a large dining room with shiny wooden floors. Large chandeliers hung from the ceilings. On the walls were paintings of the Revolutionary War. We sat by a stone fireplace. The only other patrons in the room were three elderly ladies. We'd obviously missed the lunch crowd.

It was very quiet. Spencer seemed disappointed. Bobby just laughed. He didn't believe in ghosts.

Spencer wanted to go to the bathroom, but just in case there might be ghosts, he decided it best not to go alone. I asked Bobby to go with him. Knowing the two of them liked to joke around a lot, I added, "Hey, while you're in there why not stir things up and taunt the ghosts a bit?" I winked at Bobby.

I felt a little anxious waiting at the table. I believed in ghosts, but I wasn't really sure I wanted to see one. Actually, I wanted to see one, but I didn't want them to scare the wits out of me. After all, I like jokes, but from ghosts, well, maybe I wouldn't be too amused. If these spirits showed themselves, I was hoping I could joke back with them and not panic. Facing fears is always a nerve-racking experience, and no matter how many times I've done it, each opportunity is different.

Bobby and Spencer came back from the bathroom laughing. "Well, we did like you said. Spencer and I challenged the ghosts to come out and show themselves. I think they're all cowards. Not one of them did anything."

Spencer was acting pretty confident for a ten-year-old. "Yeah, I even looked at the pictures of some of the old war guys on the wall and asked them to come out, we wanted to meet them."

"Gee, that was awfully nice of you." I said sarcastically.

At this point, nature called, and I needed to use the facilities. I didn't have the luxury of having either of the guys go with me, so I went it alone. Imagination is a great elixir. I could swear I saw the eyes on the paintings following me to the bathroom. I felt the need to make a general announcement, "Hey listen ghosts, if you are

Adrenaline Adventures

planning on doing something, do it to the guys. They really want to see you."

I was trying not to show any fear, because I didn't want them to get a kick out of scaring me. As I headed into the ladies room, I started hoping there were no perverted ghosts that were watching me as I went to the bathroom. Ghosts can be obtrusive that way. The last thing I needed was the toilet paper floating away as I went to use it. Then we really would have had a scene out of a sitcom as I came running out with my pants around my legs.

I got back to the table with no supernatural encounters. As we were waiting for our lunch to be served, the old ladies left. It was just the three of us in that big old dining room. We asked the waiter if he ever saw any strange occurrences here.

"I never did, but I'll tell you one thing, whenever I go in the cellar I can feel this weird presence. You know one of the soldiers was buried in the wall down there. Sometimes I get the feeling he is trying to come out. I try not to go down there."

Okay, I thought, this guy works here and has been paid to add to the hype; this place just has a bunch of history and nothing more. Dinner came and went, and although the food was fantastic, we were pretty disappointed we hadn't seen any celestial beings. I decided to go to the bathroom again. This time I wasn't afraid. I handed Bobby my beeper so I wouldn't have to carry it with me. As I walked past the paintings of the soldiers I said, "I guess you guys aren't in a playful mood after all." I smiled and entered the bathroom not worrying about candid camera ghosts.

When I came back to the table, I saw two very pale faces. Spencer and Bobby started to speak at the same time. Spencer blurted out, "Mom, Bobby's chair floated backward. I saw it."

Bobby jumped in, "Fran, take this beeper. What time does it say?"

I looked down at the beeper. "3:01"

Bobby grabbed it from me. He looked at it. It was flashing 12:00.

He handed it back to me. "It reads 3:02," I said. "What's the problem?"

Bobby started to explain. "When you left to go to the bathroom, my pager went off. I stood up to look at it. It read 12:00 ... no page.

Fran Capo

I'm standing there looking at the beeper and I see Spencer's face go white. I turn around and my chair is on the ground. No sound, nothing. I didn't even feel it."

Spencer jumped in. "Ma, it went backward in slow motion like someone was placing it on the floor."

"Yeah right, guys. How convenient. This happened while I was in the bathroom. No witnesses. Cute, but I'm not buying it."

Bobby adamantly continued. "Fran, you know how observant I am. I didn't hear or feel a thing. These are solid wooden floors. No carpet to buffer a sound if a chair fell. You know I would notice something like that. You know they call me the Hawk, because of my martial arts training and my observation skills. I swear to you, this was not just a normal chair falling back."

"Okay, so the chair fell back and the beeper said 12:00. So your jacket buffered it and your pager battery is running dead and is flashing twelve. It seems as if there is an explanation for everything."

"Let me finish," he continued. "I go to pick up the chair and the beeper goes off again. This time it reads 3:00 ... but there's no page. When I handed it to you, it had gone off again. 12:00 ... no page. A beeper only pages twelve when you take the batteries out of it and replace them. It only flashes when you have to reset the timer. It wouldn't switch from three to twelve to 3:01, then back to twelve again. Plus, there were no sent pages any time."

The three of us got up and tested pushing the chair back in a variety of ways. Each time the chair hit the floor, it made a sound. Since there was no music in the room, we could hear the thud each time. The only way we couldn't hear a sound is was if I stood behind the chair and slowly lowered it to the floor. We also checked the batteries on the pager and they were fine. The whole thing was a little weird and would be in line with prankster ghosts. Finally, we called the waiter over. We asked him if anyone had ever experienced this. Very nonchalantly he replied, "Oh yeah, but it usually happens at that table over there and only to doctors and lawyers. It happening at this table with this chair, that's a new one. Is there anything else I can get you?"

"Yeah, the name of the ghost."

The waiter just smiled and walked away.

Adrenaline Adventures

Bobby turned to me. It was the most serious I had seen him. "Fran, I believe in ghosts. I didn't before I got here, but I do now."

Spencer said, "Me too, Mom."

I wasn't sure yet, because I still hadn't seen it first-hand, but then I remembered how I'd asked the ghosts to only prank the guys. Maybe the ghosts were nice guys after all. The boys got their scare, and I didn't have to meet the ghosts.

The waiter came back, and Bobby paid the check. The waiter was nice enough to accommodate our request for a quick tour of the place.

"This is the haunted staircase. Some other waiters said they have seen a Hessian soldier many times walking up and down the staircase asking for a lost locket that someone stole from him. Personally I've never seen it, but that doesn't mean it's not true."

We then walked to the top of the staircase. I hoped that I wasn't walking through the guy's ghostly form as I ascended. At the top of the staircase was a chandelier I remember reading about. The waiter continued, "As you can see this chandelier has only one swinging crystal and we don't know why. There is no draft or anything that explains it." He then showed us the room where George Washington slept, and from one of the windows he had us look out as he pointed to an area in the backyard where supposedly many other ghosts had been seen."

We thanked him for the tour and left the General Wayne Inn, taking a few pictures for memory's sake.

In the car on the way home I once again asked Bobby and Spencer if they were pulling prank on me. Again they swore they weren't. They were laughing as they said it, but it wasn't a normal "I'm fooling around with you" laugh but that nervous kind of laugh that comes when something gets under your skin and you're trying to explain it, but no one will believe you. The funny thing is, I do believe in ghosts. I just didn't feel the proof was strong enough in this case.

That night when we were getting ready for bed, Bobby placed his pager on the nightstand, like he had done a million times in the past. The next morning the pager was gone. Now I was annoyed. I thought he was carrying the joke too far.

Fran Capo

For three weeks we couldn't find the pager. The day after Bobby bought a new one I found his old pager. It was clipped to a cardboard box in the basement underneath our wooden staircase. The pager was blinking 12:00.

I believe I got my proof. I ran out of the basement.

Practical joke or prankster ghost? Go on a ghost hunt yourself and dare to find the answer. We threw the pager out. We decided in the future, it's best not to taunt a ghost, because the last thing you want, friendly or not, is Casper coming to dinner and then following you home and moving in.

Adrenaline Adventures

Chapter 21
Adventure at a Glance - Dare to Do it   Mild to Wild Scale: 3
Title: Ghost Sighting
Children allowed: Yes
Length of trip: About two hours
Where to try this adventure: The General Wayne Inn on 625 Montgomery Ave in Merion , PA has since closed. But there are other places to try an adventure like this under notes.
Best time of year to go: Anytime
Approximate cost: Most haunted areas are free, unless you are staying at a haunted hotel.
Reservations necessary: No
Fitness requirement: None
Personal gear required: None, but you can bring holy water or your own medium, if you must.
What NOT to bring: Bad attitude.
Photo opportunities: Sorry, ghosts are usually camera shy.

Notes: There are many haunted places in the United States and around the world. If you go to the Shadowlands Haunted Places Index (http://theshadowlands.net/places/index2.htm) you will see a state by state, country by country listing of haunted places.

Cool trivia: The following is an excerpt from a Web site called Ghost Hunting 101 (www.ghosthunting101.com). "There are generally two types of spirits you may encounter. One was a human at one time … It may not know it's dead, may be held here by unfinished business, guilt, etc…. This human spirit is the type you will encounter 95% of the time. You could also witness a residual haunting which is just a playback of a past event. The other type of spirit you may encounter were never human and are generally bad news… the chances that you will encounter them in a regular ghost hunt are slim … be aware and protect yourself and you should have no problem." Happy hunting!

"I am always doing things I can't do, that is how I get to do them."
—Pablo Picasso

Chapter 22
"She Flies Through the Air...."
Learning the Trapeze

It was time for another adventure. Another episode to challenge myself, and push my body and mind to their limits. Some people call this living on the edge. I call it experiencing life and all it has to offer.

The destination, Xatapa, Mexico. The challenge, circus training. My compadres, my son, Spencer, and my then-husband, Bobby.

I had seen circus training offered in a Club Med brochure. I stared at the pictures of normal, everyday common folk happily suspended on a tiny trapeze. I figured if that family could do it, so could we. I called and made the reservations for a week-long training/vacation.

When we arrived in Mexico, we were greeted with the usual Club Med fanfare; songs, smiles, and a lei. It was already two o'clock in the afternoon so the Monday morning circus classes were over. As usual, I was excited and couldn't wait to check in and run over to the training area. My son, of course, couldn't wait to get to the beach, and Bobby was happy to just get a beer and relax. But they indulged me.

Adrenaline Adventures

We dropped our bags in the room and headed over to the outdoor high wire and trapeze area that was only a few hundred yards from the crystal clear, blue Mexican waters. I felt a rush of energy as we walked closer. No one was around, but there was a sign that read, "Adult trapeze class, 4 p.m." Since we had two hours to kill, Spencer played in the water, and Bobby got his beer. As for me, I anxiously sat tapping my hands, counting the minutes.

At exactly ten minutes to four we returned to the training area with cameras ready and in workout clothes to allow easy movement.

We didn't know what to expect. We sat on the tiered bleaches, which were located about thirty feet in front of the safety net. They were the benches for spectators. There were also two side benches for amateur acrobats in waiting. The side benches were right next to the ladder—the ladder that took you way up to the little tiny platform where you could access the trapeze. Next to the ladder was a chalk bin. Any acrobats who might be sweating could dip their hands into the powdered chalk and then climb the ladder without having to worry that their sweaty palms would lose grip and do them in.

As we were surveying the layout, three trainers in tights, Melinda, Ivan, and Arano, showed up. They greeted us and invited us to sit on the benches next to the ladder. Then they took their perspective positions. Arano was on the ground. He was in charge of the safety rope. Melinda climbed up the narrow five-story ladder and positioned herself on the tiny platform. From that platform you'd launch out over the giant safety net on your swing. Ivan sat on the other trapeze and his job was to shout out instructions to us newbies.

With everyone in position, I decided to go first. I always have less fear if I just get things over with. I walked to the ladder. Arano fitted me with a weight belt harness. He hooked the harness snug around my waist. Then he took a safety line and attached it to the belt. I chalked up my hands and began the ascent up the ladder.

I love climbing. This, however, was the highest I'd ever climbed on a ladder. My heart was beating wildly as I realized that soon I would have to jump off this thing. Things seem much higher up off the ground than they do when you are on the ground staring up.

Spencer and Bobby were getting real tiny. At the top of the ladder, there was a tape mark on one of the rungs. At that point you were

Fran Capo

supposed to stop and swing your body around to the other side of the ladder. As you did this you were supposed to reach out and grab Melinda's hand so that she could help you hoist yourself up onto the platform. When I finally was standing on that tiny stage, I looked down. Damn it was high. Now I know how Dumbo felt in that circus scene when he was about to leap off.

Melinda started the instructions. "Put your toes over the edge. Now Ivan is going to swing the trapeze at you. I want you to reach out till you feel you are practically falling over, and grab the trapeze. And don't worry, I'll be holding onto your waist harness so you won't fall over." Now I'm not a giant, but I was a bit worried about Melinda holding my entire weight with one hand. I sure hoped she ate her Wheaties.

She continued, "When Ivan yells 'Hike' that's your cue. I want you to jump off and grab the swing. It may seem that the swing is not close enough, but trust us. If you leap off the platform when we tell you, you will get the swing."

Usually I am good at following instructions since I figure that the instructors have done this a million times before and know what they are talking about. But in some circumstances my logic and natural survival instinct collide—especially if I think I am going to fall into the abyss. Ivan had to yell, "Hike" three times before I responded. They must have thought I was deaf. I, of course, thought Ivan needed glasses. The swing wasn't anywhere close enough for me to leap up, out, and grab. But they reassured me, and the glaring eyes of my fellow acrobats below made me jump.

The next time the swing came at me, I leaped and sure enough I caught the trapeze. As I swung back and forth, five stories above the world, things were a blur. The next thing I heard was Ivan's command, "Let go." I did and plummeted to the net below, on my butt. Now that I had the feel for it, I was ready to try it again. I went back on line near the ladders.

It was Bobby's turn. Apparently he did not have the same apprehension. He executed the move beautifully. My competitive nature was stirred. But I was proud of him at the same time.

Adrenaline Adventures

Since this was the adult training session, Spencer had to just sit and watch. He seemed fine with that, and he and another kid made fun of the way we adults were performing.

Bobby and I did this swing and release several more times. We were now getting comfortable with it since we knew what to expect.

Just as we were perfecting the swing move ... Melinda gave us a second set of instructions. "This time after you grab the swing, Ivan is going to yell out the word 'now.' When he does, I want you to put your feet through your arms and latch them onto the swing. Once you are holding on by your legs, I want you to let your hands go from the swing and arch your back and arms out. After you do one complete swing in that position, I want you to somersault down onto the net. Got that?"

Mentally I had it got it, but physically it was another thing. It wasn't that I didn't try. I tried with all my might. But no matter how hard I tried I couldn't get my legs through my arms and onto the swing. Embarrassment stormed through my body. Why couldn't I get my legs to do what they needed to do? I've hung upside down plenty of times from the monkey bars at the park. I'm athletic. Heck, I even did TaeBo.

Bobby did it on the first try. Actually, he did it so well they taught him the third move, the catch. The catch is where once you are upside down with your body in an arched position, you reach out and grab onto the arms of a trapeze artist on another swing. Once you are swinging from his arms, you do a somersault and fall into the safety net below. This catch move was the move you needed to master to get the circus certificate at the end of the Club Med week. I couldn't even get the first part down! Bobby kept on doing the move, and he mastered it so well they asked him to perform in the circus show that night. They dressed him up in tights, and he went on with other newbie performers and did a show for the Club Med guests who were watching from the bleachers. I was proud, but it only sparked my desire to try harder.

I watched through out the entire week as Bobby and Spencer did somersaults. Spencer's ten-year-old body raced up that ladder, and he grabbed the swing, did a somersault, and came down proudly with the other kids, knowing he had done it. I thought, "That's my boy." I just wished he could say, "That's my mom."

I was very frustrated, but I kept on trying.

Then something weird happened. I saw this chubby little girl get up on that swing and succeed. She turned to look for her parents in the bleachers, and her parents weren't around to watch. You could tell she was really proud of herself, and no one she loved seemed to care enough to be around to share in her glory. She was devastated and started to cry. I went over to her and told her I saw her and that I thought she was fantastic. I told her how I tried and tried and still couldn't do it. I managed to make her laugh and cheer her up, but in the process, somehow I became discouraged.

I was making this too important. I was supposed to be having fun, and all I could feel was that I wanted to give up, it was becoming too much work. I practiced at every available training session. Each time I was sure I would do it. And each time I failed. The trainers kept telling me not to give up. But I was getting very frustrated. You would have thought P.T. Barnum was judging me.

We tried different methods. I wanted that certificate. It became an obsession. At one point, I just said, "That's it. I give up. It never takes me this long to get the knack of something. I've lost my touch."

Bobby told me to lighten up, not to give up, that it would be a bad example for Spencer. He was right.

So Bobby and I stretched and trained together. Spencer was off enjoying himself with new friends, swimming and kayaking. I knew I only had this one week to get this move, and now we were down to the last two days.

Then I got sick—real sick. The Mexican water caught up with me big time. My stomach was doing the flips that I wanted to do on the trapeze. But I was determined.

It was the last session on the last day. I climbed up that ladder for the hundredth time, sick but determined. Four times up, four times plop—nada. There were only twenty minutes left to the lesson and then it was the end of Circus de la Club Med.

I said, "Okay, Capo, this is it. Repeat the instructions in your head. If you don't do it, at least you tried. Let go of the feeling of failure. Be yourself, and have a good time."

Adrenaline Adventures

With that thought, my legs easily went through my arms, over the swing, and latched on. I was swinging upside down. I heard Spencer, Bobby, and all the instructors cheering below. "You did it!" I felt fantastic, but I knew I was still one move away from the certificate.

Now I had to do the third and final move, the catch. I had broken through the failure barrier and turned off the voice in my head that said I couldn't do it. Since I had done move number two once, I knew I could do it again. I went up the ladder again, this time with renewed confidence. I latched my legs on, swung below, arched my back, and extended my arms. All I had to do was to grab Ivan's arms on the other swing. This took timing and precision. Without hesitation, I grabbed his arms as if I had done it a million times before. Then I reversed my position, flipped into a somersault and landed in the net. I felt like an Olympic gymnast. Tears ran down my face. I had done it with one minute to spare.

Bobby and Spencer ran up and hugged me. All three instructors came over to me and presented me with the certificate. They said, "We are the most proud of you ... since you worked the hardest." I thanked them and just stared at the paper. It was more than a piece of paper to me, it was a symbol. To this day that certificate hangs on my office wall as a reminder of the importance of encouragement, determination, the ability to keep things in perspective, being a good role model, and, above all, a reminder to never, never, never give up.

Fran Capo

Chapter 22
Adventure at a Glance – Dare to Do it   Mild to Wild Scale: 4
Title: Learning the Trapeze
Children allowed: Yes
Age requirement: Age six and up are welcome. Parents must stay with kids under twelve.
Length of trip: One class to couple of weeks
Where to try this adventure: Club Med (www.clubmed.com) or the New York Trapeze School (www.trapezeschool.com), which is located at the Hudson River Park in Manhattan.
Best time of year to go: All year long
Approximate cost: $47-$65 per class depending on the day and time of the week. Weekends start at $65 per class at the TSNY school, and discounts are offered for multiple classes. Club Med is a package deal that includes airfare, lodging, all meals, and most activities. You need to get individual price quotes.
Reservations necessary: Yes
Requirements: Must be good shape.
Personal gear required: Clothes that fit snugly, like Yoga pants or tight sweats, are best so they don't bunch up in the harness. If you have long hair, tie it up. Wear socks or light slippers for flying.
What NOT to bring: Baggy clothes
Photo opportunities: Yes

Notes: Doing the trapeze is a great workout and helps your body learn balance.

Cool trivia: In 1859, a French gymnast by the name of Jules Leotard invented the flying trapeze at the Cirque Napoleon in Paris. Leotard called his act La Course aux Trapeze. He started with two swings and jumped from one swing to the other. He eventually increased the number of trapeze swings to five, flying in the air and somersaulting to each one. The trapeze caught on and a catcher was introduced, like Ivan in my story. It wasn't until 1975 on American soil that a trapeze artist by the name of Don Martinez was able to achieve three and a half somersaults.

"How far would Moses
have gone
if he had stopped
and taken a poll in Egypt?"
– Harry Truman

Chapter 23
"Is that an Alligator I see?"
Everglades Airboat Ride

Most of the greatest things that have happened to me in my life have occurred on the spur of the moment. There is something exhilarating about deciding something and instantaneously knowing you will do it. The inertia propels you.

I was booked in Coral Gables, Florida to pull a fast one as an imposter at an EDGE convention. EDGE was a company run by a dedicated young entrepreneur named Scott Shickler. The EDGE convention consisted of about one hundred teachers and community leaders whose focus was Entrepreneurial Skills for Inner City Children. Scott thought it would be fun if I was to do my impostor/ fast talking routine for the attendees. You see, I happen to be the Guinness Book of World Records fastest talking female. I am clocked

Adrenaline Adventures

at 603.32 words per minute or ten words a second. When I am hired to do the imposter routine, I am introduced under a fake name, and people at the conference think I am just another "real" speaker. I start out slow and logical, and then I lunge into my fast talking, throwing out company jargon, interjecting ridiculous notions, and basically confusing the audience. They get a kick out of it, realizing they have been tricked, and everyone leaves laughing.

In preparation for my imposter show, I generally wander about the town looking for local things I can joke about. During one of my wanderings, I got roped into a personality analysis session by a persistent group of L. Ron Hubbard analysts. But while I was in their waiting room, I happened upon a fascinating magazine called *Florida Adventures*.

I had always wanted to go on the airboat rides in the Everglades. Of course, when I had read about a plane crash that occurred there a couple of years ago, I was a little nervous. I heard the disturbing news that alligators were dining on the passengers, and I was worried they might be still coming up for living morsels. The thought horrified me. Yet, I still wanted to see these ancient reptiles, up front and personal.

I decided to go into the Everglades after my performance. I just had to find a way to get there. I was only in Florida for the one night and had only a few hours before my plane took off the next day. I had not rented a car, and the nearest airboat ride place was about an hour away.

So I did the only logical thing. I announced my desire to go at the end of my speech that night. "By the way, I'm not only the fastest talking female ... I'm also looking for a daring individual to go with me to the airboat rides and go alligator gazing."

This one girl with a loud laugh volunteered. It was midnight so we made arrangements for the next morning.

Kathy and I met at eight the next morning. We drove an hour in her rented car and came to this strip of airboat places. We stopped at one place called Wally's World. It had a giant plastic alligator out in front with a beer in his hand. It was a place with a sense of humor and we both liked it.

We paid our admission, walked past the gift shop selling alligator paw keychains, and walked out to meet our tour guide. Wally's was a father and son operation. The father drove the boat, and the son— a very cute son, I might add –did the alligator wrestling demonstration.

Kathy and I got on the airboat with four other people, all Japanese tourists. We were handed headsets. "The boats are very quiet when we move slow, but when we speed up you are going to want these things."

The noiseless boat glided out on this small canal into the reedy waters of the Everglades. Not even five minutes into the ride, Wally pointed out an alligator on the starboard side.

This gator was close—finger snapping close. Airboats, by the way, have no side railings. I asked Wally, "How high do these things jump?"

He laughed. "Depends how hungry they are." We all laughed in amusement but moved closer to the center of the boat.

The gator's sneaky little beady eyes followed our every move. It was just watching and waiting. Then, without warning, Wally threw a chunk of meat over the side. The gator lunged into the air and SNAP, the meat was gone. I barely had time to see him move. That was comforting.

Wally then started to give us some facts on gators." If you saw that gator open its mouth, you'd see eighty teeth, forty on the top, forty on the bottom. As the teeth wear down, they are replaced. Alligators can go through three thousand teeth in their lifetime."

"That's a lot of Tooth Fairy money!" I joked.

He laughed and continued, "The teeth are used for grabbing and holding, not cutting. They shake their prey apart. Their jaws are strong enough to crack a turtle shell. Also, if you noticed it watching us, alligators have a transparent third eyelid for when they go underwater. They use their feet to swim slow and keep their balance in the water, but when they want to swim fast to catch prey or food like you just saw him do, he uses his tail. And despite being cold-blooded, these guys do have a heart. It's a four-chambered heart."

Wally moved the boat along again. This time we saw a mother gator. Wally told us that she was more dangerous because she was protecting her young. A mother gator watches over her young for close to two years.

I asked how big she was. He replied, "The average female is about 8.2 feet in length." We passed by her and moved on to even bigger gators.

Then we spotted it, one gator the size of a small condo. Wally explained that this one was the Capo di Tutti of gators. Being that my last name is Capo, I can relate to that. It means the head honcho, the boss, the one to watch out for. I looked at the gator to see if we were related.

Wally continued, "This guy, here, protects all the females. He's not one to be messed with. Most male alligators are about 11.2 feet in length and reach about seven hundred pounds, but this one is close to nine hundred pounds."

Since no one on the boat had the desire to leap overboard and wrestle the gator and turn him into a wallet, we were safe. We stared at King Tut for a bit longer and then moved on.

Since we were moving slow and Wally could hear me, I decided to ask the question that always had bugged me. "Hey, Wally, tell me the way again to distinguish an alligator from a crocodile."

Wally answered, "It's simple, really. The easiest way is to look at their teeth.

"Yeah, that's find if you're a dentist, but what about us common folk?"

"It's still simple. The fourth tooth on an alligator fits into the upper socket in its mouth so you can't see it. But in a crocodile you can see the protruding teeth."

"Ah, good to know. And alligators are found only here in Florida?"

"No, they have a pretty big territory. The American alligator is found from North Carolina to the Rio Grande in Texas, and they usually stay in freshwater: swamps, marshes, and lakes."

"Can they go in salt water?"

"Yes, but only for short periods of time because they don't have salt glands."

Kathy then chimed in. "So let's say we fall in the water and an alligator is near, how do we escape?"

"In the water, covering its eyes will usually make him more sedate. If an alligator has you in its jaws go for the eyes and the nose. If you tap an alligator on the mouth usually it opens and drops whatever is in its mouth. The main thing is, you don't want them to get you in the death roll. If you are not in its clutches yet, try to keep his mouth closed so he can't begin his instinctual shake. If you were on land, you'd get on his back and press on his neck; again, the main thing is to keep his jaws closed."

Everyone was quiet after that. I was picturing myself trying to hit a gator on the nose.

Wally then revved up the airboat, and we rode for about ten minutes. Then Wally slowed down the boat and said, "Okay, anyone who wants to get out of the boat and into the water can do so now."

I turned to Kathy. "What, is this guy on crack?"

She shrugged. Neither of us knew what he was up to. Wally then took off his sandals and got out of the airboat to stand in the waist-high water. Everyone on the book thought, "If the captain, here, wants to be a noon munchy for the gators, that's fine, but who is going to drive the boat back?!"

I looked around. I didn't see any fences or electric wires keeping the alligators from this section of the water. I thought it had to be some kind of trick. Maybe the guy was a distant relative of Crocodile Dundee.

Wally moved farther from the boat. He talked to us every so calmly from the water. "So, who's going to come in?"

I looked at the four Japanese passengers on the boat. They were snapping pictures of the American madman. They were speaking Japanese, and I swear they were saying, "This guy is nuts!" Then I looked at Kathy.

"Look, if this guy is standing in the water, he must know something. He's been doing this for years. I'm sure he doesn't want to be killed. It must be safe. We're here, we wanted an adventure. Let's get the whole experience."

Kathy and I rolled up our pants and slid in. As soon as we stepped into the water, the mud engulfed our toes. The bottom felt squishy, and I started thinking was would happen if this was really quickmud.

Adrenaline Adventures

More cameras flashed. I think the Japanese tourists were hoping to catch some footage for a new sci-fi flick.

The imagination is a wild thing if left untamed. I started seeing images of alligators sneaking up and dragging us away. Maybe that was why the plastic alligator in front of Wally's place was drinking a beer—he was washing down a stupid tourist!

On the outside I appeared calm and unfazed. However, I did jump once when Wally thought it was funny to grab my leg from behind.

Kathy and I loved it. After all, this was a calculated risk— calculated on the fact that this guy had done this hundreds of times before, or so we hoped.

Nothing horrible happened. No one else was even willing to try it. We had the Japanese tourists take a bunch of pictures of us with our camera for proof. We got back in the boat. We were smiling. We'd gone in the alligator-infested Everglades waters. I had to think for a second, did I really have a college degree?

Kathy and I were like schoolgirls who'd just seen the Backstreet Boys. When we got back to the dock, Wally Jr. let us hold a boa constrictor and a baby alligator. The little alligator squirmed in my hands. I could barely hold the little critter with all my strength. I said, "If this is the power of a twenty-pound gator, imagine a six-hundred-pound one."

Wally Jr. replied, "Don't doubt the gators. They can roll ya faster than a hood in Manhattan." Good thing this little guy's mouth was taped shut.

With time running out Kathy and I raced back to the hotel. I grabbed my bags, and Kathy was nice enough to drive me to the airport.

Forty-five minutes later I was sitting on the airplane laughing to myself. Life sure is fun if you take a chance. I curled up my feet and counted my toes again just to make sure. This little piggy ...

Fran Capo

Chapter 23
Adventure at a Glance - Dare to Do it   Mild to Wild Scale: 4
Title: Everglades Airboat Ride
Age requirement: Five and up
Length of trip: One hour
Where to try this adventure: Everglades National Park in Florida. Type "Everglades Airboat Ride" into any Internet search engine and a slough of places will come up.
Best time of year to go: Spring, summer, fall
Approximate cost: $45 per person (most places have a $5 off coupon available)
Reservations necessary: No, but suggested
Fitness requirement: None
Personal gear required: None
What NOT to bring: Dangling limbs
Photo opportunities: Yes

Notes: Never swim in waters that alligators are known to inhabit. Don't feed an alligator if you see it. Alligators fed by humans are more likely to attack because they lose their fear of humans and become more aggressive. If you stay in the boat, you can enjoy these creatures in safety.

Cool trivia : The alligator became the official Florida state reptile in 1987. The American alligator is listed as threatened on the U.S. Endangered Species List. Hunting is allowed in some states, but is heavily controlled. The greatest current threat is destruction of their habitat; they are running out of space to live in. In addition, there are increased levels of mercury and dioxins in the water, which can kill alligators.

"I wonder why I did what I did, when I knew what I knew."
—Fran Capo

Chapter 24
"Whatever you do, don't roll me"
Kayaking

I've gone kayaking twice in my life. The first time, which was on the Hudson River, was an adrenaline rush, and the second time was in a calm lake in New Jersey with my friend Heidi. In my trip with Heidi, outside of having a good time, the only adrenaline rush was when an attack swan came barreling toward our kayak and we had to paddle like cartoon characters to avoid getting bit. Other than that the waters were mild and it was just relaxing.

So since this book is called *Adrenaline Adventures*, I will tell you about my first kayaking experience.

The first time was with a friend of mine, Malcolm Clarke—a nationally known photographer who I met when he was doing a story for a British paper on my son, Spencer, who was three years old and the world's youngest comic at that time. Malcolm got a kick out of Spencer and we got a kick out of Malcolm's British accent and mannerisms. We all became friends.

225

Adrenaline Adventures

Malcolm and I realized that we had the same spirit for adventure. We went spelunking, hiking, whale watching, rafting, and camping together—we even thought of starting an adventure club for other like-minded people.

However, duty called and he was assigned to a newspaper in Scotland. Our last adventure together before he left this country (besides me helping him move his couch) was kayaking.

Malcolm found out about an outfit called Hudson River Recreation in Westchester, New York. They had three tour locations: Nyack, New Rochelle, and Sleepy Hollow. I had just finished writing a story about Sleepy Hollow's claim to fame, the Headless Horseman, so we chose that area. I was excited to visit the town and thought maybe imagining I was being chased by the headless guy would make me kayak faster.

The kayaking outfit had two kayaking sessions, nine to noon, and one to three. We choose the morning session. This sea kayaking program was for novices, with a smattering of advance kayakers. The tour in general was an easy one, but as it said on the Web site, "The waves, tides, wind and pace of other guests will determine the speed and difficulty of the trip."

We were told to bring a bathing suit with shorts on top, a towel, ziplock bags, a water bottle, a hat, sunscreen, and shoes that we didn't mind getting wet—an old pair of sneakers, water booties or those sufmocs. As always on any adventure that involves wetness, we were told to not wear cotton, as it gets wet easy, takes a long time to dry, and retains the wetness so you wind up getting cold faster.

We got to Sleepy Hollow an hour early as was suggested so we could sign releases and get our paddles, life jackets (or PFDs—personal flotation devices—as they are called in the business) and kayaks with a spray skirt. A spray skirt, for those of you who have never had the pleasure of wearing one, is basically a big neoprene or nylon skirt that looks like an old-fashioned hoop skirt and attaches around your waist and snaps onto the lip of the kayak so that water doesn't get in. Not a fashion statement but practical. We were also given a bailer so that when water did manage to seep in, we could bail it out with ease and not have to sit there desperately trying to scoop it out with our hands.

The hardest part of most of these types of trips is lugging your gear to the water entry point. Malcolm and I each had a single-person kayak we had to drag to the water.

Just short of the water, we were stopped for a bit of instruction by our fearless leader, Gilligan. (Yes, Gilligan as in *Gilligan's Island* ... how appropriate since this was a three-hour tour ... a three-hour tour). I knew I should have packed a lunch!

Gilligan started by asking who among us had never kayaked before. About five of the ten people raised their hands, us included. He had us come up front so we could hear the instructions. He started by showing us the standard stroke. A kayak paddle has two paddle sides, one on each end of the stick, unlike a canoe paddle, which only has the paddle on one side. With a kayaking paddle, you dip one end of the paddle in, bring it around, and then dip the other side in. Kind of like a giant figure eight. We practiced this move a few times.

He then told us some general kayaking rules. "Okay, gang, listen up.

We are going to enter the water and stay in this protected area and practice our skills. We are going to practice the strokes, a few turns, and how not to run over our fellow kayakers. You must keep your PFD on all times, even if you are an Olympic swimmer. Some general rules: please don't bump into the kayaks in front of you. I know this may be tempting ... but these are not bumper boats and you can easily damage the rudders of the kayak. Don't step over another person's kayak, especially mine. And please respect the wildlife; there are birds nesting and if they get scared they leave their young and then some unfriendly neighbors can quickly gobble them up. Don't throw anything into the water, and lastly, if you get cold, let us know immediately. And if you get stuck, we will be there to help you. Any questions?"

I raised my hand. "Are we going to be doing that Eskimo roll thing? I mean, I don't want to get stuck upside down in the water."

"No, we're not going to be learning that skill today, although it's not as hard as it looks."

"Well, what about this hula skirt? If my kayak tips over, is it going to stop me from getting out?"

Adrenaline Adventures

"Nope, those things unsnap easy. Believe me, if you tip, you'll come out and we'll be right there to help you."

"Are there any rocks or things we can bump into?"

"Outside of the columns of the bridges we go under, no. The water is high and we don't have to worry about hitting things under the water. The beginning part of getting into the water in this area is the toughest, but once you are floating you'll be fine.

"If there are no other questions, I just want to give you some final rules. I will be in the lead kayak. I'd appreciate if no one gets ahead of me. My buddy there, Simon, will be in the back, and we have other experienced kayakers who will be on the sides. For you history buffs I will be pointing out some famous landmarks.

But to start out, you all know the legend by Washington Irving involving the Headless Horseman?"

Everyone nodded yes. I looked around to see if someone was going to jump out at us.

Gilligan continued, "Irving wrote about the ghosts and goblins that haunt this town, and about the Headless Horseman who races through the Old Dutch Church's graveyard at night. You may have seen the church when you turned to drive down the path to get here. Irving is buried there. The Pocantico River runs through that graveyard, and you are now standing at the mouth of that river. This is where we begin our tour. So you are about to slip your kayak into a part of history."

It was a nice touch, a great way to start the tour with an air of mystery. I thought this would be a cool thing to do on Halloween night.

We all put our kayaks into the practice area. My dear friend Malcolm, who is very strong but not the most coordinated person in the world, banged into me.

"Oh Fran, very sorry." He got into the water and started heading toward the reeds, then quickly paddled backward and banged into me again.

"Hey Malcolm, I'm going to get you some back-up lights on that thing."

He laughed. "You know me, just stay away, then."

Malcolm and I always had a friendly competitive nature.

Fran Capo

After about ten minutes of practice, Gilligan gave the signal and we paddled single-file out of the practice area and into the main river. The current was light, but enough to give us a helping hand.

My kayak kind of zigzagged a bit until I got the strokes even. Apparently my right hard was stronger than my left, so my right-handed strokes pushed me farther.

It was a gorgeous day, seventy-five degrees, sunny but not too hot. The views on both sides of the Hudson River up in that area are spectacular. There are huge houses and even castles nestled into the hills. The river is wide and you can see a long way, and you do feel a bit vulnerable. We paddled south, toward Manhattan.

We were paddling along nicely when Gilligan pointed to a rock. "Hey guys, see that rock? That is Kidd Rock. The landing place of the famous Captain Kidd."

Very cool. I could picture Captain Kidd landing his big ship there and looking around the area with his telescope.

We continued on. I noticed we were moving slightly faster, and one stroke took me pretty far. It was awesome to see the Manhattan skyline way off in the distance. I felt as if I wanted to paddle all the way to the city, which really wasn't such an odd thing because I know there is a place that does kayaking right off Chelsea Pier in the heart of Manhattan.

Malcolm and I had our kayaks even with each other. We were enjoying the whole experience. Soon we passed the Tarrytown Lighthouse. Up ahead was the best part of the trip, the Tappen Zee Bridge. The Tappen Zee Bridge was originally opened in 1955 and is the only bridge that crosses the Hudson River between Westchester and Rockland counties. It is thirteen miles north of New York City. It's also one of the longest bridges in the United States at 3.03 miles long. It has seven lanes, is ninety feet wide, and its center span reaches a height of 157 feet above the water. I had driven over that bridge a million times (okay a hundred) but this was the first time I had gone under it.

Gilligan stopped us before we went under the bridge, "Okay guys, stay away from the columns. I want you all to go through the same middle space. The water gets a little choppy there by the sides, but nothing to worry about."

Adrenaline Adventures

One by one, we went under with Gilligan watching us like a mother duck.

I looked up at the bridge and saw the cars passing overhead. I hoped that no one would decide to throw garbage out the window or hock a luggie. That would surely ruin it for me.

We made it under the bridge. The water seemed to be moving faster. We were going down the river at a pretty nice clip. Then, about an hour into the trip, Gilligan gave us the command to turn around. He said we were going to need the extra time to go against the current. The more experienced kayakers turned around and were heading upstream in a matter of strokes. Us novices looked like one-armed bandits, spinning a few times before getting it right.

Now came the tricky part ... paddling upstream. At first it seemed easy. I was doing the same strokes and moving merrily along—or so I thought. I looked at one of the houses to my right and noticed that I had done about ten strokes and was virtually in the same location. I stroked faster and harder and barely was moving, and if I let up, I drifted downriver. A slight sense of panic arose when I thought that I might run out of steam and not be able to make it up the river.

Malcolm and I decided this was going to take some incentive. So we decided it best if we challenged each other to a race back to the bridge.

I was working pretty hard, and not moving very far, until I saw Malcolm take the lead. I then sped up, caught up, relaxed, and drifted back. Well, that stunk. It was at that moment that I wished I had eaten my spinach, because I could have used those Popeye forearms.

Again I started paddling. I looked at Malcolm's form. He wasn't struggling, he was placing the paddle in evenly and just moving along upriver. I tried this same strategy and it worked a little better. Malcolm, however, was widening the margin between us.

This was a workout and I was getting wet. For a brief moment, I wondered if I stopped altogether if I'd drift all the way backward to Manhattan. That would be embarrassing to say the least, but a heck of a lot easier. I could then just hop on a train and go home. But my determination would not let me give up; it never does.

I kept paddling, and eventually I got past the one house that seemed to be following me. Soon I was underneath the bridge. This time I didn't look up, there was no time. I kept paddling. Malcolm kept an even pace. I, on the other hand, had to paddle, rest, paddle. But even when I rested I wouldn't stop completely since I didn't want the water working against me.

At this point, I was re-evaluated my strategy of having a one person Kayak, since the double-powered kayaks were moving past me, as well. I thought of lassoing the boat ahead but figured they might notice the extra weight.

"How much further?" I yelled to Gilligan.

"Hey, don't be a New Yorker," He laughed.

"I am a New Yorker, what do you mean?"

"In kayak lingo, a New Yorker is a whiner or complainer."

"Did I mention I was from Texas?" I said. I silently kept paddling. I hate whiners.

Three hours and fifteen minutes later, we were back at our stating point. Malcolm was sitting on the beach smirking. "I think I beat you, Fran."

"Nah, I was just enjoying the scenery. It looks a lot different when you are going backward."

We returned our gear and changed out of our wet clothes. Malcolm thanked Gilligan? for the experience. And I thanked him for the upper body workout. After all, who needs a row machine when you have a kayak?

Malcolm and I headed up to the Old Dutch Church and searched for Washington Irving's grave. We found it. I laid down a flower and said, "Now I know why you said this place is haunted … it's filled with paddlers who couldn't make it back up the river."

At that moment I felt a breeze pass by me. I looked up expecting to see the Headless Horseman, but it was just the wind picking up and moving the river once again at a rapid pace. I turned to Malcolm. "At least we know the afternoon kayakers will get a run for their money. Wanna place a bet on any of them?"

"No, but I'll race you back to the …"

Before he could say 'car' I was off … this was one race I wasn't going to lose.

Adrenaline Adventures

Chapter 24
Adventure at a Glance - Dare to Do it   Mild to Wild Scale: 3
Title: Kayaking
Children allowed: Yes
Age requirement: All paddlers under eighteen must be accompanied by a parent or legal guardian. Generally, kayaking is for ages eight and up, depending on height, weight, and strength. Any child paddling must be strong enough to fully participate in the sport.
Length of trip: Three hours to full day trips
Where to try this adventure: Hudson River Recreation
247 Palmer Avenue, Sleepy Hollow, NY 10591
Phone: 1-888-321-HUDSON
E-mail: kayakhrr@aol.com
There are kayaking companies and outfitters in almost every state, so check your local area for an adventure location.
Best time of year: Spring, summer, fall
Approximate cost: $60 per person
Reservations necessary: Yes, classes are limited in size.
Fitness requirements: Must be in good health
Personal gear required: Bring sneakers, booties, or water sandals. Also need a bathing suit, shorts, synthetic shirt, windbreaker, hat, sunscreen, and garbage bag for wet clothes.
What NOT to bring: Anything that will get ruined if it gets wet.
Photo opportunities: Yes, but bring a disposable waterproof camera or a plastic bag to protect your personal camera.

Notes: Arrive half an hour early so you can get your gear.

Cool trivia: Shaun Baker is the world's foremost extreme kayaker. He holds four Guinness world records for paddling off huge waterfalls, down seemingly impossible gradients, and even the "Land Speed Record" for a kayak on snow!

"It's a great challenge in life to decide what's important and to disregard everything else."
—Author Unknown

Chapter 25
"Rafting the Magnificent Canyon"
Whitewater Rafting

In the summer of 1998 my dad visited the Grand Canyon. He was struck by the beauty and vastness of it all. He made me promise that I would take my son, Spencer, there someday soon. Always looking for ways to experience life, I thought why not raft the canyon, sleep under the stars and really get the full experience of being one with nature? How cosmic.

A friend once asked me why I do all my "crazy" adventures. My answer is simple. I want to live life as much as I can without regrets. I don't want to put off saying "I love you" to someone, or climbing the mountain, or changing a job that I hate. You have to live now ... *carpe diem*.

Adrenaline Adventures

In January of 1999, I booked a three-day rafting trip to begin on Saturday August 1, for Spencer and myself with Western River Expeditions.

In April, my dad's cancer, which had been in remission for two years, took a turn for the worse. We cared for him at home with the help of the Calbrini Hospice program. He was given three months to live. I debated on canceling the trip. My dad insisted I go. He said that his final wish would be to have his ashes spread across the Grand Canyon.

On July 30, 1999, my dad was put on the critical list. By then he weighed only 124 pounds, could not talk, could not eat, could not move. As my family surrounded him, we told him it was okay to let go. God was waiting with open arms. You have to be brave enough to let those you love go when it is in their best interest.

I bent over and whispered to my dad jokingly, "Hey dad, if you are going to go, better do it now. My plane for Grand Canyon leaves on Saturday." He raised an eyebrow and smiled a weak smile. Eight hours later he passed on with my sister at his side.

With the help of Charlie, a very caring funeral director, we expedited the cremation and made arrangements to have the ashes with us as we flew the next morning.

Spencer and I flew into Las Vegas and met with the tour group at the airport at 8:15 A.M. We checked in our regulation 14" x 21" bag that contained the recommended supplies from a list that was sent to us along with our trip confirmation. Every means of transportation possible, except maybe mule or llama, was going to be utilized to get us to J-Rig rafts waiting for us in the Colorado River.

Thirty-six people were signed up for this three-day rafting trip, eighteen on each raft, plus two crew members. At the airport our tour guides randomly handed us green or yellow slips that determined which raft we would be on once we got to the river. Spencer and I were in the green group.

From the McCarran Airport we were escorted onto a bus that took us to meet our twenty-seater scenic plane. (Say that three times fast!) After we boarded the plane and listened to the pilot make a few jokes about the airsickness bags being our personal belongings if we used them, we were off on a breathtaking audio-guided tour over the Hoover Dam and the Grand Canyon.

Forty-five minutes later we landed at a remote airport. I mean *remote--no* landing strips, just a dirt road and a wooden sign saying "Airport." Good thing the sign was up or we could have easily have missed it. From there we were loaded onto a van and driven up a bumpy dirt road to a lodge to get any last minute supplies we'd forgotten—things like candy bars, toothpaste, soap, insect repellent … whatever you really had to have for the next four days.

A few feet hundred feet from the last chance lodge was a big mound of dirt. We were told to line up near the mound. Within minutes a helicopter landed. Four by four we were dispersed into the helicopter with our bags. The helicopter rose up, creating a swirl of dust, and then zoomed off, bringing us quickly up and over the ridge of the canyon. When you first see no ground below, your stomach drops like on a roller coaster ride … then, down … down … down you go until you hit your mark in the base of the canyon. We landed at mile 188, known as the Whitmore Rapid on the muddy Colorado River—five modes of transportation later, where we met our Western tour guides. If I hadn't known better, I would have thought we'd all just participated in the witness protection program, the way they shuffled us around.

I approached the first crew member I saw, Shane Phelps, and pulled him aside. I discretely told him that I had an extra bag with me and that that bag was my dad. Before he could think I was a hit man, I told him about my dad's final wishes to have his ashes spread over the Grand Canyon. I asked if he could be so kind as to let me know the most beautiful place along the river to release him. He told me about Travertine Falls. He said he would gladly let me know when we reached it. I felt a sense of peace come over me.

Spencer occupied himself with a lizard as the waterproof bags, life jackets and camping gear were handed out. After a briefing on safety instructions, we and the rest of the green group got on our raft and chose our seats.

The J-Rig rafts were big—the thirty-seven feet long to be exact. Picture five giant neoprene-coated nylon tubes tied together, with four-stroke motors powering them. In the center of the rig was the

Adrenaline Adventures

storage area for all our supplies, including stoves and toilets for the next three days. If you sat up front you would feel all the bumps and thrills of the river. If you sat in back, you stayed nice and comfy and relatively dry.

Nine of us more adventurous types straddled one of the tubes in the front of the raft in the maximum wetness and excitement -zone. Those not wanting to get quite as wet sat up on the higher part of the rig and behind the gear. Within minutes we heard a howl from crew member Tyler, "HOLD ON! And get ready for the ride of your life." We went from the calmness of shore to the waters of the Colorado. We traveled calmly for a few yards and then saw some rapids up ahead.

We braced ourselves by grabbing the ropes in front and back of us. The raft went smashing into the fifty-five-degree water that shocked our systems as the rapids licked our faces. We looked like a bunch of wet poodles, but loved we it.

Soon, we pulled over for a taco lunch. It's amazing how much food, luggage, utensils, gear, and drinking water could be stored on this rig, they even had an extra motor.

After a delicious lunch, we were off again, this time facing rapids ranging from class one through six (with ten being the largest navigable rapids). After a few more exhilarating rapids, the water turned calm for a while. Tyler used this time to give us a brief history of the canyon. "The Grand Canyon was formed about five million years ago, and some of the rocks exposed at the bottom layers may be as old as two billion years old. The Canyon is 1,904 square miles, and the canyons width from rim to rim is 18 miles as the crow flies, cause if you were to drive from South Rim to North Rim you would cover 219 miles. The Colorado River that we are on is 277 miles in length, and there are over seventy major rapids. Ancestral Native Americans were the first people to discover and explore the Grand Canyon. Those early canyon dwellers left behind split-twig figurines that radiocarbon date 3,000 to 4,000 years old. It's nice to just think that we are floating down a river between history. Also imagine if you will what it was like for Major John Wesley Powell in 1869 when he first laid eyes upon these magnificent canyons. He was the first to have a successful expedition down the Colorado River."

Everyone was in awe for a moment until Spencer broke the silence. "Are there any animals around here?"

"There are about 1,500 different kinds of plants, 305 different birds, 88 mammal species like mountain lions and goats and 58 types of reptiles ... like that little lizard you found before, Spence."

"Are we going to see mountain lions?"

"We might, but it's highly unlikely. They don't like crowds."

We were coming up to another set of rapids. Tyler yelled, "Hang on!"

We straddled the tubes with our legs and held onto the ropes. It was like riding a bucking bronco. One rapid actually flung Spencer who was behind me over my head and to the front of the raft by the edge. I reached out and Shane lunged forward and grabbed Spencer before he went over the side. I looked at Spencer after the rapids had calmed down. He was excited. "Wow, mom did you see that? I almost went over. At first I was scared, but then I felt a big hand like Batman's swoop down and grab me out of nowhere. That was cool. Let's do that again!"

Now that he was safe, I laughed. "Yup, you're definitely my kid."

After some jokes and more historic interludes by the guides we had reached mile 202, the spot where we camped for the night.

There were no tents on this trip, just cots and sleeping bags so you could sleep freely under the gorgeous constellations. We all got off the raft and formed a human chain to unload the boat. We each picked an area and set up a cot for the night. Near the area we set up Spencer noticed a set of tracks. Shane identified them as mountain lion tracks a few days old. I suggested to Spencer that we move our cot a little closer to the raft just in case we needed to make a quick escape.

For our nature calls, a tent with a portable potty was set up for privacy, but if you really wanted to rough it, you could do like the bears in the woods. As far as bathing, there were no facilities, so we had to rinse off in the muddy Colorado River waters, not exactly a way to look like Ms. Cover Girl, but hey, when in Rome ...

Dinner that first night was hot and delicious, prepared by the fantastic four: Tyler and his brother Tanner Cornell, who had been

Adrenaline Adventures

with the outfit for over ten years, and Shane and Casey. With satisfied stomachs, we all were in bed by eight as the sun went down. To the noise of flying bats, hungry mosquitoes, and the rumbling of the rapids, we fell asleep.

The next day we were awakened to the call of "BREAKFAST!" A feast of hot eggs, bacon, fruits, and several kinds of bread was laid out. You would have thought these guys were Julia Child School graduates with a Dutch oven.

After breakfast, we loaded back onto the raft and were ready to face the river. We hit rapids with names like Satan's Gut, Bloody Finger and Diamond Creek Rapid. We laughed and felt exhilarated by the power of nature.

We stopped at Pumpkin Springs near "Little Bastard Rapid" for about an hour. The spring was warm and had a sinkhole that sucked you in waist deep, or for Spencer, neck deep. There was a seventeen-foot cliff you could jump off of into the spring. Spencer did a nice belly flop, not once but twice, and some other guys in the group choose to hold tight to the family jewels as they jumped. I hesitated for a moment then ran over the cliff yelling, "Geronimo!"

From there we headed to Travertine Canyon. Tyler, Tanner and Shane pulled me to the side and said we were approaching the place that would be the final resting spot for my dad. They were nice enough to make arrangements to let Spencer and I have some time alone to spread my dad's ashes among the pristine flowing falls. We had to climb a rope to get to the falls, but it was worth it.

In a crevice in the red-colored canyon walls, with the beautiful falls flowing, we said a prayer and let my dad go. We watched as the ashes mingled with the rest of nature. Spencer and I cried and hugged knowing we had, with the help of divine intervention, carried out my dad's last wish.

Teary-eyed, we climbed down the falls, and finished out the trip.

At camp that night, we reflected on the meaning of doing things in life with no regrets. Living life to the fullest gives you a peaceful feeling of satisfaction.

We dined on steak and shrimp, complete with personal tuxedoed service from our handsome crew (too bad they live so far away!). Warm cake, fruits, and fish finished out the evening. It was magnificent.

That night the moon shone so brightly we thought Con Edison had turned on a switch. A little nervous because of a second set of cougar tracks Spencer found, I mistook, for a moment, the snoring of a fellow camper, for the snarl of an angry cougar.

The final morning we awoke to the sound of swarming bees and the flipping of hot blueberry pancakes. We ate and loaded the raft one last time.

With calm waters, our raft floated down the river to meet a jet boat that would speed us to a beach and to a waiting bus that would take us back to Vegas, or what we called "civilization" ... indoor plumbing.

As I turned and looked back at the Canyon one last time, I saw a bird swoop down, flying freely. A warm breeze passed my face, and I swear I heard my dad laughing in heaven.

Adrenaline Adventures

Chapter 25
Adventure at a Glance - Dare to Do it   Mild to Wild Scale: 5
Title: Whitewater Rafting
Children allowed: Yes, ages nine and up are allowed on the three-day trip. Twelve and up are allowed on the trip through the Cataract Canyon.
Length of trip: Western River Expedition has trips that last three, four and six days. They can make longer trips if needed. Other rafting outfits have trips that last from one day to weeks as well.
Where to try this adventure: Western River Expeditions 7258 Racquet Club Drive, Salt Lake City, Utah 84121 800-453-7450 or visit their website at www.westernriver.com You can also go on the web and visit www.riversearch.com to find other whitewater rafting outfits closer to you.
Best time of year to go: April - September
Approximate cost: Prices range from $450-1,825 for adults and $420-$799 for kids (depending on length and type of trip).
Reservations necessary: Yes, at least four to six months in advance
Fitness requirement: Be In good health, know how to swim
Personal gear required: A complete list is sent with confirmation forms.
What NOT to bring: Jewelry, excessive baggage
Photo opportunities: Yes

Notes: There are several three, four and six day options. It's best to call and ask for a brochure.

Cool trivia: The gates of Glen Canyon Dam upstream of Grand Canyon National Park were closed in 1963. This flooded the area upstream of the dam forming what is today called Lake Powell.
   More than five million people visit the Grand Canyon every year. The inner part of the canyon is accessible only by foot, mule or by rafting the Colorado River.

"Motivation cannot be forced. The person must have the desire to change."
—From *The Two Minute Motivator* by Robert W. Wendover

Chapter 26
"Running into the New Year" New Year's Eve Midnight Run

As a comedienne, one of my biggest nights to perform is New Year's Eve. So for fifteen consecutive years, I spent that night making people laugh. It was a wonderful way to bring in the new year. Often my son would perform with me, and my mom, dad, or friends would come to the show so I'd also be spending it with loved ones as well.

In the year 2000—the big millenium year, when we weren't sure if the world was going to end, or if all computers were going to crash—I decided it was the perfect time to celebrate the new year in a different way. I looked into all kinds of options. I thought about getting all dressed up and going to a fancy party, but the cost for a dinner was the same as a down payment on a house. I thought about flying somewhere exotic but decided my family was exotic enough and I wanted to stay close to them.

Adrenaline Adventures

Then I heard about the Midnight Run, a 6K run that begins at midnight in Central Park. It was put together by the New York Road Runners Club (NYRR) and there was a whole fanfare surrounding it. They had a costume party with prizes beforehand, a live band, food, and warm-up exercises.

Then, just like with Cinderella, at the stroke of twelve, they would run through the park. And hopefully in this case not leave any shoes behind. There would be fireworks as you ran, music playing, and people cheering you on. I thought it would be a very symbolic way to begin the new year, by running in to it. The cost was only twenty dollars for members and twenty-five dollars for non-members. You could sign up online, or via phone, fax, or mail. A few days before the race, you'd get a goodie pack with your racing number, a T-shirt, a hat, some Powerbars, and other neat little gifts. And the best thing was, everyone who finished the race would get a medal. It sounded great. Of course, now I had to figure out who would want to do this with me. I wasn't dating anyone at the time, so it would have to be friends or family.

I told my mom about my great plan and her response was, "Why would anyone want to run in Central Park at night? That's dangerous."

I joked with her. "That's why everyone will be running, Ma, to keep ahead of the muggers." She did not find it amusing.

"How many people are doing this?"

I had no clue. Honestly, part of me was a little nervous. As a New Yorker you are raised to know not to go to Central Park at night. I thought, what if everyone is faster than me and I'm left behind in the dark in Central Park? I'd be a perfect target. But when I called the NYRR they said that at least two thousand people would be running; with that many people, I didn't think I'd be too far behind.

I started asking around to see who was available to do this run with me.

My sister, who is a professional belly dancer, was performing that night, so unless she was going to run in her costume right after the show, she was not a likely candidate. Although it might have worked if they would have thought she was part of the pre-run costume contest.

My mom was obviously out. She said if she entered the race she'd be still running by the time the next millennium came around.

I asked my friend Malcolm, the professional photographer, but he had an assignment to shoot the first sunrise of the new millennium halfway around the world.

Finally I mentioned it to my friend Steve Seif. He was willing and he was going to try to convince his son, Jonathan, to do it, as well. I told my son, Spencer, and he was thrilled that finally another kid was going to come along on one of these adventures.

Two days before New Year's Eve, I went into the city and picked up our numbers, a map showing the route of the race, and the goodie bags. I was a little disappointed to see that the medal was already in there. The goodie bag lady explained that since this wasn't a real timed race, the medals were given out ahead, unlike in the NYC marathon, which is strictly monitored and the medals are only given to those who actually finish the race. I decided not to tell Spencer or Steve. I figured I'd let them earn their medal, plus I didn't want any of them backing out. It'd be like getting paid before the gig.

New Year's Eve came. I called Steve S. and he mentioned that his son had bailed out on him, but that he had met a girl and that she was going to be with him until midnight. She didn't want to run, but she would hang out until we were done.

Never having run in the middle of the night, in a dark park, in the freezing cold, we weren't sure how to dress. It was twenty-eight degrees, so there was some cause for concern. We decided on the ever popular layer method, complete with earmuffs, scarf, gloves, and hat. It wasn't a fashion statement, but it would keep us warm. I brought a camera to capture our millennium moment.

At 11:50 P.M., we arrived at the park. Steve's girlfriend was waiting in a lounge somewhere near the park, and my sister, her husband, and my mom were in the club my sister was belly dancing at. Spencer, Steve, and I lined up with the other two thousand nuts to run into the new year.

Music played. Then, at one minute to midnight, I called my mom on my cell phone and wished her Happy New Year. Then we heard the countdown …10, 9, 8, 7, 6, 5, 4, 3, 2, 1 - HAPPY NEW YEAR. A loud horn went off and everyone started running. At first it was so crowed we could barely move. Within a few blocks the crowd spread out. I felt like I was in the movie *Forrest Gump*. Run ... Forrest ... Run.

Fireworks went off and lit up the crisp night air. I kept trying to look at the fireworks and run at the same time but realized that wasn't the brightest thing to do when I banged into a half-naked man in front of me.

I'm not quite sure if I was more upset I banged into someone or that the someone was a hairy-backed, pot-bellied, middle-aged man with no shirt and baggy shorts on, and he was ahead of me!

But as the next set of fireworks went off, I started to think how neat this was, that as everyone was dispersing from their celebrations we were just beginning ours.

The three of us stayed together. It was strange being in the park at night.

There were a few people on the sidelines cheering us on, but mainly it was just the runners. Some of them were still in costume from the party. I saw a guy in a gigantic rabbit outfit and thought that maybe he forgot to return his Easter costume. I saw a salt shaker and a pepper shaker running holding hands and thought that that was romantic in a funny sort of way. I saw a belly dancer and thought maybe my sister had made it after all, but I later realized it was a guy in drag.

None of our trio were runners. But we had all made a promise that once we started jogging we weren't going to stop—unless, of course, our limbs or something fell off, and then we'd have no choice. We all kept a slow and steady pace. At the one-mile marker there was a table full of water. We slowed down, took a cup, and kept running. We felt like pros.

At some points the crowd thinned out, and we could see how dark it was in the park—and that's when we sped up, just in case some mugger was looking to take down the weak ones in the crowd—you know, thin out the herd.

But muggers aside, there was an electric feeling in the air. No one was drunk, no one was wild—it was all a bunch of health nuts starting the new year off right.

At the midway point, there was a table of water and champagne. Spencer and I opted for the water, Steve S. for the champagne ... we all toasted and continued to run.

As we were running, it started to feel more like it was eighty-two degrees outside instead of twenty-eight, so we striped down. We started tying things around our waists, tucking gloves into our shirts, and wearing the earmuffs as a neck brace.

I started to wonder how much farther. My legs were burning a bit, since I hadn't practiced running for this event. Spencer's twelve-year-old body was doing fine. Steve S. and I started huffing and puffing. We laughed. "Ya think maybe we should have practiced running for this event?"

"Yeah, definitely make a note for next year," he said sarcastically.

The air was so clean and crisp that we could see our breath as we ran. And since we were breathing hard, little clouds of smoke bellowed out from our mouths. It almost looked like those cartoon balloon clouds where the words could go inside.

Spencer started egging us on, "Come on you two, you can do it."

Steve S. and I started laughing. "Three miles seems a lot longer in the dark," I said.

"I think it's been an hour, or more ... actually we've been running so long, I think I see daylight," he joked.

Just then we heard cheers and saw lights. It wasn't daylight, but something better. Yes! It was the finish line. We decided we would give it everything we had and run to the finish. We started huffing and puffing and running. We were the engines that could. We crossed the finish line in thirty minutes, eleven seconds. We all hugged each other in victory.

I took out our medals and put them on Spencer and Steve. Spencer said, "Hey, you had them all along, we didn't have to run."

"I thought you'd say that, that's why I didn't tell you until now. The point of the race is not the medal, but earning the medal. You can only wear it with honor if you complete the task. And you did. We all did."

Steve S. said, "That's a lot of bull."

I laughed. "I know, but it sounded good."

Spencer smiled. "Well, I liked doing it anyway, and at least this is one way to stay up 'til two A.M. without getting yelled at."

Steve S. smiled too. "I gotta say, medal or no medal, that was a rush. It was an awesome feeling."

I had to agree, it was a wonderful way to start the new year. And in fact, we liked it so much that Spencer and I have done it every year since—each year with different friends to share the experience.

Fran Capo

Chapter 26
Adventure at a Glance - Dare to Do it   Mild to Wild Scale: 3
Title: New Year's Eve Midnight Run
Children allowed: Yes
Age requirement: Generally seven and up. The child has to be able to run three miles.
Length of trip: Some years it's three miles, some years four.
Where to try this adventure: Central Park, New York City
New York Road Runners Club
9 E. 89th Street (Between Madison and Fifth Avenue)
Go to Web site: www.nyrrc.org or call 212-333-5050
Several other towns hold New Year's runs, including Jackson, Michigan; Worcester, Massachusetts; Alexandria, Virginia; Wilmington, Delaware; Jacksonville, Florida; and Phoenix, Arizona.
Best time of year: New Year's Eve
Approximate cost: $20 for members, $25 for non-members
Reservations necessary: Must sign up in advance and get a running number
Fitness requirements: Must be able to walk or run three miles
Personal gear required: Running clothes and shoes
What NOT to bring: Lot of things to carry
Photo opportunities: Yes, at finish line and start of race

Notes: You will get hot as you run, so don't overdo it with the layers.

Cool trivia: Central Park is 150 years old. It is 873 square miles and was designed in the mid-1800s by Frederick Law Olmstead and Calvert Vaux. The park was intended to provide a peaceful haven for the growing population. The park contains 7 bodies of water, 8,968 benches, 36 bridges, and 26,000 trees. One hundred and forty movies have featured Central Park.

"Age may wrinkle the face, but lack of enthusiasm wrinkles the soul."
-Wally Amos,
Creator of Famous Amos Cookies

Chapter 27
"A Silent Adventure"
Snorkeling With Manatees

Not all adventures with kids have to be packed with drama or filled with chase scenes. I'm the first to love an adrenaline rush, but I've found that some adventures can touch the heart and give you a rush in a gentler way and be just as rewarding.

While doing some research for a book I was working on I came across the fact that manatees are on the endangered species list. I started reading about the gentle nature of these fifty-million-year-old living fossils and immediately I knew I wanted to see them live. Any mammal that has the tenacity to stick around for that long, I'd like to pay my respects to before they're wiped off the earth by speedboat drivers pretending to be in the latest James Bond movie.

Once I got it in my head that I wanted to have a personal encounter with a manatee, I also knew I wanted to share the experience with my twelve-year-old son, Spencer. Like most kids, Spencer had a fascination with dinosaurs. Manatees come pretty close to dinosaurs, as far as the age concept goes, so I started telling him about them. I dug up an article on manatees by fellow writer Cindy Tunstall. In the article she wrote, "Every winter this distant relative of the elephant migrates to Crystal River and Kings Spring to escape the chilly waters of the Gulf of Mexico." It was February, and the season was almost over, but there was a short window of opportunity to see the manatees that winter. I decided to search the Internet for cheap flights to Florida. As I was doing that I got an IM from a guy I was dating at the time named Andre. He was a nice Polish man whose mother was a standup comic in Poland—just that alone I found funny, so we immediately hit it off.

Andre was always working, and when I told him I wanted to take my son, to see the manatees in Florida that weekend, he said, "Let's go! I need an adventure!" At first I wasn't sure if I wanted him to come, but after we made arrangements to have separate rooms and with no strings attached, I felt better.

Within two days all the arrangements were made and the adventure to see the manatees was about to begin. We left on a Friday so Spencer wouldn't miss school. (After all, you never know what grammar lesson may turn him into the next Hemmingway.) We arrived at La Guardia airport only to find that our flight to Tampa had been cancelled due to snowstorms. Something about icy runways makes the control tower very nervous. Apparently planes were not meant for figure skating.

Determined, we hung around until we were able to get on a standby flight six hours later. We had to go—our luggage had left on the last plane and was already tanning in sunny Florida. There was no way our luggage was going to have a better time than we would. I made a mental note to myself to use carry-on luggage whenever I could from then on. We arrived in Tampa at midnight. Our luggage was sitting there, sipping margaritas and smirking. "What took you guys so long?" We ignored their snide comments and picked them up.

We rented a gold convertible for the two-hour northern journey to Crystal River in Citrus County, Florida. We had our trusty Dollar rent-a-car map and plodded along. Spencer fell asleep in the back seat of the car somewhere around the exit of the airport.

We drove along the very dark Highway 75. Andre drove while I played navigator. Had I known that there would be no streetlights, I would have brought my night vision goggles. According to our map we had to cut over to the west shore to Highway 19. This was a cool highway to be on. According to a guy sitting next to me on the airplane, you could see black bears from that road. Unfortunately, all I saw that night were windshield wipers carrying off gnat carcasses.

We pulled into the Days Inn at 2 A.M. The desk clerk was surprised we showed up this late. (Doesn't every guest show up at the crack of dawn?) We asked for a wakeup call at 5 A.M. since our boat departure was scheduled for 6:30 a.m.—prime manatee time. Andre and I said our goodnights and agreed to meet in the lobby in the morning.

The next morning we drove to the Plantation Inn Dive Shop and Marina, which was a few miles up the road from our hotel. We had pre-booked our West Indian manatees encounter with them.

After we checked in, we were each fitted with wetsuits. Although the water is warm, the air temperature isn't in the early winter mornings, so even though it's Florida it's still cold in those wee morning hours. We had brought our own masks, fins, and snorkels, but Andre didn't have his own, so he rented them for a nominal fee.

As soon as the other person signed up for the encounter showed up and was geared up, we were asked to watch a video tape. The tape was about manatees, and how to act around them in the water. The tape began, "West Indian manatees are large, gray aquatic mammals. They have two forelimbs, called flippers, which have three to four nails. Their heads and faces are wrinkled and they have a snout. The average adult male is about ten feet long and weighs between 800 and 1,200 pounds. But some can get as big as 3,000 pounds.

Manatees are gentle and slow moving and mainly spend their time eating, resting and traveling. They are plant eaters, and graze along the water bottom and surface for food. When manatees are using a lot of energy, they surface every thirty seconds to breathe, but when resting they can stay submerged for as long as twenty minutes.

Adrenaline Adventures

They have no natural enemies and can generally live about sixty years. However, humans are responsible for the majority of manatee deaths with collisions from watercraft and loss of habitat as the biggest threats to manatees. For that reason they have been under the Marine Mammal Protection Act since 1972. It is illegal to hunt and capture a manatee. We understand that you may want to get next to these gentle creatures, but if a manatee dives to the bottom you are not to follow them. They dive to the bottom to either sleep or feed. If a person were to approach them at the bottom, it is considered harassment of an endangered species. We thank you and hope you enjoy your visit with the manatees." Our tour guide, a southern college kid named Johnny, took us out to the springs. Only four people signed up for the manatee encounter on that particular Saturday morning, making for one very personal experience. (Normally, you have to book months in advance.) It was cold, and we started to doubt our sanity at wanting a two-hour freezing encounter with the manatees.

As the boat slowly pulled away from the dock in the no wake zone, Johnny decided to give us a briefing. "Crystal River has several springs. Today we are going to visit two, Kings Bay and Three Sisters. This river is the home to around three hundred manatees, so you will definitely get several glimpses of them. By the way, manatees are also known as sea cows. During the winter months, because of the water's constant temperature of seventy-two degrees, the manatees feel at home here. Anything colder than that and they get hypothermia. They spend the early mornings and cold nights in these springs.

We are going to be in their sanctuary. We do not allow scuba diving here because manatees are sensitive to movement and sound, and the depth is only about ten feet. The bubbles from divers often scare them away. So it will be just us snorkelers. If you want to dive there is one place in Kings Bay where there is a cavern, but that is a totally different experience. Now, I know when you see the manatees you will be tempted to touch them right away. But please don't jump on their backs or try to ride them or go into the roped off area of the sanctuary. Also please don't try to feed them or chase after the babies. Let them come to you naturally. They will; they are like little puppy dogs."

Fran Capo

It was cold as the boat headed towards the sanctuary. A plastic canvas covered us, but it didn't do much good. There was a thermos of hot chocolate to warm us up if we wanted. There was a thin mist hovering over the water that gave it a kind of *Deliverance* type feeling. I kept listening for that banjo.

We approached the first spring, Kings Spring. No manatees were in sight. We hung around to see if any of them would wake up. After a few minutes, we realized we were probably in the coach potato section of the river, so we headed to the next spring, Three Sisters. As we pulled up, we saw other boats anchored and the bobbing heads of snorkelers in the water. We knew we had hit the jackpot.

We anchored our boat. I was the first in, and Spencer followed. The water shocked us. A wet seventy-two degrees feels very cold. It took our bodies a few minutes to adjust. But adrenaline is an excellent heater. Ever notice how you never think of the cold if a mugger is following you?

The water was about twenty feet deep around the boat. We were told we had to swim over toward the roped off sanctuary to get nearer to the manatees. As our heads were still above water and we were adjusting our masks, getting ready for our swim, Spencer yelled, "What was that? I felt something touch my leg." Spencer grabbed my neck.

"Calm down," I said with a nervous laugh. "It was probably a manatee."

I looked down but couldn't see a thing. Even though it was called Crystal River, it wasn't crystal in the area in which we were floating.

Suddenly, I felt something brush against my foot. It's a weird sensation knowing something is in the water and before you are ready to see it, it touches you. It's like being in a haunted house—you know there are actors waiting to jump out at you, but before you can get used to the dark, his hand is on your shoulder. At that point you usually do your best Scooby Doo impression and try to run away.

Since running in water is not an easy feat, we did the next best thing. We immediately submerged our heads with the masks on. Now it was crystal clear. There they were, dozens of one-ton behemoths swimming by. We didn't expect them to be so massive! The first one

Adrenaline Adventures

we saw was the size of a small school bus. Its oblong, silky body seemed to glide endlessly past us. We reached out to touch it. It was slightly slimy. It was just one giant blob. I expected to see a sign on it saying, "Goodyear Blimp."

At this point, Andre, the tour guide, and other guests were in the water.

We all swam toward the sanctuary area. The water in this part of the river was only about five feet deep. Tall grass surrounded the area and a thin morning mist laid upon the water. It was like swimming in a water hole in the Amazon River. Because we were in Florida, I had a few thoughts that a wayward alligator might have moseyed on over to manatee country. I got a little nervous when I saw a sign that had a picture of an alligator with a circle and those red slashes through it.

I questioned the guide, "Hey Johnny, do alligators come here?"

"No ma'am, they know not to."

"Whaddaya mean they know not to?"

"That sign there says no alligators in these waters."

"Okay, what if I get the one retard alligator that can't read?"

"You New Yorkers worry too much. The water's too cold for them."

"No seriously, how do you know that you don't have one renegade alligator who likes the cold? Maybe his mama fooled around and he's part polar bear or something. Or worse yet, you just get one stubborn teenage gator who just refused to go with his parents on vacation to a warmer climate?"

"Man, you have some imagination. It just don't work that way. Come on, enjoy the manatees."

I swam over to Spencer, who had attracted the attention of a baby manatee. This playful female calf took a liking to him and followed him around. When Spencer went to pet her, she rolled over on her back and let Spencer rub her belly just like our spoiled cats at home. Then she decided to really check him out and pressed her snout against Spencer's mask. Spencer tried to back up but wasn't quick enough. I laughed as the manatee kissed Spencer, leaving a smear on the mask lens. Good thing there was no lipstick!

I immediately loved these creatures and forgot all about the wayward gators.

Fran Capo

The manatees were so affectionate. It was sad to see that every single one of them, including the babies, had several scars on their backs from the boats that had hit them. For two and a half hours we snorkeled with the largest herd of these gentle mammals in the United States. The manatees let us pet them and never showed one bit of annoyance. It was truly awesome. Everyone was smiling.

As we swam back to the boat, one of the friendlier fellows followed us. I'm sure if he could have, he would have given us a parting gift, but instead he just nudged us on the leg as we climbed up the ladders.

On the boat we were all silent, each reliving our wonderful encounters. The silence was broken by our tour guide recounting some college tales of bravado with a cow stuck in mud on his dad's farm.

Back at the dive shop, as we peeled out of our wetsuits, a videotape was popped into the VCR and lo and behold, a marketer's dream. There we were ... a Kodak moment, captured on tape snorkeling with the friendly giants. We bought T-shirts, the videotape, and a stuffed manatee.

Still enthralled with the manatees, we headed to Homosassa Springs State Wildlife Park to see them once again in the parks underwater observatory. A marine biologist explained that manatees were identified by their boat scars. A sad, but true commentary.

As the people looked on amazed, we radiated, knowing that we had been in the water with them just a few hours before, without a glass barrier. We had a close encounter, and we didn't even need the Enquirer. Before we took our plane home on Sunday, we wanted one more glimpse of the manatees. We booked an airboat tour with Wild Bill's Tours. We watched a few of the gentle giants glide just below the surface as if they didn't have a care in the world. We searched around for some alligators, but none were to be found. Maybe they did know how to read after all.

On the plane home we thought about how wonderful and unique this experience was. An experience we would always treasure. And to think we did all this before class began on Monday. How wonderful.

Adrenaline Adventures

Spencer's teacher, however, did not think it was so wonderful. She had such a hard time believing what we did over the weekend that she called to ask me if it was true. She even had the nerve to say, "Ms. Capo if you do all these adventures with your son, don't you think he will find school boring?"

I responded, "Well, then you better become a better teacher, because I intend to take my kid any where in the world I can. Without missing school, of course."

She responded, "Well, it's just not a conventional lifestyle, running off for the weekend to swim with manatees."

"Miss D., I never want my kid to live a conventional life style. Secure, loving, responsible … yes. But conventional is boring. I want him to always be curious about the world. To seek opportunity when he can. Look, I can have him bring in pictures if you like so the other kids can see it."

"No, I don't think that would be good for the children. Then they'll want to be running off doing the same thing."

"So what's wrong with that?"

"Every parent is not like you …"

"There are plenty who are …"

"Please tell Spencer not to talk about it in school. Good day."

I explained to Spencer that not everyone understands the importance of seizing the day. I told him to only talk about it to his friends because they would understand.

To this day, my son still has the stuffed manatee we bought on that trip on his bed. We've done a lot of adventures since then, but this one is still ranked as his favorite. We went back once more a few years later with my fiancée, Steve, and his daughter, Jamie. The adventure will still as great. After all, where else can you cover living history, animal conservation, exercise, and a unique adventure in a quick weekend?

Spencer and I found that there are several organizations that allow you to adopt a manatee. Some start as low as twenty-five dollars. We hope that future generations will be able to enjoy these creatures. We now have a new addition to our family and another chapter in our travel book!

Fran Capo

Chapter 27
Adventure at a Glance - Dare to Do it   Mild to Wild Scale: 3
Title: Snorkeling With Manatees
Age requirement: No real age limits but parents must remain with their children at ALL times.
Length of trip: Half day to full day
Where to try adventure: Crystal River, Florida
I recommend the: Plantation Inn Dive Shop, (352) 795-5797,
Toll-free at the Resort (800) 632-6262 or
e-mail kcross@plantationinn.com
Best time of year: Late fall (November and December) and winter (January through March). Weekends get crowded, so weekdays are best.
Approximate cost: $25 per person plus equipment   (Group rates available)
$12 wetsuit rental - $7 mask, fin, and snorkel rental - $25 for underwater video
Reservations necessary: YES, only 17 people are allowed per boat.
Personal gear required: Bathing suit, towel. You can bring mask, fin, and snorkel or rent them.
What NOT to bring: Jewelry or anything valuable
Photo opportunities: Yes with underwater camera.

Notes: There are several places to adopt a manatee, you can start with www.savethemanatee.org

Cool trivia: There were 4,672 manatee mortalities documented in Florida from 1974 – 2002. Sadly, today there are only about 2,400 manatees left in the United States.
   Yet, despite all this these creatures do not seem to hold a grudge. They will play with any human who shows it love and affection. Hopefully you will be one of them. And if you really want to get on their good side, they love lettuce. They can eat an average of 54-60 heads per day.

"Never, never, never give up!"
-Winston Churchill

Chapter 28
"I'll Get You, Red Baron!"
Fighter Pilot For a Day

I remember as a kid watching Peanuts cartoons and getting a kick out of Snoopy fantasizing about his escapades as a "dogfighter" pilot attacking the Red Baron. It's one of those things you log in the back of your mind and think, "that would be cool to do someday."

With that in the recesses of my mind, I was thrilled when I came across an outfit called Air Combat USA. I sent away for the brochure. It sounded fantastic but not like an adventure I wanted to do alone. After all, I needed to have an "enemy." I filed the brochure into my "adventures to try one day" folder.

Flash forward five years. In the middle of an intense philosophical conversation, my boyfriend, Steve, said, "So what do you think about dogfighting?" I looked at him in disgust and went off into a tirade on how terrible it is to mistreat pit bulls. He started laughing. Then I realized he was talking about aerial dogfights. At the same time we said, "Air Combat USA!" We sounded like a bad infomercial. I

Adrenaline Adventures

knew I had found my "enemy"! And he was generous enough to pay for the opportunity for the kill. We had only been dating for a few months. He figured this would be a good way to impress me. He was right.

Air Combat USA is an outfit that was founded in 1986 by Mike Blackstone, a pilot with thirty-two years aviation experience who has logged 21,000 hours of flight time. With this program, you actually get to fly a light attack fighter aircraft, a SIA Marchetti SF260. You are coached the entire time by your own personal air combat instructor who is sitting by your side. Air Combat is not a simulator ride and no pilot's license is required.

The outfit travels around the United States and stays at different deployment locations. Steve and I checked the schedule and saw they'd be at an airport in West Hampton, New York, for one week.

Air Combat has three programs: The Basic—which comes in phases; the Fighter Lead-in Program, and Advanced Fighter Tactics. We booked the basic course, fighting maneuvers and tactics, for 10:45 A.M. Thursday morning.

I was just getting over bronchitis and Steve was showing his concern. "Are you sure you want to do this? Your lungs could explode since there are no pressurized cabins." He chuckled.

I called the school to ease his mind then promptly stuck my tongue out at him to let him know the fight was still on.

That Thursday, I dropped my son off at school and met Steve at his house. We decided on a light egg white breakfast—just in case one of the loops in the airplane forced the breakfast to magically reappear.

The two-hour drive to the airport was filled with anticipation. We were actually going to fly these planes. Steve, who is a licensed pilot, and I, with 6.5 hours of flying under my belt, were already placing bets on who was going to win. Such bravado!! Such machismo! Not to mention a backrub to the winner was at stake.

We arrived at the airport. We saw this guy suited up with the name Hollywood on his green jumpsuit. "You guys flying with us?"

"I don't know. Who are you, the film crew?" I said with my best New York attitude. Steve shook his head with that "there she goes again" look.

Pilot Robert Kunstmann, a.k.a. Hollywood, smiled. "They call me Hollywood, since I'm also a production manager for a Hollywood studio. Pleased to have you aboard." He shook our hands then gave us each a jumpsuit, questionnaire, and release form.

Questionnaires always ask the same basic questions: Are you in good health? Have you tried any other extreme sports? Are there any parting notes you'd like to leave your next of kin? Where's your safe deposit box?

The release was the standard, "We take no responsibility now and for the rest of eternity and longer." We dutifully initialed the items then went to the bathroom to don our identical green outfits.

Once dressed, we were sent to the briefing room. Steve and I were the only two students for this flight. We were turned over to our, twenty-seven-year-old Mike J. Blackstone, a.k.a Rocket. Cute guy—he looked like Mark Hamill from *Star Wars*. He was also a pilot for American Airlines.

Rocket picked up two model aircrafts on a stick and started briefing us. "The SIA Marchetti is an Italian-built fighter aircraft. It has 260 horsepower, can fly at 270 miles per hour, and is FAA certified from positive six to negative three G's. It can perform unlimited aerobatics with full fuel and two people wearing parachutes. It is maneuvered by the stick grip, complete with trigger controls. It's identical to the F4 Phantom. Use your fingertips, not a death grip, on the stick. We don't want to see white knuckles and have to pry your hands off with a crowbar. The planes respond quickly. Like a jet, the wings are machete thin. You'll be flying the plane ninety percent of the time."

He went on to talk about the steering, the formation flights, high and low yo-yos, the dogfighting tactics, and finally the most important rules: "Don't run into the other plane and DO NOT YAK on the instructor."

The information was a bit overwhelming, but I was determined not to let it show. Steve started making his own excuses, saying that it would be easier for me to fly since I didn't have to unlearn any traditional flying techniques.

Since the goal was dogfighting, we were told to constantly look out the windows and all around us to keep our enemy in sight. In commercial flights, the pilots are constantly checking their gages, or at least the passengers hope so. They are not busy looking around for unidentified flying objects.

Either way, I really wanted to make sure I won at least one of the fights. I was taking copious notes. Rocket assured me he would coach me all the way since he was going to be my instructor pilot.

"How will I know if I hit his plane?" I asked.

"A direct hit is registered with our patent pending electronic tracking system. In other words, you'll see smoke coming out of his plane." He grinned.

"Cool! Just like the Red Baron!"

Rocket went over a few more details. "Remember to tighten your jaw and stomach muscles when you pull back the stick and go straight up. The G force can cause you to get tunnel vision or black out if you don't, since the force doesn't allow oxygen to your eyes. If you tighten up, you will be fine. Trust me."

Lastly, he explained the parachute procedure. "If for some reason I can't get us out of a situation we would have to bail out."

I parachuted once, but that was *by choice*. Somehow that's different than jumping out of a spiraling plane. I listened closely—this was not a time to be daydreaming about whether or not I turned off the oven.

Having completed the ground school instruction, we were fitted with helmets and ready to face our airborne adventure.

Steve, Hollywood, Rocket, and I walked out on the runway and over to the planes. Rocket rolled back the clear canopy, and I climbed into the left side of the cockpit.

Embarrassingly, I was too short. I had to have not one, but three, seat cushions under my butt so I could see out the gun sight. Reminded me of high school days during Driver's Ed when I needed two phonebooks to reach the gas pedal. I guess I haven't grown much.

The engines were started, our radio transmitter headsets were made active, and we taxied down the runway to the takeoff point. I was surprised to see we kept the hatch open. Rocket explained that since it wasn't pressurized, it didn't matter. He also noted that it served as great ventilation and nausea prevention until takeoff.

Fran Capo

Once we got clearance from the tower, we were off. Steve and Hollywood followed behind. We flew out in formation. Since we were in front, we became the practice target for Steve's plane. I wanted to make it hard, maybe serpentine a bit. Rocket told me to let him hit us a few times and that it was going to be hard enough later to hit a moving target.

We practiced various maneuvers that we had discussed in ground school.

Then I heard the official call, "Let the games begin." Three cockpit cameras' red lights started blinking. They were recording the actual dogfights from three perspectives: through the gun sight, out the window, and on the student pilot.

Rocket held up one gloved finger in front of the camera and the first aerial dogfight had begun.

With Rocket instructing me, we entered fast, climbed high, rolled left, and always kept them in sight. Finally, as we were following behind them, I could see the "enemy" plane in the crosshairs of my gun sight. I had his wings leveled in the target zone, and Rocket yelled, "Fire!" I pulled the trigger. I fired several laser shots. I heard a tone pierce the cockpit as the electronic bullets were being continuously fired. I waited, and a few seconds later, I saw a trail of smoke coming out of the plane's fuselage. Yes! Bullseye! A direct hit! Rocket and I gave each other a high five as our first successful dogfight was won.

In the next fight Steve was the victor. I was bummed and more determined. I told Rocket, "Let's not let THAT happen again." Rocket gave me the thumbs up.

We were doing some pretty cool maneuvers in between dogfights. Rocket, seeing I could handle the acrobatics of the plane, asked me if I wanted to do some loops.

"Definitely!"

I pulled the stick back, tightened my jaw so I wouldn't black out, and felt the four G's of pressure push down on my face. I imagined I looked like Droopy Dog. Then Rocket said, "Bank left." And in an instant the world spun out the front window as we did two 360-degree loops. "I loved it!"

It was time to engage in the third dogfight. The gloved three fingers went up, and I quickly had to get the other plane in sight.

Adrenaline Adventures

Once again, we dove to gain speed, banked to get the correct angle, and got the "enemy" in the target zone again. The score was now 2 to 1, my favor.

I figured Steve would win the next one, because I was sure they didn't want anyone going home feeling bad. But I won the next two also. Then Rocket turned to me and said, "I don't think your boyfriend's feeling too good."

I was shocked. "How do you know?" I asked, concerned.

"I can tell by the way they're flying, they're not being aggressive. He may be using the barf bag."

That explained the "Do Not Yak on the instructor" rule.

"Oh, man. Does he want to go down?" I asked.

Rocket called over to the other plane and asked. "Negative," came the reply.

"Well then, show them no mercy!

We won the last fight and completed the mission.

We flew back in formation to the base. This time Steve's plane was in the lead.

"How many people get sick?" I asked.

"Only about one in ten," Rocket said.

"That's pretty low odds. Don't ya hate it when you have to be one of the statistics?"

We flew back in silence. It was exhilarating. I kept replaying all those flips in my head. I now understood what it would feel like to spot a plane and then dive and attack them. Definitely keeps the heart pumping. Of course, this wasn't real war, so nothing but fun was at stake.

I felt bad, though, because I wanted Steve to enjoy the adventure too. I didn't know what condition he would be in on the ground, and with his stomach already upset I didn't want to bruise his ego as well. Although I do have to admit it was tempting.

When the cockpit of his plane finally opened, I saw a very white-faced comrade get out. Yet he was smiling. "Did you enjoy yourself?" Despite the stomach flips, we both knew the answer.

We went to debriefing. They pulled our videos from the planes, and we got to relive each dogfight and see the opponent's perspective.

Fran Capo

I saw that Steve's plane was upside down for a good few seconds of flight. I'm sure the egg white sandwich wasn't enjoying that!

We changed out of our suits and back into civilian clothes. As we hopped into Steve's Jeep, I told him we could both say we won three each.

Steve smiled and said, "No need. Tell everyone the truth. Remember, after all, next week is racecar driving. And I'm going to nail you on that one."

The challenge was on once again. But for the moment I was enjoying my win and doing loops on cloud nine.

Adrenaline Adventures

Chapter 28
Adventure at a Glance - Dare to Do it   Mild to Wild Scale: 5
Title: Fighter Pilot For a Day
Children allowed: Yes, twelve and up (though children as young as eight have flown)
Length of trip: Half day—you fly aircraft ninety percent of the time and engage in six dogfights.
Where to try adventure: Air Combat USA
Website: www.aircombat.com or call 800-522-7590
Mailing Address:
P.O. Box 2726
Fullerton, CA 92837
Best time of year: Anytime depending on state and weather conditions
Approximate cost: Basic training - Phase I - $995 (Two hours of training, one hour of flight time)
Reservations necessary: Yes
Requirements: None
Fitness requirement: Must not be prone to motion sickness
Personal gear required: None
What NOT to bring: Full stomach
Photo opportunities: Yes. You get a videotape included in the price.

Notes: There are three programs. Each phase costs $995. Groups are welcome.

Cool trivia: Most of their pilots are former military pilots from the Air Force, Navy, and Marine Corps, and several are graduates of Red Flag and the Navy Fighter Weapons School. They use the military rules of engagement to establish safe minimum altitudes and distances between the airplanes. This is done throughout all their maneuvers.

"Just say yes and figure it out later."
–Fran Capo

Chapter 29
"At the Speed of Luge"
Winter Luge

I never thought of my phone bill as a source of adventure. But there under the monthly surcharge and beneath the exorbitant amount that meant I spent way too much time talking to my friend Anna in Florida was an invitation to learn how to luge with an Olympic trainer.

Normally I don't make a habit of reading my phone bill, but the word LUGE seemed to jump out at me from the page. Every time I see the word luge, jokes about the Jamaican bobsled team pop into my head. Exactly where do those Jamaicans do their practice? In the sugarcane fields?

Luge is French for sled. Well, this ain't no Rosebud. In my opinion, it's English for "idiot lunging forward at breakneck speeds without a seatbelt!" Speeds in luge can exceed ninety miles per hour, with the average luge track having two inches of ice and a vertical drop of twenty-five to thirty stories. It's the world's fastest winter sport timed to 1/1000th of a second. The luge sled can accelerate from zero to sixty in about ten seconds.

With that in mind, I opened the insert. For one weekend at the Ski Windham snow resort, this luge challenge was available. They would let you try a couple of trial runs on a plastic sled (as opposed to the real steel ones). If you qualified (which apparently means you don't break your neck, injure others, or go off a cliff), you are allowed to enter a race on a longer track, a twisting four-hundred-yard course, and compete against other novices. You are timed, and the winner in each division gets a prize. The challenge was sponsored by Bell Atlantic Telephone (which is now Verizon), the sponsors of the USA luge team since 1985. They were looking for future Olympians.

I called the 800 number and found out some more details. The luge challenge was a yearly event taught by USA luge coaches and team members. It was available for one weekend at six different northeastern ski resorts. The sleds were easy to control; they only went a mere twenty miles per hour, and the tracks were made of snow, not ice, and the event was free. I decided to go.

I told my son, Spencer, about it. He's learned from an early age that there is no such thing as a "normal" weekend with Mom. He was excited. But why stop there? Adventures are more fun when shared with good friends.

I enlisted my friend Steve S. (not to be confused with my boyfriend Steve at the time) and his son, Jonathan, as fellow luge mates. Steve's girlfriend, Claudia, just shook her head in amazement. "Where does Fran find these adventures? Who looks at their phone bill anyway?" Questions I often ask myself.

The first challenge, as with many of my adventures, was getting up at the crack of dawn. We left at 5 A.M. to start our four-hour trek to Ski Windham, which is located in Upstate New York.

Somehow our navigational skills did not quite function at their best at 5 A.M. After circling the same restaurant for the fifth time, we realized we were lost. Cows were getting annoyed. They started standing with signs reading, "That way stupid." I could hear their sarcastic mooing.

Finally, after several reroutes, we arrived at Ski Windham. Thankful to get out of the car, our adrenaline began flowing. We were about to start the real adventure.

The four of us donned our winter gear, complete with disposable camera. We wanted to make sure every part of exposed skin was covered. It's hard to enjoy something if hypothermia is sets in.

While walking toward the ski resort from the parking lot, I noticed that Spencer's socks were too small. He had a patch of exposed skin. I guess wearing the same ski outfit for four years in a row is not good for a growing boy. So the first stop was to the ski shop to get him the proper socks. These new beauties came up to his knees. Good. That oughta last him another four years. We were ready to sign up.

We went to the official luge sign-in desk. After signing a three-page standard release form, we received a luge pin, which permitted us on the trail and allowed us to practice with the Olympic trainer.

We walked over to the trail. The Bell Atlantic people had built two snow tracks—a trial run track and a racing run track. The trial track was a straight path with a small incline. The racing track was four hundred yards long. It had banks and turns and a stack of hay at the end in case you couldn't stop yourself. Impact was always one of my favorite ways to stop.

We walked past the DJ tent and over to the check-in desk to give the trial run a try. Hundreds of helmets and plastic sleds were nearby. We showed our pin and were given the equipment.

With helmets on, we sat on the plastic sleds and waited for our instructor. We came at a good time, since we were the only four at the moment checking in. A woman came over, introduced herself, and gave us basic instructions before releasing us to the official Olympic trainer.

"Okay, all I want you to do is sit on the sled with your feet in the stirrups. Now, lean all the way back until you are lying down. Keep your head up so you can see where you are going. This is the position you are to be in when you are going down the hill. Hold onto the rope that is attached to the sled. To steer right, just press your left foot down hard. To stop, sit up and dig your heels into the

Adrenaline Adventures

snow. Good luck and have fun." Talk about a crash course! Hope this wasn't a premonition of things to come.

Before she had a chance to scamper away, I asked her a question. "Are these tracks built like the official tracks?"

"No, like this course, luge courses are constructed especially for the sport. But the Olympic tracks feature a number of standard turns and curves. They have to have left and right turns, a hairpin turn, an S-turn, and a labyrinth turn, as well as straight stretches to give the racer a chance to build up more speed. The official courses must be between 3,281 and 4,921 feet long and usually have lights for nighttime competition."

"I noticed these plastic sleds are real light. How do they compare to the real sleds?"

"The competition luges cannot weigh more than fifty pounds."

She seemed in a rush, so I didn't ask her any more questions. We trekked up the trial run slope and were greeted by a trainer with a heavy accent. Now I really felt this was authentic. Something about a coach with an accent makes me feel like Nadia Comaneci.

Spencer went first. He placed his sled at the top of the run. Coach Brodoffski stood at the bottom of the sled and held it in place with one foot. "Now listen carefully. I vant you to lie back. Now show me right turn. Show me left turn. Good. Now I vant you to go left and right all the vay down the hill. Then I vant you to sit up before you come to the cones at the bottom of the hill. Understand?"

Spencer nodded yes.

"Good, then ve are ready." And with that the coach lifted his foot. Down the hill Spencer went like a drunken sailor, zigzagging left then right as instructed and stopping at the end. I could see him beaming. Jonathan and Steve followed.

I went last. I was so excited. I had listened to four sets of instructions so I knew what to do. Down the hill I went, side to side. I felt like a kid. I couldn't wait to run up the hill and do it again.

We practiced several times. Each time we were given pointers by our accented friend on how to improve. "Keep your butt close to front of sled. Good speed. Understand? Don't get up 'til last minute. You go faster. Brrmmm. Press hard with feet, you turn better. You go, now."

Fran Capo

After a few more runs we were told we were ready to try out to qualify for the race. Boot camp was over it was time to enter the battlefields. To qualify, you had to do the racing track in under twelve seconds. You were allowed two tries. There was a clock accurate to a thousandth of a second, the same one used for the Olympics. As you raced down, your final score was displayed on a giant electric scoreboard for the world to see. So there was no faking it. If you qualified, you'd come back later to get a racing number for the competition.

I went down first and did it in 10:78 seconds. On Steve's first attempt, he wiped out. On his second attempt, he did it in 10:03 seconds—quicker than the winner from the year before. Our money was on him. Jonathan was the slowest at 11:04, and Spencer did it in 11:02.

All of us qualified. We now had two hours to kill before entering our first luge competition.

The boys amused themselves by building an ice tunnel and crawling through it. Unfortunately they lost their entry pins in the process. We spent the next hour looking for the pins in three feet of snow. I felt like an arctic Sherlock Holmes, backtracking all our steps. Miraculously, we managed to find one pin, then sweet-talked the coach into giving us another one.

After a quick lunch, we were ready to compete. We trekked back up the hill. To get our racing numbers, we had to fill out a form and then stand in line in the appropriate division, men, boys, women, or girls. They checked our names off the qualifying list and then gave us our numbers. Prizes would be awarded in each category. There were about a hundred of us who qualified for the competition

There was excitement in the air. Hundreds of spectators were on hand. It really had an aura like the Olympics. I felt like I should be talking to my coach or warming up or doing something to prepare. Instead we decided it was of utmost importance to figure out a way to all do our runs and still be able to take pictures of one another. This was something we needed to capture on film. I decided I would take pictures of them first. I would wait at the bottom of the hill. The kids would compete first, and then when Steve came down after his

Adrenaline Adventures

racing run, he would grab the camera from me and I would jog up the hill and do my run before the race was officially closed.

There was a panel of judges and a group of timers in a booth. A past Olympic winner was doing the commentary. Olympic music poured out from the DJ stand. The crowd cheered, and the race began. All we needed was CNN.

Contestants formed a long line at the top of the hill behind the starting point. At the starting line, a man with a microphone asked each person his or her name, and then it was announced over the loud speaker. "Now racing in the men's division is Jeff, number 21." The racer would take off and comments were made on his style and form. Then as he passed the finish line, his time showed up on a digital display and was recorded. The crowd cheered for everyone. It was definitely not the place to be if you were shy.

We all were a bit nervous; no one wanted to make a fool of themselves in public. Jonathan was the most worried since his time had been the slowest during the trial runs. Spencer once again went first. In grand style he did an unintentional back flip over the snow bank and landed back on the sled. He continued down along the path and wiped out again, but, determined, he got up and ran over the finish line with his sled above his head. Everyone cheered at his tenacity. It was definitely a unique finish and the commentators had a field day.

Steve followed. He tried to get up a lot of speed and wiped out too. This was not looking good. But at least our team was consistent.

Jon was up third, and he handled the sled beautifully and came in at 10:58. I was busy playing Paparazzi and kept clicking away, forever capturing the race on a cheap camera. I was so engrossed in the picture taking that I was startled when Steve ran up behind me, grabbed the camera, and yelled, "Go!" I sprinted up the hill with sled in tow. There were only a few contestants left in the race.

Finally, it was my turn. I tried to get a running start. I steered over the banks and swished along the sides. I wanted the sled to go faster. I leaned back farther, trying to form the least air resistance. I felt the sled dig into the snow. I saw the haystacks approaching quickly. I was trying to maintain a straight course. I heard the coach's accent

Fran Capo

in my head. "Don't shoot up 'til the very last minute." I stopped two inches from the haystacks.

I stood up and looked at my time. I was expecting to see confetti and cheering fans. I did it in 11:94 seconds. All that work and it was an incredibly slow 11:94! Was I in some time warp or was my heart just beating faster than the sled?

I wanted to try again! I felt cheated. I had a glimpse of how Olympic stars must feel when they train for years just for those few seconds of glory, knowing only one will come out a gold medalist. Everything culminates into the one shining moment and that one chance to do it perfect.

Our foursome gathered, and all that was left to do was to wait for the results to be tallied. While waiting we noticed there were signup booths for the Junior National Olympic tryouts. Since we were in the spirit, we checked it out.

Bell Atlantic (Verizon) hosts four identical workshops in different parts of the country. Each workshop is three hours long. Ninety percent of the USA Luge National Team members are recruited through these junior workshops. They are held in the summer, so the kids can practice on luge sleds with wheels. The kids are tested on coachability, athletic ability, and luge technique. There is a twenty-five-kid maximum per workshop. The boys wanted to sign up, so we did.

As soon as we finished signing, the results were announced. To our surprise, Jonathan, the one who was the most skeptical, came in fifth place in the boys division. He won a pair of neoprene ski pants. Spencer was a little bummed. I told him in the spirit of sportsmanship that our sleds were fixed. I winked at him and we laughed.

The big winner of the day got an all expense paid trip to Lake Placid. He will get to slide down the 1980 Olympic luge run on a contraption called the Luge Rocket. I asked a nearby U.S.A. Luge Association spokesman what that was. He said that basically it's this little capsule that you lay down in, pray, and then go zooming off. After the prizes, there were some Olympic stars on hand. We got them to autograph our numbers.

In the end, we were all winners. We got an adrenaline rush. We got to experience "the fastest sport on ice," something that many

Adrenaline Adventures

people don't get to try in a lifetime, and we found our way home without having to ask for directions. A perfect ending to a perfect day, and one that left room, as always, for many more adventures.

Fran Capo

Chapter 29
Adventure at a Glance - Dare to Do it   Mild to Wild Scale: 2
Title: Winter Luge
Children allowed: Yes, ages ten and up
Length of trip: Half day
Where to try this adventure: At any ski resort that is being sponsored by Verizon. The United States Luge Association has a Web site filled with information at http://www.usaluge.org. If you go to the programs section there is a list of all the cities that hold the junior tryouts throughout the summer.
Or call 1-800-USA LUGE or (518) 523-8080 (November through March)
Best time of year: Winter for the Luge Challenge. Summer for the three-hour camp.
Approximate cost: FREE
Reservations necessary: Not for luge challenge, but reservations are suggested for the summer camp.
Fitness requirements: Must be in good health
Personal gear required: Polypropylene clothes that wick away the wetness, gloves, hat.
What NOT to bring: Cotton shirts that retain the wetness from the snow.
Photo opportunities: Yes
Notes: Get there early on competition day so you will be relaxed and have plenty of time to practice.

Cool trivia: Luging has been a popular sport in Europe since the late nineteenth century. In 1964 the International Olympic Committee made the luge an event at the Winter Olympics.
    During the November 17 International Training Week Race, American Tony Benshoof from White Bear Lake, Minnesota, a 2002 World Cup silver medalist, recorded record-breaking top speeds of 90.8 miles per hour and 91.8 miles per hour.

"Failure is not failure, but an opportunity to begin again ... more intelligently."
—Henry Ford

Chapter 30
"Just Call Me Maria Andretti"
Racecar Driving

Ever drive on a highway and have the urge to floor it? But the chance that the cops, or worse, a car with a ski rack posing as the cops stops you from going for the landspeed record?

I finally decided to give into my urge and do a rip-roaring 110-mph drive and not care about the cops. With some quick research on the information highway (where the only slow zone is your Internet connection), I came upon a bona fide racing school named Bertil Roos, headquartered in Blakeslee, Pennsylvania.

At the time, Bertil Roos had three racetracks: Virginia International Raceway where classes are held in March; Pocono International Raceway where classes run from April through October; and Nazareth Speedway that races from June until November.

When I called the outfit, I casually mentioned to Lisa, the receptionist, that I didn't know how to drive a stick. She paused. "O-

Adrenaline Adventures

kay, then you're better off doing the oval track at Nazareth. You stay in fourth gear around the track."

Good, now all I had to figure out was how to get up to fourth gear.

With enthusiasm, I enlisted my boyfriend, Steve. We were due for another adventure and he was ready to "whip my butt," as he so classically put it.

At Nazareth, the courses offered are half-day oval, one-day oval, one-day advanced, and practice sessions. We choose the half-day oval with a start time of eight A.M.

After we signed up, a confirmation package was sent with a handy-dandy Indy Style Racing School Preparation Handbook. Say that fast three times!

I opened the book: "The steering ratio is very quick and a quarter of a turn is the most you will ever have to turn the small 10" steering wheel ... place the pads of your thumbs on the top edges of the spokes with your index fingers placed behind the spokes and allow your three fingers to grip the wheel firmly, but relaxed. Your arms should be bent to the point where your elbows just reach the sides of your chest." This was starting to sound like a bad game of Twister. The handbook went on to explain shifting, rules, regulations, flag signals, and penalties.

Then came the diagrams for "ocular driving tactics." Whatever happened to just going fast around the track and not hitting the wall or other drivers?

There was a detailed diagram of the overall track with dozens of little instruction arrows explaining things like, "At this point turn left wheel on apex." Apex—isn't that a math term?

I turned the page. Ahhh! Each turn was enlarged and dissected further. I needed a yellow highlighter desperately. There was comforting news though; "You are not liable for any damage to the race car in this program." So if I hit a wall at 110 miles per hour and tumble over a few times, they ain't gonna charge me? What a relief to my broken bones.

Since Nazareth, Pennsylvania, was not around the corner from us, we decided to stay overnight in a quaint bed and breakfast place called The Classic Victorian, in Nazareth. We figured this way we'd be fresh for our day of racing.

The next morning, we drove up to the gate of Nazareth Racetrack where the gatekeeper asked, "What are ya here for?"

Steve said, "Bert-tell Roos Racing School."

The gatekeeper laughed. "You mean Berrrtil Roos."

"Hey, we're from New York," I chimed in. "We speak different."

"That explains it. Go ahead."

The gatekeeper jotted down my license plate "Fastawkr" and laughed.

Steve joked, "Fran here is the world's fastest talking female; this place is probably is the only place where something is going to go faster than her mouth!"

Ah, male bonding at its finest. I just smiled.

We drove through a little tunnel that led to a parking field. Then we saw it, the giant one-mile track: Nazareth Speedway.

According to *Autoweek* magazine, the track is the fastest mile around. It was opened in 1966 as Nazareth National Speedway and ran a weekly racing program until 1969, when its final track champion was a local lad named Mario Andretti. The track had a major renovation in 1986.

I was excited. I was going to drive on the same track as Mario Andretti. Well honey, just call me Maria!

Steve and I headed into the main building, checked in, signed the standard release forms, and were geared up.

Our gear consisted of a flame-retardant blue jumpsuit with advertising on the sleeves and chest, a helmet with our assigned numbers on it, and the thin leather racing gloves that we were asked to bring.

For an additional fee, we also signed up for the 8 x 10 photos and the onboard videotapes to capture the moment. We figured we could torture our friends with the tape later by making them watch us do eight hundred laps apiece.

We waited for about ten minutes for the classroom training to start. For some pre-class ambiance, there were video clips of real races complete with slow motion crashes on the overhead monitors. How's that for setting the mood?

I turned to look at the other students and noticed I was the only female racing. There were other gals, but they were just there to watch their boys play. Now I really felt pressure. I was the sole representative of my gender.

Our instructor, Stephan Riccaboni, introduced himself and started going over the main points of racing. "The cars go approximately 115 miles per hour; at top speed they do a thirty-four-second mile. There is no coasting like in street driving. Get your eyes up sooner on the road. Go in slow and out fast. Always know where you need to be."

Yeah, I needed to be telling them I didn't know how to drive a stick.

He continued, "After this classroom training, you are going to go out onto the track where a couple of Volvos with instructors will be waiting. We need three of you in each car. They will take you around the track and show you how to maneuver the turns. Afterwards, you will be divided into two groups. Group one will do the laps first. Each of you will do three ten-minute laps. You will be evaluated after each lap on accuracy, speed, and hitting your marks. Remember, have fun and stay away from the wall."

It was comforting to know that just in case someone didn't pay attention to that last bit of advice, an emergency vehicle was stationed by the track.

We walked out onto the track and quickly, by threes, we got into the Volvos. Somehow Steve and I got separated. I wound up with Guiseppi—kind of reminded me of that guy in Pinocchio. (Yeah, I know that was Gepetto—close enough.) Guiseppi sped around the track. "Okay, on this first turn aim straight, back off the accelerator at this line, turn your head quickly, and aim for the apex. Then accelerate, look and aim to the wall."

Am I supposed to remember all this? Can I refer to the booklet when I drive? Why didn't I take ginkgo biloba this morning?

Guiseppi continued, "Passing is only allowed on the back straight and only after the blue passing flag has been displayed to the car that is about to be passed. Acknowledge the flag, and exit the corner to let the guy pass."

Fran Capo

We took turns behind the wheel of the Volvo. I was going ninety miles per hour and pretty proud of myself when Guiseppi said, "Hey Fran, this is a race, not a Sunday drive!" Ah, that hurt.

After a few spins around the track, we got out and were passed on to the next instructor, a guy named Vince Majewski. We stood in front of one of the racecars on the track and Vince began. "This is a Scandia F2000 open wheel racecar. It has a four-cylinder, 125 hp, O.H.C. racing engine and a four-speed Hewland transmission with wide Cooper tires and wings for excellent handling."

The men shook their heads as if they knew exactly what he was talking about. I shook my head also so as not to stand out.

Vince continued, "Here you have your ignition switch, oil press lamp, alternator lamp, and starter button. To start the engine simply pull out the ignition switch and press the starter button. To shut it off, just push the ignition back in. Braking is done with your right foot. The left rest pedal is for support during braking and cornering."

So far, I was following along okay. Then Vince hit my panic button. "And finally, here is the shift lever. It's a non-synchronized racing transmission. The 'throw' from one gear to the next is very short, so be snappy in the motions. Hold the lever between your thumb and fingertips to avoid scraping your knuckles. You know the standard shifting. Any questions?"

All of a sudden I started thinking that maybe, just maybe, learning to drive a stick and then immediately going 110 miles per hour might not be the best way to learn. Butterflies were committing hari-kari in my stomach. Steve caught one of them.

I pulled Vince aside. "Pssst. Slight problem. Can you show me how to drive a stick?"

Vince looked amused. "Sure, no problem." Vince escorted me to my black number three Scandia 2000. I got in. At five foot two, I was too short to reach the pedals. I needed ALL fourteen of their cushions to prop me up on the seat. Then I was strapped in with the five-point safety system. They have to keep you tightly belted so you don't go bouncing around at one and a half G's around the turns.

Now Vince leaned over. "This is first gear, second, third, etc. Just push the start button, then ease your foot onto the gas as you lift off the clutch. Got it?"

Adrenaline Adventures

I felt as if I was starring in an *I Love Lucy* episode.

All eyes were upon me at the starting line. I attempted to start the car and ease out. I stalled. Determined, I tried again. Sputter, sputter, sputter … stall. This was highly embarrassing!

Again I tried. Start … chug … chug … chug … jerk … jerk … damn! Okay, Capo, one more time. I started it. It jerked and … YES! Victory at last!

I went out onto the eighteen-foot warm-up lane just inside the racing oval to get up to speed. You had to be in fourth gear by the time you entered the racing track. I couldn't get it into fourth. So I figured I'd fudge it and stayed in third.

Then I saw a blue flag—okay, some smart aleck wanted to pass me. I was too busy trying to remember to hit my marks and stay six feet from the wall. In the midst of my concentration, I saw a black flag, which meant come into the pits. "Wow, what did I do? Impede traffic?"

Vince ran over. "You missed the cones on turn three." I wasn't even sure which turn *was* three! But I nodded and gave him the thumbs up like I understood. Back on the track I went. This time I was willing to go a tad faster. Apparently not fast enough, though, because again the cars whizzed by.

Okay, I thought, I'm the only girl out here. I have to do better than this! Then I saw the yellow flag that meant proceed with caution. "It can't be for me, I'm not going fast enough." I was talking to myself to remember all the points. Before I knew it, the checkered flag was up, the session was over—return to the pits. Vince stood with a clipboard and went over everyone's performance. "Fran, good on turn one. Too early on turn two, and watch the marks. Not bad for someone who never drove a stick." Phew, this was worse than report card time in elementary school.

Now Steve and his group were up. He was passing cars like it was a practice run in a fireman's rally. I was proud. If I can't beat him, I don't want anyone else to.

Ten minutes later, it was time for my second session. I was less nervous this time around since I knew what to expect. The car sputtered a few times at the start, but then I got up to speed. On the straight backstretch I decided to put the pedal to the metal. I

Fran Capo

floored it. Oh man, it felt so powerful, it made me laugh. I started singing, "Go speed racer, go speed racer, go speed racer ... gooo!" I felt confident, invulnerable, and then I saw the black flag again. I made my way back to the pits to be "scolded" once again.

"Ahhh Fran, you're doing great. You just have to stay in your lane and let the other drivers pass." Other drivers? I didn't even see them. Talk about Mrs. Magoo!

The last lap around was fantastic. I finally got the feel, hit my marks, and for a brief moment made it up to 110 miles per hour. The world was a windblown blur. I loved it.

Steve did his third lap and then, sadly, class was over. We went back inside, turned in our gear, and got our achievement certificates. We were all high-fiving each other as we heard the instructor mutter in the background that the certificates were not a "get out of jail free" speed pass for the Pennsylvania Turnpike. What a party pooper!

Driving around town, we felt like turtles. We were having speed withdrawal. We were like little kids, we didn't want to go home. So guess what, we didn't.

We decided to stay overnight and do the practice session the next day. We signed up for the three ten-minute races. This time Steve and I were on the track at the same time. Now the fear was gone and my competitive nature reared its ugly head.

We raced around. And before I knew it, Steve passed me once, then twice. I was flooring it, and he was still going faster! It was most frustrating.

My fastest lap was 46:51, his was 40:20. The track record was 18:419 seconds in 1998 set by Patrick Carpentier. So neither of us were record breakers yet!

Steve said I cut him off twice intentionally. I said it was unintentional. He claimed he saw the gleam in my eye through the rearview mirror. I assured him it was only the reflection of the sun.

To this day I wink when I think about it. Either way, the racecar adrenaline made us both shine for a long time afterward. And maybe, just maybe, Steve did outshine me a little on the track. But tomorrow's another adventure. (*wink*)

Adrenaline Adventures

Chapter 30
Adventure at a Glance – Dare to do it   Mild to Wild Scale: 5
Title: Racecar Driving
Children allowed: No
Age requirement: Must be at least 16, with a valid driver's license
Length of trip: Half-day, one-day or three-day
Where to try this adventure: Bertil Roos Racing School. They have five track locations. Check out their Web site at http://www.racenow.com/home.htm, email roos@epix.net, or call 1-800-722-3669. (Tell them the fast talker sent ya.)
Best time of year: April - October
Approximate cost: Half day $495 / Full day $995 / Three day $2,795 (Prices vary slightly according to track)
Reservations necessary: Yes
Requirements: Must have a valid driver's license
Fitness requirement: Must be in good health
Personal gear required: Racing gloves, comfortable clothes
What NOT to bring: A hangover
Photo opportunities: Yes. You can also purchase video tape.

Notes: Bertil Roos is always expanding and adding tracks that they race on. Check their Web site for the most updated information.

Cool trivia fact: In 2002, Milka Duno, a beautiful naval engineer with four master degrees, became the first woman in the history of sports car racing to pilot the fastest and most technologically advanced sports car in the world – the Le Mans Prototype 900. She was also the first woman in history to pilot the fastest car in the Open Telefonica World Series – the last step on the ladder to Formula One Racing. She has established herself as one of the most disciplined racecar drivers in the world.

"You're only given a little spark of madness. You mustn't lose it."
—Robin Williams

Chapter 31
"To the Top in the Land of Oz" Bridge Climb

Before the year of the summer Olympics in the Land Down Under, the most we heard about Australia was when someone talked about Paul Hogan or koalas. But in the year 2000, Australia was the "in" place. That was also the year that the reality television show "Survivor II" was filmed in Australia. Never one to follow a trend, I went to the Land Down Under for my own reasons.

It started out simple enough when I mentioned to my boyfriend, Steve, that I didn't like to repeat adventures twice until I had several under my belt. Sarcastically he said, "Okay, Capo, what adventures haven't you tried?"

"Well, I've never been to Australia or fought with a sumo wrestler."

"Do you know any sumo wrestlers?" he asked.

Adrenaline Adventures

"Not at the moment, but I'm working on it."

"Too bad. I'd pay the guy to sit on you ... only for a moment, just to keep you still." He laughed. "Okay, why Australia?"

"Well, ever since I can remember, I've had a burning desire to climb the cables on the Veranzano bridge. Since I know I can't do it without getting arrested, I've never tried. But I heard that in Australia you can climb the Sydney Harbor Bridge."

"You want to go all the way to Australia just to climb a bridge?"

"Ah ... yes." Then I kicked into my high-gear, world-record-fast-talking mode. "I mean, that would be my main goal, but Australia has so many cool things, and if we took the kids they could pet koala bears, kangaroos, and wombats, and we could go into the jungle, snorkel in the Great Barrier Reef, and do all sorts of adventures."

Steve and I were only four months into the relationship, and at that point my enthusiasm for life didn't wear him out. He not only was game but offered to pay for the entire trip!

We looked at tour packages and chose an adventure vacation that included all the things I'd mentioned plus canoeing, a fifty-mile bike ride, an encounter with crocodiles, sleeping in a haunted resort, and lots more.

So on August 4, Steve, his daughter Jamie, my son Spencer, and I took a mere twenty-two-hour flight from New York to Sydney, crossing over the international dateline. Some fellow parents thought that taking two kids on a flight like that was in itself the adventure.

Sydney has an interesting history. It was established in 1788 when British Captain Arthur Phillip sailed 1,400 people, mostly prisoners, into the area known as The Rocks. (There goes the neighborhood!) Today, Sydney is known as the "Best City in the World" according to *Condé Nast Traveler* magazine.

Knowing the history, we decided to stay in the historic Rock District. After seeing that people drive on the wrong side of the road in Australia, and that the water in the toilet really does go down the opposite way, we headed out to explore Sydney.

We zoomed past Victorian houses, shops, and opal stores at The Rocks. We ran down the stone steps through alleys, past George Street (the oldest street in Australia), and to the main street, which lead to Darling Harbor. There before us was a gorgeous view of Sydney and the bridge!

Since we couldn't climb the bridge that day, we decided to hop a ferry and ride thirty minutes to a village called Manly known for its great beaches, in hopes of seeing koala bears. We found out we were too far from Koala Park to see the bears and instead went to Ocean World. We held boa constrictors while having an in-depth conversation with a snake keeper who sounded like Paul Hogan. No one else was there, so the cleaning lady joined in. Later we strolled along Manly Wharf (what testosterone-laden person named this?) and ate at a beachside restaurant where we were told that we "should" tip, contrary to what the travel brochures say.

The next day I was excited because I was about to fulfill a twenty-year dream ... The Bridge Climb. Since the minimum bridge climbing age was twelve, Spencer (who was eleven) and Jamie (who was nine) did not met the quota. So Steve, knowing that this was a dream of mine, told me to go ahead and that he would take the kids to Taronga Zoo instead. There they gazed at koalas and the highly evolved, bizarre duckbilled platypus, which is smaller than most people think, weighing in at about four pounds. I got ready to climb the steel structure.

The Bridge Climb tour dream was seventy years in the making. It started when the founder of the Bridge Climb Tour, Paul Cave's father-in-law, stood in line for two days to purchase the first rail ticket back in march of 1932, the day the bridge was opened. So Paul has always had a connection to the bridge. On October 1, 1998, he opened the Bridge Climb to any visitor who met the requirements and was willing to pay seventy-nine bucks for an awesome three-hour experience climbing the world's largest steel arch bridge, which has been nicknamed The Coathanger (Aussies love giving structures nicknames).

BridgeClimb is the name of the outfit responsible for the Bridge Climb. (It's not on the top ten list of original names, but it works.) There is a maximum of twelve people in a climb group, and groups depart every fifteen minutes. The climb takes place during all weather conditions except an electrical storm (which is a good rule) and you must arrive fifteen minutes prior to your climb time. You

Adrenaline Adventures

are told to wear rubber-soled shoes and comfortable clothes. Tickets are nonrefundable within seven days of the climb. I was scheduled to climb at 11:45 A.M.

The bridge was just around the corner from our hotel. Steve and the gang walked me there and waited at the bottom for a while so they could take pictures of me on the bridge from below. I checked in promptly at 11:30—there was no way I was going to miss a climb of a lifetime.

As soon as I walked in, I could tell this was one of the most well run organizations I had ever seen. They were efficient, clean, polite, and there was an air of professionalism all around.

I walked in and handed a very polite guy my voucher. I was then lead into another room with eight other people, one man and seven women, besides me—they were going to be my climb group. A staff member briefed us on the steps we were about to go through. He said we would go through about an hour of gearing up and training.

The first order of business was a breath test (and it's not to see if you're kissable). Once you passed the breathalyzer with a reading below 0.05, you were asked to sign a release form and then lead to another room. There you stood on these big, white, round dots. One dot per person. Then, like tiny elves, staff members quickly looked you over and gave you a specially designed bridge climbing jumpsuit.

With jumpsuit in hand, you were now assigned a locker. All jewelry had to be removed and placed in the locker, including watches and earrings. No loose change or cameras or any dangling items were permitted. They didn't want you getting snagged on a steel cable as you climbed, although that would make a great picture for the photo album. Once all unnecessary items were removed, you slipped your light-gray suit over your street clothes.

After we were suited up, we were turned over to our leader, Justin Hewlett. We were asked to say hi to our neighbors again, since we would be spending the next few hours together. Now the training began.

We were put into harnesses that attached around our waists. The harnesses looked like long, blue nylon belts. There was excess harness line after it went once around your waist. The excess part had a circular latch-stop on it. That circular latch at the end of the harness was your safety line. It would attach you to the bridge. You walk the entire length of the bridge attached to a metal bar on the bridge.

To practice, we were put in a room and with a big, long, U-shaped metal bar to simulate the actual bar on the bridge. We started at one end of the bar and attached our safety lines. We walked the full length of the bar, making sure the latch-stop made it over all the nuts in the bar.

The next order of business was to be geared up in a room full of bins. There were bins that had handkerchiefs, berets, gloves, hats, straps for glasses, etc. Every item has clips that attach to your jumpsuit so the item doesn't fall on innocent people below. All women with long hair, like me, had to tie their hair back—not because it was going to fall on someone below, but so that you didn't get it snagged in the bridge wires.

We were now onto the final practice area. We were lead over to the climb simulator. The simulator was a series of simple ladders that we would climb up and down. This was so we would know the proper climbing procedure once on the real bridge. The procedure was pretty simple, one person per section of ladder. This way, if anyone fell, only that person would get hurt and not take down everyone below. Rather thoughtful, I thought, and also a good way to isolate the one fool who can't climb.

We now had one last gear room to go through before the actual climb—the radio room. Once inside the room each person was told to face forward. We were then all handed radios and were told to clip the radio securely onto the belt of the person in front of us. Then we were each given ear pieces and told to test out if we could hear Justin's voice on the radio. When we all nodded that our devices were working, we were ready to begin the climb!

We were led out a back door and then through a door into a cement portion of the bridge. We went through a tunnel, and when we came come out we could see a network of steel beams. I felt like I was in the belly of the beast.

In single file we hooked our safety belts to a metal bar that we would follow to the top of the bridge. We walked a long catwalk to

Adrenaline Adventures

the pylon. Some of the walkways have grates where you can see clear down to the ground, which was about 150 feet below us. It was cool for me but would not be cool if you're scared of heights, but then why would you be on the bridge in the first place if that's the case?

With eight women in the group, there was a lot of estrogen. We were talking and having a grand old time as we walked past the catwalk and came to a series of steep ladders. Two of the women were seniors so we cheered them on as they ascended the first ladder, one at a time, just like we had practiced. When we got to the top of that first ladder, we were in for a bit of a shock. At the end of the ladder you pop your head out in between the lanes of bridge traffic. That's comforting!

Up, up we climbed. It was a perfect clear day so I looked around often. I wanted to savor every moment. We continued to the Eastern Arch, where we began the real climb up hundreds of stairs, higher and higher. It was not for the faint of heart. You are latched to the bar, which is near the edge of the bridge, and although you are fenced in, the height can be dizzying for some.

On the day that we climbed, there was construction going on, so we had the added pleasure of walking past huge construction cranes and seeing workers eating lunch and hanging out on the ledges. Two new flag poles had just been erected on the summit, as well.

When we finally made it to the summit on top of the arches, 450 feet (134 meters) above sea level, we all stopped and took in the spectacular view. From there we could see a 360-degree panoramic view of Sydney—the famous Opera House, the Olympic Stadium, the harbor, and all the people that looked like tiny ants on the ground. It was gorgeous. A dream come true.

Then, one by one, we crossed over the center walkway of the bridge. We stopped to pose for a Kodak moment (I took my hair down for the picture) and then we descended along the western arch. On the way down, instead of car traffic, we passed trains that went in between the ladders.

I bonded with two British women, Ruth and Dot, on this climb. They said they loved my accent, and of course I answered, "Wadda ya tawkin about my accent? You guys are the ones with accents." We all laughed. They said they had been to New York and had just watched a television special about it and knew all the really cool things about its history.

Since my book *It Happened in New York* had just come out, I felt the need to ask them if the special had mentioned that Manhattan was purchased from the wrong set of Indians or that Woodstock had started as a sitcom idea? They said they hadn't heard those facts. I told them that my book had cool things like that in it. They asked where they could buy a copy of my book, and I told them I had some copies back in the hotel room. Luckily they were women or this would have sounded like a pick-up line. By the time we had gotten to the bottom of the bridge, I had sold two books. It was my best sale ever! Not quite selling the Brooklyn Bridge, but close.

Three and a half hours after the start of our climb, we were back at the bottom of the bridge, where the company continued to be just as efficient. Our radios were taken off, we returned each item to the appropriate labeled bins, and we were unharnessed and then led to a seven-sink faucet to wash our hands. We were asked to step out of our jumpsuits, shown back to our lockers to retrieve our items, given evaluation forms to fill out, and then led to a line where we were given a complimentary group photo and could purchase a copy of a picture of ourselves at the top of the bridge.

The two British ladies walked with me back to my hotel room, where I sold them two autographed copies of my New York book, and as I was handing them the books, Steve and the gang walked in. I felt like I was caught in the middle of a black market deal.

I introduced everyone, and Steve uttered his now-famous words to me, "You sold a book at the top of the bridge! Capo, around you — no one's safe!" We all laughed. The kids had a great time, I made new friends, and thanks to Steve, I was able to fulfill the dream of a lifetime.

Mission accomplished ... over and out.

Adrenaline Adventures

Chapter 31
Adventure at a Glance - Dare to Do   Mild to Wild Scale: 3
Title: Bridge Climb
Age requirement: Age 12 and up
Length of trip: Three and a half hours
Where to try this adventure: Sydney, Australia
Bridge Climb - The Adventure Company, 5 Cumberland St., The Rocks.   Web site: www.bridgeclimb.com
Telephone number in Australia: +61 (0) 2 8274 7777
Best time of year: All year round, except during electrical storm.
Approximate cost: Day climb $79, Night climb $85
Reservations necessary: Yes
Fitness requirements: The climb is open to anyone who is fit enough to climb metal ladders and can cope with heights.
Personal gear required: flat rubber soled shoes
What NOT to bring: Jewelry, loose items. They supply lockers.
Photo opportunities: No. They give you a complimentary group shot.

Notes: Our trip to Australia was a fifteen-day, adventure-packed experience with a wide array of cool things to do. If you plan on going to Australia check out the full article in the archives in either www.travelnewsletter.com or www.uniquetravelstories.com.

Cool trivia: Counting the road approaches, the Sydney Harbor Bridge is about a mile long. There are 58,000 tons of steel in the bridge. The arch was built from both ends toward the middle.

Before it opened, to test its ability to support a traffic jam, its entire length was packed with railway carriages, trams, and buses. The bridge was designed to withstand winds of 200 kilometers an hour, which are equal to hurricane force. Luckily the bridge has never had to endure that pressure in real life.

"If you find that thing you love, it doesn't necessarily matter whether you do it well or not— you just need to do it."
—Stanley Tucci

Chapter 32
"Just How Long is This Borough Anyway?"
Running a Marathon

For years I had a running joke with my friend and fellow comedian Joey Novick. I would tell him all the crazy adventures I'd done, and he would simply reply, "Yeah, but have you ever run the New York City Marathon?" He'd never dove with sharks, flew combat planes, or raced professional racing cars, but he had run the New York City Marathon, and I hadn't.

Somewhere inside my competitive brain it must have registered, because in January of 2000, when I was deciding my goals for the year, I announced out loud to myself, "This year I'm going to run the marathon. Not walk the marathon, not attempt the marathon, run … or at least jog the whole damn thing."

I wrote it in my journal. Once I do that, it's a done deal.

I went to the New York Road Runners (NYRRC) Web site (www.nyrrc.org). Turns out there were several ways to register for the marathon. You could fill out an online application, fax or mail one, or wait on line on Sunday, April 2 in Central Park to get a specially marked application that gave you a slightly better chance at getting a number. At first I was tempted to do the easiest thing and register online. But I have known people who have applied several years in a row and not gotten a number, so I read on.

Since there were about thirty thousand runners from all over the world trying to get into this race, they had a very specific system set up to be as fair as possible. Some people automatically got numbers: members of the NYRRC who had run at least nine qualifying races; entrants from the previous year who canceled prior to the race; those who had completed fifteen NYC marathons or more; those who got rejected for the past three marathons in a row; and those fit individuals who completed last year's marathon and completed it under a certain time. For men, the qualifying time was two hours and forty-five minutes, and for women, it was three hours and fifteen minutes. All the rest who wanted to enter the marathon had to do the lottery system.

Out of the lottery system, those who waited on line had the best shot. Then came those who'd submitted online applications, then faxed, then mailed. Two lotteries would be drawn. After the lottery dates you could check online and see if your application had been denied or accepted.

I knew this challenge would require training, encouragement, will, determination, and stamina. I didn't want to take it on alone. Even though ultimately you run alone, training with someone could make it more pleasurable. Plus you have someone to commiserate with when it gets hard—you know misery loves company.

I called two people, my then writing partner, Anna, in Florida and my boyfriend, Steve. Anna is one of my few athletic female friends. She said yes immediately. Steve hesitated, but then agreed.

Anna registered through their Web site, and Steve and I decided that we'd go for the best odds and wait on line.

Fran Capo

I started reading some online articles about training. All the articles recommended training for about a year. It was January. I was already walking every day in my favorite park, so I figured if I slowly added some jogging, I could build up my stamina.

First, I decided I needed to assess where I was at on the running meter. To test out our running legs, I enrolled my son, Spencer, Steve, and myself in a 5K race at Baldwin Harbor in Long Island, which took place on Saturday, March 18. Spencer couldn't understand why he had to enter since he wasn't running the marathon. One quick mother look told him that his mama was not raising a couch potato, and he agreed.

I did the 3.2 miles in 33:41 minutes and I came in fifth place among the woman of my division. Steve did well, and so did Spencer. But there were only about a hundred people in this race. We knew we really had to get in shape.

My goal was to run fifteen miles by the end of April. In all honesty, I hate running, but I wanted to see what I could make my body do. I figured I had plenty of time. So I began by roller-skating. Not logical, but I figured I'd start with something I liked to build up my endurance.

As time rolled on, I kept using "legitimate" excuses for not getting into serious training. Steve was helping me put in a new kitchen and it took twelve consecutive nights of working until five A.M. to finish it. Not much energy left over for running.

Then, out of guilt to my commitment, I entered Steve and myself in another race for April 9. But a freak snowstorm cancelled the race. Steve was dancing with happiness. I was upset because now I was committed to running.

On Saturday April 22, with a ninety percent chance of rain, Spencer, Steve, and I entered another race. Spencer ran a half-mile in 04:07 minutes. Steve and I did the 3.1 miles in 33:50 and 33:39. The next day I developed a fever and was sick for a few months! It's one thing when you decide not to run; its another when you are sick and you can't give it your best effort. Now I wanted to run more than ever.

I continued to walk, each day thinking that this ridiculous cough would go away. Anna had had the same bizarre persistent cough

Adrenaline Adventures

and cold that lasted four months. Could it be psychological? New Age thinkers would say it was a way of chickening out of a challenge by manifesting a real obstacle.

At this point, Anna dropped out. She said her hip was hurting badly as she increased the running mileage. It was down to Steve and me.

On Sunday, May 2, after driving home from a Philly gig, Steve and I went to Central Park and lined up for the NYC Marathon along with about eight thousand other people hoping to get an application. The line was at least two miles long!

Only one application per person was allowed. I guess they figured if you're not strong enough to wait on line, then forget the marathon. We walked forty, yes forty, blocks to get to the end of the line, only to have it circle around and come back the same forty blocks. I think that was the pre-training itself!

When we finally reached the marathon booths, we were handed a specially stamped application indicating that we had sweated the line. Then we were told "good luck" and sent on our merry way. That's it, no big deal, just here it is, mail it in, good luck.

We sent it in that same day. Now all we had to do was wait until the lottery was drawn.

On May 4, I was still sick. I had an X-ray to see if I had pneumonia, but it came back clear. The doctor was puzzled. He gave me more antibiotics. I wasn't discouraged since the November 4 marathon date was still six months away. I figured as soon as I got better I would just double my training.

On May 20 I got the NYC Marathon acceptance card in the mail. I went online to confirm if Steve was accepted too. Yes! We were both in. We were going to be a part of the 2000 New York City Marathon. I was thrilled; Steve looked like going to the dentist without novocaine was a better option.

I read the acceptance packet with enthusiasm. It explained that we were about to embark on a journey that would change our lives. Then it went into detail explaining about the pick-up buses, how to drop out if necessary, and that a registration card would be mailed in September. With that registration card and a photo ID, you, and only you, not your chauffeur, your mother, or your bodyguard, could go to the Expo at Show Piers on the Hudson to pick up your race number and chip. There was no fooling around. This was a tightly run operation.

The information pack also explained the timing procedures. A ChampionChip would score the race. It was a small chip that would be attached to your shoelaces and worn on your sneaker. It would give you the split times at five points in the race: the start, 10K, half marathon, twenty miles, and the finish. If you missed any of these scoring stations, you would be disqualified and no amount of whining could change it. This was so nobody could pull a Rosie Ruiz, the infamous runner who started the race, took the bus, splashed some water on her face, and reentered the race at the end as if she had been huffing and puffing all the way.

I started worrying, "What if I run the whole race and my chip is blocked by another runner's sneaker during the race and the electronic beam doesn't register?"

Steve assured me that the technology has come a long way since the days of the first NYC Marathon back in 1976 when there were only 2,090 runners. He said that everyone's score would be accounted for.

At the end of the race, we would wind up having two running times: our official time and our net time. The official time was the time the cannon went off until the time we crossed the finish line. The net time was the actual time it took to run the race, because it takes a good ten minutes just to get up to the starting line with all those people.

I looked at the race course map running through the five boroughs, then reality finally hit me. This is 26. 2 miles! That's a long way by car, never mind running.

Panic set in. Let the training begin!

On June 5, Steve's birthday, we decided it was time to work out a training schedule. If we were going to do this marathon, we needed to get in shape.

To motivate us, we entered a three-month *Fit for Life* contest. It was an intense contest with before and after photos—the type of photos where you stick out your stomach, slouch over, wear your worst bathing suit and no makeup for the before photo, then get tanned,

Adrenaline Adventures

hire a Hollywood makeup artist, and suck every living breath out of you for the after photo.

We worked out six days a week. We worked very hard, but we weren't running. We were building muscles but not running stamina. Maybe this wasn't the best idea.

Our strict workout plan got interrupted from July 1 -16 when we went to Australia to do a multi-sport vacation complete with canoeing, biking, hiking, and snorkeling. We figured this would still keep us in shape and be a good cross training schedule.

In August, it was just too hot to run. So I skated and walked. Always keeping in shape, just never running.

September came. Amazing how quickly a year goes. I figured I better start doing some running if I wanted to run the marathon. They weren't going to allow canoes or skates no matter how much I pleaded.

So on September 7, I started what I considered my real training. I jogged one time around the park. Okay, it wasn't a marathon, but it was a start. My plan was to increase the amount of times around the park until I got to thirteen miles, half the marathon. I had heard that if you can do half the marathon you can do the whole thing. I don't know the logic, but that was my goal.

By October, I was jogging eight miles. My knees began to hurt, but I kept pushing it. The people in the park who had always seen me either skating or walking started cheering me on when I told them I was doing the marathon. Every day they would encourage me. I felt like Rocky.

People started offering running tips. This one park guy, Jim, who used to be a running coach, told me to alternate between the concrete and the grass to make it easier on my knees. Another guy, Little Anthony, told me build up slow. Turns out later he actually placed a bet with his friends on whether or not I could do it. I felt like a racehorse.

By the time I was up to mile eight, my knees were killing me. I decided to rest a week. On October 10 I hit a milestone. I ran ten miles! I was so proud of myself. I had come far in such a short time, but my knees were paying the price. I soaked my knees in Burrows solution, a remedy of Jim's, and used magnets, a remedy of my mom's home shopping network. The combination seemed to help. There was no way was I giving up now. I didn't want to go through this again next year!

Marathon fever was in the air. Hundreds of buses carried billboards showing a picture of the Verrazano Bridge with the masses running across it.

I started meeting people who had run the marathon before. One literary agent, Julia Lord, told me she had done it in four hours! She was very helpful and gave me hints for race day: "Put Vaseline between your toes, under your arms, and between your legs to prevent chapping and blisters. Wear a garbage bag at the beginning of the race to protect against wind. Bring a bag with dry clothes for after the race. Remember to hydrate and take plenty of power gels. As soon as the race is over, take four Advils, then three more at bedtime and two the next morning; you'll need it."

That Vaseline thing sounded pretty disgusting, but if it would save my skin from rubbing off, I was ready to get greased.

Joey Novick found out I was running and told me he was glad I was finally brave enough to do it. He wished me good luck.

I was getting excited. I felt like an Olympic trainer. This was the most I ever trained for an adventure. It was exciting to see how my body was changing and building up endurance.

By October 12, I had slowed down to just two miles. I started taking One-A-Day joint pills to help my knees. I was determined, but I didn't want to be stupid either.

On October 17, I did another ten miles. This time I did it in one hour and thirty-seven minutes. YES! I was very proud of myself. But one of my knees was still feeling weak. I decided this was my halfway point. If I was going to be able to run the marathon, I needed to stop my training. The marathon was only two weeks away.

To keep up my stamina for the next two weeks, I skated, walked, rode my stationary bike, and jogged lightly.

Meanwhile, Steve claimed he had been training on the treadmill. Because of our work schedules, we had stopped training together. A week before the marathon, he wanted to pull out. He said he'd never wanted to run it and was only doing it to make me happy.

Adrenaline Adventures

For some reason I felt betrayed. Why did he wait so long to tell me? I felt scared and abandoned. My partner wanted to drop out. This was a big challenge and I wanted someone I knew to do it with me. But at the same time, I wanted him to enjoy it, not be miserable every step of the way. And that's a lot of steps to be miserable with.

I told him I would try to find a substitute runner. At this late point, there were no takers. No one had trained who wasn't already running, and besides if any runner were caught wearing another runner's number, both people would be disqualified from all future marathons. Maybe Steve had a plan after all!

With no stunt doubles, Steve said he would keep his word and run it with me. He added emphatically that I'd owe him big time. A phrase he likes to use often. All I kept thinking is he better not have a heart attack.

On Thursday November 4, Steve and I went to the Expo to pick up our racing packs. We brought our sacred acceptance cards. Steve waited in the car and I went in first. I went through a maze of roped off lines, almost equal to that of any Great Adventure ride. The line ended at a row of tables with boxes of numbers labeled alphabetically. I went over to Box C, showed my card, and got my pack.

The pack contained my racing number, the commemorative 2000 ChampionChip, a long-sleeved T-shirt with the 2000 NYC Marathon logo on it, a UPS bag in which to keep belongings to be checked on the day of the race, a baggage tag with my name, a number to stick on the UPS bag, an invitation to the pre-race pasta party at Tavern on the Green the night before the race, an invitation to the awards ceremony and celebration after the race, and some final instructions.

After you got the numbers you could walk around the Expo center and go empty your wallet buying running related items. There were places to purchase every kind of apparel, massage tables, tables to pre-pay for video taping of the marathon, anything you could imagine that had to do with running was there, except a new pair of legs.

That night when we got home we looked over the final instructions. I felt like I was reading the instructions from Mission Impossible. "There are three start lines on the day of the race, Blue, Green, and Red. The color on your number indicates you starting assignment.

Fran Capo

Male runners with times under 4:00:00 have been divided between Blue and Green Starts. Females runners with times under 4:00:00 have been assigned F numbers and are positioned at the front of the Red Start. Any man found running with these women will be disqualified. All other runners are spread out in time order between all three starts. If you wish to run with someone who is assigned a different corral than you, you go to the highest number corral. Each corral will have 1000 numbers, line up appropriately. Runners will be called to the start at 10:20 A.M. The official start time is 10:50. Please fill out all the medical information on the back of your number in case of emergency. WNBC will cover the broadcast live for five hours, so set your VCR and look your best."

Great, no pressure, the whole world was watching. What if I took the wrong route? I wasn't that familiar with Brooklyn and the Bronx. That's when I found out about the famous blue line that is drawn for the whole length of the course. You can't get lost! With that minor detail out of the way, all I had to concentrate on was running.

The day before the marathon, I started feeling very nervous and anxious. I was getting a tight feeling in my chest. All my friends knew I was doing this. A lot of them had called to wish me good luck. I wanted to finish it, and I had never run so long a distance. I also didn't want to wind up needing knee surgery.

I prepared all my things for the big day: power bars, power gels, Advil, garbage bag, fanny pack, gloves, sports bra, anti-sweat socks, hand warmers, and running pants. I decided to put an iron-on transfer on the back of my T-shirt of the cover of my book *It Happened in New York*. Hey, with all those people out there, I figured it was great advertising. I'd be a running billboard.

That night, Steve and I loaded up on carbs (which Steve liked), but we didn't attend the pre-marathon pasta party. Why you ask? Because, thinking I was superwoman (with a bum knee), I decided I should totally exhaust myself and do a comedy show at the Cedarhurst Firehouse that night instead. Steve didn't like this. He just shook his head once again. "Capo, I don't know about you. Did you ever hear the word *rest*?"

I laughed. Okay, maybe I do push it to the limit at times. No one at the show believed I was running the marathon the next morning.

Adrenaline Adventures

I got home at midnight, which still left me with five hours of sleep. I was really feeling anxious. I finally dozed off to sleep at one. I dreamt of a treadmill chasing me and yelling, "Run! Run!"

Sunday, November 5 arrived. This was it. I woke up at five. I called Steve to make sure he was up and on the way over to my house. I ate a quick breakfast, and at six o'clock sharp, Steve rang my doorbell. He was sporting a lumberjack shirt and looking like he was going to kill me. But I did see a twinkle in his eyes; of course it might have been tears.

We drove to Manhattan and parked the car on Park and 47th Street. Then we walked to the buses at Fifth Avenue and 42nd Street near the public library. There were about five hundred city buses all lined up to transport the thirty thousand runners to the base of the Verrazano Bridge in Staten Island, the starting point for this 26.2 mile sojourn. It was extremely organized. Everyone was in a great mood. The volunteers were yelling on megaphones, "You look great! Have a great race!" People were laughing. The air was electric.

We waited about thirty minutes to get on the buses. On the bus everyone was chatty. We met a mother and daughter from Alaska. They had been training for a year. I had images of them running on the ice and sliding all over the place.

Steve sat there silent, just shaking his head and saying, "Capo, I can't believe you got me into this." But by now he was grinning.

The bus dropped us off at the Fort Wadsworth military base, the pre-start holding area. Masses piled off the buses. Instructions were being blasted from speakers in all different languages. As we got off the bus the instructions were being barked out in German. Slowly we inched our way to our designated fenced-in area. For a second I got a strange feeling that I was in a weird Twilight Zone episode and this was some cruel trick to eliminate the weakest runners from the globe. A chill ran up my spine. The instructions soon turned to English and I felt a lot more comfortable. Steve and I were in the Red area (that's for slow runners, in case you had any doubt).

The military base was enormous and was a massive hub of activity. Massage booths, food, and first aid tents were set up everywhere. A band was playing jazz on one end, and then there was a warm-up exercise routine for those individuals inclined to expend some energy before the race.

A tent for Sunday morning religious ceremonies was also set up, so no one would miss services. (I'm sure many people were praying that they would finish the race.) Helicopters flew overhead and television crews were scattered about interviewing people sprawled out along the lawn. Runners were lined up by the hundreds to use the 550 port-a-potties. And of course, to expedite the bathroom process, the world's longest urinal, a 380-foot-long giant metal pipe cut in half, was available for less modest men.

There was so much to check out. It felt like a festival. Everywhere we looked, people were doing something—whether it was getting a Breathe Right nose patch put on or just chowing down on a last-minute bagel.

Since my knee was still hurting I decided to get a massage to loosen it up. Then I went over to the television crews and tried to convince them to let me rattle off some runners' names in my fast talking style. They almost went for it until some famous world-class runner showed up and upstaged me. At least I tried. Steve just shook his head and repeated his mantra to me, "No one is safe around you Capo. No one!"

It was still only 8:30 and the race didn't start until 10:50.

We stretched out on the lawn, ate some bagels, met some people from England, and then did a last-minute pit stop. It was very windy so we kept our jackets on until the last available minute.

With twenty minutes of the start time, we walked over to the dozens of color-coded and alphabetically numbered UPS trucks to put our baggage away. This was organization at its finest.

It was time to get ready. We pinned the running numbers onto each other. I was number 39793. We donned our garbage bags, gloves, and hats and took last long drinks of water and rechecked the running chips on our sneakers to make sure they were secure. With everything in place, we stretched and warmed up. We agreed that if we got separated we would meet at the finish line. We kissed and wished each other good luck.

Then the announcement came. "Runners to your start lines." Everyone went to their respective corral just like herds of nervous

Adrenaline Adventures

sheep. We went to the red starting line and waited with great anticipation. There we were, shoulder to shoulder with thirty-thousand other people about to embark on the same journey.

My body knew the second the starting cannon went off that it was going to be put to the ultimate test of endurance—that once I started, I wouldn't stop for the next few hours. I could feel my heart pounding and my knee twitching. The tension was intense.

To keep warm, everyone was jumping up and down with their garbage bags or old clothes on.

Then the canon sounded and the crowd let out a cheer. The 2000 NYC Marathon had begun. The first few minutes we could only walk as everyone made their way across the start line. Minutes ticked away. The first few miles we had to be extra careful as runners were discarding their clothes and tossing them to the side as they got hot. These clothes would later to be donated to the homeless via the Road Runners club.

All of a sudden space seemed to open up. Steve and I had finally crossed the start line on the Verrazano Bridge. The chips recorded our time. Our race had officially begun.

My heart was pumping rapidly. I had driven over this bridge a thousand times and never realized that it was a hill. The view was gorgeous with the water gleaming on the side. The archways seemed massive as we ran under them. I couldn't believe I was doing this. I was actually going to run 26.2 miles. People were stopping to take pictures, and suddenly I wished I had my camera. This was an event of a lifetime. I wanted to capture it. Too late now—keep my mind on running.

About halfway over the bridge, I lost sight of Steve. I kept turning back but could only see him through the thousands of strange but determined faces. My self talk kicked in. "Okay, Capo, you're on your own." I didn't expect it to happen so soon. "Just concentrate on running, Capo."

By the time I got to the other side of the bridge, my knee was already hurting. This was not a good sign. I slowed down to toss my garbage bag off to get more comfortable. As I did I noticed some people had stopped to pee. Ah, the male advantage.

Fran Capo

I had already run two miles. Only twenty-four more to go. I was going to do this as much by the book as I could—drinking water at every stop, alternating with Gatorade and power gels every hour. I kept thinking, "Slow and steady wins the race."

As we turned off the bridge and onto Brooklyn's Fourth Avenue, I was shocked. There were thousands of New Yorkers lining the streets cheering and yelling out words of encouragement. There were banners and smiles everywhere. Firemen, policemen, children, old people, black, white, and Hispanic—everyone standing side by side. Such unity! I was never so proud to be a New Yorker.

People were cheering their friends on. Some runners had names on the backs of their shirts like "Goose" and "Bigman." The crowd would pick up on it and yell, "Go Goose! Go Bigman!" If only I had put Fast Talker on my shirt. Just as I thought that, a giant rhinoceros ran by, then another. Two of the runners were dressed in these big clunky costumes as the male and female counterparts. It was great, a real crowd-pleaser.

With all the cheering, it was hard NOT to run. The crowd kept you going. Little kids had their hands out so you could slap them five. Adults were smiling, and the hundreds of volunteers were standing with their arms extended out at every water station—so you could grab a cup and keep running.

The borough seemed to go on forever. At one point I asked someone if we were still in Brooklyn. Some guy answered, "Yes, you are. Now you go, girl. Only twenty-one more miles to go." Ah, didn't need to hear that. Someone else yelled out, "I can tell you where the subway is, if you like." A real wise guy. I was hoping Steve didn't hear that.

I saw the timing pad at the 10K mark, and I stepped hard on it. It registered one hour, twenty-two minutes, and eight seconds on my chip.

Eleven miles into Brooklyn I ate my first Power Bar. My knee was really hurting, so even though they recommended no Advil during the race, I took one anyway, since I felt it was buffered with the Power Bar. The Vaseline had rubbed off of my feet, and I had developed a blister. I didn't want to think about the pain. This was as

Adrenaline Adventures

far as I had run in my training. The rest was all uncharted territory. I was determined to finish.

Then I saw this old guy trotting past me and smiling. I decided I had to be able to keep pace with this guy. He told me he was seventy-five years old and this was his 101st marathon! WOW! I decided that if that guy could do it, so could I.

We ran for a while together, and then he said, "I'll see you at the finish line" and sprinted off. Talk about embarrassing.

I kept running and smiling. I felt a little on display with thousands of people watching. The experience was a load on all my senses. I'd never felt anything like this before. I could imagine how the fastest runners felt, as the world watched them run, betting on who the winner would be.

We were still in Brooklyn, and I had to go to the bathroom, but the line was too long and I didn't want to slow down my time. I decided to wait until I saw another bathroom area. I was hoping I could sweat away the sensation. As I was thinking about the bathroom, Mouaziz, the lead male runner from Morocco, finished the marathon in two hours and twenty one minutes! He was running like the wind with a gigantic lead all the way. It was fascinating to think that I still had more than halfway to go and this guy had finished!

As we headed into Queens, I looked at my watch. Not bad. Then cheers went up. Lyudmila Petrova, the lead female from Russia, who had given up running for seven years, had finished in two hours, twenty-nine minutes, and thirteen seconds. Did these people have jets for feet? I wait longer in traffic to go five miles. I was very happy for them, knowing how wonderful they must have felt not only to win, but also to be done with the race.

It truly touched me that every street, in every borough, in every neighborhood, was lined with people supporting the runners. And not just the top runners, ALL the runners. The top runners had already finished. The people were out there for us common folk.

The only place along the course that you could run without eyes gazing upon you, were on the bridges. No onlookers could line up there. It gave you time to mentally regroup. You could even walk a little, if you chose to.

As I approached the center of the Bridge Queensborough Bridge (aka 59th Street Bridge) my foot went over the third timing pad. I looked up at the clock, which read 2:55:10. I was at the halfway point. At this pace I could finish in about five and a half to six hours. I still wasn't tired. But my knee was really hurting. I was determined to finish at 5:59. I didn't want the clock turning to 6:00.

As I came off the 59th Street Bridge and turned the corner to First Avenue, I was almost paralyzed by what I saw. As far as my eye could see, down the entire stretch of First Avenue, the streets were filled with people on both sides, two and three rows deep. The runners were all spread out, so it was almost like jogging down this massive street alone. I was getting the world's longest red carpet treatment.

I was actually a little embarrassed and intimidated by so many people. Me, a performer who is used to hundreds of people looking at me felt naked running there for the world to watch. I jogged from 59th Street to 125th Street without stopping. It seemed like the easiest part of the run since the streets went by so fast and I had a way of measuring them. Besides, there was no way my ego would let me stop in the middle of a six-lane street with thousands watching.

Finally, at the Willis Avenue Bridge, I stopped and walked a bit. It was the first time I'd stopped jogging and my body felt it. As I walked over the Third Avenue Bridge, where no eyes were looking, some Italian guy next to me started talking in broken English. We didn't understand each other, but we smiled.

As I entered Harlem, I started running again (maybe that was just an old New York habit). Music was playing loud, and bands on the street were cheering us on. Kids offered us oranges and covered candy.

Then I saw a guy on crutches pass me. Okay, that was it. First the seventy-five-year-old guy in Brooklyn, now a guy on crutches is passing me. I picked up the pace again.

I started jogging next to an Asian girl from Phoenix. We ran over the twentieth mile timing pad together. Our time was four hours, thirty-three minutes, and nine seconds. At that rate we could finish in five and a half hours. She told me it was her first marathon too and that her leg hurt. Between the two of us, we had one good pair of legs. We stayed together for another three miles. Then she told me about the hill.

"What hill?" I gulped. She said that just before you entered Central Park for your final few miles there was a hill. It's not too big but after running for almost twenty miles, it seems like a killer. It seemed like a cruel joke.

I mentally prepared myself. I jogged up the hill, fighting the wind. I felt as if I was standing still. Both knees were hurting now. But I was doing better on time than I had anticipated, so I didn't want to stop. Policemen were smiling and saying, "Only a few more miles." All of a sudden I realized the winner had been finished for hours! Probably was taking a shower somewhere. How amazing is that? All I wanted to do was be done with it.

I liked the quiet of Central Park. There were no more massive rows of people, just cheerful bunches scattered around, still offering encouragement. I saw the seventy-five-year-old guy and the guy on crutches up ahead. My goal was to at least keep pace with them. I took two more Advils and ate a Power Bar so I wouldn't get nauseous.

The pain was overwhelming. I only had three more miles to go. I was five hours and five minutes into the race. I wanted to try to finish by 5:30. I tried to jog, but all I could do was a fast walk. I had hit the wall.

The last three miles seemed to go on forever. I couldn't understand how I could walk for so long and still not have gone a mile. Where were those mile markers? The clock kept ticking. Then I decided that if I couldn't run, I would use every last bit of energy when I saw the finish line.

Finally, after an eternity on that blue line, I had the finish line in sight. I knew they took pictures as you crossed the line, so I was determined to smile.

I tried to judge the distance so I wouldn't peter out at the finish line. Nothing is more embarrassing than running full speed and then dropping right before the finish line and have to be carried over with a stretcher. I wanted to come across strong.

I decided it was now or never. I started to run as fast as I could, my knees hurting every step of the way. But I kept smiling. The finish

Fran Capo

line got closer and closer. People were yelling, "Good Girl! Great finish! Almost there."

My heart was racing Only a few more steps and then YES! I crossed the finish line at 6:02:52. Two minutes after I wanted, but I didn't care. I had done it! I had run the 2000 New York City Marathon with only two months of training. I still had knees, and I had done it. They placed the medal over my head. I had never been so proud as I was then.

I kept walking, so my legs wouldn't stiffen up. It was already dark. At first I wasn't cold, but then my body started to shiver. I wrapped the thermal sheet they gave me around myself. I took two more Advils and retrieved my bag from the UPS truck. Then I paced and waited for Steve to cross the line.

I waited and waited and waited. I estimated he would finish an hour behind me. I was freezing, and my body was getting stiff. As I waited, a volunteer told me that they were thinking about getting rid of that last hill next year.

"What are they going to do, let the runners plow it?" I joked.

"No, reroute the race," she said.

Great, if I did that hill, I want everyone else to experience it. Then she told me about this woman, Zoe, the world's slowest marathon runner. She said Zoe has MS and takes twenty-four hours to run the marathon, and that there's even a McDonalds that stays open all night just for her. She has been doing the marathon for ten years. I thought maybe Steve was competing for her record.

I started to worry after an hour and a half. The marathon officials looked up Steve's name and told me he had passed the halfway point, so I knew he was on his way.

Just then I felt a tap on my shoulder. I spun around in amazement "How could you be behind me? I didn't see you cross the finish line. There's no way you could have beaten me."

He smiled and said, "I ran until Jackson Avenue in Queens, just by the half way point. Then I took the subway."

"What? You cheated. You took the subway. Who are you, Rosie Ruiz?"

He smiled and then said, "I've been freezing my butt off worrying what happened to you."

"Me? I was running."

A miscommunication of where we were supposed to meet had him calling my mom, his sister and nearly the police thinking something had happened to me. We both decided we were in too much pain to argue.

We limped slowly to the car. Even lifting our feet to the curb was painful. Steve turned to me and said, "In this moment of pain, I want you to promise me right now, you will never ask me to do another marathon. I do not want my feet pounding the pavement ever again for twenty-six miles. I mean it, Fran, or you walk home." I nodded my head and promised no more feet pounding. I just wanted to get in the car.

When we got to my house we had to climb three flights of stairs, it could have been Mount Everest the way we were holding onto the banister and pulling ourselves up.

We examined our injuries: four blisters, two injured knees and three black toenails.

The next few days we both walked like Fred Sanford, shuffling everywhere we went. My big toenail eventually fell off, and the blisters healed and went away. Within two weeks, my knee wasn't hurting as much.

I called Joey Novick, the man responsible for nudging me into running the marathon, and told him the great news. He said, "Not bad for ONE marathon. Let me know when you get to THREE marathons like me." I wanted to crawl through the phone and strangle him, but my knees still hurt. Then I asked him something I hadn't asked before. "Just how long did it take you to finish?" He hemmed and hawed and I think he said eight hours. My competitive spirit was satisfied.

Even with all the pain, the freezing, and the running, it was worth it. With will, determination, training (and maybe a few Advils) I realized that I can get through anything. I look at that medal proudly every now and then and think, "I pushed my body to limits I never thought I could, and survived. I also pushed my relationship to the limits and that survived too. The body and spirit are very resilient."

To this day, I have wonderful memories forever etched in my heart of the marathon. I proved to myself I could do it plus there's

Fran Capo

that little added satisfaction that I beat Joey's time and have a cool medal to show for it. If you've never done it, you should try it at least once in your life—even if you have to walk it.

Once is enough for me, though. As for Steve, I promised not to enter him in any more marathons, and I will stick to that.

Although, I couldn't wait to show him a brochure I had picked up. It's for a forty-two mile bike race through the five boroughs. Steve likes biking. I know he does. And I'll make sure, just like I promised that the whole time his feet will never touch the ground.

Adrenaline Adventures

Chapter 32
Adventure at a Glance - Dare to Do it   Mild to Wild Scale: 5

Title: Running a Marathon
Children allowed: No
Age requirement: Anyone 18 or older by Marathon Sunday.
Length of trip: 26.2 miles
Where to try this adventure: New York City
Call the Road Runners club at 212-423-2292, but your best bet is going to for an marathonmailer@nyrrc.org application or to visit their Web site at www.nyrrc.org. There are also major marathons in Boston, Chicago, Los Angeles, and other cities around the world.
Best time of year: The NYC Marathon is only held on the first Sunday in November.
Approximate cost: NYRR members $70/non-members $80
Reservations necessary: Yes, you need to apply for a running number; no guarantees for first timers unless you have done nine qualifying NYRRC races.
Fitness requirements: Must be able to run/jog/walk 26 miles
Personal gear required: Good broken-in running shoes, wick away clothing, blister-free socks, Vaseline for your feet
What NOT to bring: Cotton clothes, extra baggage
Photo opportunities: You can get a finish line photo and videotape.

Notes: The city streets reopen eight and a half hours after the starting canon sounds.

Cool trivia: The New York City marathon began in September in Central Park in 1970, the brainchild of co-founder Fred Lebow. The first race had 127 people entered, and only 55 finished. In 1976, to celebrate the U.S. bicentennial, the marathon moved out of the confines of Central Park and onto the streets of the five boroughs. The marathon has been run through the five boroughs every year since. Today, the race has 35,000 participants, two million spectators, and 12,000 volunteers.

"The road to success is filled with many tempting parking spots."
—Fran Capo

Chapter 33
"Don't Forget to Put on Your Back-up Lights" Backward Race

Ever since I ran my first 10K race in June of 1996 for Advil (which is rather appropriate, since I needed one afterward) I've been a member of the New York Road Runners Club. I don't really consider myself a runner since I'm not out there every day pounding the track. I'm more of an event runner, when a running event comes up, I run, rather I jog, for a few weeks prior.

The NYRRC keeps its members inspired by offering a variety of races. As a member you get a brochure in the mail or an e-mail about upcoming events. I've done a couple of midnight runs and once I ran the New York City Marathon.

As I opened a recent brochure, I noticed an April Fools' Day Run. The run was being held at Washington Square Park at 10:00 A.M. But being that it was held on the joker's day, there was a catch ... you had to run it *backward*. I noticed a warning at the bottom of the brochure: "WARNING! Running in reverse does different things to different people. Some—peculiarly—speed up, most slow down, some feel fine, some get dizzy, and a small number have been known to fall down. If you experience dizziness when retro running, please slow yourself down—walk if you need to—and the sensation will pass."

I'd never thought about running backward, and the warning only made it more intriguing. I called my adventure cohort, my boyfriend, Steve. "Nope," he said. "And I'd wear a pillow on my butt if I was you."

I couldn't believe it. He had done the marathon with me (well, half of it ... he took the train after thirteen miles) and wouldn't do one lousy mile backward. I called a few other friends—there were no takers. I was on my own with this one.

It was March 20, and I had twelve days to try this backward running thing out. The next morning, I went to the park to do my morning walk and decided to give this retro walking a try. I looked around to see how many of the "regular" park walkers were there. After all this did seem a little embarrassing. (This coming from a girl who picked Steve up at the airport dressed as Mae West when it wasn't even Halloween!) Nonetheless I was glad the coast was clear.

I began to walk backward. I had to decide which shoulder to look over to get the best view and to make sure I didn't fall in the lake. As I was walking, this Asian man stopped, looked at me with one of those bobbing puppy dog stares, and said, "Why you walk backwards?"

"Oh, it's for a race." That always seems like a good answer. You can do the craziest thing, but if it's for a world record, a race, or a good cause, people cheer you on.

Satisfied, he gave me some advice," You need rear view mirror."

"Good Idea!" I said. "And I could probably use some back-up lights too."

He nodded, half smiled and continued, "And stare at the curb so you know where you are going. You don't want to bang into tree or fall in water. Good luck."

He walked a few feet and then started to do the warm up exercises for Tai Chi. I figured if he could be dancing like a crane in the middle of the park, I can walk backward and not feel awkward.

So I started jogging backward. Just then I saw my friend Charlie, who has his own peculiar run—he runs sideways, like a car with a bad axle, but he is fast like a demon. "Hey, Fran, put more into it like a quarterback." Boy, advice at every turn.

I went backward up my first steep hill, keeping all the coaching tips in mind. Suddenly I felt muscles I never knew I had, which is always surprising when you think you are in shape.

As the hill flattened out, I had to navigate carefully because there were a lot of potholes. It was fascinating to me that I had to focus on such a basic thing like not falling down while walking, even if it was backward. I thought, "This is what it must have been like when I was a baby just starting to walk, except this time I'm not drooling."

It was odd seeing things get farther away as I ran, rather than closer. It was a totally new perspective, and I was enjoying it. I read somewhere that if you force yourself to do things differently, like brush your teeth with the opposite hand or take a different route home, it increases your creativity, because your brain says, "Hey, what's this we're doing? ... I gotta think now." So I rationalized that this new venture was good for the mind and the body.

I came to a set of stairs that I had to go down. As creative as I was feeling, there was no way I was doing a rewind motion down the steps. Even us nuts have our limits.

At the bottom, I continued backward around the park. I happened to be keeping pace with this woman and her dog, so after a few minutes, I felt the need to explain. "Hi, I don't normally run backwards, just training for an April Fools' Day fun run." We struck up a conversation and it turned out she was a fellow adventurer. She told me about a cool safari she went on where you get to live among orangutans for a few weeks in Sumatra. (I once had breakfast with an orangutan in Singapore, but that's a whole other story.) Anyway, I wasn't even sure where Sumatra was, but I noted it for future reference—I've since found out it's in Indonesia. She wished me good luck on my run, and I continued on my way.

This running backward got a lot of attention because it was different. I actually loved the kidlike feeling I was getting doing something so silly. Then it hit me. Hey, I have a kid. This would be a good time to pull rank and enlist my son, Spencer, into the race.

Adrenaline Adventures

He thought the whole thing was silly, and when I said, "That's exactly the point!" he just shrugged and agreed to keep me company.

On March 22, I faxed in our applications in. For a mere seventeen dollars for me and twelve dollars for Spencer, we were signed up for the backward privilege. We signed up as a team, and since both of us are standup comics, Spencer came up with the name "The Funnybacks".

The next few days it rained, so I didn't get to practice. Then there was a freak snowstorm, and even though I was the only one in the park with all that virgin snow, I wasn't willing to make backward footprints. I did make a smiley face and a snow angel though.

The days were passing fast. I wanted Spencer to get at least one practice run in. Even if it was an April Fools' Day race, we didn't want to be doing any pratfalls—especially ones that were unrehearsed.

Somehow, I never got a chance to do another backward practice, and Spencer didn't get to try one at all. We weren't too worried. After all, it was only one measly mile! I figured Spencer was a kid so he would have plenty of energy, and if I could do twenty-six miles in a marathon, one backward mile should be easy.

The night before the race I performed at the Comedy Cabaret in Northeast Philadelphia. Steve was with me, and we drove back that night so I could be home to get up early for the race. It was 12:30 P.M. when we arrived home—no, wait, it was 1:30 thanks to Daylight Savings Time. Ah, less sleep than I thought!

Morning came too soon, as it often does when you are sleep-deprived. It seemed ironic in a way that I was going to go backward on a day when we were supposed to spring forward.

Spencer and I got up at 8:00 A.M. and drove to Manhattan. We got there at 9:15 in time to pick up our numbers and T-shirts for the race. The numbers tags read, "NYHRC (New York Heath and Racquetball Club) Backwards 5 Miler." For a moment I panicked ... 5 miles! I thought it was only one mile. Then I read the subtext. "(P. S. It's still only a mile! - April Fools - April 1, 2001)" I was an upside down number 28, and Spencer was number 126.

It was pretty cold out, so the layered look was in order. We put on our shirts and put our numbers on the back, which was a change

Fran Capo

since in all the Road Runners races, you have to put them on the front.

Since it was a fun run, we didn't have to wear our ChampionChips. (The little devices that tie onto your sneaker to electronically record your running time as you pass the starting line and the finish line.)

There were only about a hundred runners. Some had gotten into the spirit of the day and were dressed as clowns and jesters. One guy simply put his regular clothes on backward.

A first prize of a year's free membership to the runners club was given to each of the top male and female runners. The race was divided into three categories: the masters for those forty and older and then males and females. It turned out that there was no team event.

The backward race record for the fastest male was held by Bud Badyna, who did it in 6:40 in 1994, and Barbara Brewer was the fastest female at 7:29 in 1992. I can't even do a forward mile in that time!

At exactly ten o'clock, the master of ceremonies, a British fellow, began his announcement. "Welcome, everyone, to this Fifteenth Annual New York Health and Racquet Club Backwards Mile Race. The only race of its kind, and it's here in New York. We have some repeat runners, and we even have a man who flew in from Japan just two days ago to enter this race. I ask the masters to come to the start line. Everyone is to complete four laps around the orange coned off area in the park, a total of one mile. This is the first year we are doing it here in Washington Square Park; normally it's done in the Village. It's drizzling so we ask that you be extra careful. A few years ago we had one fellow run into a light pole, so please be careful. Let's see if we can set some world records today. At the sound of the horn, we begin."

Five seconds later, the horn blew and the masters were off. One guy fell immediately, but he got right back up. Maybe a pillow wasn't such a bad idea. People did look silly running backward. As they came around the first bend, one guy was clearly ahead. Four laps later, he came in at eight minutes, nine seconds.

Now the women were up. I handed Spencer my car keys and the camera. At the sound of the horn, we began running. On first bend, my foot slipped on a manhole cover. That sent an adrenaline rush

Adrenaline Adventures

though my body. I should have brought that rear view mirror. I was jogging at the first turn. I was doing pretty good. I could see who was behind me, at least.

As I did the first lap, my thigh muscles started to burn. I didn't feel this way until mile fifteen in the marathon, what was up with that? I walked a few more steps then quickly started jogging again as I saw people gaining on me. By the second lap, my legs were really burning. This was pathetic! My self-talk kicked in, "Okay, Capo, it's just for fun. Walk if you have to."

No, my ego wanted to run. So I kept running. There was this other girl next to me, number 155, and she was keeping pace with me. I commented to her that it was less painful to run the marathon forward than this mile backward. She nodded in agreement. We both decided to race each other to keep motivated. Everyone on the sidelines was encouraging the runners. "You can do it, watch out for that curve. Careful ... you're almost there. Watch out for that pole!"

Spencer cheered me on. He had a bit of a grin as I finished at 16:42. My buddy, number 155, came in a 16:43. We hugged and congratulated each other.

Now the men were up. Spencer was there in his bright red feathered coat, ready to run with the big guys. As he rounded his first lap I saw that his cheeks were as red as his coat but that he was keeping a good pace. He had a wide stride, which I found out later makes it easier to run backward. Had I only read the manual!

Meanwhile, this one guy was sprinting backward as if he was being chased by a bear. He wasn't even bothering to look back! Wide strides, fast pace, it looked like he could possibly set a backward world record! At 6:30 this guy was sprinting around the final bend. The crowd was chanting, "You can do it!" He sprinted faster, and at 6:37 he crossed the finish line while the crowd cheered wildly. Flashes went off, and cameramen ran up to interview him. He had set a new world record!

Meanwhile, the rest of the pack was still running. Spencer was pacing himself with three guys. On his second lap, he came in at 7:08. Still red and going strong. By his third lap, he was at 11:08, and I was thinking, "Hey, my kid might beat my time! And, without any practice!"

Fran Capo

During the fourth lap, he was struggling, but when he saw the clock and the finish line just in sight, he dug in and ran like a wild man. He crossed the finish line at 14:46, beating his mom by 1:96. I was impressed.

I walked over to him, and the first thing he said was, "I think I'm going to throw up." Luckily he didn't. I had him walk around for a bit until he got his forward legs back.

Then we walked to the car, tired but full of adrenaline. It was a great way to start the day. Spencer looked at me and said, "Mom, do we have to do anything else today?"

I looked him straight in the eyes and said, "We have another race at noon." His look was priceless. I thought he was going to faint right there. "April Fools," I said.

He sighed. "Thank goodness. I'm going home to sleep!"

The way he said that reminded me of what my friend Anna always says. "Fran, that kid of yours is going to grow up to be a mattress salesman just so he can get some rest! He'll be exhausted by the time he's twenty!"

Twenty, I figured, was a long way away. But at least he had a month to rest—after all, the forty-two-mile bike ride wasn't until May 6.

Adrenaline Adventures

Chapter 33
Adventure at a Glance - Dare to Do itMild to Wild Scale: 2
Title: Backward Race
Children allowed: Yes
Age requirement: Ten and up.
Length of trip: Ten minutes to a half hour, depending on how fast you run
Where to try this adventure: New York City Road Runners Club at 212-423-2292, or visit their Web site at http://www.nyrrc.org.
Best time of year: April Fools' Day
Approximate cost: $17 adults/ $12 kids
Reservations necessary: Yes, you have to register and get a number.
Fitness requirements: Must be able to run a mile.
Personal gear required: Sneakers, running clothes
What NOT to bring: Tight clothes
Photo opportunities: Yes

Notes: I have since run backward on occasion in the park, because it's great exercise and a good way to work other leg muscles—just watch out for potholes. The backward race now takes place in Hudson River Park.

Cool trivia: In a laboratory at the University of Oregon, a Dr. Bates and a Dr. McCaw found the benefits of backward running to be: a more erect posture, improved cardiovascular function, improvement of muscle balance, prevention of injuries, and increased neuro-muscular function.

Further, backward running is used in many sports: figure skating, gymnastics, fencing, diving, rowing, skiing, trampoline jumping, football, basketball, rugby, and tennis. If athletes included serious backward running in his or her training the athletes developed better health, more energy, and more creativity.

"Inhale life, exhale pain."
—Spencer Patterson

Chapter 34
"This Ain't No Stationary Bike!"
Bike New York

After I ran the New York City Marathon, I looked for another long-distance endurance test, one that was not quite as taxing on the feet, or at minimum, one that wouldn't end with my toenails falling off.

I came across the perfect adventure in a Chinese restaurant, of all places. A brochure for an event called Bike New York. The brochure had a picture of the Statue of Liberty riding a bicycle, and I figured if that gargantuan could do it, so could I.

I opened the brochure and read, "On May 6th, you'll enjoy the awesome experience of riding 42 miles on traffic free streets through the five boroughs of New York City." Traffic free! That alone was worth seeing. It continued, "Thirty thousand cyclists ... start at Battery Park ... end up by going over the Verrazano Bridge and into Fort Wadsworth for a festival at the finish line."

I looked at the detailed map of the route on the next page. Memories of the marathon came back to me. There were five rest

Adrenaline Adventures

stops along the bike route for water, refreshments, bike repair, first aid, and portable restrooms. At the end of the tour you could take the Staten Island Ferry back to Manhattan to get back to your car. It seemed like a fun challenge.

Immediately I thought of who I could enlist to do the tour with me. Of course, my son, Spencer, and boyfriend, Steve, came to mind. We had done two twenty-five-mile bike rides in Australia and one in upstate New York. So what would be the big deal if we doubled the route? Nothing a little training couldn't fix.

They both immediately liked the idea. That's a switch. Steve didn't own a bike but said he would get one before the race, which is good since *after* the race it wouldn't have been much use. With two biking companions already established, I decided to enlist more.

I called my then writing partner, Anna, and her boyfriend, Steve S. Anna's bike was in Florida, and Steve S. didn't want to get his fixed. Okay, I called my friends Dina and Chris. Turns out they had just finished doing some mountain biking and were game. The stage was set. We had one month to plan.

I faxed in our registrations. It was twenty-seven dollars for adults who registered early, and there was a ten-dollar flat fee for kids. All we had to do was start training. I decided it might be a good idea to pick up a book on biking tips. I bought *900 All-Time Best Tips*. I figured if I couldn't get anything useful out of that book, I might as well walk.

The book had a section called "55 Tips for Better Distance Riding." The first thing it said was that "your long distance limit is about three times the duration of your average training ride." Since all of us had done twenty-five miles in the past without pain, I figured the forty-two miles shouldn't be a problem. It went on to give other useful information: "Do a negative split. Ride the second half faster than the first. Three days before the ride consume a lot of carbohydrates. During the ride eat before you feel hungry and drink before you are thirsty, with a general rule of consuming two bottles of water per hour on a warm day."

That's a lot of water! I sure hoped I would sweat it out, since I didn't want to stop every few miles for a bathroom break.

Fran Capo

I continued to read. "Vary your riding positions so you don't get stiff. Stretch before you ride. If fatigue sets in concentrate on form, not on the distance left in the ride." Then the authors talked about being prepared by having a multi-tool, a spare tire repair kit, and a spare spoke. A spare spoke, what's next, a spare handlebar?

The advice ended with them saying to bring a raincoat, stuff cotton in your ears if it was windy, roll your clothes so they take up less room in your gear bag, and to distribute weight by putting the heavy items at the lowest point of gravity on your bike.

I now felt prepared. There was one minor problem. I didn't have a bike. I had a Huffy bike from Toys R Us circa 1988 that I had bought for ninety-nine bucks and fixed several times. The bike was on its last legs, and I didn't feel like fixing it again or spending five hundred dollars on new bike. I asked my sister, Sharon, whose brand new bike was sitting in our garage silently pleading, "Ride me. Would someone please ride me?" I answered the plea, asked Sharon and she was fine with it.

For a bike that's been ridden only four times in the past two years, I was surprised it had a flat.

I was surprised it had a flat because it had been ridden only four times in the previous two years. It probably deflated out of boredom. Steve repaired the tire, and I started going on long bike rides. I went on a ten-mile bike ride to Rockaway Beach. Then Spencer and I rode about four miles to a local park. (I guess it wasn't so local.) It felt great to be on a bike again.

Two weeks before the event, we thought it might be a good idea for Steve to purchase his bike. We went to a local bike shop with Steve chanting he was only going to spend four hundred dollars on a bike. Twelve hundred dollars later we came out of the store with his new bike, complete with front and rear shocks, gel seat, front bag, blinker lights, air pump, spare tire, multi-bike tool, water bottles, and new helmets for all of us. So much for chanting.

Steve looked at me and said, "Capo, we better ride a lot more than just this one day. Every adventure you get me into requires different gear."

Adrenaline Adventures

I flashed him a smile and said, "We can go every weekend if you like, dear. And guess what? you don't even need to ask me if you decide to ride alone."

He smirked and shook his head.

Now all we had to do was get a bike rack. Even though on the day of the race, the subways were open to bikers without permits, we decided we wanted to take the car. We didn't want the hassle of lugging our bikes into Manhattan via public transportation.

On the Sunday before the race, we decided we'd better purchase the rack. It was already a busy day with Spencer, who is also an actor, shooting a film all day on location. I left the set, had my mom stand in for me as the parent in charge, and went over to Steve's to go with him to buy a rack.

Steve likes top-of-the-line stuff so he bought a really sturdy four-mount bike rack, which required putting a hitch on his Jeep. Since time was running short and I had to get back to the set before they finished shooting for the day, he crawled under the car himself and put the hitch on. That's what I like; a handyman who knows a screwdriver is more than just a drink.

I could hear Steve under the car saying, "The things I do for you, Capo."

I smiled and handed him another wrench. "It's for us, dear, not just me. You said you wanted a girl who liked adventure ... you got her."

With hitch attached, it was time to test out the bike rack. Steve loaded up his bike and drove it over to my house. Several potholes later, the bike was still mounted strong.

At my house, we unloaded the bike, and the two of us went cruising in my neighborhood. We went cruising fast, as I still had to get back to the set.

Steve's a stronger rider than I am, so he was racing ahead. I was prepared, knowing that this was one competition I wasn't going to win, at least not easily. We finished our ride. I picked up Spencer, and we promised we'd get one good long ride in again during the week. Of course, this never happened. We did a few cursory rides at night.

Fran Capo

With only three days left to race day, we started telling people that we were going to do this marathon bike ride. Steve's secretary, Lisa, laughed. "Fran, you sure do put him through a lot."

His partner Rob said, "Please don't kill my partner. I need him for a few more years."

His sister Loie said, "I sympathize for your sore butts."

As for my family, I got the usual response, an exasperated, "Forty-two miles!" Followed by, "What time do you think you will be home?"

On that Friday, I bought our energy food supply of Gatorade and Power Bars. There would be food such as bananas and oranges at the rest stops to power us, as well.

A hitch in our plans came when I realized Spencer had Confirmation practice on Sunday. Since he'd already missed last Sunday's practice while shooting the film, I didn't want him being confirmed and not knowing what to say to the priest when he handed him his wafer. The words, "Gee, that tastes delicious," wouldn't cut it. Plus, I couldn't picture myself telling the nun, "Listen sister, Spencer is going to miss Confirmation practice again, because he is going bike riding." I'm sure *that* would have gone over well. So, reluctantly, I had Spencer drop out of the bike tour. We both were disappointed.

The night before the bike tour, I stayed over at Steve's house since we had to pick up Chris and Dina at 5:30 in the morning. They only lived one mile from Steve. Instead of doing the logical thing and going to bed early, we both worked on various projects instead. We did, however, pack everything, including the mandatory blue riding vests with our numbers on them. We also packed our safety helmets as you were not allowed to ride without them.

Sunday morning we got up at five. The weather was just right, calling for a high of seventy degrees. We put on our bike shorts, drank some water, ate a bagel, and were out the door and at Dina's by 5:30 sharp.

We loaded their bikes on the rack and drove off to the city after Dina pleaded for a quick pit stop for coffee. She wound up getting into a verbal brawl with the storeowner and left her half-eaten muffin on the counter.

Adrenaline Adventures

We found a parking spot on John Street, not far from Battery Park. We took our bikes off the rack and loaded them up with the necessary supplies. Unfortunately, all the supplies would not fit into the tiny front carriers. We had layers of clothes on that we were sure to shed later, extra water bottles, a first aid kit, the recommended raincoat (to prevent it from raining), and our gel seats. Steve decided to carry these items in his blue knapsack. He strapped it to the back of the bike. It was so big he had to stuff the ends of it under his seat. Bulging, this oversized blue bag looked like it was just waiting to reek havoc. The red back lights on the bottom of Steve's seat gave the bag an evil red glow.

We rode our bikes to Battery Park, did a last-minute port-a-potty stop and then were ushered to the bike lineup on Broadway. There were forty thousand people participating in this race. That's a lot of organizing.

The line of bikes went from Battery Park all the way up to Church and Franklin Street, more than ten city blocks. Mayor Guiliani was there giving a speech about how great it was that so many people came out to support the tour. Of course, we couldn't hear a word of it since we were back in the crowd.

The tour was supposed to start at eight. It was a bit brisk out. Dina was shivering. We stood around talking, taking pictures, and looking at the other participants. They ranged in age from about eight to eighty. Some groups wore crazy things on their helmets, like giant antlers, to identify themselves and make it easier to stick together. The bikes came in all shapes and sizes, too. There were tandem bikes, rowing bikes, bikes with cushion seats, mountain bikes, hybrids, bikes with kids in tow, and some guy with a bike with a sticker that read, "B.A.D.D. Bicyclists Against Dumb Drivers. I was waiting to see a unicycle.

As we chatted, Dina reminded me of the time that we did an Advil race and I promised her that we'd stay together. At the last mile of the race, I sprinted ahead. She was mad. I reminded her that the first block of the race she got a cramp, didn't want to run, and people on crutches were passing us. We laughed about it. She made Chris promise not to leave her during the tour, cramp or no cramp.

Fran Capo

The funny thing is Dina is in great shape and a strong rider. But never the less, Chris promised.

When you do something like this it takes on a life of its own. I know that competitive feeling. When you are good at something and you get into the spirit, you want to give it your all, to see how far you can push yourself. You don't want someone holding you back. It becomes a personal mission.

I told Steve he could go ahead of me anytime he wanted. I didn't want to hold him back. I also didn't want to be pressured to go beyond my limits. I needed to pace myself. I told them I was planning on eating power gels and drinking water every few miles just like the book recommended to keep my glucose level up and energy supply high. I would have pulled out a chart and timetable, but they already thought I was nuts.

It would be interesting to see how this was all going to play out. We all seemed to be going in with a different mindset. Some for the joy of togetherness, some for self-victory, and some just to come along for the ride.

At 8:30 a.m. the tour officially began. A big cheer went up as forty thousand bicyclists inched their way up the city streets. It was a little anti-climatic, but it's hard to move quickly among so many people. It was a good five blocks before we could even get on our bikes to ride. At Central Park, the congestion cleared up and finally the *walk your bike tour* turned into a *ride your bike tour.*

We had all agreed to stick together. In case of emergency our plan was to call each other on our cell phones. That was a good plan except Dina and Chris didn't have their phones with them. Okay, plan two, if we got separated we meet at the Ferry.

Dina trusted Chris would stay with her, after all he had the Power Bars, money, and water on his bike. Surely, he wouldn't leave her stranded. I, on the other hand, not being so trusting, had my own separate supplies. After all, I had beaten Steve in a lot of these endurance challenges, and you just never know when that male ego might kick in.

We stayed together in Central Park. We were slowed down due to an accident and bikers rubbernecking. Some kid and an old lady had collided. Don't know if anyone was hurt but the ambulance was

Adrenaline Adventures

there. After we passed the collision, we once again picked up the pace.

Then Dina wanted a Power Bar. She and Chris stopped. Steve and I didn't notice at first that they had stopped so we kept riding. Then we realized they were gone and looked around. Suddenly we saw Chris at our side.

"Where's Dina?" I asked.

I think I lost her accidentally." Guilt was all over his face. "Do you think she'll be mad?"

"Yup." Just then Dina sidled up, all smiles. She wasn't even mad. Something wasn't right in Denver.

We rode together for about five minutes, and then Dina zoomed ahead. Chris noticed and said, "I better catch up to her." Now that's a trained man. He zoomed off and that was the last we saw of them for the duration of the tour—the happy couple peddling off into the sunset.

Steve and I rode side by side, peddling at a decent clip, slowing down every now and then for me to snap a picture. Steve would rather have his toenails pulled out than have his picture taken. But I snapped photos anyway. You never know when they can be used for blackmail.

The cool thing about biking though the five boroughs is going over the same streets that you drive on. It's a totally different perspective when it's you and not some car engine powering the vehicle. Hills feel like mountains when your legs are doing the work.

From Central Park, we went over the Madison Avenue Bridge into the Bronx. We were in the Bronx maybe a total of ten minutes, just enough to say we did that borough. Then we darted across the Third Avenue Bridge and once again we were back in Manhattan. One borough down, four to go. Just as we were building nice even strokes, all the bikes came to a halt. We were stopped at 125th Street for the car traffic to go through.

This was totally unlike the NYC Marathon. Once the canon goes off, the clock is ticking and you don't stop for no stinkin' cars. Even though I knew it was a bike *tour*, I kept thinking bike *race* in my head. When I finally settled down, I was able to enjoy the scenery more, although my competitive side wanted to know how far ahead Dina and Chris were.

When we were allowed to go again, we had to rebuild our momentum. We peddled along FDR Drive and went through one of the underpasses. A big red banner hung over the entrance way, "Bikers Use Caution, Expansion Gaps in Road." As everyone went through the tunnel, instead of watching for the expansion gaps like we were supposed to, we all screamed at the top of our lungs to hear the echo. Maturity at its finest. Of course, I joined in.

When a thousand people are screaming at the same time the echo gets pretty loud. I think the vibration for the echo must have sent powerful sound waves out because it was at this juncture that the first blue bag incident occurred. As Steve was merrily peddling his way along FDR Drive, his demonic blue bag decided to take a nosedive for the pavement. It went rolling along the street and stopped precariously in the middle of the road, just daring other bikers to run over it.

We carefully darted in and out of bicyclists and retrieved the bag. It's amazing that no one ran over it, or us. Steve reattached the bag, this time more securely. The bag still had that evil glow.

Sporadically along the route there were safety marshals yelling out things like, "Potholes up ahead" or "Slow down, construction ahead."

We left Manhattan via the Queensborough Bridge. I remembered how steep this bridge was from the marathon. I started peddling really fast so I could get some momentum to get up the hill. I was determined that I wouldn't walk the bike up any of the hills. It was my own personal goal.

Not proficient at gear changing, I did the best I could. Then, when my legs started to hurt, I did the next best thing. I stood up and used my body weight to push down on the pedals. It seemed to help.

When we had made it through the third borough, I wondered if Dina had decided just to ride home since we were already in Queens; she had been complaining about the cold, and it was totally in her nature to stop home and get a jacket.

At Astoria Park, the bike traffic slowed down once again as we approached one of the major rest stops. Even those people not stopping were instructed to get off their bikes and walk through the park. We could pick up the trail on the other side and continue, if we liked, or stop first to use a port-a-potty or grab a bite to eat.

Nature called, so we dutifully waited on the long lines. No matter how you slice it, those portable toilets are disgusting. Toilet paper runs out fast with forty thousand people.

Forty-five minutes later, with bladders relieved, we continued on our sojourn. We readjusted the infamous blue bag and were on our way. It was 10:45. We had been riding for about two hours, and we weren't tired!

Not even five minutes after we'd departed from the rest stop, I noticed that the bag from hell was slowly slipping off Steve's bike. Again we stopped to fix it. Steve took it in stride, but I could see a silent storm brewing.

We apparently weren't the only ones losing our stuff. All along the tour we saw various bike parts; a reflector here, a glove there, a spoke here, a bent tire there. Steve commented that there were so many bike parts that if someone picked them all up, by the end of the tour they could build a new bike.

Our next bridge to cross was the Pulaski Bridge, or Penny Bridge as Steve calls it. Great, another incline. All I kept thinking was what goes up must come down. The hill has to end sometime. Coasting down was fun, but those marshals were always on hand to warn you to slow down — party poopers. Just once it would have been fun to whiz by them, leaving them in a tail-spin.

Now we were in the borough that never ends — Brooklyn. Brooklyn is half of the entire tour, and the streets are pretty rough, just like its tenants. All I can say is I was sure glad I was wearing a sports bra.

After bouncing for about an hour, the blue bag became dislodged again. This time like a cartoon character with steam coming out of his ears, Steve dismounted the bike, grabbed the bag and rolled it into a ball. He started mumbling curse words. Then he looked at the bag and said, "The next time you come off, I'm throwing you off the highway." Poor bag. He was just trying to hold on. It wasn't meant for the back of a bike. I decided to kiss Steve. I had to do something to calm the savage beast. Not sure if it worked, but the bag winked at me.

We continued our forty-two-mile trek. We were slowed down at the four other rest stops when we had to again walk our bikes. People commented that there hadn't been so much stopping the year before. But overall, people were in good spirits.

We were on the last leg of the tour—the Belt Parkway. We could spot the end in sight, the Verrazano Bridge. It was a gorgeous day to be riding alongside the water. Boats were racing up and down the river. With the bridge in sight I sped up. I was anxious to get to the end. Steve was about one hundred yards in front of me. I could spot him by that blue bag which was now flapping a strap and waving at me.

Every now and then Steve would turn around and I'd wave to let him know I wasn't too far behind. I figured by now Dina and Chris were over the finish line.

As we got to the entranceway of the bridge, everything came to a halt. Apparently, all the bikers were being funneled into two lanes. Anxiously we waited half an hour as we inched up toward the bridge.

Finally, when we were able to ride again, we met with our last hurdle, the toughest hill of the ride, the Verrazano Bridge. I had learned to work the gears and was able to do it without much of a struggle. As we got to the apex of the hill, I looked around and took in the view. Then I sat back and enjoyed the smooth ride downhill.

I crossed the finish line at Fort Wadsworth at 2:10 P.M. Steve was waiting on the other side of the line with a big grin. "Just for the record, Capo, I beat you."

I smiled and tapped the blue bag. "And just for the record, this little guy almost beat you."

The bike festival was in full swing, complete with music and food. We looked around for Dina and Chris. We went to the reunion center, but there was no sign of them. We hung out under a tree, waiting, eating, and watching for our two compadres until three o'clock. We figured by now they had crossed the finish line.

We headed over to the ferry. To my surprise the ferry was not just around the corner; it was another three miles away. Sneaky how they do this. Getting to the ferry completed the forty-two miles. There was really no place to meet at the ferry. We searched the tanned faces of the people hanging outside the local delis and bars. None looked familiar.

Finally we decided to cross the river. On the ferry the atmosphere was relaxed. Everyone seemed to be in a contemplative mode. One old guy was talking about doing a hundred-mile race. My ears perked up. Steve noticed and just said, "C-A-P-O! Can you at least wait 'til we get off of the ferry to plan our next adventure?"

"Okay, I can wait that long." I smiled teasingly.

Once in Manhattan we figured the only logical place to meet the missing duo was at the car. We biked to the car, and this time it was very different because we had to dodge pedestrians—there were no blockades clearing our path.

We arrived at the car and waited and waited. Finally, at 5:30, they showed up. Dina wasn't in the best mood. Chris had his head dangling like a whipped pup's. "You left her, didn't you?" I asked. Apparently they had hooked up briefly and then Chris went peddling ahead. He finished at noon. Dina, in hot pursuit, stopped to leave messages at the message board and crossed the finish line at 1:30. She was waiting at the reunion center, but we never saw her.

Chris had spent the rest of the afternoon crossing and re-crossing the ferry to find Dina. He was panicked knowing she had no money, no food, no phone, and no water. He wanted the police to put out an APB on her, but the woman cop just laughed. "How old is she?

"Forty," Chris replied.

The cop put her hand on his shoulder and assured him that Dina could handle herself. The question was, could Chris handle the wrath of Dina?

We all sat in the car. Dina vented, Chris apologized, Steve added some quick comments, and I sat in silence thinking about how I would write all this down.

Eventually things were smoothed over. No one was sore, the blue bag survived, Steve suffered a sunburn but a heavy dose of aloe cured that. And I had a forty-two-mile-stone to put down in my chapters of life's adventures.

Fran Capo

Chapter 34
Adventure at a Glance - Dare to Do it   Mild to Wild Scale: 2
Title: Bike New York
Children allowed: Yes
Age requirement: Fourteen and under must be accompanied by a parent. Children under one year old may not participate.
Length of trip: Half day to full day, depending how fast or slow you ride.
Where to try this adventure: New York City
Bike New York, 891 Amsterdam Avenue, New York, NY 10025
Phone: 212-932-2453
Web site: www.bikenewyork.org or E-mail: info@bikenewyork.org
Check out other bike clubs around the country for similar rides.
Best time of year: Bike New York is held the first Sunday in May.
Approximate cost: $34 early registration/$39 late registration, for adults. Kids under seventeen - $20.
Reservations necessary: Yes, the race takes place rain or shine.
Fitness requirements: Must know how to ride a bike and have the stamina to do 42 miles.
Personal gear required: Bike, safety helmet, tool repair kit, spare tire, pump, water, Power Bars, blue vest with number that they send you, whistle
What NOT to bring: Excess baggage
Photo opportunities: Yes

Notes: Spencer was confirmed and joined me for the 2004 bike tour.

Cool trivia: The Five Borough Bike Tour began in 1976 as a program of American youth hostels. This organization produces the largest cycling tour in America. They have added two other tours for those who want to ride outside the city: The Twin Lights Ride based in Monmouth County, New Jersey, and the Harlem Valley Rail Ride operating out of Millerton, New York in northern Dutchess County. Both of the new tours have optional lengths between 25 and 75 miles.

"Life's a compromise of what your ego wants to do, what experience tells you to do, and what your nerves
let you do."
—Bruce Crampton

Chapter 35
"Everything You Always Wanted to Know about Survival But Didn't Know Who to Ask" Survival School

Ever since I was in college I had a desire to take a survival class. It's always good to know survival skills just in case your plane crashes, or if you're out taking a three-hour tour and the next thing you know you're on Gilligan's Island. I for one wouldn't have had all that luggage, so I sure as hell better know how to survive.

I had taken a one-semester survival course at Queens College where the final exam was a weekend camping and trekking trip. But after one of my teammates showed up in high heels, claiming they were the most comfortable shoes she owned, I felt I wasn't really getting my money's worth on survival education.

Adrenaline Adventures

Then when the television show "Survivor" hit the airwaves, they made eating rats look like the only delicacy of the day. I thought there had to be a better way to survive.

I logged onto an Internet search engine and put in "survival schools." After sorting through the list, I came to Tom Brown Junior's Tracking, Nature, and Wilderness Survival School. What caught my eye about this school was the quote, "The school is based on Tom's experience of living in the wilderness and the teachings of Stalking Wolf, encompassing over twenty years of his life."

If I was going to learn from anybody, I wanted to do it from a guy who'd lived in the wilderness and who had a teacher named Stalking Wolf. I didn't want some college professor with a degree in nature who owned some *National Geographic* back issues and had a teacher named "Sitting Butt."

It also helped that the school was in New Jersey, close to my New York home. I called and asked for their brochure. There were twenty-six different classes, but everyone was required to take the Standard Course first. The seven-day Standard Course taught stalking and tracking skills; nature observation (including camouflage); survival techniques covering: making a shelter, finding water, making a fire, finding food, trapping, tools, and tanning (and we're not talking Coppertone); and the oneness-with-nature philosophy that later I found out was the driving force of the school.

I read through the brochure. The note, "No animals will be trapped during the course, but participants will learn how to trap if necessary" was the clincher. I signed up for a July course. After all, I wanted a school that respected life, not some Rambo institute.

About a week later I received a confirmation letter and list of necessary equipment: tent, sharp knife, sleeping bag, pad, mess kit, clothes (that's good!), rain gear, towel, biodegradable soap, notebooks, pens, bathing suit, and flashlight. Also recommended were a tape recorder/tapes, camera/film, extra batteries, snacks, and a seat cushion. (I guess those pine needles can get pretty rough).

I had no preconceived notion of what this school was going to be like, but I was excited. One thing on the form caught my eye: the directions to the school. "From I-78 in either direction, look for the large TA TRUCK STOP sign. Using a pay phone, call the Tracker School (908) 479-4681 for directions."

When I called the school in advance, I was told we would only be given directions on that day, since they didn't want anyone coming to the school early. Interesting, a tracking school that didn't want to be tracked. Maybe this was our first test.

I told friends and family I was going. Everyone had these images that I was going to be out in the wilderness and they'd never see me again. I told them surviving the Jersey tolls would be a feat in itself. Little Anthony, a guy from the park I run at, said, "Hey, I could get some of the boys to go with you, you know kind of like a bodyguard thing ... just in case."

My boyfriend, Steve, wanted all the details and swore he would call me Frambo upon my return; my son, Spencer, cried, thinking some bear was going to eat me, and my then writing partner, Anna, wanted to make sure I'd make it back to finish the project I was working on. My mom, Rose, just wanted me to call when I got there to make sure I was safe; she stuck a protection prayer in my sleeping bag just in case. People sure do have overactive imaginations. But to be safe, I sharpened my knife.

I packed and checked my list the night before. I washed my hair and showered not knowing how often I would get a chance to do it at the school. I also took off my jewelry and nail polish. I didn't want them to think I was some prissy New York girl.

I had a bad cold, and people suggested I back out. But I couldn't picture calling a survival school and canceling because I had a cold. They'd probably be snickering and thinking, "She's dead" as they hung up. So I put some Contac and cough drops in my bag to get me through.

DAY 1

Check-in time was four P.M. on Sunday. At 3:30 I pulled into the TA TRUCK STOP and called for directions. I saw other people with backpacks using the pay phones, as well. I smiled thinking, these are my fellow survivalists. I drove the few miles to the school.

Adrenaline Adventures

As I pulled into the dirt parking lot there was this guy in cutoff jeans looking very friendly. He casually directed us to the parking area. "This is the parking lot; you can drive up the road, drop your gear off, then park back here."

I asked if there were any other women signed up. "You're the only one," he said. I guess my look of shock made him tell me the truth. "Nah, there's about fifty-five people signed up, and at least twenty or so are women."

Yes! That meant I'd won the bet with my boyfriend!

I drove up the dirt driveway, passing the port-a-potties on the left behind the cornfields. I drove a bit more, surrounded on both sides by forest, and finally made a left onto the grass behind a two-hundred-year-old red barn house. I saw others getting out and walking around the barn, so I followed suit. As I turned the corner of the barn, past the wood shed kitchen on my right, I saw it. My home for the next seven days ... tent city.

Everyone was picking their place in the sun to pitch their tents. Most of the tents were modest. I had a deluxe four-person tent and a black wheeling suitcase. I was not exactly a poster girl for nature. Then I saw this older women with Little Orphan Annie hair and a tent as large as mine. Immediately I knew I would like her. Her name was Elisa, and she was from New Jersey.

As I was setting up my tent, two guys, Ben and John, offered to help. Everyone was in a great mood and friendly. And contrary to popular belief, they were not the "good ole boys, pick-up truck, gun-carryin" type. They were more of the nature set.

After a few minutes, my behemoth tent was set up. I threw my bags inside and parked the car. As I walked back to the tent, I thought, "This is it. Let's see what this survival thing is all about."

I took a shortcut back to my tent that lead past the shower stalls. Immediately I thought about Petticoat Junction. The attached wooden stalls were the type where your head sticks out and your shins are exposed. You had to get the water from a cold water garden hose and from a sprocket attached to a hot stove. You mixed the two extremes in the ideal proportions into a bucket, hauled the bucket across the lawn, and viola...you had a shower.

Yup, I could tell this was going to be a memorable week.

Fran Capo

At seven that night, after everyone was settled in, we were called into the barn, which was to be our classroom for the next seven days, for our orientation. Everyone had a nametag. I sat in the front row flanked on the left by Elisa and on the right by Liz, a haircutter from Kentucky. Behind me sat an architect named Joy who had an infectious laugh.

The barn had rows of wooden benches surrounding a stage. The stage was simple: a wooden planked floor. On the stage was a wooden bench and a large overstuffed armchair with a big paw print on it. Over the chair off to the left was an oval sign reading, "Tracker Survival School." On the wall directly behind the stage was a dry easel board with a two big signs, "No Sniveling" and "Quit yer whinin'." A sign that wouldn't have been there if they didn't need it.

The rest of the barn was decorated with an assortment of newspaper articles, some animal skulls, artifacts, and pictures of native tribes from around the world doing various primitive activities.

Sitting in the chair was Kevin, the director. He looked more like a state police sergeant who took no prisoners, a big guy with short, reddish hair. Joe Lou, the senior instructor, was next in line, and he was much smaller than Kevin and looked laid back. He'd had EMT training. Next were Billy, who had long, black hair and glasses, and Ivory Snow–type blonde girl, Ruth Ann who had her nose pierced, a tall, slim blonde fellow named Tom (not Tom Brown), and Betsy, who has an herbalist. Interns named Yanus, Scott, Emily, and several other volunteers rounded out the crew, our survival trainers.

Kevin told us the basic rules after everyone was introduced. "We've been around for sixteen years, and all the classes will be held in this barn. You may want to grab a seat cushion, as you will need it after a while. All meals will be eaten outside. Breakfast will be around seven, lunch at twelve, and dinner at six. Each of you will sign up to be on a crew all day for two days. There's a clean-up crew, pot crew, fire crew, water crew, and shower crew. When something is called out loud—for example 'Clean-up crew!'—repeat the words wherever you are in camp. This way the word goes out to everyone. If anyone is allergic to anything let us know. Only bathe in the showers, not the streams or lakes ... and organic tampons are available if anyone needs them."

Then Tom (not Tom Brown) went on to talk about the four hazards to watch out for: ticks (those tiny bugs smaller than a pen prick that can cause Lyme Disease); poison ivy (the three-leafed plant); dehydration (if your urine is any color but clear, you are dehydrated); and that you have to wear shoes at all times except during certain exercises. We were told what signs to watch out for to avoid the four dangers. Since the closest hospital was forty-five minutes away, we all took heed, although there was trained EMT staff.

They had a bookstore for any emergency items: toothpaste, snacks, film, etc. And if you ever needed a staff member at night, they were in the house behind the barn and in the trailers.

We took a short break and then were called back in. Everyone was seated again and getting rather chatty. Then, all of a sudden, the ambiance in the room shifted as Tom Brown walked in.

A silence fell as this tall, tanned, fifty-year-old man with white short hair, looking very lean and intense, entered from the side door and took center stage. He was passionate, yet low key. A very dominant personality relating an important message. A message that said we're running out of time to save Mother Earth. "You know we as a people have to get back to nature; we are destroying it faster than it can heal. To me, eating and sleeping are a waste of time. I have you people for only one stinking week, and I want to give you as much information as I can, but it's up to you to learn."

Then he told of how he met Grandfather, his mentor (a.k.a. Stalking Wolf, a Lippen Apache and real grandfather to his best friend Rick), when he was seven. He also told about his ten years alone in the woods, after Grandfather's death, in full survival mode. He paused for effect. "Full survival, not a backpack, not a knife ... nothing. Living with nature, fully wandering over North and South America until I came back to 'civilization', feeling out of sorts with people who didn't understand the things I saw or how I could see them."

He told of how he helped the police track lost people and criminals, and the dead bodies he'd pulled out of places because people just didn't know how to survive. There was an urgency in his voice when he spoke of the wasted lives. He continued, "You know I've been shot at four times and stabbed three times." He wasn't bragging; he was stating a fact. Then he talked about how the school had come to be and how he'd picked this farms' location because of its biodiversity and tracking terrain to help the students learn. He continued, "I am proud of every one of my students, and they have never let me down. I may even call on one of you in this group to help in tracking a lost person." Elisa and I shot each other a quick wide-eyed glance as if to say, "we better take good notes."

Then he talked about awareness and how important it was to observe all things. "You know since you people have gotten here, I've been observing you, watching your behaviors. My scouts are watching you, too. Some have been right under your feet and you didn't even know it." (As long as they are not watching me in the shower or bathroom, I'm okay.)

He talked more about tracking. "By the time I'm through with you students, reading a mouse track on gravel will be as easy as seeing dinosaur prints in peanut butter." He paused to let that thought sink in then said, "I'm a frontline warrior, and that's why I'm here in New Jersey, to be a watchdog to the most populated state per square mile."

He ended by looking us squarely in the eyes. "It's your job not to believe me ... prove me right or prove me wrong. I believe people must live it before they can teach it. This is going to be the most intense week of your lives." Then he told us to relax.

Whew. We all took a breath.

There was a ten-minute break. Then the call came out ... "Five minutes!" Everyone yelled, "Five minutes." Then "Come on in!" And everyone promptly took their seats. These people meant business.

Now the lessons began. Kevin was back up. The first lesson was on various types of knives, from clip point, which was a good multipurpose knife, to skinning blades, which have a broad sweep but are hard to carve with. He talked about blade geometry, how to grind knives, safety, the handle styles, and which knives were good for what. Kevin said the best type of knife to have in the wilderness was "the one you had with you!" That I can relate to!

Adrenaline Adventures

Then he examined our knives. I needed to purchase one that was good for carving the next morning at the school store for fifteen bucks.

Class ended at eleven. I felt like I was in boot camp. This was going to be intense, but at least I knew no girl would be wearing high heels. I put bug spray on and walked down a narrow trail to the port-a-potties in darkness. A display of fireflies danced above my head. One lady from Utah had never seen fireflies, so I caught one and let her hold it. The night was hot. When I got back to my tent, I crawled in feeling sticky and itchy, wondering if I was being watched. I decided I'd get up early and take a shower.

I was awakened a few hours later by rain pounding on my tent. Thunder rumbled but soon subsided. Then the rain faded into a dull monotone melody, and I fell back asleep, glad that I had waterproofed my tent on my last camping trip.

DAY 2 -FIRST FULL DAY - MONDAY

Got up at five A.M. Took shower. Felt self-conscious because I could peer over the door. Not comfortable yet in the natural setting being naked. Wondered if Tom had gone naked in the woods.

Breakfast was called at 6:30. We stood by a wooden table outside and received our meals. We all had this lump of oatmeal/rice concoction put on our plates. No one said a word ... remember "No Sniveling."

I met people from all over: Canada, Tennessee, California, and Maine. It was amazing. A lot of people had read at least one of Tom's sixteen books. I had read none of his books, so this was a totally different experience for me. I learned snippets of his life from his admirers.

I was on clean-up crew, so I got to wash down the tables, put the food away, sweep, and do general cleaning.

At 7:30, classes began. Tom Brown was up, and the room again was quiet. He was a seasoned storyteller, and he mesmerized his audience as he spoke. He talked about Grandfather's philosophies, and how at first he felt funny teaching them at the school until a student of the school told him how to do it in a way that wouldn't offend people. Then he spoke a passage that he had memorized from his book *The*

Fran Capo

Quest about Grandfather's philosophy. "It was not enough that man just be happy in flesh, but he must also be happy with and joyous in spirit. For without spiritual happiness and rapture, life is shallow."

He then talked about the universal consciousness that all of us have, similar to the way a flock of birds all turn at the same time, and called it The-spirit-that-moves-through-all things. He felt that a spiritual person must take the wisdom and philosophy of the earth and bring it back to a modern society.

After a quick break, Tom moved on to the topic of survival. Tom said, "Grandfather felt awareness is the doorway to survival, and survival is the doorway to the earth."

He said man can survive in every conceivable landscape, be it tundra, desert, or mountain. Tom had taught Navy Seals in Virginia how to survive in pine oak forests for ten days with nothing, then he'd taken them to Nevada, then to the jungles in Panama, and finally to Alaska.

He looked at us intensely, making eye contact with every one of us as he spoke. "If you are dressed and have a knife, you are NOT in full survival. Scuba divers and backpackers have too much gear— they use crutches. I am a survival purist—naked, that's it." (I don't even like to go naked in my house!) "If a survival situation is anything other than the Garden of Eden, then your skills - SUCK. "

Hey, then my cooking skills at home suck, because without a microwave, I'm sunk.

He continued, "Survival skills are universal and have been perfected by primitive man, so don't reinvent the wheel. Take the time to perfect the skills.

This class will teach you to deal with the what-ifs. What if my tent blows away? What if a bear eats my food?" (Yeah, what if I'm trying to get rid of a spouse and he finds his way out of the jungle?)

Tom continued, "This class takes away your apprehensiveness because you become a child of the earth. You will truly no longer fear anything. You will eat when you're hungry, sleep when you're tired, and play to exhaustion."

Actually that didn't sound too bad.

Tom got down to survival. He talked about the sacred order of survival and to think of it in terms of the number three. First, get shelter (you can live only three hours without shelter, then get water (you can live only three days without water), then get fire (you can live only three weeks without fire) then get food (you can live three months without food).

Up to bat next was Joe Lou with a fire-making workshop. Joe had this drawing of a stick figure man gathering wood. Every one of Joe's classes began with a stick figure drawing. Joe talked about the natural laws of fire preparation and maintenance. He gave us an equation, Form = Natural Law + Environmental conditions. For example, if the natural law is you need water and all you have is rocks, then the form is boiling rocks to purify the water. If you do, you will have good drinking water; if you don't, it can be contaminated. There is always a reward and penalty system in place in nature. Follow it, and you will live; don't and you will die. He said, "There are twenty-three ways to make fire, nine are common like the bow drill and hand drill, and fourteen are regional like bamboo fires." He also said we needed to follow the law of conservation of energy by using whatever materials were close at hand to make fire. He showed us how to build a fire pit.

He went on and on...I now had temty-five pages of notes in my book and it was still morning.

On break I ran to the bathroom, sniffed the fresh air and was wondering what I got myself into. My brain was already feeling a bit overwhelmed. Just as I was starting to feel a bit relaxed I heard the familiar cry …"Come on in"…

Ruth Ann was now in the lead, teaching barefoot. She taught us how to make a bow drill. She told us to think of the coal as the infant, how to gently put the coal inside the tinder once we had gotten one, and blow on it until it becomes a flame. She made it seem so easy. I started thinking of Tom Hanks in *Castaway* and how excited he was when he finally made fire. This was a skill I wanted to conquer. It was something we take for granted with the flick of a lighter and yet most people couldn't reproduce in the nature.

She showed us how to dig the hole for the fire and the four parts to making a bow drill: the bow and string, handhold, spindle, fireboard, and notch. The whole shebang. Then she told us to make sure once we put out our fire to scatter the ash and never let it just sit because when ash becomes wet it turns to lye and can burn you. I figured I wouldn't worry about that; if I started a fire, I wasn't going to put it out. I'd let mine burn like the eternal torch.

Another ten pages of notes and we were ready to go outside and create fire.

We went outside in pairs and had to axe a cedar block into two separate parts. Then each of us carved our spindles, fireboards, and handles. I had never carved with a knife before, or used an axe, so those were lessons in themselves. I was still carving when lunch was called. Some of the more experienced knife people had their firemaking sets ready.

Lunch was a stew. We all looked at each other. No one sniveled.

By 1:15 we were back on the benches. We were reminded that we had all week to try to make fire. Good thing, I figured it might take me that long to carve the set! We were also reminded, "Hey folks, it's still only Monday. Day One." Was that possible? I felt like it had been at least a week since I'd been home. I believe a time warp had begun.

That afternoon we learned how to make rope, traps, clothes, and shelter. We learned how much water we needed and how to purify it. We were told that humans lose three and a half quarts of water in an average 24-hour period, through skin, respiration, urination and excretion ... so we need to stay hydrated.

They also told us that if you don't have water not to eat, that by eating food alone without water you will die faster. But if you do have a little bit of water only take eight swallows then wait fifteen minutes before you take the next swallow because that's how long it takes the body to absorb it.

Finally it was dinner time, and once again we got stew ... MMMM was this a lesson in thankfulness or did the chef only have one trick up his sleeve?

Everyone looked starry eyed. No one dared complain. Actually we were enjoying it, in an exhausted kind of way. It was overwhelming, and this was only day one ... would this day ever end? Would I ever retain all of this information? Or would it go the route of my trigonometry equations?

Adrenaline Adventures

After dinner Kevin taught the ethics of hunting and trapping. He emphasized that all life is sacred and valuable and that everything has a spirit that you must be respectful of. He said to hunt like the Apache's. Study the herd, and take the weak link out, the animal that was going to die anyway, so you are not hurting the propagation of the species.

My mind started to wander, and I watched a bat flying around the barn. I was on overload, yet I was listening. After Kevin's talk, we went outside to practice some trapping skills. Then it was back into the barn.

Fifty pages into my notebook, the day ended. At eleven, I went into my tent, snacked on walnuts, did a nature call, and noticed the fireflies again. The woods were very quiet. I went to sleep thinking about what it would be like to do a full survival—definitely a different kind of adrenaline rush, totally relying on yourself I drifted off to sleep determined to make fire the next day.

DAY 3 - TUESDAY

Got up at 5:30. By 6:10, I had showered. I saw a groundhog scurry under a shed. My feet got wet from the dew on the ground and I thought, "Ah yes, morning dew is good for water collection." A shift in my thinking.

I worked on my bow drill. I was trying to burn a hole in the wood when David came over and said, "You want to know what you're supposed to do?"

I joked, but it sounded like a New York snap, "Yes, please tell me WHAT I'm supposed to do!"

David said, "My, that sounded hostile," but was laughing as he said it. I could see that my New York aggressiveness and my impatience at my lack of skill were going to need a bit of work. David said he knew I didn't mean it. We worked together until the call for breakfast came. Again, we got a lump of rice and oatmeal. I felt even my meager culinary skills could surpass this. Then I wondered if I could ever bring myself to kill an animal in the wilderness. I decided I'd look around for plants first, but if I had to, I would if I was in full survival with my son, Spencer. Now, I'm sure *that* is an animal instinct.

Fran Capo

That morning we had a lesson on tracking, direct from the Tracker himself, the man that has been tracking for 44 years. Tom began, "Tracks are found on every environment, gravel, dirt, grass etc." He said he could see the tracks all over the stage floor. We all just stared. All I saw was wood.

Tom continued, "Walking over to the barn this morning I could see where a snake slivered, and where a fox emerged and paused to watch a rabbit." To him tracking was awareness, the doorway to the spirit.

I was trying to be aware, but the only doorway I could see at the time was the one leading into the barn. I looked at the stage again, as a performer I've stood on a thousand stages, and never saw any tracks. I looked once again. Nope, just wood. He told us not to get frustrated. It must be neat to have that kind of vision, and lonely at the same time.

Then he taught us how to read pressure releases (an impression made by the foot in the ground) and identify prints.

Kevin then took over and got down on the floor and imitated different animals' gaits. He drew the line when it came to portraying a gallop. And here I was ready to throw a saddle on him.

We took a break and everyone worked on their bow drills for fifteen minutes. Calls of "I've got fire!" came as people achieved the task, followed by applause from fellow students. I really wanted to get the fire but my spindle kept falling out as I was pushing it back and forth. I wasn't getting the knack of it, and was allowing myself to worry. I kept thinking if I was out in the wilderness I better be able to make a fire. I was creating my own friction, and it wasn't on the bowdrill.

The 10:30 workshop continued on animal gaits and pattern classification.

. It was then time for lunch. Lunch was stew again. This time, however, it didn't bother me; it was food, and it was filling and not fattening. I also finally burned the hole in my fireboard. A step in the right direction.

At one, cartoon Joe was up again with his identifying stick drawing on the board. He told us animals live by the natural law of conservation of energy. Their first instinct in danger is to freeze, the old deer in the headlight syndrome, then to run. For every deer you see walking away, three more are frozen somewhere nearby.

Joe then showed us how to measure the age and weight of a track. He ended the class by explaining that each of us has a dominant side. If you were to blindfold someone without any reference point, like a mountain or lake, the person would walk in a giant circle within one square mile, on the side of their dominance. Which explains why so many people lost in the woods wind up in the same spot in which they started.

Seventy-three pages into my notes it was time for Ruth Ann to take over. It was 3:45. She taught us about stalking movements and told us about Apache children who could run three hundred miles without stopping. And I thought running a Marathon was impressive!

We went outside and all fox-walked in bare feet, talking sixty-six seconds to do one step. (I know some government agencies that move that slow naturally!) For me, it took a lot of concentration, as my natural tendency was to move faster. We all walked around trying to get the move down. Then we graduated to the crawling stalk and the belly crawl.

By dinnertime, thunder clouds had rolled in. It began to pour. So we did the only logical thing we could as tent people ... we played tag in the rain.

That night we learned brain tanning. I envisioned a brain sitting on a little beach chair taking in the rays. But instead it was the name for obtaining a skin, gutting, and preserving it. I liked my vision better. But then again, my vision wasn't going to clothe me in the woods if my plane crashed.

DAY 4 - WEDNESDAY

By now we were all settling into the routine. No one was wearing their nametag anymore. We were at the midpoint. I didn't even care that people were in the shower stalls next to me. I noticed several spider webs had formed on some branches and dew had created a beautiful bowl in which the sunlight was reflected. I snapped a picture. People were practicing their stalking moves and foxwalk. Everyone was busy working on a skill.

Fran Capo

Today for sure I would make fire with my bow drill. I felt I had to, time was running out. Many people had accomplished it already. I ate the normal wad of oatmeal for breakfast. They told us some of the volunteers were practicing their scout skills and that one of them was under the table at breakfast, throwing things at our feet. No one noticed. Talk about unaware!

We spent the morning at several survival workshops, learning more methods of making fire, how to use camouflage, and how to de-scent ourselves by washing in pine needle tea. I made note to see if Lipton had that in a teabag.

Then it was time for lunch. I saw one of my classmates practicing stalking by the outhouse. I walked past him, and then doubled back and decided to stalk him. I got within five feet of him before he noticed me. It was kind of cool. I remembered that the main thing in stalking is to allow your pace and your route to be dictated by the landscape, and to surrender your will to the earth. My lessons were bouncing around in my head, and I was hoping some of them would sink in and take root.

During lunch I once again tried to make fire. I saw I was trying too hard, so instead I walked around the cornfield. I spotted one of the scouts and saw a chipmunk in a tree. We just looked at each other for several minutes. I stayed perfectly still.

Our afternoon consisted of Tom (not Brown) teaching us two types of stick-throwing methods, and then we practiced on stuffed animal targets like Barney. I aimed for a stuffed donkey and whacked him right off the stool.

Tom said that we had to do better and to use our awareness. Then Tom upped the stakes. "Okay, if all the targets are *not* knocked down, there will be no dinner." He laughed, but he meant it. Even though it was only stew, we wanted it. There were fifty-five of us and only twenty-five of them. When the stick supply was exhausted and still five targets remained, I asked if we could throw our shoes.

He only laughed, so I did. Soon dozens of shoes were flying and all the targets were down and we got our meal.

After supper, we went back into the classroom to learn how to build a debris hut, which is a hut made out of debris, sticks, and leaves. We were told that if the debris was mounted two and a half feet high it can keep you warm in thirty-degree weather; if it was four feet high it can keep you warm at negative thirty degrees.

Then we went into the woods to actually build a debris hut out of hay. A short raffle was held, and three winners got the privilege of spending the night in the debris hut.

Then they announced that tonight was going to be a special night. We were going to do a sweat lodge. For some reason the name reminded me of something the Flintstones would be involved with. This sweat lodge, however, was to detoxify our bodies and to center our minds. There were four ceremonies Tom had learned from Grandfather, and tonight we were going to experience one. So in a sense this was a gift from Grandfather to us.

We were to wear bathing suits and bring a rag to cover our faces if we thought we couldn't handle the heat. And if at any time during the ceremony we had to leave, we were to raise our hands and say, "I need to leave." The ceremony would be stopped and they would not think any less of us. I, for one, didn't want to interrupt any ceremonial prayer to leave.

We all waited on line as the sweat lodge was prepared. Stacks of hay in a circle formation, with a pit in the middle, were already set up, as were the skeletal wooden slats that formed an outline of a ceiling. A large blue tarp was placed over the ceiling slates, forming a cover. Then hay was placed on top of it to keep the heat in. Barrels of hot rocks were brought into the lodge and placed into the center pit. There was an excited anticipation among the students.

It was a nice cool night. One by one we crawled into the sweat lodge, circling around in a spiral until every seat was taken. We all sat in the dark with our legs folded, waiting to experience what was next. The air in the lodge was already stifling hot.

Tom was seated, and when we were ready to begin, he said, "Doors," and the tarp was brought down to cover the two exits. Then Tom led the ceremony, sometimes in English and sometimes in Apache words he'd learned from Grandfather. He spoke blessings to Mother Earth and asked that each of us cast out our baggage so we could become one with nature again. I sat there in the dark, sweat dripping down from every pore of my body, closing my eyes and trying to focus on the words and form images in my mind of what was being said. I was psychologically glad I was near one of the exits. I didn't want to cough or pass gas or do anything to disrupt the ceremony. I noticed one person leave very discretely.

As the sweat inched its way down my body, the heat and the sound of water sizzling on the burning rocks was hypnotic. Peppermint seeped into my nasal cavity, and then it seemed my cough was gone. Time seemed suspended. The message was ringing out, "Learn to survive with the planet, not against it, and you will thrive and be more aware and live in harmony."

More words floated around, and then it was over. We were supposed to go off and be with ourselves and not talk.

Everyone walked away slowly. The night air was refreshing, and the stars seemed brighter. I can't say I was transformed, but I did feel an inner peace.

There was a lot more going on at this school than just physical survival. This was the survival of the soul, the mind, and the body through nature. All the great leaders of the world, Jesus, Buddha, etc., spent time in solitude in nature. It was their vision quest.

DAY 5 - THURSDAY

Once again I announced to myself that this was the day for fire. I knew in my heart I wouldn't leave without having had a coal ignite. I had created smoke many times, and I kept telling myself "where there's smoke, there's fire." I just had to coax the fire out.

We went over the pressure releases that tracks show. The pressure releases have nothing to do with the size of the animal but more to do with his motion ... which direction was he moving in and why. The foot is like a tiny map where every movement is recorded.

There was a lot to take in with tracking. I felt like I was back in geometry class without a slide rule. We played in the outdoor sandbox, identifying different tracks. They were easy to identify ... why? Because they had little index cards next to them telling us what they were. If only it was that easy in the real world. I was on page 137 in my notes.

Then we went to the Julia Child of primitive cooking, Billy. He had prepared an outdoor feast using primate stoves, hot rocks to boil water, hollow tree stumps as containers, a flat rock as a barbeque,

Adrenaline Adventures

an array of cooking variations from materials nature supplied. He gave safety tips such as, "Never use wet rocks in your fire. They explode when heated." He showed us cooked vegetables, meats, and plants. They smelled delicious. We were tempted to grab them, but he teased us with nibbles. Ultimately he let us taste them, and after three days of stew, they tasted heavenly.

They emphasized once again that this class was an insurance policy in case we ever got stranded. We would have the knowledge to survive.

That afternoon, we learned more about footprints and tracking. Kevin told us, "There are 63 indicator pressure releases in a person's foot that are unique to a person, and they never change from birth to death." (Unless of course you loose a leg or something.) He continued, "No two people's footprints are alike. There are only 13 indicators in a finger print. A footprint then is far more accurate". True, but I somehow couldn't picture cops toe printing Al Capone.

We were sent into nature to observe and study the world around us. I was fascinated by the purple color of one particular bug on a branch. I'd never seen a bug that color! I realized I was using tunnel vision on the bug when I should be using my wide-angle vision to heighten my awareness. The second I mentally switched gears, I noticed hundreds of those bugs all over the tree. Hundreds that just seconds earlier I did not even realize existed. I now understood the power of wide-angle vision. I felt another shift in my learning.

Plants 101 as taught by bubbly Ruth Ann came at the close of the day. "Since we cannot survive in a parking lot," as Tom Brown puts it, we have to know what to eat in nature that won't kill us. For example, you can eat the cherries off a black cherry tree but the rest of the tree is poisonous. Ruth told us how to make teas, spices, and medicinal remedies, as well as how to identify the plants and use plant guidebooks. She mentioned that our ancestors ate around one thousand different plants. Today, we are stuck with about twenty.

By ten that night, I was starry eyed and visions of sugarplums were dancing in my head. In this survival school you didn't go to sleep, you passed out.

Fran Capo

DAY 6- Friday
Woke up at 5:30 A.M. and decided to go to the creek to see if I could spot any animals. I saw a rabbit. He hopped away in a hurry as he heard me coming. Then I started to walk really quietly toward the creek. Something immediately to my left in the bushes darted away. Wow, so close and I didn't even see it. It's amazing to think how many animals are in the forest invisible to our untrained eyes. But with the power of full awareness and by learning the tracks, the invisible world becomes as plain as day.

For breakfast we graduated to eggs and pita bread.

The first class began at eight, and Kevin taught it wearing a shirt that read, "Shut-up and Track." He covered debris tracking, stone and gravel tracking, and dust and grit tracking. Kevin told us that when someone steps on grass, it creates a compression, and the grass will never reach the same height again. The compressions in turn create some kind of order and you can read them.

To prove this, we were sent out on the trail, the same trail we took to go to the creek, the same trail that always looked devoid of animal life. The interns and volunteers had set down popsicle sticks pointing to and identifying different animals' tracks. In one section about a foot by a foot wide, there were tracks from a bobcat, bear, deer, squirrel, weasel, chipmunk, and housecat. It was a major thoroughfare of animal life, yet we could not spot a single creature with our eyes. It was amazing how with the popsicle sticks, the actual tracks popped out. I wondered how much I would notice them without the sticks. I did notice later in the day that the ground seemed to hold more meaning than just something to step on.

Soon it was lunchtime. This was the last full day of survival school and I had still not created fire. Many people over the course of the week had tried to help me, all offering advice, slowly getting me closer to my goal. Don kept reminding me that it's a journey not a destination. Amy offered words of encouragement such as "You are almost there." David kept telling me to stay centered and to think of a special place where I felt peaceful.

I tried everything, I whittled down my spindle, I opened up my fireboard, I pretended I was a concert violinist so my arm wouldn't get tired.

Adrenaline Adventures

Then the call came, "Ten minutes!" I drilled faster. Bill kept saying, "You can do it! Keep going. Just a little more."

Smoke started several times just as my arm was giving out. I was praying to the fire, thanking the fire, pleading with the fire. And then, I just let go. My mind drifted to my place in the park that I love, and I just drilled.

"Five minutes!"

I wasn't going to stop. The friction was building up; the coal had been lit and little wisps of smoke were raising from the fireboard. We carefully breathed air onto the hot spot and placed the tender.

"Come on in!"

I wasn't leaving when I was this close. Then, in an instant, the tender turned to flames. It felt awesome! I felt like dancing and hollering all at the same time. I ran into the classroom where an intense Tom Brown was waiting. I was slightly embarrassed, but I didn't care ... I had created fire! And it felt great.

Tom gave his final lecture to us; it was on "coyote" teaching and awareness. He told us about how Grandfather would create a passion in Tom by never answering his questions, but rather making him have the desire to go out and find the answer himself, and ultimately learn something he would never forget.

Tom told story after story in a way that captivated the audience. Yet each story had a lesson. Tom ended with, "It's not dying that one should fear, but never having lived at all." He left the stage. Everyone sat, jotted things in their notebooks, and pondered. I was now up to page 180.

At one o'clock, Betsy, the herbalist, talked with a passion about harvesting the plant kingdom. We went on a nature walk and had a serious of plants identified for us. Then we were assigned to teams and picked plants, taking only the leaves so the plant could live on. We all gathered these edible plants, and a wild dinner feast was prepared. Along with our feast we were each given a fresh trout and told how to gut it. I was the first at the cooler for the trout, but as I looked in the cooler I was immobilized. They were beautiful in color. I touched one. It was cold and slimy.

Elisa stood next to me and we debated if we wanted to do this or not. *We* didn't' want to.

I had never gutted a fish, and really wasn't that anxious to try. Yet I eat fish, so I felt I was being a hypocrite. After a few minutes I picked up a trout. Elisa picked up one as well. Okay, first stage done. We had it in our hands.

I wasn't squeamish, but something about it being dead just bothered me. I couldn't stand to have it watch me cut it, so I chose the cut-the-head-off method. Brad, the scuba instructor, was near me. He held the nose of the fish to steady it as I cut. But as he held it, I saw its eyes bulge and I knew I was about to cry. The head was now off. I took a breath.

I then started to cut the stomach from the anal cavity up through the center. Somewhere in the middle, I just started crying. "I hate doing this." Something about it really bothered me. (Good time to see a shrink or at least decide if I need to become a vegetarian.) Brad took the fish and gutted it for me; Liz washed it off. Elisa, meanwhile had gotten by with a little help from her friends as well.

I seasoned and cooked it on the open flame. I can't tell you how many times I thanked the fish for its life and apologized to it for cutting its head off.

After dinner, a few more lessons on advanced shelters and some slides of these gorgeous primitive huts that would put some ski lodges to shame. They talked about all the other classes offered that took place in the Pine Barrens and were eighty percent field work and twenty percent lecture. Classes that would really put your skills to the test.

We stayed up late on our last night. Cowboy Joe played the guitar, and people sang and talked by the campfire.

I had bonded with three girls ... my motley crew, Liz, Elisa, Joy, and myself. We decided to walk to the creek at night, remembering all the tracks we had seen that day. The creek was beautiful, but we still had some fear of the forest. We spooked ourselves. Then we shifted gears and imagined staying by the creek all night, but we weren't comfortable because we weren't yet confident about our skills.

Then one of us made an announcement. She hadn't gone to the bathroom all week for fear of sitting on the bowls. We had a laughing fit making fun of her and imagining what she would have been like in the covered wagon days, waiting months until she got to her

Adrenaline Adventures

destination to go, while the wheels and ruts jarred her insides upside down.

We laughed until one in the morning. We were the last to zipper our tents.

DAY 7 - THE FINAL DAY - SATURDAY

I was up at 3:30 to go to the bathroom. Trish, whose tent was in front of mine, was unzipping her tent. I saw her with a flashlight all covered in mud and ash. She was out to touch a deer. Tom had offered an incentive earlier. If anyone could stalk a deer and touch it, remember its markings, and then tell Tom, he would go out, track your prints and the deer's to make sure you really did it, and if you did, you'd get the next class for free. In all the years the school had been around only twenty-eight standard-class students had done it. The gauntlet was thrown, and Trish was up for the challenge on the final night. I wished her luck.

I got up officially at six to start breaking down my camp. I evened up my tab at the school store for miscellaneous items over the week and saw another rabbit.

Just because it was the last day didn't mean we would be slacking. At 9:15, we learned about two more animal traps, the rolling snare and the baited T snare. Billy and Ruth Ann impressed upon us once again that it was our responsibility to make sure that we tested the traps and that the animals didn't suffer. We owed it to them to be efficient, since we were eternally indebted to them for giving their lives so we could live.

Our final lesson was from Kevin. It was on dust and grit compressions. "Okay, people it's the last day, we are going to show you tracks. First off, you always look at a track from a low angle so you can see it."

We all looked at the wooden stage again and still saw nothing.

Kevin asked us to walk around the barn and then come back in. While we did that he changed the lighting inside the barn. Sure enough when we came back in, with the new lighting and at the right angle we saw the prints. We saw dry foot marks on a wooden surface where we had seen none all week. It was as if a proverbial light had been turned on.

Fran Capo

Two hundred and twenty five pages of notes later the classes ended.

Kevin told us one farewell story about a promise that Tom had made to Grandfather upon the birth of his first son; it was a story that only Kevin could tell in such a way, a story of a beautiful place turned into a mound of garbage, a story that forever locked Tom into his destiny to pass on the message of Grandfather. Then we watched this big police dog of a man, cry, moved by the passion of this story. There was not a dry eye in the room.

Kevin begged us not to just put our notebooks away after the class was over, but to pass on the word for people to get back with nature and save Mother Earth so that all our children in the future may enjoy it just as much.

Then, one by one, Ruth Ann, Billy, and Kevin gave us their final messages. Each of them told us to be patient with ourselves and with our loved ones in communicating what we had learned, and to allow ourselves seedtime to understand and explore all we had been taught this week.

We gave the instructors a standing ovation. They had touched our lives and taught us a new appreciation and knowledge of nature and survival. They taught us to be caretakers of the earth, not destroyers.

We all packed up our gear, cleaned the grounds, took pictures, and hugged goodbye.

As I pulled out of the parking lot, I saw a groundhog scurrying across the road to his hole. I stopped my car next to him. He looked back over his shoulder and then raised his paw to his head as if in salute, and then he continued on his way. Maybe animals can recognize caretakers.

I came to the survival school for a physical survival class. I left with not only the skills but with the knowledge that I had begun a journey inward.

I knew that that week of lessons moved me in a way that would truly last a lifetime, and I did one better: I passed the lessons on to my son, who later that year took the junior coyote track class. Now we both see the world from the same perspective ... thanks, Tom!

Adrenaline Adventures

Chapter 35
Adventure at a Glance - Dare to Do it   Mild to Wild Scale: 3
Title: Survival School
Children allowed: Yes. There is a separate program for kids.
Age requirement: Must be at least 18 to attend the adult class
Length of trip: One week
Where to try this adventure: The Tracker, Inc.
Tom Brown, Junior's Tracking, Nature, and Wilderness Survival School, P.O. Box 173, Asbury, NJ 08802
Phone: (908) 479-4681 Fax:(908) 479-6867
Web site: www.trackerschool.com or E-mail: TrackInc@aol.com
There are also Tracker schools in California and Florida.
Best time of year: All year round
Approximate cost: $800 for the seven-day Standard Course
Reservations necessary: Yes
Fitness requirements: Good physical health
Personal gear required: Tent, sharp knife, sleeping bag, pad, mess kit, clothes, rain gear, towel, biodegradable soap, notebooks, pens, bathing suit, and flashlight. Also recommended are a tape recorder/tapes, camera/film, extra batteries, snacks, and a seat cushion. (They supply you with an equipment list.)
What NOT to bring: Radios or any nonbiodegradable products.
Photo opportunities: Yes

Notes: The school is the largest of its kind in the United States. Courses run the gamut from the standard class to a philosophy workshop to a winter survival course.

Cool trivia: Recently, Tom Brown Jr. was the technical advisor on *The Hunted*, a major motion picture starring Tommy Lee Jones and Benicio del Toro. In 1978, Tom founded the Tracker School in the New Jersey Pine Barrens. He has helped the police find many missing children and track criminals.

"Every one of us has a special talent inside. Find out what it is and let it shine!"
—Fran Capo

Chapter 36
"There's Still Gold and Ghosts in Them Thar Hills"
Panning for Gold

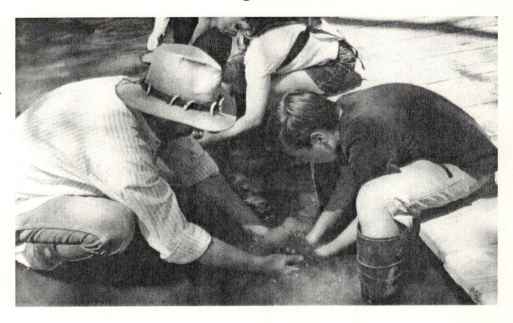

As part of a ten-day trek through California, my son, Spencer, my boyfriend, Steve, his daughter, Jamie, and I went to Yosemite National Park. We were in awe of the magnificent giant redwoods and the grandeur of the mountain faces like El Capitan. It was just one leg of many we had plotted along the way.

After leaving Yosemite, we drove along the famed Highway 49, The Mother Lode, the route to Jamestown, for the main reason of our trip—a gold prospecting adventure. It was an adrenaline rush of a different type ... finding money in its purest form, gold.

At the time we were driving, The Mother Lode was just a term we had heard of. We had no idea that it referred to the biggest vein of quartz in the world, stretching 123 miles. Why is this important? Because gold sticks to quartz ... and this was *the* place to find it. The Mother Lode was the area that drew thousands to California during

Adrenaline Adventures

the 1849 Gold Rush. Had we known we might have parked the car right there and taken out our picks.

But, being oblivious to the wealth beneath this "gold" highway, we just enjoyed the gorgeous mountains and the one-lane, curvy roads. Earth tones—brown, red, and beige with splashes of green—penetrated our eyes as we drove. The scenery itself was gold for the soul.

Not having total blinders on, we did notice a lot of iron pyrite shimmering in the mountains ..."fool's gold." The sun playfully bounced off it as if to say,"Take me! Take me, you fool. I'm what you're looking for."

As we got closer to Jamestown, we became excited about the possibility of finding gold, and we talked about the best method to split whatever we found. Spencer thought we should split it evenly. Jamie thought we should each keep what we found. Steve and I figured no matter what, we'd follow that unwritten law of parenting and wind up giving our stuff to the kids. But things don't always work out the way you plan them.

We arrived in Jamestown by noon. A town that was founded in 1848 when gold was discovered one mile south along Wood Creek. Nuggets as big as seventy-five pounds were found there. After the surface gold was gone, it was the quartz mines, rich in gold, that kept this town booming. Today it has a population of 950 people.

It still had the feel of a small western town. The main street (appropriately named Main Street) is about four blocks long. I could picture horses tied to the wooden rails outside the local establishments, and ladies in their finery strolling down the streets with budding tycoons. The town is just two hours east of SanFrancisco, but the feel is a million miles and hundreds of years away.

We quickly checked into the Jamestown Hotel, an eleven-room Victorian bed and breakfast owned by a young married couple. Each room is decorated differently, filled with antiques, and named after famous women of that era, such as the Diamond Lil room.

Before the place became a bed and breakfast, it was the Mother Lode Hospital. It is said that a woman, Mary Rose Sullivan, and her baby died during childbirth at the hospital. Her ghost haunts room number seven, the Diamond Lil room. That's a bit of information I conveniently forgot to mention to the gang. Besides, we were in the Vade Phillips room, room number eight. Clear on the other side of the hotel.

We dropped our luggage (and I did a quick ghost check just to make sure the ghost knew which room was which), and then we went across the street to the world famous Gold Prospecting Expeditions headquarters. It was the coolest shop on Main Street, a huge, wooden, yellow, barn like building with a giant gold nugget replica on the roof and a mannequin of a scrawny looking man hanged by the neck beside it for effect. Just in case you got any ideas about stealing.

There was also a free gold panning station outside the shop to give tourists a taste of prospecting.

We gazed at the exterior for a few minutes then went inside where we scheduled to meet one of the owners, Bryant Shock. He was going to be our gold prospecting mentor for the next two days. The woman behind the counter, Beverly, was expecting us. "You must be Fran. Bryant will be with you in a few minutes. He told me to give you this." She handed me a thirty-five-page booklet, the "Prospector Course Companion Manual." With a smile she said, "Bryant said to read this tonight."

Geez, I wasn't even there ten minutes and already I had homework! "Couldn't I have a nugget instead, sort of as a sample study?"

She just laughed.

We amused ourselves in the shop while Bryant gathered some tools for the day's outing. The shop was like a journey back in time. Everywhere you looked were flashes of the past ... artifacts found on local gold digs, wanted posters from days gone by, mining tools, gold pans, an endless array of things to look at.

We leafed through a book of hundreds of newspaper clippings that was in the front of the store. It contained clippings about the town, the Gold Rush, and about Bryant's father, Ralph Shock, who was a gold dealer himself and the original owner and operator of both the gold prospecting tours company and the shop until his recent death. There were also several articles about the wonderful programs that Gold Prospecting Expeditions offered to kids nationwide.

As we were leafing through the book, Bryant came out from behind a black curtain and introduced himself. He fit right in with

Adrenaline Adventures

the décor. He had on a white cowboy hat with a brown band with several coyote teeth in it (which I found out later belonged to his dad). He sported a reddish brown beard and mustache, a blue and white bandana around his neck, a white long-sleeved shirt, and jeans.

We shook hands and made our introductions. Then Bryant gave us directions to his mining camp a few miles down the road. He told us to grab some water and hats and douse ourselves in sunscreen since we'd be working outside for hours. We also snuck a bite to eat.

Ten minutes later we were standing outside the "Jimtown 1849 Mining Camp." Bryant pulled up in his car with his trusty little dog and let us through the gate. We walked through and saw what appeared to be a mining camp from the Gold Rush era. Once again, we felt transported through time.

Since it was a private lesson, the atmosphere was casual. The five of us sat down on the wooden picnic benches in the campsite. Bryant began by giving us a history of the town. "You may wonder why our camp is called Jimtown. The town was originally named Jamestown after a shrewd San Francisco attorney, George James. But after stealing from the miners, he snuck out of town. The citizens wanted to rename it, but unfortunately the old name stuck. So locals call it Jimtown, while on the map it's Jamestown."

"I bet those citizens wanted to do more than rename the town. Maybe string him up like that mannequin outside your store," I said.

Bryant laughed and continued, "If you look around, you'll see that my brother Brent and I went to great lengths to authenticate this camp. We went through diaries and archives dating back to 1833 to make sure it was set up just the way it would have been."

He pointed out boot hill, an old gold mining tunnel, a Studebaker freight wagon, a grave yard, a saloon, an outhouse, a mining supplies tent that was made from Levi canvas, the original material from the 49er days, and a replica of Mark Twain' cabin, the one he stayed in from 1861 to 1868 during his mining days. The real one was located on Jackass Hill in Angels Camp, where Twain wrote his famous Jumping Frog of Calavares County story.

"The neat thing," Bryant continued, "is this replica camp is located on land that really was a camp and also occupied by Indians at one time. When we started setting up this teaching camp and digging we found artifacts that are now displayed in our store like the old pistols and gold digging equipment. We also found grinding rocks (used to grind corn) with deep holes, which meant that Indians had camped here for a while." The excitement of his find, all these years later, still shone in his eyes and was reflected in his voice.

Bryant proudly explained, "My dad started this school twenty-nine years ago. The purpose of our school is to teach amateur gold seekers the scientific methods of locating gold and the basics of geology, the knowledge which many of the 49er's lacked. This also explains why so many of them went home broke or empty-handed. With what I teach you today and tomorrow, you guys will find gold … I guarantee it."

We were all getting excited. Now if he could only guarantee the size of the nugget we'd be set!

He saw that we were getting anxious to start, so he briefly explained our itinerary for the next two days. "Today, we are going to learn the physics and hydrology of placer gold deposits. Placer deposits is just one of the types of gold deposits found on the earth. For our purposes, you'll learn how to pan for gold in our creek. Then I'll show you the sluice box method, which we will work on around the Indian grinding hole area of the creek. Tomorrow we will drive to Table Top Mountain, and I'll show you the Mother Lode vein, then we will do some more gold prospecting farther down along the creek. Now let's get started."

He handed us each a vile for our gold finds and a black, plastic, fourteen-inch pan. Then he walked over to a cupboard full of black, knee-high rubber boots and handed us each a pair, so we could put our feet in the stream as we sat on the dock and learned panning.

With equipment in hand, we got up from the picnic benches and walked over to a nearby pile of dirt that had been brought in from a site outside the camp. He put several shovelfuls in a white, plastic bucket and instructed us to walk the few feet over to the wooden boardwalk that ran the length of the creek.

Then he filled each of our pans with the dirt. We all sat down on the dock and the lessons began. "The most important thing to understand is that gold is very heavy; it's almost twenty times that of the same volume of water. So as we pan and get rid of the sand, gravel, and rocks, the gold will go to the bottom of the pan. After we are done, all that's left in the pan, hopefully, will be the gold. Now start panning."

Bryant sat in the stream facing us, so we could imitate his moves.

"Panning is an important skill for a gold miner to master. First, place your pan in shallow water deep enough to cover the pan."

We all obeyed, eager to find our gold.

"Next, use your hands to break up the dirt, clay, and root clumps."

We did this as Bryant watched our technique. Immediately, the water above our pans became very cloudy. I was nervous to break up too much dirt, thinking I would wash the gold away accidentally. He came over and roughed up my pan. My heart sank.

"You can be rougher ... trust me."

I smiled.

He continued, "Now, I want you guys to wash the larger rocks. Look at them first to make sure they're not quartz, and then discard them."

Steve was briskly throwing away his rocks, and Spencer was discarding them quickly too. Jamie and I looked more like we were doing a geological report on the stones.

"Now that you've gotten rid of the larger stones, hold the pan level underwater, and with both hands, shake it from side to side so all the gold can settle to the bottom. "

This I was very intent on doing.

"Okay, with both your hands, I want you to lift one edge of the pan out of the water. Then, by moving the pan back and forth like waves on a beach, wash away the lighter sand that is on top. This is called sloughing. Repeat this process three or four times. Each time, you'll have less and less dirt in your pan as it gets washed away."

Spencer, Steve, and Jamie had the knack. I was taking my time ... still not trusting in the heaviness of the gold.

Fran Capo

After we sloughed a few times, we put the pans back underwater, then took out any remaining larger pebbles, sloughed some more, and finally, we had about a fourth of a tablespoon of dirt left in the pan. We were now ready to "read the pan." Read it! At this point I was so excited I was ready to recite *War and Peace*! This was the moment of truth ... the time you'd see if all your hard panning had left you with even a speck of gold in your pan.

As instructed, I held the pan with one hand in front of me. With just enough water to cover the tablespoon of material left, I slowly swirled the water then quickly let it bring down the sand. If there was any gold dust it would stay at the top of the pan.

I swirled and swirled, waiting and hoping and then I heard,"I got gold!" Jamie was the first one to get gold in her pan. It was a small speck, but it was gold. She carefully put it in her vial. We congratulated her then quickly filled up our pans once again to see if we would be the next lucky gold dust winners.

I was the next gold lady with a few specks sticking to my pan. Spencer followed and finally Steve. We kept panning until Bryant had to pry the pans away from us for a late lunch.

After lunch, we moved onto the sluice box method. Bryant explained, "The sluice box is a long metal box that can move the equivalent of thirty pans at a time. You feed shovelful by shovelful of dirt into the box, making sure you don't clump it all at one end. After you have done a full bucket, you check what the box has caught and then pan out the rest."

Deciding to add a little friendly gender competition into this, Steve and Spencer worked one box, and Jamie and I worked another.

In the boys' box were dozens of small pieces and two nice-sized chucks about as big as a pinky nail, worth about seventy-five dollars each. Bryant was amazed they found chunks that size. Jamie and I stopped to look at the booty.

Spencer wanted all of the smaller pieces in lieu of the two big pieces found. He went for weight, and Steve went for size. That was when the first bit of gold fever hit me ... I tried to convince Spencer to split the small nuggets equally with Steve and for each one of them to take one big chunk. Somehow I felt Spence was being cheated. While they battled it out, Jamie and I went back to check the progress of our box. Unfortunately, we had found very little, which, of course, wasn't our fault since the boys had obviously taken all the good dirt.

But, with gold found, we diligently continued to work the boxes until five when the class officially ended. Bryant took the sluice boxes but told us we could stay at the camp and pan more if we liked. One look at the kids and we knew we were staying. They were happily digging and shoveling until eight, filling up their vials with gold found by panning. Now if we could only figure out a way to harness this energy to clean their rooms!

That night we all compared our finds. We needed a magnifying glass to see mine. Spencer offered to give me some of his, but I wanted to find my own, not take from my kid. Even though I knew it was the logical thing to be happy for the kids and Steve, I kept wishing I'd find some too. A nice chunk would be good. I didn't want to have to go back to the highway and bring home some of that pyrite.

After reading the manual that night, we could see how the gold rush fever grew. Once you had the taste of finding gold ... you wanted to try again. Back then, people could make more money in one week panning for gold than they could make in a year, and the anticipation of finding it was very exciting, not knowing which shovelful could turn you instantly wealthy. The weird thing is I'm not a gambling casino–type person, but there was something very different about working with nature, and bringing up its natural treasures in what looked like common dirt.

We met Byrant at nine the next morning for day two of our gold prospecting expedition. This time we drove to various locations to see where gold had been dug for in the past, including Table Top Mountain and Negro Hill. Then we saw where they were mining for gold once again, only this time with high tech equipment, including using infrared satellite photos taken in 1980 to determine where to start digging.

Then he showed us the Mother Lode. "What makes the Mother Lode so unique is that, in the 123 miles, there are consecutive changes from mariposite to slate to serpentine sandstone. This is the only place in the world you will find these changes. It's the largest vein of gold in the world."

Fran Capo

With that history lesson behind us, we went back to the mining camp anxious to continue our search for gold. Steve, Jamie, and Spencer went back to the sluicing box. Bryant, the dog, and I went down creek, crossing thigh-high water to look for bedrock and learn how to "read" a creek or, simply put, to learn how to determine where to find the gold.

Since this creek has seen thousands of his students over the past eleven years, we had to really look and be observant.

Bryant said, "Remember, gold is usually the heaviest material and therefore works its way to the bottom of the streambed. There are certain drop areas for gold. One is where water flows through a wide area then slows down, and the other is inside a curve on a creek bed. So just look for bedrock. If it's smooth, it will be at the points I told you. If the bedrock is uneven or has cracks, the bedrock itself will have natural traps for gold."

Okay, there was only one problem. To me, bedrock is where the Flintstones lived. I wasn't sure what it looked like. As we both stood there, he nudged me, "It's the solid rock beneath the soil or surface."

Ah, gotcha!

He pointed out a rock near the creek and had me follow it down with my hand into the water. I found rocks going along that line. Then I dug out the mud, stones, and gravel in between with my hands and a shovel. I placed the material in my pan just in case this was an untouched hole and therefore a spot for gold. I got to the bottom of the creek. I had to do all this by feel since it was a creek and the water was cloudy since I was stirring all the bottom stuff up. I felt that the rock on the ledge and the rock in the water had an underground connection. I had reached bedrock. I dug in the crevices where gold was likely to have settled. Bryant told me to dig until there was nothing left in that section.

The first hole yielded nothing after three panning sessions. We went a few more feet and found two more bedrock holes to try. Bryant and I dug underwater in side-by-side holes. He told me his hole had been previously dug in; at the bottom there were leaves, which meant they had fallen from the trees and settled in with the other stuff. Had it been undisturbed no outside things would be at the bottom.

Adrenaline Adventures

I had three pans of mud, gravel, and sand from my hole. I went to the shallow creek and started panning the way Bryant had told us to the day before. I carefully inspected the rocks, making sure none was quartz and then tossing them into the flowing river. Just as I was about to toss a rock, I stopped. "Wait! What is this?!" Bryant came over. Sure enough, it was a quartz rock about the size of a dime, but thicker, with shining chunks of gold stuck to it.

Bryant said, "Man, where did you find that?"

"In the hole I was digging in," I quickly said.

He laughed. "You got yourself a piece worth about three hundred bucks, and if you make it into jewelry it's worth more. Nice find."

To say I was a happy camper is an understatement. I tucked the rock into my pocket, trying to be careful not to wipe the gold off it. We walked back through the creek. I was being extra careful not to fall in and lose my newfound treasure.

I couldn't wait to tell everyone. It was an awesome feeling. If I had not been taught the proper skills, I would have walked right by that place in the creek and not thought another moment about it.

Now what was our ruling again on the gold we found? Clearly I was away from everyone. I sure hoped they had a successful day as well or this was going to get real sticky.

I got back to the camp and showed everyone my gold. Brent, Bryant's brother, was there and gave me a bag to hold the gold in for safekeeping. "You guys did all right." Brian laughed. Then he took out this gold nugget that he had found a while back. It was big. I was tempted to run back into the creek to look for more, but I was satisfied.

Turns out Jamie and Spencer had found a fair amount too. They agreed to split it. But since Jamie had lost hers from the day before, she now had less than everyone else did. Steve said he'd buy her some gold chips from the gold store, and she was happy with that. But in addition, Spencer said she could keep what they found together. Steve then offered to buy Spencer some gold chips since he was so generous, but he wanted some postcards instead. (Gotta teach that boy the value of gold.) Jamie got her chips and then wanted to surprise Spencer and give him back the gold he gave her that they split. All the time Steve and I kept our mouths shut about our finds.

Later I found Jamie's vial. Spencer still didn't want his split back. He was happy with his own personal find, and everyone went back to the hotel with a taste of gold fever and a nugget in their pocket.

Of course, why would I be satisfied leaving the adventure there? That night in the hotel we had to change rooms because of a maintenance problem. Instead of one big room, we had two separate rooms, Spencer and I in one room, and Steve and Jamie in another room, which happened to be directly across from the haunted room, number seven.

It was right before bedtime that I decided to spook my child. I told Spencer about the haunted room. He wasn't thrilled with my timing. "Did you have to tell me right before bed?"

I laughed, but it wound up spooking me more than him.

At midnight, Steve and I agreed to meet in the hallway after the kids were asleep to have some down time. It was then that I told him about the ghost as well. "Listen, Steve, back in 1897, this was a hospital. Supposedly this young red-haired woman who called herself Mary Rose Sullivan got off the train and came to the hospital looking to speak to a doctor. Turns out she was pregnant out of wedlock. She went into labor, something went wrong, and both she and the baby died. The father was a British soldier, and their families disapproved of their love and sent the guy to India, where he was captured and tortured during the Hindu/Muslim troubles. Embarrassed and hurt, she fled her family and came to Jamestown where her grandfather had struck it rich years earlier, and died here. Supposedly all three, the soldier, the mother, and the baby live in room seven, happily ever after, as ghosts. Many have seen the ghosts."

Steve looked at me and said, "Let's go in. I've seen ghosts before."

He was serious, he had. But I hadn't. It was one of those you-don't-want-to-but-you-want-to moments.

The way the hotel was set up, all the doors of the unoccupied rooms were open and had a roped chain so you could look in and see the room. The door to number seven was open as we spoke.

The hotel was quiet. The kids were asleep. To be honest, I was scared. I'm not afraid to jump out of planes, but I don't really want to meet someone who has passed, even if they are a happy ghost family.

Adrenaline Adventures

I told Steve of my fear, and he said, "I'll never let you live this down." With that, I walked into the room alone. I don't know if it was my imagination or if the room had an aura, but I felt uncomfortable.

I stayed about a minute and then said, "There!"

Steve still felt I was a chicken. I was about to go back in the room when we heard a loud scream ... we both jumped. It was Jamie. She had woken up and saw Steve was gone and panicked.

Saved by the waking child, we went back to our respective rooms.

All night long I couldn't sleep, feeling I hadn't faced a fear. Me, who lives by the philosophy of "fear nothing." This was not sitting well with me at all. At six, I heard a tap on my door. It was Steve.

He smiled. "Want to try again?"

Part of me didn't want to disrespect the owners or the ghosts. But my curiosity got the best of me (my apologies to the owners). We went in the room again and just stood there. It was still dark, but knowing that the day was coming, somehow made me feel safer. After all, it was a gorgeous room, and the ghosts were lovers. I tried to picture Casper in my head, but somehow Poltergeist sneaked in instead.

Then Steve said, "Let's try to lure them out." And with that he kissed me. I wasn't quite sure how this was bait, but I didn't want to open my eyes and see I was kissing an apparition. We kissed for what felt like five minutes. I had one eye open, of course—someone had to play lookout. When I felt I had stayed sufficient time to claim overcoming my fear, we left.

I went back to sleep wondering if the ghosts were watching. Later that morning, we were in rush packing and had to check out. Steve noticed the door to room number seven was closed. He remembered that we had left it opened the entire time. He opened the door so it would be the way it always was. The door slammed shut. He opened it again, and again the door closed. He tried it several times, and each time, as soon as he let go, the door forcibly closed. He knew the door was capable of staying open, because it had been open the entire time we were at the hotel. The ghosts were not pleased.

Steve didn't tell me this until we had checked out. I was curious to see if the door would close if I pushed on it as well, but figured I'd just take his word. Why have them angrier and decide to follow us to San Francisco?

We went across the street and said goodbye to the Shock brothers. We bought some final gifts, exchanged last minute stories, and headed on to the next part of our California adventure. I did look over my shoulder once to see if we had any spiritual hitchhikers, but the coast was clear. But then again, it would be since they were ghosts. I put all thoughts out of my mind and concentrated on the road ahead. I looked back at the kids, and they were happy playing their new video games with their old gold dust in their pockets.

Adrenaline Adventures

Chapter 36
Adventure at a Glance - Dare to Do it   Mild to Wild Scale: 2
Title: Panning for Gold
Children allowed: Yes
Age requirement: No age limit
Length of trip: Half hour to full week
Where to try this adventure: Gold Prospecting Adventures LLC. 18170 Main Street , P.O. Box 1040, Jamestown, CA 95327-1040 209/984-4653 Reservations 800/596-0009 www.goldprospecting.com
-Jamestown Hotel, PO Box 539, 18153 Main Street, Jamestown, CA 95327 Phone 209-984-3902   Rate: $65-$95 per night
Best time of year: Summer, spring, and fall
Approximate cost: Half hour - $10, Course 1- $595, Family plan - $390
Reservations necessary: Yes
Fitness requirements: None
Personal gear required: Hat, sunscreen, notepad, pen
What NOT to bring: Clothes that you don't want to get wet
Photo opportunities: Yes

Notes: If you are planning a trip to California you can read my complete adventure which includes many exciting spots in the archives of either www.uniquetravelstories.com or www.travelnewsletter.com. You can also pan for gold in most of the other mountainous states, Vermont, North Carolina, Colorado and Maine.

Cool trivia: Native Americans who bathed regularly called the 49er's en route to gold country the stinky trail west. The 49er's were in "bumper to bumper" traffic from sunup to sundown in ninety-degree heat day after day with no shower or bath. The women wore long dresses, and the men wore long pants. They wore the same clothes every day for six months. They had no choice but to drink rancid water, which lead to diarrhea— The Indians thought the emigrants uncivilized because of their poor hygiene.

"Age is of no importance, unless you are a cheese."
—Billie Burke

Chapter 37
"A Dolphin Adventure and Other Marine Encounters of the Best Kind" Swimming with Dolphins

Several years ago I did a dive with dolphins in the Bahamas. I remember the experience being anticlimatic; all the hype of interacting with these brilliant creatures and instead it was more like an underwater bus tour had dropped off a group of thirty humans and we were told we had ten minutes to shop. We were instructed to sit in a circle on the sandy ocean floor and extend our hands out as a dolphin swam around the inner circle a total of three times. We each got to touch it in passing. That was it. The total dolphin encounter. I'd be better off looking at a picture of a dolphin and splashing water on my face. I vowed to find a better place someday to interact with these wonderful creatures.

Well, I found it. It was called Dolphin World in Key Largo. They offered a three-day marine animal workshop for people ten and

Adrenaline Adventures

older which included a reef snorkel, an environmental tour, and two dolphin programs.

I called up my trusty boyfriend, Steve, and told him about this great adventure idea and how the kids (his daughter, Jamie, and my son, Spencer) would love it. He knew by the tone of my voice that it was just a matter of when. He gave me the typical, "Yes dear, I don't have a choice, do I?" response.

The only logical time to go was during the kids' mid-winter recess break. Who knew that that was the hardest time to book a trip unless you called the nanosecond the school calendar came out? We were able to book a flight to Fort Lauderdale, no problem. However, getting back was another story. Not one airport in Florida had four round-trip tickets available during that week. We were even willing to go two at a time like Noah's Ark. Nada. We tried every airport in Florida—we tried the Internet, my travel agent, other travel agents, even chanting. No luck. We could go Amtrak, but it would take twenty-two hours. We could fly to Australia in that time!

Finally, determined to do this, we decided we'd drive back to New York. That's when we found out we could fly out of Atlanta, Georgia. Hey, it's better than driving the whole way back to New York! With driving cutting into the trip, I asked if the workshop could be done in two days. Jan over at Dolphin World said, "No problem." Too bad she didn't work for the airlines.

We flew out on a Tuesday and got to Fort Lauderdale at eleven P.M., then drove over to Steve's mom's house for a quick overnight stay (he had to be a good son and say hello to mommy).

The next morning, after a quick dip in his mom's pool, shaking down some grapefruits from her backyard tree, and a quick visit to her antique store (with the kids getting some good bargains), we started our sojourn to Key Largo in our rented car. The drive down was a mere two and a half hours. Nothing compared to rush hour in New York. Besides, the kids were busy with Pokemon. We knew we were getting close when we passed Jewfish Creek Bridge (I'm not kidding that's the name).

For those of you unfamiliar with the Florida Keys, they are located at the southernmost tip of Florida and accessed by the Overseas Highway (US 1). They consist of Key Largo, Islamorada, Marathon,

Lower Keys, and Key West. Everything in the Keys is marked by these green and white mile markers (MM), beginning with MM 126, which is one mile past Florida City, and ending with MM 0, which is Key West, only ninety miles away from Cuba.

Key Largo is the largest of the Florida Keys (about thirty miles end to end) and is the first key you hit as soon as you cross over the bridge to Route One. The Spanish originally called it Cayo Largo, or Long Island. Key Largo is acknowledged as the "Diving Capital of the World." It is famous for its beautiful offshore reef, found in John Pennekamp Park (the nation's first underwater park) and the Key Largo National Marine Sanctuary.

Our hotel, the Marina Del Mar, was at MM 100, just off the main highway. It was the place that Dolphin World recommended, since it was near the activity sites. Plus, we got ten percent off, always a nice incentive.

As we went to check in, however, we found out our one-bedroom suite was occupied by some rude people who refused to check out. Of course, I'm thinking, knock on the door and throw them out Soprano-style, but the hotel had different plans. They said we'd get a regular room that night with twin beds and the next night we would get upgraded to the deluxe two-bedroom suite for the same price. We agreed. Why not, it came with a whirlpool.

After a six o'clock wakeup call the next morning, we headed down to the dock by the hotel to meet the captain of our snorkel expedition. After a briefing on how to put on snorkel gear (I've never seen anyone put the fins on his face but there's always a first time) and emergency procedures, we were off for a pleasant forty-minute cruise to White Banks Reef. We were fitted with wetsuits and had our gear ready for the fish encounter.

Not that we were anxious or anything, but Spencer and I were the first to dive off the back of the boat into the water. We were told to swim to the front of the boat and off to the left to see the reef. The water temperature was seventy-three degrees, and the depth only about twenty feet. Jamie and Steve soon followed.

The Keys are the home to the only living coral reef in the continental United States. They lie primarily within two protected areas: Biscayne National Park and John Pennekamp Coral Reef State

Adrenaline Adventures

Park. These reefs are living, breathing natural wonders that are as much as seven thousand years old. They grow at the incredibly slow rate of one to sixteen feet every one thousand years (I think I'm on that same growth plan!) So were told to keep our hands off!

You can see the reef by snorkel, SNUBA (which is a tethered SCUBA diving where you can go down twenty feet below the surface as you breathe air piped down from tanks on a boat), or you can SCUBA dive the old-fashioned way, with tanks on your back. Since we had the kids with us, we snorkeled. As responsible parents, we each stuck with our own child. So much for romance.

Spencer and I spotted all kinds of fish: clown, angel, parrot, neon, and my favorite, the polka-dotted puffer fish. We also saw sea fans, sponges, and brain coral. There are more than six hundred species of fish in these waters. I was hoping to see a nurse shark to get the adrenaline flowing, but I didn't.

Then I spotted a barracuda. I've seen them many times before, so I wasn't alarmed. They usually just stop, stare with their cold, beady eyes, and aren't very much interested unless you have glittering jewelry dangling from your neck. Then they come in for a closer view. I knew Spencer would think it was cool to see a barracuda so I pointed it out to him.

He was so excited he lifted his head and blurted out to Jamie, "Look, barracuda." That's all she needed to hear. She swam swiftly back to the boat like one of those cartoon characters, with Steve by her side. She happily sunned on the deck of the boat. I have to teach Spencer the art of skillfully keeping his mouth zipped since Jamie's still new in the adventure division.

We enjoyed the gorgeous coral reef and all its multicolored fish for a total of one hour. Then we were given the signal from the boat captain and we headed back to shore.

After an hour break for lunch, we dried ourselves off and got ready for our afternoon adventure, The Florida Everglades Park Environmental Tour. This time it was only a cozy party of six.

The two-hour tour took us to the Mangrove Islands, to Hemingway's Pass where *National Geographic* has shot footage of one-thousand-year-old trees, and to salt water marshes with no soil, just thousands of tangled tree roots that constitute the island.

Fran Capo

Since it was winter, we were safe from the bloodthirsty mosquitoes. But we were warned that if for some reason we ever got stranded here in the summer, the only way to survive would be to cover our heads with our shirts dipped in water, so as not to get eaten alive.

On the way back, the captain pointed out a floating junkyard, which was actually the residence of a ninety-three-year-old man who has lived on that boat for twenty years. Amazing—and I thought trailer parks were bad.

We were also told that if you took the Intercoastal Waterways north, you could head straight to New York. Finally, we searched the waterways for a manatee. We spotted two. The kids loved it. I snapped some shots, and we headed back to shore.

That evening, we checked into the gorgeous two-bedroom suite. The kids swam in the pool as Steve and I watched.

That evening we checked into the gorgeous two-bedroom suite. The kids swam in the pool as Steve and I watched.

I was reading a book by Nora Roberts appropriately called *The Reef*, as Steve conducted business via cell phone.

As we sat poolside enjoying our vacation, we got THE call. The call you dread. The call you hope never happens, but eventually always does. Steve's mom's husband, Gary, had died unexpectedly. We'd just seen him yesterday, happy and healthy, and now he was gone from this world—Heart attack. We were shocked. After many discussions, we decided not to tell the kids until after the dolphin swim tomorrow. Then we would cut the trip short and head back to Fort Lauderdale to offer support. His sister was with his mom already.

The reality of things like this puts everything into perspective and makes one realize that doing things at the spur of the moment in life and not putting off the adventures you dream about is important, because in the end, we never know when God will call in our chips. The lucky thing is, the morning we left their house, we heard Steve's mom, Alice, and Gary telling each other, "I love you."

With an odd mixture of sorrow and passion for living, we got up early the next morning, rushed through a continental breakfast, and drove over to Dolphin Plus (the marine mammal research and

Adrenaline Adventures

education center that Dolphin World hooked us up with). We began our first encounter with the dolphins, the structured swim.

After we signed our waivers, we were lead out the back door of the office/gift shop and down a ramp to a large area with several fenced-in pens. The walls surrounding the dolphin pens were made of ancient coral reef, not cement as it first appeared.

An instructor sat all twenty of us under a tent and began a forty-five minute orientation about dolphins, their anatomy and general hands on behaviors for us humans to do during the program. "We have two sea lions and thirteen bottle-nosed dolphins at this facility. The funny thing is the area that is shaped like a bottle on a dolphin isn't really his nose at all; it's his mouth. His nose is the blowhole. Dolphins can stay underwater for about fifteen minutes but usually only stay two to three minutes before coming up for air. They do not have vocal chords; all the noise comes out of their blowholes. They have eighty-eight cone-shaped teeth, but they don't use them for chewing. They swallow their fish whole, head first, so they don't get the scales caught in their throats. They have no circular motion in their jaws. Dolphins have thirty-five to fifty layers of skin. They also have taste in the parts per billion, where we have it in the parts per thousand. Which means if you put one drop of lemon in an Olympic-sized pool, they can taste it. They lack the sense of smell and only can distinguish bitter and sour, which is good since otherwise they would always have that salt water taste in their mouths."

She started flip flopping a stuffed dolphin while pointing out parts of his body. "When you go in the water, the dolphins will be doing a series of behaviors with you. Look them in the eyes, that's the way of connecting to them. They will sense everything about you through echolocation. They know how dense you are (and we're not talking IQ—fat quotient is more like it), and they can see through our bones because we are made up so much of water. They know if you are pregnant or had any kind of weird surgery or operations."

Great, we have a date with the Clark Kent of Dolphins. The instructor told us that one lady accidentally found out she was pregnant through the dolphins. The dolphins hung around her because they could see the fetus! So girls, if they just pass you by, be thankful!

Fran Capo

Then we were given our final instructions before being divided into groups. "Please don't reach out for the dolphins. They have no way of protecting their eyes, so if you reach out, they will run away. Also, when you grab onto their dorsal fins, grab the base, which is the strongest part. Relax and enjoy."

After the orientation, we were given flotation vests. There is no free swimming or diving, and no snorkeling equipment is used during the structured swim.

Our trainer was Betsy Madison. She introduced herself and carried two buckets of fish as we followed her to the pen where the alpha male, Dingy, and the alpha female, Elby, and their six-month-old offspring, Cosmo, were waiting. Alpha, by the way, means the dominant one.

We all stood on a wooden platform. Betsy kneeled in the middle and asked us to go in the water two at a time. Spencer and I went in first, me on her right, Spencer on her left. Steve was on 35 mm camera duty, and Jamie watched. Steve is a computer guy; pictures aren't exactly his strong point, although many other things are. So we hired Dolphin World's videographer to tape the session also. After all, how many times in your life do you swim with dolphins?

Plus it sure beats watching a video of the family birthday party, with someone taking one too many slices of rum cake and singing "Feelings" on the karaoke machine.

We lowered ourselves into the water. It was cold! As I was getting used to the cold, Elby popped up. Wow, I was three feet away from a dolphin. I actually started to giggle. We were told to hold out our hands. The dolphin's sleek, silky body passed over our hands. My grin got wider.

Next, one at a time, we were told to lie on our backs with our feet spread apart (oh yeah, I want this on camera!). The dolphins were instructed to nuzzle their bottle-nosed mouths to our feet and give us a toe push ride. Then we were told to wait in the middle with our arms spread out in a T-like fashion. All of a sudden Elby and Dingy popped up. The next thing we knew we were holding onto their dorsal fins and headed toward the platform at torpedo speed. I could feel the strength, yet gentleness, of these beautiful creatures.

Driving lessons were next. As we held onto a kickboard, the dolphins pushed our feet, and as we steered, they zoomed us around the pool. Now Betsy had us engage in a little mischief. We were told to start a water fight with them. We splashed them with our hands, and they soaked us with their fins. It was like a thimble compared to a water bucket. I swear I heard them laughing. The interaction continued as they jumped over hoops and gave us more rides. It finally ended with them kissing our hands. After using loads of film, it was time for Jamie and Steve to have their encounter.

I never saw Steve smile so much. There's something about getting in the water with dolphins that just makes you laugh out loud. It's like having the ultimate cool playmate. At the end of their session, instead of kissing Steve on the hand, Elby went for his lips. She looked up at me, winked, and laughed. Good thing Steve likes brunettes.

Betsy was fantastic, friendly and she really wanted to make sure we got the most out of our encounter. We had such a great time and an experience we'd never forget.

After a quick lunch and dip in the hotel pool, we were back at Dolphin Plus for our natural swim. This time Holly led the informational briefing. The anatomy information was the same (it would be scary if it wasn't). The rules for the natural swim were totally different, however.

The instructor explained, "In this swim you are not allowed to touch the dolphins. Let them come to you. You are in their home. You will be given a mask, fins, and snorkel. Don't stay on the ceiling of their homes, dive down into their living room and look them in the eye. You are their playthings. This is their time to play with you. They like children first, then women, then men. Do crazy things in there. Make noise, be goofy, be different. They will come over out of pure curiosity. Enjoy."

This time our encounter was with three other dolphins, Jessica, Squirt, and Tracey.

We were divided into groups of six. As we all entered the water, we were told just to swim around without using our hands.

The dolphins, all three of them, were immediately attracted to Spencer. Every time I looked up, Spencer was snorkeling with a dolphin swimming on each side. They were even jockeying for who could play with him more. Steve tried diving down to get their attention. They came over briefly. Jamie and I tried swimming out with a long pole to attract their attention, and they came over briefly. We even tried singing. That probably made them run more. At one point Jamie got out, and Jessica seemed to be waiting for Jamie to get back in the water and play. As for me, I resorted to my last-ditch effort. I broke into my fast talking rendition of the "Three Little Pigs" underwater through my snorkel. Believe it or not, that attracted them. I guess even dolphins find my fast talking an oddity. But soon, they went back to magnet boy. The half hour went quickly.

After the natural swim, we drove straight to Fort Lauderdale.

We got back, hugged Steve's mom, and the kids' natural playfulness with the family dog seemed to distract everyone.

The next morning we drove to Atlanta, stopping briefly at the Kennedy Space Center where we got a chance to chat with an astronaut. He told us how awesome it felt to see the earth from space and how hard on the body it was to come back. They have to drink forty-eight ounces of salt water upon reentering the earth's atmosphere so they can hydrate. He ended by telling the kids, "I am nothing special. I had a dream and never gave up on it. I studied hard and kept applying myself. You can do the same."

We finally arrived in Atlanta, Georgia, at one in the morning, after twelve hours of driving. After a few hours of sleep, Jamie, Spencer and I were on the red eye flight. Steve flew back to Fort Lauderdale to be with his mom.

As Spencer, Jamie, and I sat on the plane headed toward New York, I thought about all that had transpired. The kids were playing again, Steve was supporting his mom, and I was thinking about how everything in life is what you make it. Our adventures, our dreams, our desires, our relationships all come from putting ourselves out there and giving it our best.

Whatever you perceive your adventures to be, live them today, to the fullest because you never know what life may hold. Create your own destiny, share your adventures with those you love, and allow yourself to totally enjoy it all with laughter and the heart of a child; if you do, you will look back on a life with no regrets.

Adrenaline Adventures

Chapter 37
Adventure at a Glance - Dare to Do it   Mild to Wild Scale: 3

Title: Swimming with Dolphins
Children allowed: Yes
Age requirement: Ages eight to twelve must be accompanied in the water by a parent. Ages thirteen to seventeen must have a parent on facility grounds.
Length of trip: Half day to three day workshops
Where to try this adventure: Dolphins Plus - Key Largo, Florida (305) 451-1993, or toll-free at (866) 860-7946
email: info@dolphinsplus.com, or Website: www.dolphinsplus.com
Best time of year: All year round in Florida.
Approximate cost:. Cost for the natural swim is $125 per swimmer. Cost for the double natural swim is $210 per swimmer. Cost for structured swim is $160 per person. You can participate in both swim programs for $240 per swimmer.
Reservations necessary: Yes
Fitness requirements: Must be comfortable in water.
Personal gear required: Bathing suit
What NOT to bring: Anything you don't want to lose in the water.
Photo opportunities: Yes

Notes: They have a variety of packages to choose from so you can call your own shots. Other places around the world offer dolphin swims also, just make sure you will get maximum time with minimum people in the water or you will be disappointed.

Cool trivia: Dolphins Plus has educational summer camps, rescue programs, and they also have a therapy program called Island Dolphin Care, which is a not-for-profit organization. Island Dolphin Care was developed to help children and their families who are coping with various developmental, physical, or emotional difficulties. They provide a recreational program that focuses on the emotional and physical well-being of the participant and his/her family.

"We are not retreating – we are advancing in another direction."
—General Douglas MacArthur

Chapter 38
"Zorro for the Day"
Fencing

I remember one night while I was in high school staying up until three A.M. watching a Bob Hope movie. I don't remember the name of film, but what I do remember was that he fenced in it. Something about the way he comically but gallantly did it, inspired me so much that the next day I joined the fencing club in school, and then went onto join the fencing team. To think, Bob Hope, not Zorro was my inspiration.

Since then I have tried many sports and crazy daredevil adventures but never went back to fencing. So one day when my thirteen-year-old son, Spencer asked, "Are we doing anything new and exciting this weekend or are we finally going to relax?" Out of the recesses of my mind came, "Relax? Sure. After you and I take a fencing lesson."

He just shook his head. "Where do you come up with these ideas, Ma?"

Adrenaline Adventures

I'm not sure why fencing popped into my head at that moment, but inspiration can come from anywhere. I remembered saving a flyer I'd found a year ago from a place called Metropolis Fencing in New York City. I dug up the flyer and called the place. They were not only still in existence (as they had been for seventy-five years) but were thriving, and reasonably priced lessons were available in three different types: foil, saber, and epee. We chose the standard foil lesson.

In the meantime, a very impromptu friend, Dee called, "What adventures are you guys up to this weekend?" I told her and she was game to come with us.

Dee, her son John Michael (J.M.), Spencer, and I headed into the city for the 2:30 class.

Upon arrival we were amazed how big the place was. It was a two-level space with six thousand square feet and twelve-foot ceilings on one floor and another nine thousand square feet with a twenty-foot ceilings on the other floor. That's a lot of fencing space!

When we walked in, teams were dueling. Apparently we walked in at the end of some kind of electronic fencing tournament. A wire was hooked up to the fencers, and if they hit their opponent tip on in the target area, they scored a point. We watched for a few minutes, which made us even more anxious to play.

Leroy, one of the operators of this family-run place, greeted us. We told him that we wanted to try fencing. "You came to the right place. New York is the fencing center of America."

"We'd called about the foil class," I said.

"Good choice. Foil is the training device, kind of like rubber nunchucks," he responded. "Foil has the most rules and regulations and the smallest target, the chest area. It's also the fastest paced, which the boys will love."

"Refresh my memory," I said. "What are the other two, epee and that saber-tooth tiger thing?"

He laughed. "Epee is taught on Saturdays. The epee sword has a bigger guard. It was derived from a dueling weapon." He took out an epee sword, which had a triangular blade. "As you can see, there is a blood groove left in this sword where the blood from the victim would drain out and not get on the fencer."

"Geez, how nice. You can kill with no messy stains. O.J. would have liked that."

He continued, "The epee is a puncture and dueling weapon, and the whole body is the target with this sword. There are no rules in a real duel."

"Well, that's good. The last thing I want when I'm about to go in for a kill is to be told my feet were crossed the wrong way."

Leroy chuckled.

"Okay, Leroy," I said. "Tell me about this saber thing?"

"The sabre was used while someone was on horseback. It was a slashing weapon derived from the Calvary. The blade is made to do both a forward and backward slash. With this sword, the target is everything from the waist up."

"That makes sense, since the guy on horseback wasn't going to aim for the feet." I added, "Well, then I guess we picked the right course, since the horse I came in is a Saturn, and we aren't signing up for the gore today."

"Great. It'll be the four of you, then?"

I turned to Dee. She shook her head no. After hearing the sword summary she quickly decided to play photographer and sit this one out. That left just the two boys and me taking the lesson.

Leroy handed us over to his wife, Georgine, who was one of the instructors.

Georgine took us to the back of the room, carefully making sure we walked to the sides of the mats, staying clear of the fencers. All we needed was for some amateur to poke us in the eye by mistake.

In the back of the room was a rack of protective gear. We were each given a white padded vest. Some of the vests slipped on through the front, and some in the back, like a straitjacket. (Now that's two things you definitely don't want together, a nut and a sword.)

Since I was the only female of our group, I got an added piece of gear—a breast guard. For those of you who have never seen this thing, it looks like a giant, clear, plastic bra made for some Amazon women. It was huge. I looked like a size 40DDD in it. I was trying to get Dee's attention to take a picture of me posing as Pamela Anderson but she was busy guarding our personal belongings.

Adrenaline Adventures

After we put our chest gear on, we were each given a fencing mask and a glove to wear over the hand we were fencing with. Then we were instructed to walk back along the wall to the front of the place and get our foils.

Georgine gave us background information and some ground rules. "The roots of fencing go back to the Middle Ages and beyond. While skill with a sword was crucial for fighting on the battlefield and in the arena to stay alive, there is evidence that fencing as a sport took place in Egypt approximately two thousand years before the birth of Christ. In the Middle Ages in Europe, with the rise of chivalry, rules for sword fighting among noblemen were set. When it wasn't used for combat, it was considered a sport that every gentleman should know.

The good thing about fencing is it doesn't rely on physical force. So a man and woman can fence and be equally matched."

I liked the sound of that!

She smiled and continued, "Timing and speed are the most essential elements in fencing. Today you are going to begin with the foil. As you were told, the foil is a training device. It has the most rules and regulations and the smallest target, the chest area. It's also the fastest paced. The foil is a puncture weapon. Of course, this one has a rubber tip." Thank goodness, or it would have been on hell of a lesson.

She looked at the boys and added, "This is not a toy. It's a weapon. It's loaded at all times, so the rules are no swinging it or aiming it at anyone. When you're walking or when the foil is otherwise not in use, it is to be held TIP DOWN."

In my head I heard the typical mom's line, "Or you could poke someone's eye out. And this time I mean it!"

It was time to get on the mats and begin the lesson. There were five of us taking the class; the three of us and two other guys. One guy was tall and lanky and the other looked like he could be a henchman on Wrestlemania.

Our instructor was Amrou Ahmed, an Egyptian National Olympic Fencing Coach who was with Metropolis for eight months. He was very trim, friendly, spoke quickly, and had a bit of an accent that at first was hard to understand.

Amrou began, "Okay, first we practice without the foil and mask."

We all just stood there with our equipment.

Amrou looked at us. "Why are you waiting? You need to put your equipment down."

Immediately, feeling like fools, we complied. This was going to require careful listening.

Good naturedly, he laughed and continued, "We are going to begin with the En Guarde stance. Now, you face your opponent standing sideways. Your front foot (usually the right) is pointing forward directly toward your opponent in alignment with your body. Your rear foot (usually the left) is perpendicular to your front foot, forming the letter L. There is about a eight inches, or one foot length, distance between your two feet." He went around checking our feet and making sure we were in an L position, not Z or T or any other letter of the alphabet.

"Okay, now bend your knees, lowing your center of gravity."

I heard someone's knee creek. I felt like yelling, "Get an oil can for the Tin Man!" But I thought better of it, just in case I did something embarrassing later on, like spear Amrou in the groin.

Amrou continued, "Now bend your right arm at the elbow about forty-five degrees. Keep only a fist distance between the side of your body and your elbow."

We all looked down. Spencer's fist must have been swollen that day because he had about a yard in between his elbow and his side. Amrou quickly adjusted Spencer's stance.

"Keep your wrist straight. Think of the foil as an extension of your arm."

(Okay, just call me Edward Scissorhands!)

"Your foil is to be pinched or held with your thumb on top and your index finger on the bottom of the handle, with the rest of your fingers all grasped behind the guard plate."

We all checked our grips.

"Now this is very important not to get hurt. Take your left arm and keep it behind you. It is to be curled as if you are making your hand touch your shoulder. There. Now you are done!"

Adrenaline Adventures

It sounded more complicated than it was. This was definitely an instance where a picture is worth a thousand words.

After we were in our correct stances—which by the way is great for the thigh and butt muscles—we were taught three basic moves: advance, retreat, and lunge.

Amrou demonstrated. "Watch me. To advance, simply take a step first with your right foot and then with your left. No jumping. No dragging feet. Separate steps. Keep your center of gravity low and your arms in the same position."

We all nodded then he yelled, "Advance!"

No one moved.

He looked puzzled. "What happened? How come none of you moved?"

I, for one, didn't understand his command. He said it so fast that I didn't realize that he was telling us to advance—and I'm the fast talker! We looked at each other as if we had single digit IQs.

"Okay," he said, "let's try this again. Advance!"

Like an army of well-trained soldiers, we all jumped at his command. Once he saw we had the knack of it, he kept repeating, "Advance, advance … advance …" He corrected our form as we did it. "You, keep your arm curled. You, don't jump. You, your feet are too far apart. Try to correct yourselves."

We practiced a few more times.

"Excellent! Very excellent!" he said. We were ready for the retreat … which was the same thing only in reverse.

To get us used to the moves, he mixed them up with a quick game of Simon Says. "Advance. Advance. Retreat. Advance. Double retreat." Ah, he got us on that last one. Soon we were all in the fencing groove. Meanwhile, Dee was taking pictures, capturing our efforts on film.

Finally, we were ready to don our equipment. We put on our headgear and took up our foils. En Garde! A few more advances and retreats and we were onto the final move of the lesson, the lunge.

The lunge was just like it sounded. You take a big step forward with your right foot, lunging forward but keeping the center of balance over your right knee, not past it. You extend your arm, aiming for the protected chest area. As you lunge forward, your left arm straightens out behind you and goes down by your side, keeping it out of harm's way. Sounds easy enough ... just takes some coordination. I had an advantage because my limbs were starting to remember my high school fencing moves. But Spencer did have to nudge me a few times to put my left arm down in back. Picky, picky.

The kids and the other guys were doing their own variations on the theme. Arm staying up, jumping forward, leaning too far, and dragging the leg. But eventually, with Amrou's encouragement, everyone was happily lunging.

Next came the real fun ... contact! Amrou stood in front of us, and each of us had a chance to jab him in the chest. I lunged right in. All I had to do was imagine a few ex's and it was a done deal. "Excellent!" he said. Although at one point he did tell me not to go for the throat.

As he was practicing with each of us individually, the rest of us had to do the exercises. After a while, holding my arm up started to hurt. But there was no way I was going to let my foil drop. I looked over at Spencer and J.M., they were sweating, and eager to be teamed up.

After a few bouts with the instructor, we were paired off. We worked our way down the mats, alternating between advances, retreats, and lunges. I worked with the tall guy, who was a bit timid. I told him to toughen up, I could take it. The next thing I knew he was lunging full force. Me and my big mouth! I retreated and was barely touched. We switched partners.

Finally, we had a chance at a "match" with just the instructor. He explained that in a match we had to have proper fencing etiquette. We would only score points if the tip, not the side of the blade, hit the chest area.

We each were instructed to approach the mat, fencing masks in hand, and shake. He said, "Ready?" And we had to reply, "Yes" before we could begin. Then, with a nod and a smile, he said, "Fence!"

With a flick of swords, each person tried for the target area. It was obvious that Amrou was letting us get hits in to build our confidence. I got one hit to the chest and scored a point. Then I hit him in the groin. Not good, and no points were scored for that one. He scored a

Adrenaline Adventures

point for getting me in the miracle bra. The score was now 1-1. Then I hit him again below the belt. He said, "Where did you hit me?"

I replied, "Ah, you tell me. It's your body."

He smirked. Luckily, Dee didn't get my hit on film so there was no photo evidence. I made one final contact with his chest and the bout was over. We shook hands to end the match with a sign of good sportsmanship.

The boys then each fenced with Amrou. I rooted for Spencer to be more aggressive. I must have been Roman in a previous life.

After the last bout, the boys fenced for a while with each other under Amrou's supervision. He encouraged them, and they obviously were enjoying this live video game version of ancient times, with them as the heroes.

When the hour was up, we put away our equipment. Leroy strolled over to us. "Well, did you enjoy it?"

The boys both said, "It was great! We want to come next Sunday."

Leroy smiled like the cat that ate the canary.

I said, "This is a great school you have here, Leroy."

He corrected, "Thanks, but technically it's not my school. It was passed down from a fencing master to me, a gift with a unique price tag."

"A unique price tag?" I inquired. "How so?"

"The school was given to me by a fencing master with one provision, 'Don't let it die!' So my family and I have been running it ever since. That was ten years ago. We've had famous fencers from all over the world come here, even Zorro's son. We train Olympic-style and have had students compete on high school, college, and national levels. I love it. I am a man of my word. So we are keeping the tradition alive."

"Wow, that's a lot of responsibility," I said. "Just like the eternal Olympic flame. You don't want to be the person that lets that thing drop."

Dee said, "We did our small part today. By introducing fencing to our kids, we gave it to the next generation."

We all left feeling that we had stepped back in time. We enjoyed and experienced a sport and lifestyle from long ago. Whether we go

Fran Capo

back again or not, life is about experiencing new things, for a mind exposed to something new is never the same again. Seek out new adventures and explore your world.

Adrenaline Adventures

Chapter 38
Adventure at a Glance - Dare to Do it   Mild to Wild Scale: 2
Title: Fencing
Children allowed: Yes
Age requirement: Seven and up with parental consent
Length of trip: Classes range from twenty minutes to one hour.
Where to try this adventure: Metropolis no longer exists, but these New York City fencing clubs have picked up the slack:
New York Athletic Club, 180 Central Park South 212-247-5100
New York Fencers Club, 119 West 25th Street 212-874-9800
The Fencing Place, 173 East 75th Street   212-244-3090
www.thefencingplace.com (This school is only a few months old.)
Best time of year: All year round.
Approximate cost: $25 for a twenty-five minute private lessons.
Reservations necessary: Suggested, but not necessary.
Fitness requirements: None
Personal gear required: Flat shoes
What NOT to bring: Tight clothes
Photo opportunities: Yes

Notes: When double checking the information about Metropolis Fencing, I was surprised to find out they had been shut down. New York City rent became too expensive. Representatives of the fencing community said they have felt a huge void since losing Metropolis.

Cool trivia: Aldo Nadi is considered by many fencers to be the greatest fencer of all time. He was the undefeated European champion for twelve years in a row and won a silver medal in the Olympics. His brother won five gold medals in the same competition. He fought an actual duel with rapiers.
   Their father fought against another highly experienced fencing master in a very famous "duel to the death."

"The difference between fiction and reality? Fiction has to make sense."
—Tom Clancy

Chapter 39
"The Hidden World of Akumal"
Cavern Diving

Being an advanced scuba diver, I'm always looking for new and exciting underwater places to explore. So when I saw an article in *Scuba Diver Magazine* about cenote diving, a.k.a. cavern diving, in Mexico, I clipped it out and decided one day I'd go.

Flash forward five years. I was driving in my car and heard an advertisement about a new IMAX movie called *Journey into Amazing Caves* Since I'm also an avid spelunker, I called up that same afternoon, bought tickets, and took my mom, Rose, and my son, Spencer, to the showing. Little did I know that the movie was about the very same caves in the Yucatan Peninsula in Mexico that were written about in the article I had cut out several years before. As I watched, glued to the screen, I knew this was the year I would go.

That night I went online and my e-mail buddy from Louisiana, Todd Williams, a dive master and photographer who I had never met, happened to IM me. I told him about the cenotes. Even with over three hundred dives to his credit, he had never even thought about trying them. We talked about going in the summer when our kids were out of school.

Adrenaline Adventures

When I get something in my head, I tend to be impatient. The summer was seven months away! If I went now, I could get it into this book before the deadline.

I found the magazine article I had cut out and e-mailed the dive shop listed. Unfortunately it was a bizarre defunct website. With my adrenaline flowing, I was now on a mission to locate a place to do the cenote diving. Of course, there were a few other small details I had to work out.

One, I wanted Spencer to experience this wonderful world, but he wasn't scuba certified. Two, I had to plan it in between my lectures, gigs, and his schooling, and three, my boyfriend's daughter, Jamie, was too young to dive.

A search on the Internet led me to a place called Maya Ha Resort, and the owner, John, was nice enough to lead me to Hidden Worlds, the very same dive shop where the IMAX people had filmed *Journey to Amazing Caves*. This was fantastic! It was meant to be. I also noticed on their Web site that they offered cavern tours to snorkelers, so non-divers like Jamie could go too.

As the pieces were falling nicely into place, I sprung the idea on my boyfriend, Steve, about the cenotes and all of us going with Todd, my Internet buddy. Steve didn't feel Jamie would be up for that kind of adventure, so after some discussion, we decided to take separate vacations. He'd go to Florida with Jamie, and I would go to Akumal, Mexico, in the heart of the Yucatan Peninsula with Spencer to explore the underwater caves and the Mayan ruins. And get this, Steve didn't mind that Todd would go with me; he even thought it was a good idea so that a mother and son wouldn't be roaming around Mexico themselves! Just the kind of guy I like; confident and not possessive.

I e-mailed Todd, told him plans had changed, and that I wanted to dive in February during Spencer's school vacation. He was game. This was going to be interesting, a slow-talking Southern boy and the world's fastest talking female hanging out together with boy in tow. Someone was going to speed up, slow down, or burn out. Of course, Todd said he figured he could just let me do all the talking and nod occasionally. That's one way to solve it.

There was still one minor challenge. Spencer wasn't certified and spring break wasn't very far away. As luck would have it, I called a local dive shop named Danny's. The classroom and pool training classes were starting the following Monday. It was five consecutive weeks, which left us one week to spare before his spring break. Todd could do his open water certification, the final part needed to get certified in Mexico and we were set. Perfect! Again, this trip was meant to be.

I called Hidden Worlds and spoke to this guy named Kevin. I told him I was doing a story on cenotes. Kevin gave me a quick rundown. "To safely dive a cavern zone, the scuba diver must either be trained and certified as a cavern diver or participate in a cenote dive with a qualified professional cave diving guide. No open water instructor can take you through the cenotes, the reason being that a cavern dive in a cenote means diving into an overhead environment, which does not allow a direct ascent to the surface. All my divers are cavern trained.

Hidden Worlds has been around for many years and has not had one bad incident, so you are in good hands. We have all the equipment you need here, just let me know when you want to go."

Now this is the kind of operation I like to dive with, perfect record and efficient.

Kevin was nice enough to turn me onto this wonderful place called Vista Del Mar Condos and Hotel. With the Vista Del Mar, you have a couple of options; you can stay in the two- or three-bedroom condos or get a hotel room. All are private, beachfront rooms. We chose the simpler hotel room. I spoke to Heidi, the sister of the owner, Jamie Cost. After my I did my "Three Little Pigs" fast-talking demo for her mom, via phone, we were set. A quick search on the Web showed the place had the nicest rooms and the best rates in Akumal. I had two frequent flyer tickets that I book, and all that was left to do was to get Spencer certified.

The five weeks went quickly. Spencer passed his written exam with flying colors and the next week we set off to meet Todd in Mexico.

At the Cancun airport, a dark, tanned, mustached man with a bright, flowered shirt and tons of Mardi Gras beads around his neck greeted us, "How y'all doing? Great to finally met you." As the words rolled off his Southern tongue, he put tons of beads around our necks. I felt like we were getting inducted into the Louisiana Hall of Fame.

Spencer's thoughts were more simple. "Great, now we look like geeks."

Todd explained that these beads were great bargaining tools, and while he'd waited for us, he had given out a bunch to the local children. All of a sudden I had flashbacks to Club Med, when a bead could get you anything. I figured I'd wear them just in case I lost my American Express card.

Since Todd had arrived several hours earlier, he had already arranged for our transportation, a two-door jeep for our exploring pleasure. The only problem was that two doors, three persons, and ten bags later, we looked like a family of gypsies. Spencer was so contorted in the backseat that I was ready to sign him up for Ringling Brothers. With a crow bar and a straw, we managed to get him some breathing space.

It was a one-hour drive south from the airport to the town of Akumal. Todd drove.

We turned left at a sign that said "Akumal Village." Heck, it was easier to find Akumal than it was to find the long-term parking at the Newark airport.

We passed a closed reception center, some shops, and then went under an archway with a gate with no guards. It was ten o'clock, and everything was dark. We saw a statue, and at that juncture the road forked. We took the right fork, but it looked like a residential district, so we backed up and then took the left fork instead. We headed down a main road scattered with condominiums and residences along the beachside and jungle on the other side. We passed a few more shops and restaurants. I looked at the map that Heidi had sent me. There were two bays in Akumal, Akumal Bay and Half Moon Bay. Vista Del Mar was on Half Moon Bay. We saw a few people, some walking and some riding bicycles in the dark with no lights. Brave souls. We kept driving, absorbing the whole atmosphere. Finally we spotted our hotel. We checked in at the desk, got our rooms, and were totally thrilled.

Fran Capo

When they said beachfront rooms, they weren't kidding. The rooms were right on the water—okay, not right on it or it would be flooded, but it was about five feet from the beach and twenty yards from the water. Our room was painted a peaceful aquamarine color, with smooth stucco walls and Guatemalan décor.

Spencer and I walked out our back patio door that faced the water and met Todd, who was two rooms down. He had made vacation T-shirts that said "Chillin' in Paradise" and handed one to both of us. He was like a walking clothes designer. I was ready to put in my shoe order.

Even though it was late, we decided to explore the area. A short beach walk, still on Vista Del Mar property, we passed the closed dive shop, Akumal Dive Adventures. We passed the pool and then stopped to climb these really cool towers that overlooked the ocean.

Since we were hungry, we followed our noses to their two-floor bar and restaurant, La Buena Vida (which means the good life ... how right they were.) The beach bar downstairs was really unique. Everywhere you looked there was something neat to see. Right outside there were a bunch of hammocks so you could be served and relax at the same time. If you chose to sit barside, they had wooden swings hanging from ropes. Over the bar was a giant skeleton of some kind of sea serpent. A chain of miniature skeleton lights hung around the bar area. On one wall was a great white shark's head coming out of a circular saw wheel. In the back of the bar was a giant melted candle about four feet high with drippings that looked more like a lava flow.

After using about a roll of film, we went upstairs to the restaurant. Our stomachs were growling by this point. The restaurant had this thick, thatched, high roof with wooden beams and had a jungle atmosphere to it.

Everything was going great until the waiter came over and spoke to us in Spanish. Imagine that, Spanish in Mexico? What a surprise. Good thing we had our Spanish dictionaries handy. I made Spencer order in Spanish. That lasted for about a minute. He then resorted to pointing, while Todd nodded. The waiter smiled and spoke in English.

Adrenaline Adventures

After dinner, we decided to walk off the calories and headed down the dirt road in front of our hotel. We walked past the other hotels and into the darkness. There was virtually no light pollution in Akumal, and for good reason.

Akumal means "the place of the turtles" in Mayan. Their beaches are an important nesting site for endangered sea turtles and are protected by the ecological center. Between May and October, the female turtles come to Half Moon Bay, dig their holes, lay about 120 eggs each, and about sixty-five days later, seventy thousand baby turtles are hatched. Then those little tykes make a mad dash to the sea guided by the moonlight. Artificial light like streetlights, porch lights, indoor lights, even flashlights, would guide them away from the water, resulting in unnecessary deaths.

Seeing those swarming turtles must be awesome. I made a mental note to come back to witness it. But for now, in this season, we had another sight to behold, the wonders under the sea. Tomorrow was Spencer's first dive with Todd.

Day 2 - Monday

I immediately knew this was going to be a good trip when Spencer got up early. On school days I have to drag his butt out of bed, but here he was walking on the beach with Todd and it was only eight.

We went over to Vista Del Mar's dive shop, which was called *Akumal Dive Adventures*, and met Kris, the owner and Esteban, a dive master from Canada. It's always convenient when a resort has its own dive shop, so you can easily book trips, get certified, or plan excursions.

Kris had been told by Heidi that I, the fast talker, was coming, so at 8:30 in the morning, I found myself once again rattling off "Three Little Pigs." He was very accommodating, and by nine, we were geared up and on the dive boat just a few hundred yards from our room. We were ready to head out for Spencer's first taste of diving in open water, and what a great place to start because the coral reefs surrounding Akumal are part of the second largest barrier reef in the world. I bought an underwater camera to use, since Todd would be busy testing Spencer.

It was only the three of us and a woman named Rinda, a psychologist who was into these unique breathing techniques. She had been happily married for forty years … her secret? She didn't live with her husband. Now there's a technique I gotta try.

Since the dive boat was small, we had to do a backward roll entry. I was a little nervous since I hadn't dove in a while, and I had been having ear problems. I was hoping they would equalize, thus allowing me to go down.

Spencer, Todd, Kris, and Rinda went down, no problem. I bobbed at the top of the water. Why? Because I forgot to take into account that I had a new wetsuit and that it was going to take more weight than usually to get me down. I had to go from nine pounds of lead on my weight belt to sixteen. Then I was able to sink. Thank goodness it was that and not that I had accumulated extra blubber.

I watched from the ocean floor, which was only about a depth of thirty feet, as Todd did the check out dive with Spencer. I was so proud that my kid was getting certified. It's like an underwater graduation, minus the cap and gown.

Every now and then, I would look around and check out the fish. I spotted a barracuda slowing swimming by. I swear I saw him shake his head in disgust. "Again with these divers! Can't they find somewhere else to go?! I'm going to start charging rental space." But he just kept on trucking, with one glazed eye on all of us. He was like the Sammy Davis Junior of barracudas.

After the fundamentals were out of the way, we were ready to scuba around. We checked out some coral reefs but were careful not to touch them since the oil on our hands can kill these ancient and delicate ecosystems that have been in existence for more than fifty million years.

As we floated through the water, we saw sea turtles, blue tangs, yellow-tailed snappers, eagle rays, and parrot fish. We surfaced, came back to shore for some interval time (when you dive, you have to let residual nitrogen out of your system), and then after an hour's rest, we were ready to dive again.

Adrenaline Adventures

The second dive was a little rough since the waves were getting pretty high. My ear started to hurt, and Spencer banged his head on the back of his tank. But despite our minor physical discomforts, Spencer did a great second dive and mastered all his skills. Todd was smiling ear to ear. "Like I always say, happiness is being in over your head." Then he turned to Spencer and said, "You're a natural. You've done just fine."

We all had to shower after our morning dives. Scuba is not a glamorous sport. Sometimes you come up and your nose is runny, sometimes you have seaweed in your hair. As Todd said, "Scuba is a sport where you have to park your pride." After all, in what other sport is it acceptable to spit into your mask then put it on?"

Refreshed we drove over to *Hidden Worlds Cenotes*, confirmed our two cavern dives, then explored some of the Yucatan Peninsula's famous Mayan ruins. It was a perfect day.

Day 3- Tuesday

We got up at seven and headed over to Hidden Worlds. Got there half an hour early so we hung around, took pictures of the IMAX movie signs they had proudly on display, and pondered over the local fruit tree. We saw one of the dive shop guys bring his two pets with him and tie them to a tree. The pets? Two spider monkeys who were having a grand ol' time swinging from tree to tree.

As soon as the dive shop opened, we went in and were greeted by Kevin, the Hidden Worlds guy who I coordinated this whole trip with. He showed us around the shop, complete with pet snakes, hundreds of colorful t-shirts and huge pictures of the cenote dives.

The shop was bustling with the activity as everyone was preparing to go on the cavern dives. We got geared up in our 5mm wetsuits. Since the fresh water temperature is seventy-five degrees and the water is still, we had to wear thicker wetsuits to stay warm. Also, we needed lighter weights in fresh water, than in salt, because salt water tends to keep you buoyant.

With gear ready, we were introduced to Richard Allen, a tall, lanky, blonde from New Zealand who had come to Akumal with his writer girlfriend on vacation and wound up getting a job. He would be our dive master for the day leading us into the two caverns, Dos

Ojos and the Bat Cave. In cavern diving, for safety reasons, there is a maximum of four people to a dive master.

After the introductions, we loaded everything onto these open jungle trucks. These trucks looked like tractors pulling wooden carts. The engines had no cover, just a canvas thrown on top of them. The wooden carts in the back were painted with zebra stripes or cheetah spots. The carts were big enough for about twenty people to stand in. They had six big tree branches that acted as rails for us to hold onto.

The jungle mobile lurched forward and we were off on fifteen-minute trek into the heart of the Yucatan jungle, over a bumpy dirt road. We had to really hold on, or we'd be thrown off the truck. It was like being on roller coaster ride standing up. It was fabulous.

As we drove, Richard started giving us the orientation. First, he talked about the animals in the woods. Then he started to talk about the history of the area. "The Spanish conquerors were amazed to find out that the Yucatan Peninsula had no rivers. They wondered how the Mayans living in so many cities and villages could survive in this dry and harsh land, especially since it scarcely rained in the area and was subject to long, intense droughts. And then they found the secret. The cenotes ... which is the native word for 'natural wells.' It derived from the Mayan word *d'zonot*, which literally means 'subterranean cavity that contains permanent water.' (By the way, it's pronounced seh-NO-tays.) Besides using them for their water supply, the Mayans also thought the cenotes were entrances to the underworld. Some cenotes, like the Cenote Sagrado, were used for human sacrifices; virgins were hurled into the cenote from an altar placed at the edge."

"Don't think I want to dive in that cenote, although with Spencer by my side, I don't think anyone will be mistaking me for the Virgin Frannie."

Richard continued as we trekked on through the jungle. "In some cenotes, new animals have been discovered, and a really interesting thing is that, though these animals are usually blind, they follow a twenty-four-hour biological cycle just as if they could perceive day and night."

Adrenaline Adventures

"Cenotes are found only a few places in the world, because they are uncommon geological formations, but here in the Yucatan, they are abundant.

The cenotes themselves are small in diameter, but they link to massive underground cave systems, as you will soon see. You guys are lucky because Hidden World is the largest cavern diving and jungle snorkeling park in the world. The Dos Ojos Cavern dive is through an extensive system of underwater caverns and caves, and that's why they chose to film the IMAX movie here. We will be going in some of the sections where the movie was filmed, but not into the cave section because you have to be specially trained for that. In those sections is where you will experience the haloclimbs, which is the layer of water in which the fresh and salt water meet and form an blurry area, almost like looking through Vaseline."

Richard was about to continue when a giant bump in the road made us all jump up and hold on tighter. Todd said, "Hell, if these are the paved roads, I'd like to see what the unpaved roads looked like."

Spencer was just enjoying the ride, and I was trying to keep notes, which was impossible, and my notes looked more like hieroglyphics.

In between bumps, Richard managed a few more words, "The cool thing is that scientists estimate these caves were flooded about thirteen thousand years ago when the surrounding sea level rose. As of the year 2000, there were a total of sixty cave systems, with the longest being listed in the *Guinness Book* as Nohoch Nah Chich at 225,000 feet."

At the mention of Guinness, my ears perked up. So these caves made it into the book as well, very cool.

"Well, folks, we're here." And with that, we pulled into the camp area in the jungle. We looked around, taking it all in. Todd commented on the stone bathroom house that was a hundred yards back. "Imagine a fancy place like this has a bathroom." Actually it was an elaborate outhouse.

Closer to the dive area were a bunch of benches in a semicircle to put gear on, a makeshift changing room made out of canvas off to the left, and then there was the pit—the pit that led down into the cenote. I had imagined a big water hole in the middle of the ground that we'd dive into, not a pit we'd have to climb down into. This was exciting.

The pit was about four feet by five feet. It was surrounded by a wooden fence so no one could accidentally fall in. A yellow rope hung from the center. We later found out it was used to raise and lower heavy dive gear. There was a ladder, or "stairwell system," as they called it, that was built in 1996 to make access for divers easier. Good thing because it was at least a fifty foot drop to the water.

After we donned our scuba gear, the groups paired up with their cavern-trained dive masters. We let the other groups go first. Then I climbed down with my mask, fins, underwater lights, and weight belt on. No snorkels are allowed or needed in the caverns. Spencer followed, then Todd with his big, bulky camera.

Once we were inside the pit, Richard told us, "Welcome to the most beautiful experience in diving. We are going to enter Dos Ojos; we are now in the Bat Cave section of Dos Ojos. These two giant cenotes are considered the best in the world. The depths we will do today are no deeper than twenty-eight feet. It is crystal-clear water, which means you won't have to rinse off your gear from salt at the end of the dive, a nice perk in cavern diving. Now I'm going to go over some safety rules while inside the caverns. One, we keep our lights on at all times; if you wish to see what the caverns look like in total darkness, cover your light with your hand. Two, we are going to check your buoyancy as we enter the open pool area here to my right. Deflate your BC (the buoyancy control jacket the divers wear) and take a full breath. If you sink to eye level you are fine. Three, since there are delicate formations here, please don't touch them. They have stopped growing and the human touch can kill them. If you feel yourself floating up, put your hand over your head to protect your head from hitting a rock and for the safety of the cavern formations. If you feel yourself sinking, use only one finger to push yourself away from the cave floor. We don't want the silt rising, as it will obscure vision. Also, unlike in regular diving, in caverns you need to keep your knees bent upward as you swim; it prevents you from kicking up silt.

Adrenaline Adventures

Last, we will use some simple signals as we would in night diving, using our flashlights to circle for okay and back and forth to get my attention. Shine your light to where my light will be because that's where I'll be looking. We will go in single file. Any questions?"

I jumped in, "How far will we be from air?"

"You'll never be more than 150 feet from air; there is 1,500 feet of cavern we can see today without ever leaving the light zone. Remember, we are diving in the cavern portion of the cave since you are all open water–certified divers; you have to be cave-certified to go into the cave sections of the cenotes. Cave diving is one of the most dangerous sports in the world, so I hope no one will be foolish and exceed their training and venture off. That really puts a damper on things. There is a yellow guide rope so it will be easy to follow. Just don't go below it, and don't hold onto it. Follow the rules for safety and you are ready for one of the best adventures in your life."

We all got in the pool area, put on our fins, and were handed our BCs and tanks. The water felt cold at first, but in our thick wetsuits, we quickly got acclimated. We tested for buoyancy, got the okay, and were on our way, Richard, followed by Spencer, then me, and Todd covering the rear.

We swam through a small opening and immediately we were in the beautiful environment of Dos Ojos. There were ancient cave formations, stalactites and stalagmites, everywhere, big and small, straight and curved. We were floating through this crystal-clear underwater paradise. We followed the yellow rope, equalizing the pressure in our ears as we made subtle rises and drops around the formations. There were little crevices everywhere, crawl spaces to explore that held mysteries from centuries long gone. We shined our flashlights and used or imaginations as we peered in.

Time stood still in the cave. It was so awesome. I looked at my PSI gauge and saw I still had 2,700 pounds of pressure. How could that be? We started with 3,000. Wasn't I using any air? I was sure we'd been down there awhile.

I was aware of Todd snapping pictures and was thrilled he was capturing the beauty. I was also proud watching Spencer handle himself in this foreign environment. I don't know if I was more excited showing him the adventure or experiencing it myself. All I thought was, of all the adventures I have done, this is my finest moment. It was as if I could feel the ancient forces of nature. It felt so primordial.

The sunlight from the outside world shown in through cracks in the rock formations creating a gorgeous blue silhouette. Rays of sunshine danced on the water. We kept gliding through, always keeping an eye on the golden rope.

Then, just when all was calm, we turned a corner and spotted an alligator. It was lying still on a rock. My heart jumped until I saw the Barbie Doll in its mouth, very cute. I floated closer to get a better look and then for some reason I couldn't move any farther. In getting closer, I went below the rope and my tank got caught. Luckily the boy from Louisiana was there to save me from the vicious rope and rubber monster. Todd smiled, and I gave him the okay sign. Good thing he didn't take a picture of that!

We floated through a few more formations, and forty-five minutes later we surfaced back in Bat Cave's open pool section, and I still had 1,500 pounds of air left.

We took off our gear, climbed the ladder, joked about my bout with Barbie, and ate lunch. The local jungle cats seemed to enjoy dining on Spencer's sour onion Pringles, a delicacy for Mayan cats. As they purred, at Richard's request, I gave my fast talking "Three Little Pigs" rendition.

Since it was a shallow dive we didn't have to wait long for our second cenote encounter. This time we were headed into the bat cave section of Dos Ojos.

After lunch, we descended the ladders into the pit. It really did have some resemblance to Bruce Wayne's Bat Cave. For the second dive, I put on a second wetsuit; after being in the water awhile, your body temperature drops, and people often get colder on a second dive.

We went into a different entrance, since we were exploring another section of the sixty-kilometer cave system. This part of the cave was just as awesome, but darker. It had huge columns, and stalactites hanging down. One part looked as if we were entering the mouth of a dragon.

Adrenaline Adventures

I decided this is the closest you can come to being on another planet without leaving the Earth. There were sand dunes with jutting stalagmites, and we were just floating through it like an astronaut. When you walk in a dry cave, you see things on the cave ceiling and say, "Wow." In an underwater cave, you can float to any point of interest and see it up close and personal. There is no other feeling like it. I was in awe the whole time and kept saying, "Remember this feeling, Capo. Take it all in."

As we swam through, I noticed there were these pockets of air on the ceiling that looked like mirrors. I remembered reading about some stranded cave diver who got lost and said that when his air ran out in his tank, he took some sips of air from the air pockets. Those tiny bubbles of air made the difference between life and death until he was rescued. As for me, I'll stick by the rope and use the sacred thirds rule; use one-third of your air going in, one-third coming out, and have one-third left for reserve. I didn't want to be sucking no stinkin' air pockets.

We continued our journey until we surfaced at one point to check out the place where the snorkelers enter. It was paradise in the jungle, gorgeous lush plants and this crystal clear water with an overhang for the snorkelers to swim around in. The snorkelers seemed unaware of our presence. With all my gear on, I felt a like a sea monster rising up on them, and then descending again unseen.

This dive was over in about twenty-five minutes. It was truly the best dive experience I've ever had. It was inspiring to know that in the jungle, under the land, laid such vast beauty that God created and that man is privileged to see.

If you never dive in your life, then at least see the IMAX movie, but if you want to explore one of the most remarkable places on earth, come to a cenote.

We rode back through he jungle, jostling and laughing. We turned in our tanks and thanked Kevin for the wonderful experience. We all left with T-shirts as parting gifts.

For the rest of the day, I did something I never do. I just hung out on the beach. Todd and I just watched the ocean, enjoyed the view, and reflected on how beautiful the world can be. It all depends on your focus.

Fran Capo

Spencer, of course, being a kid, was busy playing in the water. He found this rock with these weird life formations on it. They were about two inches long and had a hard shell like a turtle. They were crimson to greenish yellow with some orange in them. The shells were sculptured and had a pattern to them. We called Estaban from the local dive shop to identify these creatures. He had never seen anything like them before. After we came home, Todd took a quick look in his underwater information book and found Spencer's sea monsters were a thing called ornate chiton. Some natives use them as bait or food. Speaking of food, it was time to head back the good life at La Buena Vida and chow down, the end to another perfect day.

Day 4 – Wednesday

When you are in a place you try to see all the best it has to offer. With that in mind, we decided to see another cenote—a cenote considered the second best in the world, The Grand Cenote. It had a maximum depth of thirty-two feet, with lots of small passageways and openings accessible to lure open water divers into big trouble. But if you follow the permanently installed golden rope line and are with a professional cavern tour guide there's no problem.

This trip our tour guide was Esteban from Akumal Dive Center. We also decided to hire a videographer, Victor, from Hidden World.

Grand Cenote is a privately owned cenote, so you have to pay to get in. Wooden tables are set up outside in the parking lot, so you can take your gear right from the car to the table, get ready and then enter the fenced in facility.

Once inside the property you walk down this beautifully flowered path for about five minutes (with all your gear on), and then climb down a steep wooden ladder. This was a bit tricky. At the bottom of the ladder were two wooden boardwalks with large gaps in some areas. Carefully we walked across one boardwalk to the edge. At the edge was a platform. Attached to this outdoor platform were two ladders that led into the water. We climbed down the ladder, t swam a few feet and were at the mouth of the cavern.

Esteban gave us a set of safety rules and told us to follow the yellow line. Esteban was in the lead, followed by Spencer, myself, Todd and Victor floating around taking video pictures.

Adrenaline Adventures

We entered the cavern. It was much bigger in scale than Dos Ojos, so the natural light was more prevalent. The blue green halo effect really shone on the surrounding formations. I had to remember to keep my knees bent like in the last dive, which felt awkward, but eventually got used to.

As we came to the other side of the cenote we did a three-minute decompression stop, as Esteban's computer required. We surfaced, looked at the location where the snorkers were and then submerged like the diving machines we were.

I asked Todd if he minded always being in the back on the dives, he answered, "Hell, if you're not the lead dog, the scenery never changes."

On the way back we passed a sign at the beginning of another cave area—an area with no golden rope. The sign read, " ALTO prevenga su muerte! No continue." Which means, STOP, prevent your death, don't continue (pass this sign.) To punctuate the point there was a picture of the Grim Reaper on it. Need more be said? That area was for experienced certified cave divers ONLY. It looked ominous, yet I'd be lying if I said a part of me wasn't curious what was in that part. But as I say, I like calculated risks, and my calculations said no tickee, no goey.

As we were about to surface and conclude the dive, with Victor taking his parting shots, Todd mentioned that he knew how to break dance under water. Well, there's a photo op, not to be missed. So we all went back to the bottom and started to do flips, spins, and dosey does for the viewing camera on the sandy bottom. It was a regular hoe down under water, with the fish mouthing the word "LOCO" to each other.

We surfaced having enjoyed the best cenote dives in the world!

On the way back to the airport we agreed that that was one of greatest adventures of our lives.

I thought about how this trip came together so quickly after all these years of dreaming about it. Then I thought about an expression that Todd repeated several times during the trip. "If you want to do something you find a way. If you don't, you find an excuse." I knew one thing for sure, there were no excuses on this trip!

Fran Capo

Chapter 39
Adventure at a Glance - Dare to Do it   Mild to Wild Scale: 5
Title: Cavern Diving
Children allowed: Yes, but only if he or she is open water certified.
Age requirement: Twelve and up

Length of trip: Half day
Where to try this adventure: Hidden Worlds in Akumal, Mexico
Web site: www.hiddenworlds.com.mx or
E-mail: info@hiddenworlds.com.mx or Tel: (52) 984-877-8535
Best time of year: All year round.
Approximate cost: One tank dive is $50; two tank dive is $90. Dive prices include the tanks, weights, and guide, but does not include open water dive equipment, dive lights, or wetsuits.
Reservations necessary: Yes
Fitness requirements: Must be able to scuba dive and have good buoyancy control.
Personal gear required: Mask and fins, open water dive equipment, 3 mil full wetsuits, and flashlights, but you can always rent this equipment if you need to.
What NOT to bring: NOT RECOMMENDED FOR DIVERS WITH CLAUSTROPHOBIA OR BUOYANCY PROBLEMS.
Photo opportunities: Yes, if you are a professional underwater photographer. Otherwise you can hire a photographer.

Notes: I recommend staying at Vista Del Mar; it's not a big chain hotel, but it's right on the beach, has a great restaurant, and allows you to get a feel for the town. Call 1-877-425-8625 or e-mail heidi@akumalinfo.com or visit www.akumalinfo.com.

Cool trivia: Buddy Quattlebaum is one of the pioneers of the professionally guided cenote dives and is the founder of Hidden Worlds Cenote Park. Buddy has recently discovered a new cenote, Dreamgate, which became available to the public in September of 2003 and is only open to Hidden Worlds divers.

"One who gains strength by overcoming obstacles possesses the only strength which can overcome adversity."
—Albert Schweitzer

Chapter 40
"A Hot Weekend of Glass"
Glassblowing

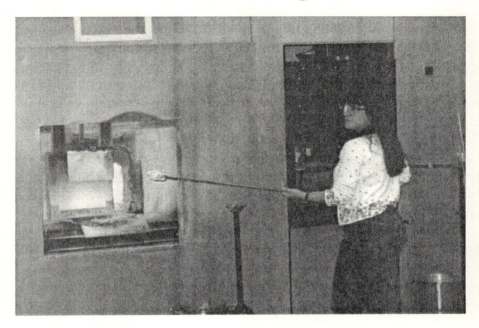

It's easy to take everyday items for granted. Take a drinking glass for example. When's the last time you thought about what goes into making a beautiful drinking glass, or even a simple one? And if you break one, while you may be somewhat upset, the general attitude is, "Oh well, it's just a glass; we can always get another one." While we can't stop every minute of the day to admire the beauty around us, it's nice every now and then to look at the craft behind the beauty.

With that in mind, when my boyfriend Steve said, "Someday I'd like to take a glassblowing class," my mind started ticking. Sure, why not? That would be fun. I went on the Internet and in a short time had located The Studio of The Corning Museum of Glass, which is in south central New York State in a town called Corning.

Now, you may be thinking, how the heck does this qualify as an Adrenaline Adventure, and here's my logic on it: to me, adrenaline happens when the body experiences something new or exciting.

Adrenaline Adventures

While I'm more the fast-action type, I do like to put myself in new situations to stimulate my brain, and this was one of them. Plus, not everyone always wants a level-five rush.

The Corning Museum studio offered a wide array of glass classes, from beginning glassblowing, to paperweights in the furnace (and no, that's not an anger management technique), to flameworking. Since Corning is the premier institution of the art, history, and science of glass, I figured it would be a good place to begin our education.

I soon found out that these classes were highly in demand and filled up almost immediately. It was only November. The next available classes, which weren't even listed yet, wouldn't be until March. We decided to do a mini test run a few weeks later to the Crystal City (as Corning is also known) for the Crystal City Christmas Celebration (say that three times fast) which happens during the three weekends immediately following Thanksgiving. We thought maybe we could sneak into a class, you never know.

Upon arrival, we strolled along the five-block strip known as Historic Market Street. The nineteenth century architecture combined with the lit-up tree, carolers, horse-drawn carriages, live reindeer, a parade of lights, and Santa's glass house in Steuben Square made it feel like we'd gone backward in time.

The next day we were ready to make our move. First, we went to a few museums and then saved the bulk of the day for the main attraction of Corning, The Corning Museum of Glass. The museum is a ten-minute walk from Market Street, over the river and right next door to the Finger Lakes Wine Country Visitor Center. Which can prove convenient for some people—they can make a glass at Corning then go next door and fill it with wine and drink it!

We went inside the museum and asked if anyone had dropped out of the workshops. You never know, maybe someone got into a fight with their spouse and a glass was chucked at them, and they decided glasses were dangerous. The guy at the front desk checked the list, and no one seemed to have had marital disputes that weekend. But they did have a twenty-minute intro flower-making workshop available. We were game, even though it was not included in the admission price.

We walked across the parking lot to the separate studio building. We were directed to the workshop area. We were the only two there, which made it nice and personal.

In the workshop, we were asked two simple questions: what type of stem we wanted our flowers to have and what color we wanted the flowers to be. Then we watched a quick demonstration, the type of demonstration where professionals make it look as if this is the easiest thing in the world to do—just like the Olympics, where after you watch the pros, you go out and buy a luge. After the demo, we were each given goggles, an apron, and a sleeve to protect our arm from the heat. Not exactly the Marilyn Monroe look, but necessary.

Once we were properly attired, the instructor casually walked over to this furnace, placed a stick in it, took out a blob of molten glass, rolled it, added the colors we wanted, and then quickly handed the stick to us. Then we turned, pulled, and yanked at the glass before it cooled, thus forming it into a beautiful glass flower. The flower then had to cool overnight, and we were told to pick it up in the morning. It seemed simple enough. That's all there was to it? Ah, so little did we know.

We were now anxious to do the whole process ourselves. When we picked up our flowers, we asked if we could sign up for the beginning glassblowing weekend workshop in March. We had to wait until Monday when registration officially began. On Monday, we were the first to sign up via phone, and within one week, the class was filled with the maximum of nine students for safety reasons.

Three months later, on the Friday night before the workshop, we drove the four hours to Corning, so we could stay overnight and get a good rest. The two main hotels in town, the Days Inn and the Radisson, both have competitive rates and are about a five-minute drive from the studio. We stayed at the Radisson.

The next morning we got to the studio at 9:50 A.M. We walked past several classes in progress to our studio in the back of the building.

Our work area was large, with furnaces, tool benches, and a separate area with tiered seating behind a shoulder-high glass shield for those who wanted to watch. One guy was sitting there with a camera. Apparently his girlfriend had dragged him along as payback

Adrenaline Adventures

since she'd taken pictures of him at his motorcycle conventions. I asked him to take pictures of us as well. Why not? He was already playing photographer.

The class didn't start until ten, but everyone was already there and they had begun the instruction. This was a bunch of anxious hot-air blowers.

The instructor, Matt, was a young, tall guy with thick brown hair. He had a very casual attitude in his teaching, but he expected you to be on top of your game. There were nine students altogether, plus one interpreter for Alan, a hearing-impaired guy who was taking the class. Proves you can do anything if you keep excuses out of the equation.

Matt quickly brought Steve and I up to speed. He went so fast, I thought he was competing with my world record. "Hi, glad you could make it. This here is a marver table. It's made of steel, but marver means marble in French. This is where you will roll your hot glass."

Then he walked over to another shorter table that was near the benches. "On this table you see six tools. They all have a different purpose. These long, pointed ones are pinches and are used to pinch the glass outward like you did when you made the flowers. These other long ones that look like longer pinches are called jacks. Then we have these scissorlike things called shears, and these other bizarre scissorlike things are called diamond shears. This paddle is called a Taglia, and finally we have this odd-shaped tool called a Sophietta. Don't ask me how to spell it. It's also known as a puffer. I'll explain later what each one is for."

Now we were up to speed. (Yeah sure, just don't test me on it.) As the class stood in front of the closed 2,100-degree Fahrenheit furnace, Matt gave us a short history on glass. "While the process of glassblowing has been known to humans for about two thousand years, the individual studio movement has only begun in the past fifty. Our ancestors have been manipulating natural glass like obsidian since prehistoric times."

Somehow picturing a caveman named Og with a delicate little glass tube didn't seem right.

Matt continued, "However, the Egyptians are credited with the first use of glass as an art form around 3.500 B.C." (That explains it. Leave it to the Egyptians. It wasn't enough for them to build pyramids; in their spare time they had to make beads and glass vases, too.)

Then the Romans got in on the act. After they conquered the neighboring lands, they adopted the technology, and glassmaking spread throughout Europe. By the Middle Ages, Venice was the glassmaking center of the western world. Desperate to keep that world title, in 1271 a city ordinance was passed that banned foreign glassmakers from entering and working in Venice. (That's one way to stop the competition.)

But nothing stays the same. When the Industrial Revolution came, it did what it did best, changed a craft into an industry. Soon, with the invention of the tank furnace and automatic bottle-blowing machine, mass production glass pieces became commonplace. The artist was tossed aside. Then, in 1960s, the Studio Glass Movement began to reintroduce the artist of this craft. These two guys named Harvey Littleton and Dominick Labinor created a smaller kiln combined with a new low melting point of glass, and thus allowed artists a medium to use to create their art. And so, because of all this, we were standing in the studio, novices ready to do something that cavemen began.

Matt gave us some safety tips. "Burns and cuts are possible when working with glass and when glassblowing." (I'd say—2,100 degrees of anything can be dangerous.) "Use common sense, and keep your work area clean and free of unused materials. If you have someone working with or next to you, stay centered at your glassblowing bench, and be aware of all activity. When coming through with material you just gathered, say, 'Coming through' or 'Watch your back.' You are in control when you have the substance. But just in case something does happen, we have first-aid equipment close at hand.

"You'll want to spend as little time as possible in front of the furnace. The heat can kill ya."

At this point I felt like yelling, "It's not the heat, it's the humidity," but I didn't think anyone would appreciate it. So I just let him continue.

Adrenaline Adventures

"The punty pipe is a long metal tube on which you will gather your molten liquid glass."

Matt had an assistant slide the two-by-two-foot furnace door open, which allowed him to gain access to the liquid glass inside. He slid it open only enough to get the punty pipe in but not have to be subjected to the intense heat and get burned. As soon as the door was open, the intensity of the heat could be felt in the room. Matt stepped in and proceeded to gather some glass. As he did, he explained, "Think of this in five steps. First, put the pipe on the ledge, making sure you are already rotating it before you even step close to the furnace. Then tilt the pipe at a forty-five-degree angle and dip it into the liquid while you are rotating the pipe. Count to three. Then take the pipe out at the same forty-five-degree angle. Level the pipe (which now has a gather of glass on it) and pull it out, turning it all the while. Now go back in and get a second gather. Keep turning the pipe as you step over to the marver table. Then, nice and even, you will roll the pipe off your palm and onto the table. Using the full length of the table, you will roll the hardening glass into a cylindrical object. Our goal by the end of these two days is to make a cup. It's a big goal, but we can do it. Okay, who's up first?"

We all stared at each other. Steve, who hates standing around for instructions, rushed to the front of the line with goggles in hand. He took a heated punty pipe from another oven and stepped up to bat.

I had clocked Matt, and he was in and out of that furnace in twelve seconds flat. Steve went in and looked like he knew what he was doing. He was there for about eighteen seconds. In that short time his pale white arms turned a nice shade of red. From that point on, he wore his long-sleeve sweatshirt to protect his arms.

Soon it was my turn at the liquid tanning machine. The heat was immense and uncomfortable. I didn't like it. I wanted to get it over with, but I also had to concentrate on what I was doing. As soon as I was away from the furnace, I realized I had to go back in for a second gather. AHHHH! Whatever happened to mom's advice, "Don't play with fire!"? I knew there was a reason I stayed away from that hot thing in my kitchen called a stove.

Determined, however, to make the glass cup, I, too, even with my olive complexion, donned a jacket. I was prepared for battle.

Fran Capo

One older lady in the class said she was uncomfortable, but she wasn't sure if it was the furnace or she the fact that she was having hot flashes. Man, if that's what they feel like, I'm putting in my application now for skipping that period of life.

Soon it was my turn again. I tried different methods to get this intense heat thing conquered. I tried opening the door just a tad, but it became troublesome getting in and out of the oven. I tried moving quicker, but then I didn't gather enough material. Finally I asked for one of those sleeves that I wore when I made the flowers. That made all the difference in the world.

After dealing with the heat, the next challenge was to make sure the honeylike glass we gathered didn't drip off the end off the pipe. (You can't very well make a cup with something that looks like spaghetti.) We did this by trying to evenly turn the pipe. It's harder than it looks because if you go too slow, it becomes uneven, and if you go too fast, you're not allowing it to settle. The glass was in constant threat of warping due to uneven turning while hot.

Next to conquer was the marver table and getting this honeylike glass to conform to a cylindrical shape. For each second you wasted, the glass would cool and be harder to manipulate. If you weren't careful, you could wind up with some odd golf-club-like shape, a shape that Matt kept telling us he didn't want. Yeah, well, neither did we! The concept was easier than the execution.

A bit frustrated with our progress, Matt had us each stand and practice the movement of rolling the punty pipes from our hands onto the table and then back up and onto the table again in one continuous roll. Grace of movement was never one of my strong points. I kept winding up with a triangular object, which Matt would tell me wasn't the shape they were going for. Really? I didn't get that message the first five hundred times he told me. I felt like smacking him on the head, but didn't think he'd like that shape either. Displaced anger? Who's to say?

Maybe the heat was getting to me. Eventually I got the knack of applying even pressure.

Luckily, we kept recycling all the glass by putting it in these garbage bins to cool. We'd crack off the glass from the punty pipes and start all over.

Adrenaline Adventures

We went to and from the furnace and the marver table until lunchtime. All I kept thinking was ... all this to make a glass cup! We ate at McDonalds for lunch. The cups were paper.

Back from lunch, we practiced gathering some more. At least now my liquid glass had some semblance of a cylindrical object.

At one point, Steve, always the businessman, commented that the heating bill in this place must be astronomical. That's when we found out Corning owned their own utility plant. Talk about good business sense.

We were ready to move on to phase three: getting from the furnace to the table to the workbench, all before the glass cooled. It was like playing "Beat the Clock."

Why was I not surprised there was a special way to get into the bench too? But first let me describe this bench. It was like a giant armchair with no back. You sit on the cushion part, which in this case was made of wooden slats. The two waist-high "armchair" sides are made of steel and are only about three inches thick and three feet long. They have a ledge on the top of them. The purpose of these armchair sides is so you have a place to roll your punty, or glassblowing pipe, back and forth to keep the glass centered as you work. Got that?

To get into the bench, you first had to make sure you were holding the punty pipe, with your liquid glass on the tip, level while still rotating. Then you quickly placed the end with the glass on one "armchair" ledge holding the other end up so you could slide into this bench and sit down. Once you're on the seat, you place the cool end of the pipe on the other side, kind of like locking yourself into a roller coaster. Immediately you start to roll the pipe along the ledge. You roll with only your left hand, as the right hand prepares to grab for your tools. Your tools are conveniently located on the tool table, which is flush against the right side of your workbench.

The first tool we worked with was the jacks. We made a line in the glass with the jacks by lightly applying the jacks to the glass blob as we spun it. Slowly we increased the pressure on the jacks, thus making a deeper and more noticeable line in the glass. We did this for the remainder of the day.

Fran Capo

At the end of class, Matt made a sample glass cup to show us the entire process. He said, "See how simple?"

In my opinion, it was simpler to walk to K-Mart and buy a cup. But I was here, and come Hell or high water I was going to make a drinking cup. Since I already felt the intensity of Hell with the heat, I simply just had to wait for the flood.

The next day, we got to class early. We practiced a few punty runs and then were onto the blowpipes. The first thing we had to learn how to do was blow into the blowpipes. You'd think you'd just blow. Nah, that's too simple. You hold this five-foot-long hollow steel pipe sideways from your mouth like you would a flute. Then you quickly blow into one end and then cap it with your thumb. That traps the air and forces it to the front of the pipe, where hopefully it will blow your molten glass into a nice bubble. While practicing, when you let your thumb go, you hear this little pop sound. That's the sound of trapped air. When you have glass on the end, of course, the proof is in the bubble.

The first thing I didn't like about this was the fact that we were all putting our mouths against the same blowpipe. While I don't mind sharing, I do mind having my mouth where every else's has been. For some reason, I seemed to be the only person that this bothered. So when in Rome ... I puckered up and put my lips to the pipe. One would think a fast talker would be good at blowing hot air. But it took a couple of good tries to get it consistently. I noticed the men were better at the hot air stuff from the start, something I'd suspected all along but was glad to see confirmed in the class.

Now, with glass globules on the end of our blowpipe we all began to produce bubbles. It's cool to see the bubbles form for the first time. It's quite a feeling of accomplishment. It takes a few seconds for the air to travel down the pipe, then all of a sudden it's there.

We took our bubbles and went over to the bench and started putting jack lines in. This was the first step to creating our cups. We did this until lunch. Then it was time for our skills to be put to the test.

After lunch, we were put into three working teams. Steve, myself, Al (the deaf guy), and his interpreter were assigned to Jason, an assistant instructor and first grade teacher. You always want a first

Adrenaline Adventures

grade teacher by your side, because you know they'll have patience and can explain everything using cartoon characters.

We worked together to create our individual glasses. Steve was up first, so I could take pictures. He started by doing two gathers of glass on the blowpipe. Then he went over to the marver table, gave the pipe a couple of good rolls, then blew into the pipe and created the initial bubble.

Then Jason took the blowpipe and put it in the glory hole. (A glory hole is a furnace with a round hole; the furnace is set at 2,300 degrees Fahrenheit. It's used to re-heat the glass and make it pliable again.)

While Jason did that, Steve sat down on the bench. Al was the assigned blower, so he kneeled down on the left side of the bench, and as Steve rolled the pipe against the ledge of the bench, Al blew into the pipe, making the bubble bigger. This was all carefully orchestrated by Jason's instructions.

As Al was blowing, Steve had this big wooden spoon that had been dipped in water, and he was putting it along the growing bubble to form the initial shape of the cup. Steam oozed off the glass as the contrast of hot glass and cold water collided.

The jacks were used next to created a line where eventually the cup would separate from the blowpipe. The back end of the jacks were used to smooth out the cup. The heat coming off the cup was intense, so we used one of the tools as a makeshift guard to protect our arms from burning. (I don't know how Matt and these assistants worked in short sleeves.)

Next came the transfer. A punty pipe was attached to the open end of the glass right in the center. A drop of water was plopped onto the line that was previously made with the jacks. Like magic, the glass piece was transferred onto the punty pipe and off of the blowpipe.

Once again, Jason placed the glass substance in the glory hole, heating up just the end so it would be flexible to work with.

As soon as it was out of the glory hole, the pipe was handed back to Steve, who was still seated on the bench. Al's blowing serves were no longer needed. With jacks once again in hand, the prong end was used to start making a hole that would eventually become the mouth of the cup. Slowly, as the pipe was still being rolled back and forth against the ledge, the prongs were opened wider and wider until the top and bottom were of equal size. Then the outside was smoothed out as the pipe was still spinning.

Finally, Steve took the wooden paddle and laid it across the top of the cup to smooth out the part you drink from. With that last bit of craftsmanship, Steve handed off the pipe to Jason, who took it and placed it in another oven to set overnight. All I kept thinking was, "ALL this to make ONE stinkin' cup!"

Al was up next. He made a gigantic cup, large enough to quench the thirst of a family of four. Seeing the size of Al's cup, Steve turned competitive. Men always feel competitive with anything involving size. Luckily, I was up next. Steve had time to plot his next cup. In the interim, my first cup went fine.

However, the second time up, Al blew too hard and my cup became distorted. It extended, drooped, and died. So, I tried it again. On my third attempt, I burned myself on the blowpipe while it was on the marver table. I grabbed it up too high. Pain shot through my body. I didn't want to let on that I was hurt, because I was determined to get a second cup out of this class. I plodded through the motions.

When it was time for the glory hole procedure, Jason went to pull it out of the hole, and my masterpiece plopped to the ground. We all just looked. Jason said, "Oops, sorry, it happens."

Kidding around, Steve said, "Go get it."

I think the shock of what Steve had said made Jason go for it. He came up with this pear-shaped thing with a tiny opening. "This is what you call abstract art."

Steve said, "We'll take it home; we can put a candle in it."

So Jason shrugged, put my name on it, and shoved it into the overnight oven.

With me out of the way, Al and Steve both made second cups. A battle of the biggest was now in session. Steve made a cup that looked more like a barrel. Matt nixed it, saying it was too dangerous and would explode in the overnight oven, jeopardizing other people's work. Steve looked injured. It was like telling a boy his bike is too big and can't be allowed in the park with the other bikes. In the end, Al's and Steve's second cups were about equal in size. They both smiled.

Adrenaline Adventures

    I was happy with my cup and the makeshift artwork that, to me, symbolized the whole process. As the class ended and I was applying burn ointment to my hand, Matt was desperately trying to make a vase to show us his handiwork before the four o'clock buzzer rang. At 4:05, he showed us a finished vase, complete with fancy doodads. Once again, he made it look easy, but now we knew the real truth.

    Five days later, our glasses arrived in the mail. I took mine out and carefully put it in my cabinet next to my store-bought glasses. Though it in no way can compete with the beauty of the professional's glasses, there is a special pride in knowing I made it. I haven't taken a drink from it yet, but when I do, I'm going to be really careful because I know for sure that if I ever drop that it, the last thing I'm going to say is, "Oh well, it's just a glass; we can always get another one!"

Fran Capo

Chapter 40
Adventure at a Glance - Dare to Do it   Mild to Wild Scale: 1
Title: Glassblowing
Children allowed: Yes, but not for the workshop Steve and I attended.
Age requirement: Eighteen and up
Length of trip: Weekend workshop
Where to try this adventure: Corning Glass Studio
One Museum Way, Corning, New York 14830-2253
Phone: 607-974-6573 or 800-732-6845 (ask for the studio)
Web site: www.cmog.org
There are other glassblowing classes around the country. Type "glassblowing" or "glassmaking" into any Internet search engine.
Best time of year: All year round
Approximate cost: $200 weekend workshop/kids' workshops $20
Reservations necessary: Yes, and make them way in advance
Fitness requirements: None
Personal gear required: None, but wear long sleeves
What NOT to bring: Easily flammable clothes
Photo opportunities: Yes

Notes: The museum offers family-oriented workshops where kids can make glass paperweights, marbles, and other cool things. The actual museum is nice to visit, too, with many of the artists' work for sale in the gift shop.

Cool trivia: New Jersey is also famous for glassblowing, and in a big way. The Museum of American Glass located in Millville, has a bottle that was made on site in 1992 during their Glass Blast Weekend. This bottle can hold 188 gallons of liquid, stands 7 feet, 8 inches tall, and holds a Guinness world record as the biggest blown bottle ever made. (You can read how it was made in my book *It Happened in New Jersey*.) Yes folks, I am shamelessly plugging my other book.

"Life has no plateaus.
You either grow or die."
— Author Unknown

Chapter 41
"Horses and mules and jeeps ... oh my"
A Western Spirit Adventure

My constant search for adventure has always been sparked by the desire to push myself beyond my physical limits, and to use that as a metaphor for breaking through any fears I might have. But just exploring the physical limits, although mentally challenging at times, can be a narrow experience. I feel every person should balance family, career, physical, mental, and spiritual to truly explore all life has to offer.

With that philosophy in mind, I was intrigued when I received an e-mail from a place called Western Spirit Enrichment Center in Prescott, Arizona, ninety-six miles northwest of Phoenix. The owners, Marian and Gary, had read my story, "Just Say Yes," in *Chicken Soup for the Women's Soul* and wrote to say they shared my philosophy on life.

Adrenaline Adventures

I checked out their Web site, and the place looked wonderful. A ranch set in peaceful surroundings, where the deer and the antelopes (and jackrabbits thrown in for good measure) play. (And I thought I was special in New York with stray cats and gray squirrels.) Their motto caught my eye: "Connecting people to spirit and nature." That was right up my alley, a mixture of inner and outer adrenaline.

I read further to see exactly how this worked. I didn't want to be chanting every morning, shaving my head, or wrapped up in some super religious vacation where I wasn't allowed to talk. (After all, a fast talker not talking is a fate worst than death, although my boyfriend might disagree.)

The site said, "Reclaim or enhance your spirituality by participating in daily morning workshops on a variety of spiritual and personal growth topics that will inform or empower you. Enjoy many adventurous outdoor activities in the afternoon, such as horseback riding, river rafting, Grand Canyon tours, jeeping in Sedona, Indian ruins, lake kayaking, hiking, biking, and skiing. Evenings may include massages, yoga, Tai Chi, cowboy singers, or stories of Native American culture." Sounded like a full week to me. I was intrigued.

I e-mailed Marian, and before I knew it, a date was set.

Since I don't believe in coincidences, I felt this opportunity came at exactly the right time. My relationship with Steve was good, but not spiritual enough, and since we didn't have to shave our heads, I felt this would be the perfect setting to explore that avenue.

A few weeks before our departure, a welcome packet arrived. "We are looking forward to meeting you and Steve ... Check-in time is Sunday at 6 P.M. If you are driving from Phoenix Sky Harbor Airport, directions are enclosed. It is approximately a two-hour, mostly scenic drive. Upon arrival at the ranch you will be greeted by our Australian Shepard, Dillon. He's a very friendly two year old, but if you don't like dogs we'll put him on a leash."

The letter went on to give the week's schedule, weather conditions, and a list of suggested items to bring. It continued, "Everything is inclusive in the week-long retreat, and participation in any workshop or activity is optional. As a reminder, there are no televisions, telephones, or computers available in the rooms. We promote a

Fran Capo

philosophy of 'Getting away from it all.'" Wow, they weren't kidding. This seemed like a good place for the witness protection program. No phones or communication with the outside world—that in itself was going to be a challenge, but one that I've met before on my outdoor trips and loved. I was very impressed with their attention to detail. It looked like a first-class operation.

I was all set to go. But then it happened. Once again fate intervened. At one in the morning on Friday, just two days before our departure, Steve had an emergency at work that would take a few days to repair, and he would not be able to come. I called Marian and explained the situation. After a great deal of scrambling, I had Spencer, my son, come with me instead.

Spencer wasn't thrilled about this. It was his week off from school and he had made arrangements to hang with his friends, plus he had an audition for an ABC television pilot and a Bar Mitzvah to go to.

I tried to make him happy by having his friend come over the night before, mailing a present to his friend at the Bar Mitzvah, and doing a video audition for ABC that we Fed Exed just an hour before we had to catch the plane. Nothing like getting totally tense before spending a week on a spiritual retreat ... it's enough to send your system into shock.

Spencer tried to talk his way out of going. "Ma, it's not that I don't appreciate going with you, and I'm sure once I get there I'll have a good time, it's just I wanted to relax and enjoy myself at home."

I felt bad, but this was a wonderful opportunity for him to get in touch with nature. If the truth be known, I was very disappointed that Steve couldn't make it, but I figured in the grand scheme of things there must be a reason.

So, at 6:15 on Sunday night, Spencer and I were on a flight to Phoenix. Miraculously, Spencer had a totally different attitude after he realized our seats were in business-class and he could move his seat, play video games, and watch his own movies.

When we arrived in Arizona, we set our watches to Mountain Standard Time, rented a car from Hertz, and drove to the Marriott Hyatt and plopped down for the night.

Adrenaline Adventures

Sunday - Day 1, Easter

After a late breakfast, we were on the road to Prescott. The drive was gorgeous, with Saguaro cactus and desert plants along the way. There was one sign that caught our attention, "Prison nearby, don't pick up hitchhikers." That made us feel comfy. I sped up.

After a few wrong turns, we arrived in Prescott, home of the world's oldest rodeo. It was eight o'clock and pitch black. Marian called on my cell phone to say Gary was at the security gate waiting for us. We didn't see him, so we entered the code they'd given us and started to drive into the community and up the dark dirt road to their house. Immediately, as if on cue, hundreds of jackrabbits darted in front of the car. I felt like I was in some western video game trying to avoid them. They were worse than New York City cabdrivers, cutting us off at every turn.

As if that wasn't stressful enough, we noticed a car following us. We were praying it was Gary, since the last thing we needed was some sick stalker attacking us on the first day of our peaceful retreat. We slowed down. He slowed down. Finally I stopped. The car pulled up next to ours. The window rolled down, and I heard a voice, "Fran?" I nodded. "I could tell it was you by the way you were driving past them rabbits. Follow me." Spencer sighed with relief. I obediently followed, letting him clear the way.

We continued about two miles to their ranch, which was at the end of the road. We parked the car and were greeted by Marian and Dillon, their Australian Sheepdog. After our hello hugs, we unpacked the car and were shown to our bedroom.

For some reason I'd pictured the place as more commercial, with a dozen or so guest rooms and a reception lobby. But I was pleasantly surprised. It was actually more like a bed and breakfast, with only two guest rooms, each with separate entrances to the outside porch.

Our bedroom was a nice, simple wooden bedroom with a dream catcher by the bed, a handmade quilt, a writing pad, candles, an alarm clock, a miniature babbling brook, bath gels, self-help books by the bedside, and two Easter baskets on our bed as a welcoming gift.

In the closet was a refrigerator with complimentary bottled water, fruit drinks, and sodas. There were also his and hers bathrobes, yoga mats, hairdryers, rain ponchos, flashlights for night walks, and water bottles and fanny packs to use on hikes. Sure enough, no phones, though there was a phone in the main part of the house.

The other guests hadn't arrived yet, so dinner was held. Meanwhile, Spencer and I took the opportunity to scout out the place. We stood on the wraparound porch listening to the night noises. It was so peaceful, then a coyote howled in the distance. This would take getting used to.

We were at an elevation of 5,300 feet. In the distance, in front of the house and way down the hill, we could see the city of Prescott with its lights twinkling. It was strange to see civilization and not be able to hear it. The moon was very bright, and the night air was chilly. Spencer and I debated about using their hot tub on the porch but decided to wait until another night.

Finally, the other couple, who wish to remain nameless, arrived. The girl was very friendly, and the man was reserved. Once they settled in, the table was set in the dining room, and we all chose places to sit. Gary was the cook that night. He had whipped up a delicious chili recipe that he had gotten from some famous cowboy. Before we ate, Gary and Marian led us in a simple prayer of thankfulness for the food we were about to eat, for our safe arrival, and for a week filled with love and enjoyment. That said, we dug in. The food was fabulous. The meals alone were worth the trip!

We were handed an itinerary for the week and then given a brief set of rules, "This is your vacation; because of the atmosphere, people have a tendency to feel the need to clear their own dishes, or help … don't. We want you to relax. The kitchen is off limits unless of course you want something, then we will be more than happy to get it for you. Behind you, on that table by the mirror, you will see deserts and fruits set up. They are always there for your enjoyment, as well as fresh water."

We all turned. There was a giant carrot cake with lemon frosting, fresh-baked chocolate chip cookies, red juicy apples, oranges, and an assortment of other tempting treats.

After dinner, and after all our questions about the coyotes, snakes, and other wildlife had been answered, Spencer and I went back to the outside porch. He played with Dillon, who seemed thrilled to have a kid with as much energy as he did, and I sat and gazed at the millions of stars. I looked up at the dark mountain behind the house and decided that in the morning I would climb to the top and have a look around.

Day 2- Monday

Last year at this time, Spencer and I were running backward in Central Park. What a difference a year makes. I was up at 7 A.M., and it was a gorgeous day. The yellow grass in front of the house glistened, and the contrast of the black cows made me want to take up watercolor.

At 8:10, the breakfast bell rang. Breakfast was an array of eggs, bagels, fruit, yogurt, cereal, fresh-squeezed orange juice ... the works. Once again we said a morning prayer. The prayers are sent to them daily by none other than Miriam Williamson from a "Course in Miracles." Each day it was a different message and something beautiful to ponder. It set a nice tone.

After breakfast, there was an hour before the first workshop, so Spencer, Dillion, and I hiked up Angel Hill, which was behind the house. It took us about twenty minutes to get to the top—just enough time to work off breakfast. Then we heard the bell signaling the beginning of a workshop. We went down with Dillon leading the way.

The first workshop was the gratitude journal workshop. Spencer and I took this class alone. Marian, with her very calm and peaceful demeanor, leads all the workshops in their spacious living room. During the workshop, Marian, who has developed her intuition very strongly, said that she had an intuition that Spencer was an old soul, wise beyond his years. It was not the first time I'd heard that from a spiritual person. I only wish he could transfer that knowledge into homework, but then again, who knows, maybe Buddha was an inattentive student as well, too busy figuring out the meaning of life and not worrying about pi R squared.

After lunch, Gary took Spencer out by the stables, where there was an imitation bull made out of two stacks of hay and a bull's head replica. Gary took some lasso ropes and showed Spencer how to rope it by the horns. They practiced for a while, and Spencer finally got the hang of it. It was a good prelude for what was coming next because that afternoon was the first adrenaline adventure, an authentic cowboy horseback ride through the Arizona desert. We piled into Gary's van and drove for about an hour to a place called Rafter6 U Ranch, a fifty-thousand-acre ranch with two cowboys named Steve and John as the head honchos.

These guys were very colorful characters, the real McCoys. Because of his authentic look, Steve was asked to be in the movie *Getaway* with Kim Bassinger. During the seventies, he worked on a wagon train herding thirty thousand cattle. He told us it was a tough life and the one thing you learned early on was to never to insult the cook or pass the dead line, the line you cross by getting too close to the chuck wagon.

John led our ride. We were all saddled up our horses except for Spencer, who was given a mule named Bingo. Turns out mules are more sure-footed, so Spencer was happy.

Unlike rides back home, this ride was in the desert, no trails, just desert. How the hell they knew the way, I'll never know. Comes with the territory, I guess. We passed a dead cow that had wilted down to the bones, with that famous skull head just sitting there. Or course I took a picture, no shame.

After seeing the dead animal and some tumbleweeds roll by, John asked if we were ready to get some real ridin' in. We all nodded yes. With a quick sound to the horses to get them in motion, we picked up the pace.

I have been on horses many times in my life but have never really mastered the trotting part. On this day, I felt like Billy Crystal in that movie *City Slickers*. I was bouncing up and down, opposite of the horse's movements. Thank goodness I was wearing a sports bra!

I know horses can sense when someone is inexperienced, so I tried to talk my way out of it. "You know, horse, I'm doing this for the exercise." The horse trotted faster, and I kept smacking the saddle, making that plop … plop … plop noise. It was a western saddle so after a few more plops, I decided to hang onto the horn in front. I know you're not supposed to do that, but it always gives me a feeling of support.

Adrenaline Adventures

Then John asked if we were ready to gallop. Now, galloping I could handle. For some reason, I am better able to get into that rhythm. Like a scene right out of the movie, John gave a "yeehaw" yell, and we all went galloping across the desert, kicking up the dust. I looked back half expecting to see a posse chasing us. I saw Spencer's mule was keeping up nicely, and that Spencer was grinning from ear to ear.

After a few minutes of galloping, we slowed down and let the horses rest. Out of the corner of my eye I saw a jackrabbit hop by. I turned to look and he was gone. Man those things are everywhere! The way he suddenly popped out, I felt like I was in a "Where's Waldo" cartoon.

The ride lasted a full two hours, with more trotting, galloping, and resting.

Antelope occasionally passed us, as if on cue. I looked around to see if there was a director yelling, "Okay, bring in the antelopes—nice touch, now cut."

After the ride, we were treated to a cowboy cookout. There in the middle of nowhere, a table was set up, and there was a delicious meal cooking on the barbecue behind an authentic chuck wagon. The cowboys took turns telling us stories about their wild adventures as we chowed down on the grub.

We drove back to the ranch, having had a full day. We were ready for bed at—get this—ten o'clock! I haven't gone to bed that early since I was in kindergarten. This western dude ranch type living sure does knock you out.

DAY 3 – Tuesday

This day was filled with more workshops, fantastic gourmet meals, a laid back afternoon adventure of a hike up Mingus Mountain, the mountains in which General George Crook chased Geronimo and his band of Chiricahua Apaches, and a tour of old Indian ruins and the artsy town of Jerome.

At night, a Native American singer came to the ranch to entertain us. This place was truly magical with its wide variety of experiences. That night I laid in bed and thought about a sign I had seen during our hike in the mountains; it said, "Take nothing but pictures …

leave nothing but footprints." I think that summed up the spirit of the day.

Day 4 – Wednesday

By 8:45 we were on the road for our long haul to the South Rim of the Grand Canyon.

We talked about ways in which we could make work a better place and how to deal with people who are not quite pleasant. Of course, my idea of smacking some sense into them wasn't exactly spiritual and didn't go over too well. I was just kidding. Some good ideas were tossed around and a handout of suggestions was given out.

Upon entering Grand Canyon National Park, we stopped at a lookout called Mather Point. There is something very fascinating about this giant hole in the ground. This ancient chasm, carved over a millennia through the rocks of the Colorado Plateau, is awesome. I think it's the size that humbles you and makes you realize how we are just a dot in time.

Since Spencer and I had rafted the canyon before, it was interesting to see it now from this perspective. We had flown over the canyon and rafted it, but we had never stood at the top looking down.

With physical exertion in mind and plenty of water in our bottles, Marian and Gary led the way on a hike down into the canyon with gravity helping us every step of the way.

We passed these massive archways and stopped for a photo op. Then we spotted something that Gary and Marian on their many treks there had never seen. We saw an endangered California condor. Condors were recently (1996) reintroduced into the wild, and there are now about twenty-five condors living on their own in the Grand Canyon.

What is cool is that the condors released into the wilds of Arizona have come to the Grand Canyon, which was once their native habitat, as proven by condor bones found in caves around the canyon.

After about an hour of hiking, we stopped, made a 180-degree turn, and headed back up the trial. This was a one-lane dirt path, but people were going in both directions. I looked behind us and noticed there was the mule train. A very slow-forward-moving mule train.

Adrenaline Adventures

Gary and Spencer were way ahead; in fact, at times Spencer was sprinting up the mountain trail. Marian and I were keeping pace, and then, for some reason, I got really winded. (Gee, could it be the steep ninety-degree angle of the hill?) I hated slowing anyone down so I told Marian to continue ahead, while I stopped and rested. Yes, I rested! But not for long because, every time I stopped, I noticed the mule train getting closer. The last thing I wanted was to be behind a bunch of asses. So I kept on going. At times I'd even leave the trail and sprint up the mountain. I felt like an ex-con trying to keep one step ahead of the law. Finally, I made it to the top, and not even five minutes later the mules arrived too. I swear they looked like they were laughing at me.

A quick trip to the gift shop made me feel better about the hike. I saw a shirt that said, "I hiked, dragged myself, complained, nearly passed out, and barely made it out of the canyon." It was the confirmation I needed that I wasn't the only one feeling weary.

That night our destination was a surprise, and I'm not going to tell you where we went. You'll have to try this adventure and find out for yourself. Just trust that it takes place on the famed Route 66, the highway that runs 2,400 miles, through eight states, starting in Chicago and ending up in Los Angeles.

Back at the ranch, Spencer and I decided to try out the hot tub on the porch. It was pitch black out, and we could hear coyotes howling. Spencer commented, "I know you'd rather be here with Steve, Ma."

I looked at Spencer. "You know, in the beginning I thought that, but I can't say that's true anymore. It's a totally different experience with you than it would have been with Steve. I think it's cool that we are spending this time together."

Spencer and I were experiencing things together that bonded us more as mother and son. I was appreciating my time with him. Although I missed Steve, I felt there was a reason the trip had happened the way it had. I think in my quest to be the perfect mother, sometimes I get so wrapped up in work that I don't get a chance to spend as much quality time with Spence as I'd like. This was giving me the opportunity. I looked at Spencer and said, "Come on, let's go inside and play a game of Spit."

He smiled. We played cards until we fell asleep.

Day 5 - Thursday

Today was the day of high-adrenaline adventure.

Our adventure took place in the beautiful red rocks of Sedona. Sedona is considered by the Native Americans to be the spiritual vortex of the Southwest, an excellent place for meditation, located in the high desert at an elevation of 4,500 feet, under the rim of the Colorado Plateau. But don't let that fool you. There is an awesome adventure that awaits.

Marian drove us to a jeep tour outfit. On the way, she put on her historian hat and told us how this lovely town got its name. "Back in 1902, a man by the name of Theodore Schnebly arrived in the city with his wife, Sedona, and his two children. There were a few families already there, and they were eager to have contact with the outside world. Schnebly wrote to the U.S. Postmaster to establish a post office in the town, and his request was approved. The only thing missing was a name. He tried to have Schnebly Station but was told it was too long to put on a cancellation stamp. So he choose his wife's name, Sedona."

Good thing, because there is nothing attractive about the name Schnebly.

As she finished the story, we came upon Bell Rock, a red rock that looked like, you guessed it, a bell. I saw people climbing it and was tempted to get out. We snapped some pictures but had to hurry to catch our two P.M. jeep appointment.

Sedona is off the beaten path, but Hollywood made it famous with John Wayne's *The Angel and the Badman* film and Robert Mitchum's *Blood on the Moon*. Since then, many commercials and TV shows have been shot in the surrounding areas of the city. It's now a big tourist attraction with quaint marketplaces, golf courses, and chapels. But it hasn't become over-commercialized to where it has lost its charm and grandeur.

Ten minutes before our appointed time, we arrived at the office of Pink Jeep Tours, the original jeep tour company in the United States, operating since 1958. It was started by a few guys who thought this four-wheeling stuff was fun. They kept bringing their friends out for an afternoon adventure and soon realized they could make a business out of it. The rest is adventure history. I had no idea what to expect.

Marian took care of the financials, and we piled into one of the many bright pink jeeps in the parking lot. Marian, who had done the tour many times before, decided to go hike instead. An elderly couple joined us. Our tour guide, Gus, greeted us, and we were on our way.

At first it seemed rather normal, driving on the paved cement highway out of the small town of Sedona. But then, at this Broken Arrow Road sign in Coconino National Forest, we made a left turn and everything changed. The road became a dirt road, a very bumpy dirt road, filled with large stones. Gus stopped the jeep, lowered the glass windshield, turned and smiled at us, and said, "Fasten your seatbelts, folks, and hold on."

We just laughed; a few bumps weren't going to scare us. He shrugged, obviously knowing something we did not know.

At first, we just bounced down a set of stone steps. Not a bad start, but then there was this giant boulder in the way, and I mean GIANT. Instead of going around it like a normal car would, we simply went over it like one of those tricked up toy cars with rubber tread wheels goes over the cat's bowl. We went up and over this boulder as if it were a mere pebble. Seat belts were not an option on this trip.

I thought that was a cute trick, and we all looked at each other and laughed. Little did we know that was just the warm up. I had heard of four-wheel drive many times in my life, but I never actually experienced it. After all, what's the most you are going to use a jeep for in New York, to go over a sidewalk or two?

We four-wheeled up more forty-five-degree-angle stone staircases and then up and over more red rocks while the magnificent canyon walls were all around us. At one point we stopped at a plateau with some lookout points. We got out, took pictures, and just took in all the beauty.

After a few minutes of communing with nature we were back in the jeep. We figured we had reached the high point ... but nooooo. We couldn't have been more wrong. We were in for even more intense jolting and bouncing. It was fabulous.

Fran Capo

We drove up this humongous hill on which there was a giant rock perched. They called it Mushroom Rock. We figured it was a nice rock to look at. Next thing we knew, Gus drove the jeep up to the edge of Mushroom Rock. Less than a few hundred feet from where we were gallivanting around was a sheer drop-off of more than two hundred feet. I'm serious, one wrong move and we would have been splattered like Wile E. Coyote on the canyon floor.

I looked to see if there were any safety nets, or gates, or if maybe this was a hologram. But no, this was the real thing, and Gus was driving around like it was a Sunday stroll. He was getting a kick out of our white-knuckled grips on the side of the jeep.

Spencer and I were holding on tight but were laughing at the same time. I looked at the old couple and they were having the time of their lives.

Just when I thought the terrain couldn't get any steeper, we continued up rocks the size of a two-story house! I didn't know this kind of driving was even possible. I had to ask Gus, when it was safe of course, a question. "Excuse me, what kind of jeep did you say this was?" I figured if it's this good on boulders, the streets of New York would be a cinch. Turns out it was a Wrangler Jeep that had about ten thousand dollars worth of work added to the suspension to enable it to make this trek—that and a lot of skilled driving. I don't remember that course being offered back in driver's ed, and if it was, that would be one hell of a road test!

Then Gus thought it would be fun to scare us. He took us up this one rock that seemed like it was at a ninety-degree angle. He started to go up and then pretended the tires lost their grip, "Oh no, folks ... this has never happened. Hold on!"

He let the car slide slowly backward. We all looked at each other with panic at first, but then Gus started to laugh and we all realized it was a joke. Good thing I had my Depends on.

We bounced, lunged, and jolted for about an hour, with the bumpiest downhill route saved for last. We felt every nook and cranny of the last path down. It was like being in a runaway bumper car. Our bodies got knocked around a bit, but it was fun.

Spencer and I were laughing all the way. This would not be good ride for those with a delicate stomach.

Adrenaline Adventures

Finally, after being bounced in every way, we once again were back on the paved road. Gus put the windshield back up and then drove back to the Pink Jeep Tour office, just as if we had been out for a Sunday stroll.

I'm telling ya, you can't go to Sedona without experiencing this ride. It's a must. Gary and Marian sure knew how to show their guests a good time.

DAY 6 - Friday

Since we had rented a car, Spencer and I decided to go solo and explore Arizona on our own on Friday. Actually I had it in my mind all along that I wanted to see the Painted Desert and the Petrified Forest because my dad had visited those places on his trip to Arizona. And even though he'd said it was disappointing, and Gary and Marian said the lack of rain would make the colors less than brilliant and that it was a good three hundred miles away, I was determined to go.

Well, the naysayers were right. The drive was cool, and two-million-year-old trees that had turned to stone were awesome, but the place didn't live up to the hype. The petrified forest was just stumps; I was expecting trees.

We did stop along the way, though, to see the Meteor Crater in Winslow, the planet's first proven meteor impact crater that left a 570-foot-deep hole nearly three miles wide. That was pretty intense.

We got back to the ranch by 6:15 P.M., and a nice treat was waiting, a Swedish massage. Spencer couldn't partake in this luxury since he was underage, so he played cards with Marian instead.

It was very peaceful, and I felt my body and spirit both enjoying the treat. Forty minutes later, I felt like melted wax—warm and pliable. It was a wonderful way to end a very full week.

That night, Spencer and I said our goodbyes to the couple, for we were leaving at five A.M. for our drive back to Phoenix to catch our plane. We packed and had a very restful sleep.

DAY 7 - THE FINAL ENCOUNTER

The next morning, we tiptoed around, left a small gift for Marian and Gary, and were on our way. Dillon came to say goodbye, and

Fran Capo

then we realized Gary and Marian had gotten up to give us one last breakfast and some treats for the road. We hugged, we joked, and then we left.

As we pulled out past the sign, '"Western Spirit Enrichment Center," we thought of the full week we'd had and all the fond memories we'd carry. It was a wonderful experience for the mind, body, and soul, and we felt as if we'd made a lasting friendship with Marian and Gary. We hoped to keep that feeling of peace with us for a long time. I knew one thing, I would at least say thanks at every meal and be grateful for all the wonderful things I have.

As I was contemplating how my life had changed, a jack rabbit darted out into the road and took me out of the dreamy state. The rabbit looked back at me as if to say, "It's all part of life, folks. Sometimes you got to stop and smell the roses, and other times you have to be quick like a rabbit and grab opportunity when it knocks."

All I know is that that little critter was lucky I was quick and swerved to miss him, but I wasn't so quick that I didn't stop to glimpse the sunrise.

Adrenaline Adventures

Chapter 41
Adventure at a Glance - Dare to Do it   Mild to Wild Scale: 3

Title: A Western Spirit Adventure
Children allowed: Yes, but not during couples only week.
Age requirement: Ten and up
Length of trip: One week
Where to try this adventure: Western Spirit Enrichment Center
P.O. Box 25252, Prescott, Arizona 86312-5252
1-800-ONESPIRIT (663-7747)
Web site: www.westernspiritranch.com
E-mail: info@westernspiritranch.com
Best time of year: All year round
Approximate cost: $1,395 for the week, which includes lodging, all meals, all workshops, and all adventures except skiing. Airfare not included. If you mention you purchased this book, you will get a $200 discount! And don't think you can just read this and call, there will be a test ☺
Reservations necessary: Yes. You have to book in advance, because there is a maximum of four guests unless it is a day workshop or a corporate event, in which case they utilize a different space.
Fitness requirements: Good physical shape for adventures.
Personal gear required: Comfortable clothes, hiking shoes
What NOT to bring: Work
Photo opportunities: Yes

Notes: For the purposes of this book, I kept this chapter to the more active things that we did. To read the full article on the Western Spirit Center, check the archives of www.uniquetravelstories.com.

Cool trivia: It is well documented that either quick or constant stress can induce many mind and body disorders. Besides prescribed drugs, there are extremely effective holistic methods to tackle stress. Yoga, meditation, relaxation, massage, outdoor exercise, fresh air, healthy food, and prayer can help. The Western Spirit Center has all these things wrapped into one week.

"There is absolutely no benefit in worrying about things that are beyond my control."
—Author Unknown

Chapter 42
"A Leap of Faith"
Tandem Skydiving

One of my very first adventures was doing a static line parachute jump in Lakewood, New Jersey, right out of college. Doing a static line was exhilarating, because you had to have the courage to step out of the plane, but you only had to deal with a free fall for a total of eight feet, the length of the static line. Since the static line is attached to the plane and deploys your chute, you don't get the feeling of free falling or the worry of pulling your own chute in time. That was fine for then. I figured it would be nice to free fall through the clouds sometime in the future.

I didn't have a definite time of when I wanted to do a tandem jump. It just came up one day when my friend Heidi asked, "So what's your next adventure?"

Adrenaline Adventures

Without thinking, I blurted out, "Maybe a tandem jump." Once said, the idea stuck. All I had to do was get some friends to do the daring deed with me. I looked at Heidi; she shook her head no.

I scanned my e-mail list and remembered that a couple of months earlier, at a high school reunion, two former classmates, Alex and Eugene, had mentioned that if I ever decided to jump, they'd come along. I e-mailed them and, conveniently, they were both working that Monday (okay, they are stockbrokers, so maybe they really were but still, they could have called in sick; after all, some people think it's sick to jump out of a perfectly good plane). I guess I'll have to ask them on a weekend and see if the results differ.

I tried a few more friends, but they all said they needed their feet to be solidly on the ground at all times.

I once again went back to Heidi, since I felt she was the one who'd started this in the first place. Heidi thought about it and said she might give it a try. At the time, we thought we might want to make my adventures into a television show (and that still might be a possibility), so we enlisted the services of her friend Evan, a very laid back guy and fellow producer who thought I was totally nuts but wanted to come and watch.

With no takers, but at least spectators, I phoned a place I had heard about called The Ranch in Gardiner, New York. The Ranch is about a two-hour drive north from Manhattan and very close to my favorite rock climbing place, Mohonk, which is in the neighboring town of New Paltz. I figured if I jumped out of the plane near The Ranch, I'd be able to get a bird's eye view of Mohonk. Of course I could stay inside the plane and do that too, but then it would be more like a bird's eye view inside a cage, and I don't do well in captivity.

I called and spoke to Joseph Richards, the owner of The Ranch. He was very upbeat and enthusiastic. He gave me the rundown. "We've been in business for over twenty years and have never had a fatality, but before you do a tandem jump, we'd like you to go to our Web site, www.skydivetheranch.com, and review the information. Go to the release forms page, read them, print them out, and then sign them. Then if you could watch the instructional video, you'll know what to expect before you come up here. It's that simple."

He sounded very confident. I thanked him, picked a tentative date two Mondays from then to avoid the weekend rush, and said I'd get back to him to confirm. Immediately, I went to the site.

I clicked on "Your First Tandem Skydive – Tandem 1" and read the following: "With this introductory jump, you will skydive from our usual altitude of 13,500 feet with a free fall of approximately 60 seconds." (That could seem like a lifetime!) "You will then enjoy a five to seven minute canopy flight with a spectacular view of beautiful upstate New York ... During the tandem jump, you are physically attached to one of our highly skilled USPA certified tandem instructors for the entire skydive. Your tandem training will take about fifteen minutes and you will jump from one of our Dehaviland Twin Otters or Pilatus Porters. That's planes for us laymen. We can easily accommodate any number of friends you may want to bring." (Mmmm. Any number of friends! I was having trouble getting one!)

It ended with, "You must be 18 years of age and weigh 225 lbs or less."

Not a time you want to lie about your weight ... next thing you know you and the instructor will be one big police chalk mark on the ground. Then again, you can use the weight issue as an out by going to your local Dunkin Donuts and consuming everything in sight. "Oops, 226! My, my. Oh well, can't jump!"

With that said, and my devotion to dieting increased. I downloaded the release forms. The were the standard type of adrenaline sports release form, warning you that you can get killed, you are fully aware of it, and you want to do it anyway and p.s. you can't sue.

With the legalese out of the way, I clicked on the video. For some reason my finicky Mac didn't want to witness the rush of freefall, even though I downloaded the files. So I had to move to plan B: anxiously wait until I got to my boyfriend Steve's house to view it on his PC.

In the meantime, I continued to try to recruit fellow jumpers. Again, there were no takers, just a lot of well wishers.

A week before the jump I had a chance to finally see the instructional video. Steve and I watched it on his computer. It was the owner, Joseph, playing the part of the newbie jumper, with one of his instructors, Carol Sternberg, as the tandem instructor.

Adrenaline Adventures

Joseph explained, "Your instructor will have on both a reserve and main chute. The ripcord handle will be by the instructor's right leg. The harness will connect you and the instructor at four places; two snaps at the shoulders and two snaps by the thighs. You will have an altimeter on that will be set to zero while you are on the ground. Each number on the altimeter represents a thousand feet. You will wear a helmet and goggles."

I decided to start writing all this down, since I wouldn't be able to view the video again later at home. I felt like I was studying for a final exam, and in reality, if something went wrong, it would be a FINAL exam.

The video went on to show how to get ready once you are in the plane. Each of the jumpers sits in between the legs of the person behind them. You are handed a helmet to wear. When it's time to get ready, you are asked to get on your knees (and no its not to pray) so you can get hooked up to the instructor.

Then you put on your goggles, tighten them, stand up one leg at a time (which is quite a feat since you are now attached to another person), head to the door, do the countdown, and jump."

The video explained in detail how to stand at a forty-five-degree angle in the door and to look at the propeller while getting ready to jump. Then, once you heard, "Ready, set, arch," you were supposed to jump out the door. The video stressed that at six thousand feet YOU pull the ripcord and then happily flare and land softly on the ground and hopefully on your target.

Honestly, I was okay watching the video until I heard the part about me reaching back and pulling my own ripcord. I started having visions that I'd be reaching back there and grabbing for the wrong thing as I went spiraling down to earth. Why can't the instructor just pull the ripcord? Must I be responsible for our lives my first jump out?

Steve saw my panic and said, "I'm sure the guy will pull it if he sees you don't."

Even still, I decided I needed to watch the video *several times* and memorize the information. Steve rolled his eyes and went downstairs to watch TV. Sure, he could stay calm, he wasn't jumping! But I did notice he was eating a big box of Dunkin Donuts just in case.

As "Jump Day" got closer, I started to think about my mortality. I'd never thought about it before with my other adventures, I kind of just did them. I guess I never looked at the risk or danger, just the thrill of overcoming a challenge. But, for some reason, 13,500 feet was sticking in my mind. Strange, I didn't worry when I jumped from 2,500 feet. I guess it was the splat factor that was bothering me. I thought maybe I should prepare just in case; after all, I did have a lot of projects in the works.

With that thought in mind, I sent letters to my editors telling them to publish my books anyway and to give the money to my son, Spencer. Then I wrote "just in case" letters to my son, my mom, my sister, and my boyfriend telling them how much I loved them, where the cash was stashed (all two dollars of it), about my will, and that I'd haunt them if they didn't behave.

Finally, I sent out a mass e-mail to my friends telling them I was jumping, I kidded, "So if you don't hear from me on Tuesday, you know what happened."

The responses ran the gambit of emotions; "Good God girl, you are amazing!"; to the spiritual, "While you're up there maybe you can pray for those people who never get their prayers even close to heaven"; to sheer honesty, "No way, Jose, I'm a total sissy ... a ground lover—but enjoy if you must"; to the cautiously funny, "BE CAREFUL FRAN ... WE HAVE TO STILL HAVE LUNCH. DAMMIT! IF YOU DIDN'T WANT TO MEET – JUST SAY SO ... DON'T GO JUMPING OUT OF A PLANE!; To the encouraging, "Good luck! I have jumped from a perfectly good airplane over eighty times, and have comeback fine each time! You will have a blast!"; and finally to some facts I really didn't need to hear, "The human body bounces ten feet when dropped from thirteen thousand feet on a good day." Good day? Seems like anyone who is bouncing out of a plane when dropped is having a bad day.

The amazing thing was no one was shocked I was jumping. I guess I've been doing adventures for so long, it's like Betty Crocker announcing she's going to bake a cake. In this instance it could be an upside down layer cake.

Anyway, I felt better knowing my business was all tied up and my friends and family knew what was going on. I also wanted to

Adrenaline Adventures

make sure that I didn't fight with anyone the night before. The last thing I wanted was bad karma on the jump.

The night before the jump, I lifted weights just to be ready in case the ripcord was hard to pull or something. I didn't want to be messing with that thing in the air. Nope, I didn't want to leave any stone unturned, or any cord unpulled.

After my workout, Heidi called. "Fran, they say it might rain tomorrow afternoon and it's supposed to be cloudy. I know your jump is at eleven so I think we will have to play it by ear."

I was already a bit nervous, and the thought of jumping without being able to see the ground wasn't one I was fond of. I didn't want the ground sneaking up on me, and my last words being, "Oh there you are … damn … splat."

Luckily, the weatherman was wrong. This was one time I was really happy that weather is not an exact science. Jump Day was gorgeous and clear.

Now all I had to think about was the list of people that had made me promise to call them upon landing—safely, that is.

My son, of course, wanted to know if he was still going to have a mother by the end of the day. I told him, "Think of it this way: then you won't have to clean your room." That's how we respond to fear in our family, with jokes. But to make him feel better, I gave him a cell phone to take to school (even though it has to be turned off by school law), so at least I could leave a message to let him know I was all right. My mom, who had been saying novenas since I told her I was going to jump, made me promise to call her at work as soon as I had two feet on the ground as well as the rest of me in one piece. And finally, my boyfriend and two close friends, Anna and Janette, wanted me to call just for peace of mind.

That morning, I dropped Spencer at school at eight. I reassured him that everything was going to be fine. I also told him that in life you have to practice what you preach, and if I'm telling him to go out and live his dreams, as a mom, I have to lead by example and not just give it lip service. I kissed him goodbye and then drove upstate by myself. My friends Heidi and Evan were driving up together from Jersey to watch me jump and also to act as photographers to capture this moment for eternity.

Fran Capo

On the ride up, to pass the time, I called Anna, who, like a true friend, said, "Don't worry, Frannie. Everything is going to be fine. This is just another crazy Capo adventure designed to give you a few minutes of peace and quiet where no one can reach you. But I gotta tell you, there isn't enough money in the world to make me jump. Unless the plane is on fire, is spiraling down, and the captain is dead, I'm not leaving the plane."

I arrived at The Ranch before the other jumpers, which was surprising because somehow I had missed the road to the place a couple of times and had to loop back. Maybe it was my subconscious mind saying, "Why not just go to Mohonk and rock climb?"

I sat in the parking lot for a few minutes and said a quick prayer. Then I decided to get out and check out the place. There were a couple of people underneath this huge canvas. Some were just hanging out, some were preparing chutes, and some (gorgeous half-naked men) were planning their skydiving aerobic dance number.

Everyone was upbeat, happy, and calm. I went into the trailer, which doubled as an office, and handed in my release forms. The office girl told me she had jumped a few times and loved it. She said, "The oldest guy that jumped was ninety-six and the oldest woman was eighty."

My competitive nature kicked in. "Well, if they could do it, so can I. They did live right?"

She just laughed.

I looked at all the pictures and cartoons on the wall. I had a flashback to something I'd seen on one of the videos on their Web site. I just had to ask the question.

"Hey, by the way, who was the guy on the video with the long, gray beard, the Amish-looking guy with the Grim Reaper personality of death? He scared me."

"Oh, that guy is Bill Boots. He's known as the father of the three-ring release system that allows you to safely cut away from the parachute if necessary. He was also one of the first guys to do a tandem jump."

"In the video he mentioned tandem jumping was still experimental, is that true?"

Adrenaline Adventures

"Well, it was experimental from around 1983 to 2001. Just last year it was changed from that status."

"Maybe they should update that video." I felt a little better knowing I was no longer a guinea pig.

Shortly after, Heidi and Evan arrived. They had brought a friend, Cassidy, who was thinking of jumping too. I asked them if they had changed their minds about jumping, and Evan shook his head. "I still think you're nuts."

Heidi said she'd watch and then maybe do it another time.

Cassidy said, "She was game, but her attentions seemed distracted by the half-naked men running around."

Another nice office girl, Bernadette, gave us an overview of what was going to happen; it sounded pretty similar to what I'd heard on the tape I'd watched ad infinitum.

I was introduced to Carol Sternberg, a gold medallist in skydiving who was going to act as my cameraperson. She would be jumping out of the plane with us, wearing a helmet equipped to take both stills and video. She started rolling tape right away. "So Fran, why are you jumping out of a plane today. Are you nuts?"

I played to the camera. "Nuts? No, my son said, 'Ma, you've been bugging me about the homework lately, you sure you don't want to jump out of a plane?' So I took him up on it."

She taped as I took the instruction lessons. My instructor for the day was James Leonard. James had jumped 3,500 times before and had been skydiving since 1992. He said sometimes, depending on how many students there are, he jumps as many as twelve times a day! And here I was worried about just one jump! But still, in my defense, the first time is special and particularly scary. You only need one mistake.

I casually asked James if was happily married. I just wanted to make sure that he didn't pick today to get out of his marriage without the hassle of a divorce. With a twinkle in his eye he said, "Well, my wife left me, the kids won't talk to me, my house burned down, and my dog ran away with the neighbor's cat."

I felt like I was listening to the lyrics of a bad country and western song.

Then he laughed. "Just kidding. I'm single and my girlfriend and I are very happy."

With his sanity and sense of humor checked, I suited up in a blue jumpsuit and had an altimeter—a device that measures altitude—strapped to my left wrist.

We went around the back of the office/trailer to a training area. There was a platform to simulate the door of the plane where you could practice your stance and jump.

James began, "Remember to stand with your feet at a forty-five-degree angle to the propeller. Hold onto your harness in the door. You will hear a count of 'ready, set, arch.' Then we will jump. The arch is important because it helps the center of gravity to be in your stomach and helps control the free fall. A few seconds after, I'll pull the drone chute, which will stabilize us. I'll tap you on the shoulders to let you know that the drone is out. Then you put your arms in a W position. Give a quick check to your altimeter, and reach your left arm over your head and your right arm back for a practice grab of the ripcord. Then relax and enjoy the ride. Remember, the two most important things are to have a good time and smile for the camera."

Easy for him to say. I would be his cushion if we landed without a chute.

The final things we practiced were flaring and the steering of the parachute. Steering was pretty simple. To turn right, turn your head right and pull down on the right toggle. The farther down you pull, the faster you turn. Same thing on the left. The only difference from the static line jump (besides the fact that I had a guy constantly on my back) was in the landing. In a static line, you look at the horizon, and as soon as you feel your feet touch the ground, you drop and roll. In a tandem jump, you land on your butt. Since that area of my body has more padding, I was okay with this.

To land on your butt you do this thing call flaring where you pull both toggles of the parachute down at the same time. As you pull the toggles down, you raise your feet straight in front of you so you can glide into the grass. Hopefully you do it right and don't get any butt burn.

James asked, "Any more questions?"

"Yeah, I know what happens if you pull the chute too late. What happens if you pull too soon?"

"Nothing. You just float longer."

"Oh, okay."

"Anything else?"

"What if I pull the rip cord at five thousand feet instead of six thousand?"

"We have beginners pull at six thousand because we figure by the time they remember what to do it is five thousand. A professional can pull as low as 3,500."

"Good, I like a little leeway."

"You'll be fine, Fran."

"Just one more question. If for some reason when I'm putting my right hand back looking for the rip cord, I happen to grab for the wrong thing, you are going to pull the cord, aren't you?"

James just nodded and laughed. I laughed too, but I checked the location once again.

It was time to don the parachute and harness. We walked under the tent where all the equipment was laid out. Carol was taping James, who was getting ready, and asked, "Isn't that the chute that doesn't work?"

James gave a coy smile to the camera. "I'm sure it's good for one or two more jumps."

James put on the backpack that contained the drone, the main chute, which is checked every day, and the reserve chute, which is checked on cycles of 120 days even though it is rarely used. I checked again to see where the ripcord was. It was kind of hard to miss since it had an orange golf ball attached to the end of it. But still, when I was jumping, I wouldn't be able to turn my head back like Linda Blair and look for it.

I put on my harness, which had the hooks to attach to James in the four places. James made sure it was tight. I felt more secure that way anyway.

We headed over to the plane. Only one other guy and I were doing a tandem jump. The other twenty people on the plane were professionals. We tandem jumpers were to be the last to jump and, therefore, needed to be the first on the plane.

Carol took pictures of my walk to the plane. I did a little dance number to show I wasn't nervous. Yeah, right!

I sat in between James' legs, and Carol sat in between mine. Everyone was laughing and joking. I was joking, too, but inside I was nervous. After we took off, James gave me my helmet to wear. It was a leather helmet, nothing that could prevent brain injury. I kept checking my altimeter as the plane was climbing ... 8,000 ... 9,000 ... 10,000. I was handed my goggles and asked to put them on.

James, sensing my nervous energy, said, "Don't worry, you'll love it. It will seem surreal."

I couldn't imagine how falling 120 miles per hours could seem surreal, since my cheeks would be pressed against my face and the earth getting closer by the second.

I was too short to see out the window, so I really couldn't get a sense of how high I was. I started wondering how all of us were going to jump out at the same spot. I mean, it's not like the plane could stand still over the target.

James said, "We all try to jump as quickly as possible when the pilot feels we are over the target. If he has to, he will circle around and then the next batch will jump."

I saw the door roll open and the first group of guys leap out of the plane. Just like that. No thought ... nothing. Some of them jumped backward; some did somersaults. They made it look so easy.

My heart pounded. The plane was more than half cleared of divers. But we had to circle around again. The waiting was killing me and giving me reprieve at the same time.

Within minutes, we were ready for the next batch to be regurgitated out of the plane. Then I heard Carol say, "Fran, any last words?"

As she pointed the camera at me, I choose to joke. "Ma, I never told you about the time I ... oh well." I figured if I was going to have last words on camera, might as well make em funny.

At this point, I knew I wouldn't turn back. I heard James say, "On your knees." It was the only time in my life I would obey that command. He hooked me to himself in the four spots, two on the shoulders and two on the hips. Then he said, "Ready, let's stand." We both put our right foot first, then the left. We made it up without tumbling over. We headed toward the door of the plane.

Adrenaline Adventures

I watched the tandem guys go before me. For the first time, I saw how high up thirteen thousand feet was. I couldn't believe I was about to jump. My adrenaline was working overtime.

Carol went outside and hung onto the side of the plane so she could capture our jump. The moment of truth. I stood in the door of the plane, holding onto my harness. The wind was blowing in my face. I put my feet at a forty-five-degree angle and looked at the propeller.

James said, "Don't forget to smile." I nodded. Then I heard the command, "Ready, set, arch … JUMP!"

In one giant step, with no turning back, we were out of the plane, spiraling toward the earth at a dizzying rate of 120 miles per hour.

The next few seconds were a blur. I know my eyes were open, and I must have seen the plane, but I can't even recall the sensation of falling hundreds of feet. It's like I saw everything and nothing at the same time.

Then I felt the tap twice on my shoulders that signaled the drone chute was open. I put my hands in the W position. Then James pointed to Carol, who was a few feet away from me, waving and smiling and recording my every move. It was then that I looked down for the first time and realized I was above the clouds. I checked my altimeter; it showed eleven thousand feet. I did my practice reach for the ripcord and then, for some reason, a peace came over me.

I started to laugh. I loved the feeling. I was floating in the air, or at least it felt that way. There was no sensation of falling. It felt like two giant invisible hands were bouncing me slightly and holding me suspended in air.

The closest sensation I've ever had to this was when I would put my hand out the car window as I was driving down the highway and the wind would push it backward as I tried to push it forward. The play of forces.

I looked all around and saw the gorgeous Mohonk Mountains in the distance. The ground was still so far away, and I could see for miles. I waved and smiled at the camera. I had every faith that the chute would open. The first step, as they say, is always the scariest.

Fran Capo

Since James saw I wasn't scared, he pushed down on my right hand while we were free falling which spun us around quickly to the right. Then he pushed

with the left hand and we spun the other way. I was having the greatest time. I felt totally free.

Then I remembered. Ah, I better check my altimeter. I looked and saw it was showing six thousand feet. I reached back for the ripcord. I found it immediately and pulled. It was so much easier to pull than I'd imagined it would be. When the chute opened, we were pulled slightly upward. I looked down and saw Carol rapidly drop out of sight. That is when I realized how fast we were going. A few seconds, and several hundred feet later, I saw her pull her chute.

We floated down. At this point, we were going only fifteen miles per hour and could talk. James unhitched our two bottom hooks so we could land easier. We made right and left turns, practiced a few flares, and then spotted our target, a big sandy circle. When we were ready, James said, "Flare." We did and landed ever so smoothly on our butts.

Carol was waiting with the camera. "Hey, you did it! How was it? Would you do it again?"

"Absolutely. That was a true adrenaline adventure. I loved it. It was the greatest feeling just floating for thousands of feet and seeing the world from a whole different perspective."

Heidi, Evan, and Cassidy came running up. "It looked awesome," Heidi said. "I wish I did it."

Cassidy chimed in, "Girl, I wish I did it too. But for now, I'm gonna see if I can jump on one of those half-naked hunks and see what we can arrange for the near future."

Evan just shook his head. "You're all nuts. All I know is I kept looking for the plane up there and the next thing I know a bunch of people were just plopping out of the plane like ants."

We all laughed.

I felt fantastic. It was the scariest and most rewarding adventure I'd ever done. I wanted to go again. Carol came over and congratulated me and handed me the video and a roll of still pictures. That was quick. We watched the video on their VCR.

Then James handed me a certificate, "My First Parachute Jump."

Adrenaline Adventures

He also handed me a logbook and wrote, "Nice exit, had fun, pulled and Yahoo!"

I walked away feeling I had conquered another fear, and this time I could literally say I had stayed on cloud nine for a long time—well, at least a minute.

I called everyone as promised. Spencer was relieved and couldn't wait to see the video. He said, "Everyone at school thinks I have the coolest and craziest mom."

"And what about you? What do you think?"

"I think it's great, because life is always exciting. Scary sometimes, but exciting. It also teaches me not to take things for granted. I love you, Mom."

"Love you too." I smiled and drove home thinking about my adventure.

At home, I saw my "just in case" letters sitting on my desk. I was going to rip them up, but then I thought twice and decided to keep them, because knowing me ... tomorrows another adventure.

Chapter 42
Adventure at a Glance - Dare to Do it   Mild to Wild Scale: 5
Title: Tandem Skydiving
Children allowed: No
Age requirement: Eighteen and up
Length of trip: Half day
Where to try this adventure: The Ranch
Phone: 845-255-4033 or Web site: www.skydivetheranch.com
Best time of year: Summer, spring, fall
Approximate cost: $185 for first jump
Reservations necessary: Yes
Fitness requirements: Must weigh under 225 pounds
Personal gear required: None, besides courage
What NOT to bring: Tight clothes
Photo opportunities: Yes

Notes: Of all my adrenaline adventures, I found this one to be the scariest. There are skydiving places around the country. Thoroughly check out the outfit first before agreeing to jump. Find out their safety record.

Cool trivia: The "sport" of skydiving began shortly after World War II when returning Airborne GIs found civilian life a bit tedious. While they weren't fond of getting shot at while they jumped, they did think the jumping part was fun. So when the United States government started dumping surplus parachute equipment into the civilian market in the 1950s, the paratroopers took up parachuting as a sport.

After a while of just tumbling any old way down, a Frenchman by the name of Jacque Istel brought the concept of a controlled freefall to the United States. The "box man" fall that skydivers do today was originally called the "French Frog" position. Istel introduced the first skydiving course for civilians around 1957.

"Live every day as if it's your last, and one day you'll be right."
—Martha Orellana

Chapter 43
"Leader of the Pack"
Learning to Ride a Motorcycle

At the age of two I was on my first motorcycle. My dad used to ride me up front on his bike and drive me over to the Hudson River so we could skip stones. This was, of course, before the helmet laws or really any safety laws were in effect.

If someone saw a two-year-old on a motorcycle today, child welfare soon would be involved and the perp would be on *60 Minutes*. But back then, it was just a father showing his daughter a good time, and I loved it. My dad said I used to go around making the sound of the motorcycle and I was always bugging him to go for a ride. Who knows, maybe that's the root of my becoming an adrenaline junkie.

My dad had two motorcycle accidents during my childhood, one on a rainy night while he was rushing to see my ballet performance (yes, believe it or not, I took ballet—took it, wasn't good at it—grace is not my forte). And the other time, a trailer slammed into him. He injured his knee one time, and the other time he wound up with a broken arm. Lucky, I guess, because it could have been worse.

But that didn't deter me from someday wanting to ride a bike, because I figure in life you have to go after your dreams—something is going to kill you anyway, might as well be doing something you

Adrenaline Adventures

like, within reason. Not talking about drinking or drugging yourself to death here.

Anyway, over my lifetime I've ridden on many people's motorcycles, and in high school I even got my learner's permit, but I never had a bike to practice on, so the permit expired and I kept doing other adventures.

Then a few years ago, my friend, Heidi, and I were working on a television pilot for an adventure show. Heidi was the producer on the show, and she had a motorcycle. I was the host, and she thought, for the opening credits, it would be cool for me to ride into the opening shot on her bike. I was game.

So before the shoot, I went out to her house and we took her bike into a vacant parking lot. I got on, and it just seemed to come naturally. Her bike was small, and I felt comfortable on it. I was up to second gear in no time. Confident that I could handle it, we made arrangements and did the shoot. Heidi and I talked about how much fun it would be to ride together—two motorcycle mamas ridin' down the highway. At that moment, I vowed to get my motorcycle license.

I called my boyfriend, Steve, and told him what I was going to do. He used to have a bike and was thinking about getting another one someday. My enthusiasm was obviously contagious and we both decided to get our class M license. Steve had been riding since he was a teen, but at the time, a separate license wasn't required, or if it was, no one checked. I liked the fact that we were both going for it, and it sparked a little friendly competition.

The first thing we both had to do was pass a New York State Department Motor Vehicle learner's permit test. This required picking up the manual, studying it, and then going in and taking the written test. When I went to pick up the book, the guy there told me that we also had to pick up the driver's manual, because a lot of questions from the regular driving test were on the motorcycle test as well.

We both took the test on the same day but in different locations. There were twenty questions on the test, and you could get up to six wrong before you failed. It was multiple choice, which is always easier. They tested you on rules of the road, safe driving techniques, road signs and their meanings, and about the use of alcohol and drugs while driving.

After the test, you had to wait a few minutes, and then they let you know if you'd passed. If you'd passed, you would then take a vision test, and then be given your permit.

Steve called me while I was waiting for my test results. He told me he'd passed, got a hundred. I knew this wasn't just information, but rather a little digging point. Great, so the pressure was on. I waited to hear my number called. There was this big bingo-like board and when you saw your number, you'd walk up to the counter. It's funny because most people almost run up to the counter, like they've just won the lottery or something. I saw my number light up and skipped to the counter. The lady looked at me and said, "You passed. Next."

I asked if I could look at the paper. She said, "No."

I said, "Could you please tell me what score I got? I have a little wager with my boyfriend."

She smiled. "You got one hundred, dear."

"Yes!" The playing field was even.

I walked over and got my vision checked, took care of some paperwork, and was then on my way. I called Steve on my cell phone to share the news. We both laughed. We knew the game we were playing.

The next step was to take a motorcycle safety course. The benefits of taking this course were that you would get a road waiver test. (In other words, you'd take your road test with them at the completion of the course, and you'd get an insurance reduction of ten percent off your policy, or four points off your license if you have any infractions.)

We contacted the Motorcycle Safety School (MSS) and they told us about a local course given in Westchester County at Yonkers Raceway by MANYS (the Motorcycle Association of New York State).

We called and enrolled in the Beginner Rider Course, which was a twenty-hour course given over two days, from 7:30 to 5:00 both days—so it was intense. The guidelines for the course were many; you had to be able to ride a bicycle, possess a current and valid driver license, possess a current and valid motorcycle permit, maintain full attendance for the entire course, successfully pass a

Adrenaline Adventures

written knowledge test of one hundred questions, successfully pass a riding skill evaluation test, and be sixteen years of age or older.

The total cost was $375 per person. To enroll, besides paying the money for course, we had to send in a copy of our license and interim learner's permits. They weren't just going to trust your word or go on good looks and charm. They were very strict.

In about a week, our registration arrived. The instructions read, "Arrive early! If you are late due to any excuse (traffic, directions, etc.) you will not be allowed to continue (there is NO rescheduling or refunds due to your being late.) We recommend you arrive before start time. Be prepared for all weather conditions; bring food and WATER. You must have PROPER RIDING GEAR that includes over-the-ankle boots, gloves, protective eye-wear, long pants, long-sleeved shirt, and helmet. Helmet liners must be purchased if you are using a MSS helmet, and bring your NYS drivers license and motorcycle permit; PHOTO ID'S WILL BE CHECKED. The class cannot commence unless all students are present, so be there promptly."

Whew, I wasn't sure if I was taking a road course or boot camp.

The day of the class Steve and I arrived forty-five minutes early. It was already hot and we had on our long-sleeved jackets, pants, and boots. The course, except for classroom training, was outside, so this was going to be interesting.

Once everyone was assembled, we were led into a classroom for our first part of the training. There were seventeen students; five women and twelve men. There were also two instructors, Dan and Brian.

When we entered the classroom, our licenses were checked. Then a roster was read and a Basic Rider Course handbook was passed out. We were told to put our names on it immediately. Yup, this was just like back in elementary school. I was wondering if we were going to have to put a book cover on it.

Then we were asked to introduce ourselves to the person next to us, find out about their experience on bikes, and then relate it to the rest of the class. We had five minutes to complete the assignment.

Once Brian called "time" we started one by one and told the tales of our newfound companions to our left. I was lucky enough to be able to relate Steve's story. "Hi, to my right is Steve. He has been riding motorcycles since he was sixteen. When he was seventeen, his mom left him under the care of his older sister. She was supposed to baby-sit him. She instead had a boyfriend over and wasn't paying attention to Steve. Steve didn't like that, so to scare them, he rode the motorcycle up the stairs of his home and busted in on them, shining the headlights and beeping the horn. His mom didn't find out 'til years later." Everyone laughed, but I think they thought they had a hellion on their hands.

We all went around the room, and everyone was very relaxed. We watched a few videos on driving. I am always curious who writes the copy on these things. They all have that same voice, same dry presentation. I think they should add a little humor into the videos—maybe have a ninety-year-old lady on the bike popping wheelies ... or giving the finger to drivers as an example of what not to do—something to spark these tapes up.

Anyway, after the videos we spent the morning going through the manual, talking about the different kinds of motorcycles, risk management strategy on a bike by using the acronym SEE—Search, Evaluate and Execute, choosing riding gear, the parts of a motorcycle, how to start and stop the engine using the acronym FINE-C—Fuel, Ignition, Neutral, Engine cut-off switch, Choke/clutch, the correct turning posture, stopping distance, braking and swerving, and the dangers of alcohol. We were told to study the manual that night because there would be an one-hundred-question written test on it at the conclusion of the course.

During lunch, I bonded with this one girl, Kate. She told me that her boyfriend told her she wouldn't be able to handle a bike, and she shouldn't even try. I told her to give it all she had and show him she could do it. She was really nervous, and she told me she didn't have any faith in her abilities. So I told her she should be proud she was here and in the worse case scenario at least she tried, and she could always try again. After all, motorcycles are not just for men.

After lunch, we were marched out into the hot July sun to a huge parking lot behind the racetrack. We were each sized with bikes and then divided into two groups.

The first thing we had to do was carefully walk our bikes out to the practice area. Once in the practice area, we met with our field

Adrenaline Adventures

instructors, Johnson and Patricia. Johnson was tall, lean and looked like a state trooper with his shades and high boots on.

"Okay, listen up. I'm going to make bikers out of you — safe bikers. If I see anyone doing anything that is against regulations, they will be asked to leave. Today we are going to get through as many exercises as we can. The course requires that we finish seventeen exercises. You will be skill-tested on five of them. If we have to stay late, we will. The course is not complete 'til each one of you successfully does these training exercises. If we reach a point that someone cannot do the exercises, they will be asked to leave and allowed to join another class at a later date. Do not take it personally. Motorcycle riding is a serious thing, and we only want to put people on the road who can handle it. There are to be no cell phone calls during class, or anyone getting back late from lunch. Be aware at all times of what's happening around you, and keep an eye on your bikes. If you drop your bike for any reason, you are automatically out of the class."

Man, talk about pressure! What if a good strong wind came and knocked it over? Or what if some stray carrier pigeon crash landed into my bike ... the list could be endless. But I decided to watch guard just in case.

Johnson then had us stand beside our bikes, and he went over all the parts so we would become familiar with them. He pointed out the throttle, clutch lever, gearshift lever, electric starter, engine cut off, and on and on.

After we became familiar with the parts, he had us put on our gloves, goggles, and helmets and mount our bikes. He had us use the FINE-C procedure we'd learned in class. F is for fuel supply valve. We turned the valve on. I is for ignition, and we turned the ignition switch to the on position. N is for neutral. We can make sure the bike is in neutral by rolling the motorcycle with the clutch lever released. He told us NOT to rely on the green light on the instrument cluster. E is for engine cut off, and we put the switch in the run position. And finally C is for choke. Have to set the choke on, on a cold engine. He said it's a good habit to squeeze the clutch as a precaution against starting in gear.

He made us practice this several times.

Then we were finally ready to get the bike moving. He told us to walk the bike a bit, then slowly use the throttle and let off the clutch.

The first exercise was to measure everyone's coordination and how we handled going in a straight line. Some people wobbled, some went too slow, some too fast. Most people had never ridden before, but they at least had the balance from learning how to ride a bike.

We then moved onto the four basic steps of a turn on a motorcycle; the slow, look, press, and roll. This was the procedure we were supposed to follow for a turn. If we were above ten miles per hour, we were supposed to lean with the bike. Under ten miles per hour, we were supposed to counter our weight against the bike and not turn. Johnson and Patricia would tell us what we did right or wrong during each execution. After each turn, we waited like anxious puppy dogs to see whether we were getting a biscuit or a newspaper on the nose.

The instructors were good but tough. They watched for our posture and to make sure we were keeping our backs straight and eyes and heads up. There was a lot to remember, it was hot, and the process was tedious. I was dying to rip off my long-sleeved shirt but thought flashing might not be appreciated, so I opted to roll up my sleeves. Immediately, the instructors were by my side. "Put those sleeves down please, Ms. Capo."

I did as I was instructed, but I was not pleased.

Then the lecture came. "Ms. Capo, if you do fall, the sleeves are for your own protection, so you don't get scratched."

I thanked Johnson and continued to sweat.

The instructors would jot down little notes on each of us. I felt like I was being inspected with a magnifying glass, and I was curious to see what they wrote. I felt like taking out a pad of my own and making some notes, but I thought they might not appreciate the humor. By the fourth exercise, two girls had been asked to leave the class.

One was Kate. I saw Johnson walk over to her, and then someone escort her and her bike off the practice course. I saw that she was crying. I mouthed to her, "You tried! Don't give up." All of a sudden,

Adrenaline Adventures

I felt like I was on the show *Survivor* and she was doing an immunity challenge.

We continued with more exercises: going around cones, and stopping and braking exercises. Steve was handling his bike like a pro, and I was doing okay. I was wide on some of the turns and they kept telling me to lean in more. I felt that if I leaned any more, I would fall over, and I didn't want to drop the bike. I was trying to do what they said without being thrown out. I knew they were right, but getting my body to do what my mind was saying wasn't always easy. It's kind of like going for that piece of cheesecake while your mind is saying, "That's not good for you."

Patricia was very encouraging, though. She told me I was doing great. Later she told me that she took this course a few years ago, then followed it up with fifty practice hours. She got so good, she became an instructor. I couldn't even conceive of fifty practice hours. I just wanted to get through this initial day.

The class ended at 5:30, and we had gotten through eight of the seventeen exercises, which meant we needed to get through nine the next day plus the written test and skill test. I knew tomorrow would be a long day.

I went home and studied my notes. Steve briefly looked over his. He explained that since he had ridden for so many years, a lot of it was second nature. I called Heidi to tell her my progress, and she said she was rooting for me to finish the class and get the license.

The next day, we were there early again. One guy showed up half an hour late and was not allowed to partake in the day's events. The guy started whining, then threatening, then pleading, but it was of no use. These people were serious. I later found out that this course used to be the police training course, and that's why it was so strict. Believe it or not, they said they had lightened up the intensity somewhat ... hard to believe. What did they make you do before, sleep on your bike in the rain while not tipping it?

This day we reported straight to the practice area. After our gear was checked, we were given bikes. I wound up with a different bike and didn't feel quite as comfortable on it, but I figured if I'm gonna ride, I should be able to ride any bike.

I noticed there were only twelve of us now. Somewhere along the way, others had been asked to leave. I was glad I'd made it this far, but the day was young

Joining us today was an older hardcore biker guy. Turns out this dude, Buddy T., had been riding for nearly forty years, but he had never gotten a license. He was the quintessential biker with the long hair, tattoos, leather jacket, etc. And he had attitude. He was not happy he was there. Apparently he had failed this class twice before. He kept mumbling, "I can outride any of these instructors. This is bull them trying to teach me how to ride after all these years."

You see, the problem was this. The motor vehicles department started matching up registered bikes, insurance, and driver's licenses. They found that almost fifty percent of the insured bikes did not have licensed drivers, so they sent out letters to all the bikers telling them to get a license or their bikes would be impounded. Well, no biker wants that, so they all started taking classes. Only problem was they were used to riding their own way—not the "proper" way. So a lot of them were flunking out, and Buddy T. was one of them.

We started day two with a couple of exercises on shifting, stopping, and cornering. There were a bunch of cones set up and we had to go in between them without knocking the cones down or going out of bounds. It actually was a fun exercise.

Steve kept getting corrected on his head position. They said he had to turn his head more and he was keeping it straight. Later he told me that he would do whatever it took to pass the class but ride the way he felt safest later. I was getting a bit nervous because all these experienced drivers were being told they were doing it the "wrong" way. It's hard to teach an old dog new tricks, especially if the tricks have been working for years. I, on the other hand, only had to learn it, not re-learn it.

The hardest exercise came later in the day when we had to do two figure- eight turns in a rectangular box. We were not allowed to go outside of the box, nor let our feet hit the ground. We were going extremely slow, and it took a lot of effort not to let the bike fall.

Buddy T. was swearing up a storm. "I ain't never had to do figure eights on the road. This is one stupid exercise." He did it, but his feet hit the ground once. He got off and slammed his bike to the ground. He was disqualified again.

After all the exercises were done, it was test time. We had made it through without getting thrown out. They set up five skill courses for us. We would be scored on position, staying within the bounds, and maintaining a certain speed.

I started to get really nervous for the test part. They lined us all up, and one by one we would do each exercise. We had two chances at each skill to get it right.

The first skill involved starting at one point, getting up to second gear by another point, and then shifting back down to first and braking within two cones. If you passed the cones, you failed. If you didn't shift, you failed. If you braked before the cones, you failed. They actually measured with a stopwatch how long it took you to brake. I felt like this was the Olympic tryouts. "Okay judges … show us the scores."

I talked myself through it. "Okay, Capo, get up to first, now shift to second, okay, cones coming up, now brake." I thought I did fine. But apparently I had to do it again, but faster. Imagine a fast-talking person like me not going fast enough.

This time I made sure I made it up to twenty miles per hour. Whoa baby, I was speeding now. I stopped within the cones and saw the instructors smile. Yes … one down, four to go.

Oddly enough, the hardest skill, the figure eight, I did great on.

We went through all five tests. I watched Steve, and he was breezing through them. I saw other people stumble but recover. We weren't sure exactly when they were taking points off. I started to get a worried feeling in my gut.

After the tests, they told us to go to the classroom. While we were taking the written test, they would tally up our road scores.

It was very nerve-racking taking the written test when we didn't even know if we had passed the road test. Within forty minutes, Steve handed in his test. Two minutes later, I handed in mine. There was one question I kept debating on.

With all the tests in, we now had to watch one final video with these two wholesome young kids talking about the dangers of drugs. They were so doofy, it looked like they were on drugs. The information was good, it was just the execution.

Then the instructors gave us some final words. "It was a pleasure having all of you in this class. Congratulate yourselves for making it this far. For those of you who do pass this class today, note this is still not your license; you are still a permit holder. MANYS will mail you a three-part form in the following weeks. This form is recognized as the road test waiver, and the DMV will endorse your license once the form is turned in."

With that said, they handed back the written tests. Steve got his and smiled. I got mine and smiled. "You show me yours first?" I said.

He turned his paper over; he had gotten a hundred.

"Now it's your turn, Capo."

I turned my paper over. I had gotten a hundred.

All that was left was for us to pass the road test.

An instructor came in and announced, "Two of you did not pass the course. I will be calling each of you individually out into the hallway. For those of you who did not pass, you can take a retest next week, and a private lesson in between, if you like."

Everyone in the room looked at each other, all of us trying to guess who did not make the grade.

I was really nervous. One by one, people were called out. Steve went out and came back saying he not only had passed, but came in number one in the class. Now the pressure was really on, the best I could be was number two. Three other students were called and then it was my turn, the moment of truth.

I walked out to the hallway and over to the instructor. He looked up at me and said, "Fran, sorry, but you didn't pass this time."

I was devastated. All that hard work and *nada*. I held back tears.

"How come?"

"You went too slow on two of the tests. You didn't get the bike up to twenty miles per hour."

Me, the adrenaline junkie, bungee-cord-jumping mama ... couldn't get the bike up to twenty. What was I thinking?

Adrenaline Adventures

I was too embarrassed to go back into the classroom. So I walked out to the car. Steve figured out what had happened and met me in the parking lot. I was crying.

"Capo. What's the matter with you? Why are you crying?"

"I HATE failing at anything. I tried my hardest. I made it through all those stupid exercises and got hundreds on both tests. But I didn't make it when the real road test came, and you did. I'm embarrassed, angry, and hurt."

"Fran, I've been riding a bike for years. You did great, I saw you. You just needed to go a little faster, that's all. I know you can do it."

"Forget it. What am I going to tell Heidi? This is so humiliating."

"Capo, are you going to give up?"

"Yes!"

"That's not the Capo I know."

"Can you just let me cry and be miserable for a few minutes, and then I can talk myself into feeling better and retaking it? I just need time to feel bad."

"Women!" He walked away and left me alone for twenty minutes.

When I composed myself, we went back inside and registered for a retest and a one-hour private practice session for the following Wednesday.

That whole week I studied the manual again. I kept all the details in my mind. I didn't tell Heidi that I had failed.

My son, Spencer, came with me to watch my retest. It was another hot day.

This time the instructor was a real laid back guy. He went through a one-hour private practice session with me. The whole time we practiced the exercises that were going to be on the test. I was doing fine. A couple of times, the bike stalled and I got frustrated with myself. He told me to calm down and that I could always take another lesson. But I didn't want to. I wanted to conquer this thing now.

Spencer saw my determination and later commented that there was no way he was getting in my way. He took pictures of me on the bike like I'd asked him too.

Fran Capo

At the end of the lesson, the instructor came over to me and said, "Congratulations, you passed."

"What?"

"That was the test."

"No, really?"

"Yes, if you like we can do it again."

"No, no. Wow, this is awesome." I ran and told Spencer.

He smiled. "I knew you would. Actually, I was praying you would because I knew how upset you'd be until you did pass it. You get very focused, Mom."

I thanked the instructor and left feeling like I was on cloud nine. I called Heidi and told her the good news. She said she was proud of my determination.

Two weeks later, Steve asked me to come up to his house. I went and there sitting in his driveway was a brand new Harley. It was gorgeous. We went for a nice, long ride, zooming down the rode with the wind in our faces … it felt like freedom and it was totally legal. It brought back all the memories of those nice, long bike rides with my dad long ago.

We rode around, and I felt that I had finally conquered something that for a long time I had set out to do. I was so proud. As we drove, I realized that sometimes dreams don't come true right away, but they always come true in the end if you don't give up.

Steve's bike was too big for me to handle—it was the type with the couch on the back, but at least I knew that I now knew how to ride and soon my license would arrive in the mail.

On November 21 of that same year (2002), Steve called me and told me his bike was having problems and was in the shop. He wanted to know if I could come and drive him to the Harley shop so he could pick it up. I said, "Sure, no problem."

I got to his house, and then we drove to the shop.

Before we were about to get out of the car and go in the shop, Steve turned to me and said, "Oh, by the way, my bike's not here. Can you hold onto this?" He handed me a key chain.

"What's this?"

"I know you said you always like to design your own ring, and you don't like my taste in jewelry, so I thought that maybe you would wear this key chain instead." He put the key chain on my finger. "Fran, I bought you a Harley, oh, and by the way … would you marry me?"

I was speechless on both accounts. I joked with Steve, "So if I say no, do I still keep the bike?"

He smirked. I hugged him and said, "Yes. I would be happy to marry you."

We kissed and then he said, "Okay, come on, they're waiting."

We walked inside Reggie Pink's. Waiting for me was a gorgeous blue and gold Sportster with all the trimmings. I hugged Steve.

"You said you wanted a different kind of proposal, one that you could always remember. Do you think this qualifies?"

"It sure does, and from now on if anyone says, 'So where's your ring?' I can happily say I'm finally riding it."

Fran Capo

Chapter 43
Adventure at a Glance - Dare to Do it   Mild to Wild Scale: 4
Title: Learning to Ride a Motorcycle
Children allowed: No
Age requirement: Sixteen and up
Length of trip: Two intense days – twenty hours
Where to try this adventure: Any Motorcycle Safety Foundation course. To find the one nearest you, call 800-446-9227 or go to their Web site at http://www.msf-usa.org/
In New York: MANYS – 212-579-5543
Main office:809 Metropolitan Avenue
Brooklyn, NY 11211 or Tel: 718-599-1079
Best time of year: Summer, fall, and spring

Approximate cost: $375
Reservations necessary: Yes
Fitness requirements: Must be in good health, have a valid driver's license and a learner's permit, and be able to ride a bicycle.
Personal gear required: Helmet, gloves, long pants, long-sleeved shirt, goggles, ankle-high boots.
What NOT to bring: Tight clothes.
Photo opportunities: Yes

Notes: Do not be late to class, you will get thrown out.
   Although you can go straight for your road test, this is a fantastic course to teach you how to safely operate a motorcycle. It covers everything you need to know to be as safe as possible.

Cool trivia: If you think riding a motorcycle is dangerous, try riding it blindfolded. Billy "The Whizz" Baxter from Britain lost his sight after an eye infection he picked up while serving as a staff sergeant with the army in Bosnia in 1997. With the help of the Royal Artillery Motorcycle Display Team, he developed a way to ski while blind using a three-way radio system. He set a record on August 2, 2003 on his Kawasaki Ninja bike by reaching a speed of 164.87 miles per hour. The record is opened to both the blind and blindfolded.

"You gain strength, courage and confidence by every experience in which you really stop to look fear in the face. You are able to say to yourself, 'I lived through this horror. I can take the next thing that comes along.' You must do the thing you think you cannot do."
—Eleanor Roosevelt

Chapter 44
"Who You Calling a Blimp?"
Blimp Ride

One of the reasons I love e-mail is because you never know what surprises it may hold or who you might meet. It was one surprising e-mail that lead to my next adventure.

A polite man by the name of Alan Gross had read about me in the local paper and wanted to purchase my book, *It Happened in New York*. One thing led to another and through a couple of emails, I found out he was an airship enthusiast, or for us lay people, he loved blimps. Actually that's putting it mildly since the man practically has a museum of airships (not actual size, of course) in his apartment and has been riding in them since he was thirteen.

I told him I was working on a book called *It Happened in New Jersey* and that I was doing a chapter on the Hindenburg. Being that he was an airship historian, I wondered if he had any information that wasn't common knowledge. Turns out, Alan had worked in the very hanger, Hangar One on the Lakehurst base in New Jersey, where the Hindenburg had been stationed. (It's now a registered historic landmark.) While on night duty as a crew member at the hangar, he used to hear muffled voices but never saw anything unusual until one night when a friend brought a Ouija board into the hangar. As Alan put it, "Bright red eyes without a body are not usual, right?" Turns out he had seen what many others before him had seen, a ghost s from the Hindenburg era. The hangar was known by many to be haunted. The information he gave me was a wonderful addition to my chapter.

Over the next few months, Alan came to my book signings and we became friends. Then one day, as I was doing some errands, I spotted a blimp in the air (not that I had to strain to see it). Since you don't see them often, it's hard not to stop, look, and imagine what it would be like to be inside of one of these behemoths. Then the idea hit me. Why not go inside one? That's something I've never tried. There has to be a place that gives blimp rides.

I asked Alan if he knew of a place, and that's when he told me he was working on a project to get the Old Flushing Airport in Queens designated as a blimp port, to be able to give rides to the public from there. What a great idea! He wanted everyone to share in the joy he had when he took his first ride. But, unfortunately, he was running into the usual political red tape.

But I was determined. I wanted to ride in a blimp and then write about it for this book. That way, even if people couldn't ride in one, at least I could give them a no-holds-barred first-hand account of what it was like. I asked Alan if there was any chance he could arrange a ride. He said he'd look into it.

True to his word, I received an e-mail from Alan a couple of weeks later. His letter was filled with exclamation points! The Saturn blimp was coming to New York for a few days to shoot the MTV Music Awards. He was ninety-nine percent certain he could arrange for me and two of my friends to go for a ride. The Saturn Lightship was the perfect ship for the job. I drove a Saturn at the time. How fitting that my own car's blimp should save the day. I treated my SL2 to a car wash since it was going to meet its big brother in a few days.

After some quick rearranging of schedules, I had the troops together for that tentative Sunday, August 25, blimp ride date.

Fran Capo

There is a lot more preparation to riding in a blimp than one would think. First I received an invitation through e-mail from Diana Meyer, a Saturn Lightship representative. This combination congratulations and formal invitation invited us to enjoy a flight aboard the Lightship, which was based at Solberg Airport in New Jersey for its stay in the tri-state area. The invitation had a list of rules for the ride:

- Please be punctual, the Saturn Lightship cannot delay take off for late arrivals. Punctuality is crucial. (In other words, buy a watch that works, pal, and no excuses!)
- Please DO NOT approach the Lightship without an escort. Doing so can result in a $50,000 fine and possible imprisonment. (Man, at that price, I'll bring an escort just to make sure.)
- Please wear comfortable clothing and shoes; you may be expected to walk through grass or sand to get to the airship and you will climb up a few steps to board. (As long as I don't have to swim in shark-infested waters, I'm okay.)
  - The temperature outside the Gondola (the area where the passengers are) is equal to the outside temperature. (Good to know.)
  - Be prepared, there are NO bathrooms on board or in the airfield area. Flights last about an hour. (So either wear your Depends or don't drink beforehand.)
  - Weather may cancel the flight.
  - Please bring photo ID with you to present to crew prior to boarding. (Does my YMCA card count?)
  - You can bring a camera or video camera. (We'll bring both.)
  - This is a flight of a lifetime … ENJOY!

I was excited. To put it in perspective, there are more astronauts than blimp pilots in the world. And there are only ten blimps flying in the U.S. (only twenty-five worldwide). The Saturn Lightship is the newest blimp in North America, and I was not only getting to ride in it, but I was also allowed to bring those near and dear to me. It was an honor.

After I received the invitation, I spoke to Diana via phone. We had to go over a few logistics, and I had to give her the names of

Adrenaline Adventures

my guests. She told me I could bring two, possibly three, guests depending on whether or not a reporter was coming to shoot the Yankee game from the blimp. Nothing against the Yankees but I was hoping the guy would be a no-show so I could bring my three people.

I tried to convince my mother, the woman who walked on hot coals with me and told me nothing is impossible, to go. There was only one minor detail—my mom is scared of heights. I told her, "Ma, what better way to get over the fear than in a nice, fluffy looking blimp. This is a chance of a lifetime! Not everyone can go on a blimp, and I don't know if we'll get a chance to do it ever again."

She wasn't convinced, unfortunately fear is a powerful elixir. She reasoned, "I'd be afraid I'd fall out of one of those windows and land on some poor, innocent person below, and besides the whole Hindenburg thing makes me not want to go."

"The Hindenburg! Ma, that was years ago. This Lightship is totally different than the Hindenburg. They don't make them like that anymore. The Hindenburg was a rigid dirigible that had a metal framework that supported its solid shape and it was filled with hydrogen, a highly explosive gas. The Saturn Lightship is a non-rigid dirigible filled with helium, a NON-combustible gas. It's totally safe. And even in the worse case scenario, if the engine goes out, we could still float down to the earth safely."

(She wasn't thrilled about the engine going out part ... not a good selling point, I realized later.) She was still unconvinced.

So when the final arrangements were made and Diana asked for my guest list, I told her my boyfriend, Steve, and my son, Spencer, were going. I mentioned that Alan was coming along to video tape us going up. Diana asked a few more questions, and then came the show-stopper.

"By the way, Fran, how much does your boyfriend weigh?"

I laughed. "Why? Do you want to make sure he isn't a blimp himself?"

She laughed. "We just have to know weight for distribution inside the craft, and we can't have over a certain weight."

Fran Capo

Boy, can you imagine not being able to go on a blimp because you are one?! Talk about needing a diet. I mean, if you stand next to the airship and they can't tell who is who, you are in serious trouble.

I assured her that Steve wouldn't cause the ship to sail sideways. Diana gave us the scoop on our blimp pilot. "A guy named Carl Harbuck, 'Squirrel' for short, will be your chief pilot. He's from Alabama." She laughed. "I wish I could be there to hear the two of you talk."

Yeah, that's a combination sure to make the balloon hyperventilate, the world's fastest talker and a New Yorker and a blimp pilot from Alabama. This trip was going to be very interesting.

The morning of the flight I convinced my mom to at least come with us to the airport. She agreed. We got up at seven, picked up Alan by 7:30, and were then on our way to New Jersey for our eleven o'clock launch.

On the way, Alan amused us with tales from his previous blimp flights. He told us how on one flight the entire blimp crew took helium before the guests came on board. When they greeted the guests like the munchkins from *The Wizard of Oz*, everyone laughed. You could see the sparkle in Alan's eyes when he spoke of the blimps. His excitement started when he was a kid, the first time he helped grab the ropes of the Goodyear Blimp to help it land.

On the final leg of the journey, we drove along a one-land highway to get to Solberg Airport. As we pulled into the parking lot, we saw it, all 165 feet of the red and white Saturn blimp with a big ION logo on it. It was surrounded by orange cones, and there were several small Cessna planes off in the distance.

Since we arrived before our escort, we decided to get a quick breakfast, make one last pit stop (because from here on, in it would be bladder control central), and bring some donuts back for the ground crew. Nothing like bribing the crew to ensure a smooth takeoff and landing.

When we arrived back at the airport, our escort, Jeff Capek, was there. Jeff was a pilot himself but wasn't doing the flying today. He made us fill out release forms and show ID.

After several minutes of chatting, he casually remarked, "By the way, we have room for two more."

Adrenaline Adventures

Yes! The Yankee cameraman stayed home … hooray!!!

Jeff turned to Alan and my mom. Alan's face lit up like a kid's at Christmas. My mom looked at all of us, grinned, nodded her head, and said "Ohhh … really?" She turned to me as if I'd plotted this. Then she looked back at Jeff and said, "Sure, why not?" I was so proud of her.

After the preliminaries were done, we got into a van and were driven out to the airfield where the blimp and crew were waiting.

We drove on the grass, and then we got out and walked toward the blimp. When we were still about two hundred feet away, Jeff said, "Okay folks, let me give you a little background and some safety rules and then you're good to go." He started, "Saturn is the only North American auto manufacturer to use a blimp. The Lightship weighs 6,335 pounds and is an A-150 blimp. The Lightship follows a year-round touring schedule providing aerial camera platforms for major sporting events nationwide, like the Yankees games, etc. It was launched in 2001, is 165 feet long, fifty-five feet tall, and forty-six feet wide. It's filled with 150,000 cubic feet of helium and has a special internal illumination system so it glows at night."

We all nodded at one another … pretty cool.

Jeff continued, "The average cruising speed is forty miles per hour with a maximum speed of sixty-two miles per hour, and it climbs about 1,400 feet per minute. On an average day, the ship will travel 350 miles."

(That's about how far I drive for some of my gigs! Imagine pulling up to a comedy club in a blimp. It'd be hell to find a parking spot.)

Spencer asked, "How many gallons of fuel does this thing hold? You know, just in case we need to turn around or the engine goes out or something."

I looked at Spencer. He shrugged his shoulders and said, "Grandma told me to ask."

Jeff laughed. "It holds 148 gallons. You guys could go about 531 miles before you'd be in trouble."

I heard Ma say, "Good, let's go about two hundred miles only to be on the safe side."

Spencer and I looked at her, then she laughed at herself for saying it.

I noticed that the airship was attached to a big pole by just the tip of its nose. I commented, "That pole is holding the blimp in place?"

"Well, that mooring mast keeps it steady, but the airship is still free to move back and forth with the wind, so keep your eye on it when walking up to the steps. If you just stay with me, I'll tell you when it's safe to get on."

I looked at the blimp. It was swaying in the wind. Getting on was going to be like waiting your turn to enter a game of Double Dutch. The timing had to be just right.

Jeff gave us a few more details. "When you get on board, find a seatbelt. You'll need to be sitting for takeoff and landing. There will also be a headset hanging up over the window. You need to put that on over your ears. There's also a boom microphone, put it really close to your mouth since it's voice activated; this way you can talk to the Captain. When you come back we're not sure yet if we'll have you come back to the mast or not."

"What is the alternative, to jump?" I asked.

"No. Don't worry, I'll warn you when to get off, and you'll be able to use the steps."

Good thing, since parachuting was my last air adventure and I hadn't packed a chute.

"By the way," I said, "I read that some blimps have water ballasts to weigh them down, and that when they take off they dump the water, sometimes on the innocent on-lookers below. Any chance we can do that today?"

He laughed. "Well, we have ballasts, but we won't be using them today."

"Oh well, there goes a good photo op." I know Spencer and Steve would have found it amusing.

Alan asked if we could take a picture lifting up the blimp. Jeff didn't think that was possible today. At this point Jeff must have thought we were a bunch of delinquents.

Just as he was forming opinions about our motley bunch, the head honcho, the chief pilot, Carl, our Alabama contingency walked up. He introduced himself, made some cute gestures at the video camera that Spencer was using, and said, "Ready to roll, folks?"

We all nodded.

Carl went on board. There were wires holding the blimp. Two crewmembers turned on the two 180-horsepower engines that were located on each side of the gondola. (The gondola is the cabin that is suspended from the airship for crew and passengers.) After the twin five-foot props were turned on, the crew physically rolled the blimp back. The wind made the gondola lift slightly off the ground, but the crew still held on.

Then another crewmember climbed up the mast. He had on a safety belt. He put on his gloves and then, once we were all on board, he would release the nose pin.

We got the all-clear signal from Jeff and walked over to the blimp. One by one we climbed up a three-step metal pull down staircase that was swaying in the wind. I felt like I was getting on the staircase in a fun house, trying to time my foot with the stair. It made me laugh. As we are climbing on, crewmembers were literally hanging on to the blimp underneath to keep it down.

The staircase led into the eight-seat gondola. I always had imagined that I would be sitting inside the balloon itself, not below it, for some reason.

We had to distribute our weight on both sides. There were two seats up front for pilot and sidekick and three individual seats lined up on the right side and a bench that sat two in the back and one seat on the left. Carl, Ma, and Alan were on the left. Spencer, Steve, and I were on the right.

There was a crew of sixteen people, including the crew chief and gondola crew. We sat back and watched them prepare for takeoff. Like a well-oiled machine, immediately they each took their place.

The mast guy unpinned the ball-and-hitch mechanism that attached the nose cone to the blimp. On each side, three crewmembers held down the blimp with rope. One guy was pulling the gondola and was awfully close to that propeller.

Two guys up front were giving signaling directions to Carl. Then one guy in the back was taking out weighted bags to give us lift power. The sound inside the gondola got a little louder. Then, leaving ropes dangling, the crew let go and we were up and on our way.

A blimp sounds like a small airplane but doesn't fly like one, it kind of lumbers around, moving side to side. The control panel is up front like on a small craft, but the steering device is totally different. Carl was sitting in what looked like a wheel chair. The steering wheel is really an "elevator wheel" that makes the blimp go up and down and is on the pilot's right side. It is operated like you would the wheels of a wheel chair. The left and right direction of the blimp are controlled by rudder pedals that are located on the floor in front of the pilot.

Carl told us that the aircraft is off course ninety-eight percent of the time and that the pilot is constantly making minor adjustments to get to the destination.

I noticed a window in the ceiling of the gondola where you could look up and see the actual balloon part. Carl explained in his Alabama accent, "The airship's outer shell consists of three fabrics laminated into one. The same company that makes spacesuits for NASA fabricates that material. So we're using Space Age material for something a little bit more down to earth. This thing here is like the world's biggest windsock."

"So then this thing is pretty tough, blowing in the wind like that?" I said.

"Well, actually it's like a big baby. The ship is never left unattended because the wind and sun can play havoc on the blimp. So it's always gotta be minded like a baby. And then there's also a matter of security."

I laughed. "Security? Well, its not like someone's going to sneak away with this thing under their jacket."

He looked at me and realized I was kidding. "Hey, it's part of my sarcastic New York makeup," I said.

Spencer asked, "How often do you fly this blimp?"

"A couple of times a week because it has to go in for a maintenance check every week. "

My Mom piped in, "That's good. Better safe than sorry."

After Carl played the answer guy to our questions, Carl and I talked about different adventures we've done and about his family and how he has two kids, Jessica and Clint. In between his cool stories and my fast-talking, we covered a lot of ground. The rest of the gang listened on the headsets, and Spencer was happy playing cameraman.

Adrenaline Adventures

The windows on the blimp are big, so there is no problem seeing out. There was a sign on one window that said, "Don't lean on windows" which, I think, would be a good idea anyway.

I started to get used to the humming noise and feel of the blimp. It felt more like sailing instead of flying, as if gentle waves were swaying us back and forth.

I turned around and saw that everyone was smiling, even Ma. She was looking out the window like a little kid. At times, she was so relaxed I even caught her dozing off.

Steve was watching and observing Carl's maneuvers since he is a pilot himself. He was noting the way Carl handled the craft in the wind and the thermals. Since blimps don't go that high, the gondola isn't pressurized. We stayed at a cruising altitude of one thousand feet.

Our destination was New York City, with a quick stopover by the Meadowlands. When we were approaching the Meadowlands, Carl turned off the propeller and we just floated and enjoyed the silence. (A moment of panic rushed through my mom's face, but then she realized it was under control.)

After our moment of silence, we swung around and were cruising over the Hudson River. Because of heightened security, we weren't allowed to fly directly over Manhattan, so we stayed over the river, with Manhattan on one side and New Jersey on the other. It was an awesome view.

At one point, I looked down and saw the shadow of the blimp on the water; it looked like a large shark or submarine was following us.

We headed downtown first. We passed the Empire State Building, passed the Intrepid with all the planes on its deck, passed the South Street Seaport and Chelsea Pier where the new trapeze school is, and finally headed down to Ground Zero.

We all stopped talking at that point. It was very humbling seeing it leveled out like that, a gaping, silent hole in the midst of the hustle and bustle of plenty.

A little farther on, we saw the Statue of Liberty. There was symbolism all around us, and we were getting an up-close and personal bird's eye view, a very low bird's eye view, of the city. Some touring helicopters were flying level with us.

A little after passing the tip of Manhattan, we turned around and headed back up along the Hudson to Upper Manhattan. The water of the Hudson glistened (yes, even dirty water can glisten) and looked beautiful. We were cruising along nicely, and we passed Madison Square Garden, passed Grant's Tomb, and passed Saint John the Divine (the largest cathedral in the world). Just as we were admiring more sights, we spotted it—the enemy ship, another blimp; it was the Fuji Blimp!

"Hey, get out of our sky!"

Steve told me to play nice.

I asked Carl if there was anything that blimps try to avoid besides birds and other aircraft while in the sky. He said, "Yeah, we usually don't like to go into the side of mountains, and we try to keep out of storms. Although one pilot I know liked to play it rough and fly under bridges with his blimp."

Boy, that's not something you want to misjudge. Imagine how embarrassing it would be if your blimp got stuck under a bridge! Try to explain that to your supervisors.

We floated around for another hour, and then it was time to land. The ground crew looked like a bunch of running dots.

As we got closer, they grabbed the dangling ropes and ran with the ship like it was a giant balloon on a string. One guy was giving hand signals to Carl. Carl had to get on the throttle because there were heavy winds. Finally, we landed after almost four hours of cruising around in the skies.

When it was safe, Jeff told us we could get out. One by one, we de-boarded the blimp. We all were smiling.

Carl got out and we said our goodbyes and thank you's. He told me his daughter, Jessica wanted to be a writer one day. I told him she could start by writing about her dad, who is a really cool guy from Alabama. He smiled.

I turned to look at everyone. Alan had this glow about him, having had his blimp fix. Steve was asking about the details of some of the maneuvers. Mom was really happy she'd faced her fears, and

Adrenaline Adventures

Spencer was shaking hands with the ground crew. And I was happy to have experienced another great adventure.

As we got back into the van to be driven to our car, we turned around and looked back one last time. The Saturn Lightship was again heading skyward. A feeling of satisfaction came over us all. No matter what happened from that day forward, we knew we would never look at a blimp the same way again. And I knew that my mother would never again say (at least not with a straight face) that she was scared of heights. Not bad for a day's work. Thanks Alan!

Fran Capo

Chapter 44
Adventure at a Glance - Dare to Do it   Mild to Wild Scale: 3
Title: Blimp Ride
Children allowed: Yes
Age requirement: None
Length of trip: Half day to full day
Where to try this adventure: Saturn Blimp (but only by invitation)
The Lightship Group
Tel: +1 407 363 7777
Website: www.lightships.com
Email: info@Lightships.com
Best time of year: All year round
Approximate cost: Negotiable
Reservations necessary: Yes
Fitness requirements: There is a weight limit, depending on how many people are on board.
Personal gear required: ID, invitation, camera, flat shoes
What NOT to bring: high heels, uncomfortable clothes
Photo opportunities: Yes

Notes: As of this writing, Alan Gross is still working on securing an airfield that would allow public blimp rides. For now, corporations can rent blimps for events and aerial advertising.

Cool trivia: Blimps were used during World War I by the Germans for spy missions and bombing England. Later, the Americans built military airships for use by the Allied forces. Fleets of Navy blimps protected both U.S. coasts from enemy submarine attacks during the war.

"You come to love not by finding the perfect person, but by seeing an imperfect person perfectly."
—Author Unknown

Chapter 45
"Skydiving without the Splat Factor" Simulation Skydive

I've been to Orlando, Florida, several times, and while I have nothing against Mickey or Universal Studios, I find the trip to places like that a little too "normal." So when my fiancé, Steve, suggested that we go there for winter vacation with the kids, I asked if we could spruce up the trip with some cool excursions. He was game.

I knew he and his daughter, Jamie, had never snorkeled with manatees, and while it wasn't exactly around the corner from Orlando, we plugged that in as the first leg of the adventure.

Next came the amusement parks, and airboat rides complete with baby gators. But I was still looking for something out of the ordinary for us to try. Then I remembered that on a business trip with Steve a few years ago, we had seen a brochure for simulation skydiving in a wind tunnel. I looked on the Web and found it. It was a place called Skyventure, and it was smack in the heart of Orlando. Perfect!

Since I had just done the tandem skydive earlier that year, I thought it would be cool for the rest of the gang to experience what I went through without the "splat factor" risk involved. I checked with everyone, and they thought it was a great idea.

I called and found out there was practically no age limit—okay, if you're under three you can't go. The only real limits were weight—if you are over six feet and weighed more than 250 pounds, then just like in real diving ... this might not be the best sport for you. Gravity would suck you to the ground—not good. If you are under six feet but weigh more than 230 pounds, you still might not want to try this adventure. I noticed when I told Steve about the weight limit, he reached for a pack of Twinkies ... such a wise guy.

We made reservations for the four of us. Reservations sold out fast. The place opened up at two and we had a 2:30 appointment. I found a five-dollars-off coupon in one of the tourist attraction brochures, which was pretty cool. The same company also had a Skycoaster, but Steve felt that Jamie wouldn't be up for it.

Adrenaline Adventures

We pulled up to the building, which had a huge metal box on the bottom and a cone-shaped part on top, with a bunch of metal stairs leading to the top on the outside. That crazy-looking building was where we were about to do our simulation skydive adventure.

The office was a separate building. We checked in, filled out forms, waited for our 2:30 group to be called, and then headed up the stairs.

We stopped briefly in the observation room.

There we could watch the other groups through a big glass window.

After a few minutes, we were all called into a training room for a briefing. There were twelve of us in the 2:30 group. The instructor introduced himself and gave us the low down. "Skyventure has been around since 1998. This is the original site, and we now have sites in California and Malaysia. (I didn't realize skydiving was popular in Malaysia.) Today you guys are going to get a feel for what it would be like to free-fall from 13,000 feet. Has anyone here every skydived?"

I raised my hand.

Steve smirked and said, "Showoff!"

"Hey, I didn't say I was Evil Knievel."

The instructor continued, "That's great. Then you will be able to vouch after the experience that this will feel like the real thing. Actually we have the best skydivers in the world come to train here on a regular basis, and many world champions have worked out their routines here. So you are going to train amongst the best. We're very laid back it. It's about having fun.

Now we're going to practice here the arch position. That's the position you need to be in once inside the tunnel. Like in real skydiving, it puts the center of gravity at your stomach and you are in better control. Positioning is very important."

He climbed up on a table that was centered in the middle of the classroom. He was face down. He stomach was on the table and he went into a spread eagle position with his legs bent at a forty-five-degree angle.

Then he hoped off and asked each one of us to try it. I felt a little stupid getting up in front of a group of strangers and lying on the table, but hey, ya do what ya gotta do.

As each one of us went, he corrected our positions. After we had all tried it once, he gave us a bunch of hand signals to practice. They were so that he could communicate with us inside the loud wind tunnel. He showed us signals that meant to lift our heads, spread our legs wider, and become more arched. Then he had us get on the table again. He gave us a series of sign language signals and we had to respond accordingly. Once he was satisfied, the lesson was over.

Then we went outside the training room into a lobby area. We were all given lockers to put all loose items away in. Girls had to tie their hair back, and no jewelry, cameras, change, etc. were allowed in the tunnel.

Once we were rid of any dangling articles, we were each given a helmet, flat shoes with no laces, and a jumpsuit with these wide, salami-like, rolled-up-material things attached to the outer thighs and the upper arms. I later found out that was for teams; they hold onto those things when doing those fancy formations.

Jamie, Spencer, and I had nice aquamarine suits. Steve was decked out in a bright red getup. There would be no missing him.

Once we were ready, the instructor lined us up by size and gave us numbers. Apparently the wind tunnel has a control panel and a live engineer who controls the intensity of the wind. The wind speed is lower for the lighter people and more intense for those more robust.

We were marched in line upstairs to the actual simulator. We walked through a metal door and were in the outside chamber of the simulator. There was a long wooden bench, and we were asked to sit in numbered order, with number one being closest to the entrance door of the wind tunnel.

The wind tunnel is cylindrical in shape and has fourteen sides. There are glass panels three quarters of the way around. The area without a glass panel contains the control room with a window. The instructor inside the tunnel and the control operator on the other side of the wall can see each other and communicate through the window.

The wind tunnel has two doors, an entrance and an exit. From the bench we were seated on we could watch the other students. On the other side of the wind tunnel were the spectators.

Adrenaline Adventures

A video camera captured all our movements, and, of course, a video would be for sale later for our viewing pleasure.

Each one of us would get two chances in the tunnel. Each simulated dive lasted one minute. We were worried that as soon as we leaned into the tunnel we would be sucked to the top, or worse, that as we headed for the exit door we'd be flung out. But these fears were all unfounded, as the tunnel, although powerful enough to lift us, was rather gentle on our bodies. But to demonstrate the point, the instructor went first to show us how it was done.

He stood in the entranceway door, leaned into the wind tunnel, and then was immediately airborne. He was in the arch position and was flying up and down inside the tunnel. It looked like fun. Then he deiced to do a few acrobatic flips and spins. Then, with ease, he aimed toward the exit door like superman and stepped out. We all applauded. We were ready to go. I wanted to try a flip.

The first student was up. It was this tall, lanky man who was rather uncoordinated. He jumped in, and his arms and legs flailed all over the place. The instructor was hand signaling him left and right, and the guy was just spacing out and not responding. He quickly exited out the door.

Jamie was up third. She went in, arched her back way up, and hovered around ten feet off the ground. The instructor grabbed her, spun her around gently, and then exited her out the door. Nice job.

Spencer was now the flyer on deck. He arched, not quite as much as Jamie, and shot up about twenty feet headed toward the ceiling. I don't think he expected he'd rise so high. The look of shock on his face was priceless.

I was up next. Being the pro of the group, I thought it would be a cinch—NOT! I kind of wobbled a bit before I was airborne. I swear it was much easier in real life! It was cool, though, to feel the sensation of weightlessness again. And, in fact, that alone is worth the price of admission.

Steve was up last in his bright red jumpsuit. He hovered near the ground. Then the instructor gave him a signal and Steve put his hands in a superman position, which was fitting since he was in red. He rose three feet, not a world record but a good first try.

Fran Capo

We all had a second go of it, and we did better the second time around. Jamie went flying high the second time, and her mouth went wide open. Spencer purposely aimed for the ceiling.

I tried to do the spins I did in the air during the tandem jump. Steve wanted to give his second chance over to his daughter, but then he thought we all might think he copped out or it was unfair.

The hour flew by, no pun intended. We were led out of the room, and then we de-geared, took our possessions out of our lockers, and were given a certificate for our achievement. The instructor came up to me. "Well, what did you think?"

"I have to admit, it was the same sensation as the real thing except you didn't have to jump, didn't need experience, and didn't have to worry about parachutes and possibly stopping on impact. All the fun, none of the hassle."

"That's what I like to hear!"

I asked Jamie and Spencer what they thought. They said it was the coolest thing they had ever tried. Jamie high-fived me, and Spencer hugged me. Then we all thanked Steve for the treat.

Jamie, like Steve, was satisfied with the simulation skydive and felt no need to ever do the real thing. Spencer, however, got the bug and decided that when he turned eighteen, he would jump. I was right there along with him, because now more than ever, I wanted to jump again. I guess it's all in the genes. Kids see the enthusiasm from their parents about certain things and get subliminal signals about life. Or maybe, it can be just as simple as the old cliché the apple doesn't fall far from the tree.

Adrenaline Adventures

Chapter 45
Adventure at a Glance - Dare to Do it   Mild to Wild Scale: 2
Title: Simulation Skydive
Children allowed: Yes
Age requirement: Three and up
Length of trip: One hour, 2 simulated dives of 1 minute each
Where to try this adventure: My SkyVenture (original location) 6805 Visitors Circle, Orlando, Florida 32819
Tel: 407-903-1150
Web site: www.skyventure.com or E-mail: info@skyventure.com
They have also have locations in Paris, California, and Malaysia.
Best time of year: Open all year around – from 2:00 P.M. to midnight, 365 days a year.
Approximate cost: $38.50 plus tax per person for adults, $33.50 for children 12 and under
Reservations necessary: Yes,
Fitness requirements: Weight limit of 250 pounds if you are over six feet, 230 pounds if you are under six feet
Personal gear required: None
What NOT to bring: Tight clothes
Photo opportunities: Yes

Notes: This adventure is a great way to feel what it's like to skydive without the stress factor.

Cool trivia: The inventor of SkyVenture and Skycoaster is Bill Kitchen. He, along with Alan Metni, a former U.S. World Champion skydiver, own the investments. They also have a tunnel camp (check out www.tunnelcamp.com) where they train champions for competition.
   The oldest person who has tried this simulation was a fellow Guinness holder, Banana George Blair, at age eighty-nine.

"Nobody other than you can make you a quitter. There may be people who will try and discourage you, but only you can decide to listen and allow them to succeed by giving up."
—Fran Capo

Chapter 46
"That's Just Bull!"
Riding a Mechanical Bull

Ever since the movie *Urban Cowboy* with John Travolta came out in the eighties, I've had the urge to ride a mechanical bull. Unfortunately, the only places that seemed to have them at the time were bars, so I opted to wait until a better place to try it came along.

I almost forgot about wanting to try it until Kenny, a fifteen-year-old, red-headed kid from our neighborhood told me one day that he rides a bull down at the local stable. This was when we first moved in, and I didn't even know they had a stable down my block – after all, we live in Howard Beach, not in the country.

Turns out there is a stable right off the highway, and they have fundraising rodeos during the summer. Kenny was one of the kids that rode the bull to raise money. I gave him credit. He said he got thrown off plenty of times, and, luckily, had never broken anything ... kids are agile.

The adventure was fresh in my mind again. So, naturally, while my fiancé, Steve; his daughter, Jamie; and my son, Spencer, were happy from trying out the simulation skydive, I was still looking around for other adventures.

Then one night in Orlando while we were at this crazy upside-down interactive museum called The Wonderworks I saw across the street a cowboy with none other than a mechanical bull.

Steve saw the look in my eyes and said, "Go ahead, find out how much it is."

I went up to the cowboy, and he said, "Young lady, it's only five dollars a ride."

"For how long?"

"Two minutes." He smiled.

"Is it safe?"

"Yup, never had an accident. You tell me how fast or slow you want to go."

I walked around the enclosed area, which looked like a well-padded boxing ring. The bull was in the middle, and if you got tossed off, you would fall onto the cushioned mats. Steve, meanwhile, was checking out the construction of the ring.

"Can kids go on?" I asked.

"Yup, if their parents are willing to sign a waiver."

Man, is there anything that I do in life that doesn't require a waiver? I was game. I asked the gang who wanted to go.

Spencer's hand shot up, and Jamie said she wanted to try it.

Steve shrugged and said, "I'll hold the bags."

There were several people ahead of us, so I used the time to find out some things about the bull. "How much does this thing cost?"

"This here is a hydraulic bull, and those air mattress are state of the art; it's very sophisticated, not like in the *movie Urban Cowboy*. This baby here cost me ten grand."

"Man, that's a lot of five-dollar rides."

"Yup, that's why I'm out here every night."

"You should rent to parties or corporations."

"I do. And those suits are the wildest. Cooped up in their offices all day, they want the bull set on high. I've got one guy, though, who can ride it to a count of ten, no matter how high I put it up. But I tell ya one thing. This bull is very intense, but it's also very safe. I can stop this thing fast if I have to. You can't always do that with a real bull. Plus, you gotta be careful where you ride; some places, like Indiana, are not regulated, and their rides are not subject to periodic inspections or licenses. This here is one legit, grade A bull."

"Well, that's certainly good to know. By the way, are there any rules?"

"Yup, you can only keep one hand on the bull."

"Ah ... always a catch."

Then the cowboy cranked up the music and invited the next rider into the ring. A burly guy got on the bull, and the cowboy asked him, "Do you want it higher?"

The man yelled, "Hell yeah!"

So the cowboy cranked it up a notch. The man held on tighter. "Faster!"

The cowboy cranked it up faster. We could see the man was about to fall off. Stubbornly, he yelled, "Fast—" and then he fell off.

His girlfriend was laughing at him.

Jamie wanted to go first out of our bunch. She got on the bull, held her hand up, and the cowboy went nice and easy on her. He made it sound like a contest. "Come on, Jamie girl ... you can do it ... only one more minute..." He cranked it a bit faster, and she held on. She stayed on the whole time. She came off smiling, and Steve hugged her.

Spencer was up next. He got on and had this real laid back movement to him. Almost like he was dancing with the bull. The cowboy asked him if he wanted it faster, and Spencer just said, "Yup." So faster it moved, and again Spencer looked like he was just riding a wave. He had one hand in the air like a pro. The cowboy upped it a notch, and I saw Spencer's thigh muscles tighten on the bull. They gave a countdown, the bull spun around trying to buck him off, and he stayed on the entire time. Two down, one to go.

I was the last up in the bunch. I got on the bull, and my first instinct was to grab the horn on the saddle like I do in horseback riding. But I knew that was against the rules, so I fought the instinct.

Since I was an adult, the cowboy started the bull at a higher notch. The thing was spinning around and bucking me. I had to really hold on tight with my leg muscles. I could feel myself slipping. There was no way I was going to fall and embarrass myself. I dug in tighter.

Adrenaline Adventures

I managed to get myself back upright. And then came the dreaded question. "You want it faster, cowgirl?"

"Sure, why not go full tilt?"

So he upped the notch. I had ten seconds left. I was slipping, but I was holding on. Ten … nine … Eight …I saw the ground getting closer. Seven … six … five … I dug my legs into the sides. Four … three … two … one! I fell. But it was right after he said "one", so I felt okay. Man, talk about making it in the knick of time.

The cowboy applauded my efforts. The gang was laughing. Steve just looked at me and shook his head.

"Are you happy now, Capo?"

"Yes, very. Thank you."

"One question. Are you ever going to grow up?"

I looked him squarely in the eyes and said, "I sure hope not."

Fran Capo

Chapter 46
Adventure at a Glance - Dare to Do it   Mild to Wild Scale: 2
Title: Riding a Mechanical Bull
Children allowed: Yes, with parental consent
Age requirement: Seven and up
Length of trip: Thirty seconds to two minutes
Where to try this adventure: Across the street from The Wonderworks in Orlando, Florida, 9067 International Drive Pointe

Rockin' B Bucking Machines, Box 220, Cheyenne, Oklahoma 73628 (580) 497-2727 or Web site: www.buckingmachine.com (Rents mechanical bulls to television companies, movie shoots, fundraisers, fairs, parties, and for teaching. The company comes highly recommended by many champions in the bull riding field.)
Best time of year: All year round providing there's no rain.
Approximate cost: $5 for two minutes
Reservations necessary: No
Fitness requirements: Can't have back, neck, or heart problems, or be pregnant.
Personal gear required: None
What NOT to bring: Loose items
Photo opportunities: Yes

Notes: You can rent mechanical bulls for parties. Type "mechanical bull" into any Internet search engine and a bunch of places will come up. Also watch for them at local festivals and fairs.

Cool Trivia: For the filming of the movie *Urban Cowboy* (1980), the movie that started the mechanical bull riding craze, John Travolta had a mechanical bull installed in his home two months before production began. He became so good that he was allowed to dismiss the stunt double and do the takes himself.

"Life is a mirror. What you see lacking outside must first be lacking inside."
—Wally Amos

Chapter 47
"Sleeping with the Fish"
Sleeping at an Aquarium

As I was searching the 'Net for a weekend adventure, I came across something that caught my eye, "Sleep with the fish." At least that's what I thought it said. I started to have visions of a *Sopranos* episode where some poor guy gets whacked and winds up with cement shoes on the ocean floor.

Upon closer examination, I saw that the New York Aquarium was having one of its tri-yearly public sleepovers; this one was the "Bedtime with the Belugas Sleepover." It's one thing to sleep next to your goldfish, quite another to sleep next to a pod of beluga whales.

Intrigued, I called and booked a space for myself and my son, Spencer. I was told to bring a sleeping bag and a change of clothes.

We pulled up to the aquarium entrance at six P.M., an hour before the fun was to begin. The security guard had our names on the list.

Adrenaline Adventures

We signed and were instructed to turn left, go to the gate, and ring the bell. As we turned, we saw the Cyclone, the famous wooden roller coaster of Coney Island fame, peering over the fence on the right from a few blocks away.

The parking lot was dark and empty. It was weird seeing the aquarium with no one around. An air of excitement filled us. We drove alongside the main fence, parked the car, and walked to the gate. A sign read, "Authorized personnel only." I spotted a bell, so I rang it. I felt like I was in *The Wizard of Oz* and some munchkin was going to pop his head out. "Who rang that bell?"

Two guys walked up to the gate and escorted us in. There is something terribly fun about going where you are not supposed to go and not getting into trouble. It's like belonging to a secret society.

We were the first to arrive. Susan, the main instructor and volunteer coordinator, greeted us cheerfully. She quickly introduced the crew. "This is Becky, Crystal, John, Chris, Mike, and Matt. They are the docents."

I tried to pretend I knew the word, so I casually repeated it. "Ah, the docents." Where's the German dictionary when you need it? Turns out it's just a fancy word for volunteers.

Crystal and Becky led us through two metal doors and into a cement hallway and told us to dump our sleeping bags and belongings there. Since no one else was there, we felt a little weird. They assured us others would be coming. Then they led us into a room *formally known as* the Discovery Room (sounds like Prince); since the name was sold to some other operation, we just called it the DC Room. We were told we were allowed to wander around until the rest of the sleepover participants arrived.

It was so neat being the only two people in the room. It was like having the ski
slopes all to yourself; you don't know whether to zoom downhill at full speed or go zigzagging across the mountain.

Spencer zoomed off to parts unknown. I zagged on over to a tank that housed a miniature crocodile who was floating eye level in the water. Turns out it was a dwarf caiman. Still, it looked like a crocodile to me.

Then an African clawed frog caught my eye. He looked exactly like the test tube mail order frog, Stinky, that Spencer had for a pet. Stinky used to put his stick food in his mouth and hold it like a cigar. Stinky was the only frog I knew that could do a Groucho Marx impression.

We wandered around in the peaceful environment. I spotted my two favorite fish, the puffer fish with their big eyes and innocent round faces, and the bright orange and white clown fish. Clown fish ain't all jokes. They're one of the few fish that know they can't protect themselves, so they buddy up with the sea anemones, which are poison to other fish. It's like having a bodyguard with a dart gun.

In a nearby tank, a bizarre-looking fish called the leafy sea dragon floated around aimlessly. He looked like a seahorse wearing a bad Halloween costume.

As we walked around, the room started to fill with other parents and their offspring. At seven, we were all asked to go into the classroom for orientation. There were a total of twenty-nine people, fifteen of them kids.

Susan sat down with her back against a case filled with model animal jaws, sample flippers, and shells. The kids sat around her in a semi-circle on the rug, while the less flexible parents opted for the wooden chairs. She laid out the rules. "We will be sleeping in the DC room. Keep your shoes on in the hallway. You have to have fun, and you must learn at least one thing."

One of the kids wanted to know if he could run around like a maniac, and to my surprise, she said, "At some points ... yes."

She also pointed out that there were two security guards there all night. Now I felt better. No one could take the belugas, or my purse!

She also mentioned there was an around-the-clock, on-the-job maintainer—the aquarium's personal plumber whose job it was to check the pipes, the exhibits, and make sure the fish weren't doing the dead man's float.

Now that the rules were laid out, it was time to venture into the cold night air and into another of the aquarium buildings to boldly go where few spectators have gone before.

Adrenaline Adventures

After radioing security, Susan cleared the way for us to enter one of the buildings. The alarm went off anyway. The kids thought it was great. I pictured us trying to explain to the cops. "Honest, officer, I'm here to sleep with the fish. No, I don't owe anyone money."

The alarm was quickly shut off, and we went over to see some sea otters. These sixty- to eighty-pound sea otters were brought from the wild and were being rehabilitated to be put back in the wild. Unfortunately, three of the otters at the aquarium had flunked otter school so they remained permanently spoiled at the aquarium, with no desire to leave. And why would they want to leave? Even an animal sees a good deal, free room, board and medical, and a no clam charge. Considering otters eat one-third their body weight in the wild, that's a hefty fee. And if they are really moody, they even get their own private sleeping quarters. I know some humans who would go for that deal.

Next we headed over to the 94,000-gallon tank that housed the walruses. Walruses' lips are like Hoovers. They can suck the meat out of claims without opening them up. Thus their other name, "sea pigs."

Susan had all the kids face her with their backs toward the walrus tank. Then the strangest thing happened—Ivack, the only male walrus in that tank, had an ego attack. The more we ignored him, the more he tried to get our attention.

With the grace of a sumo wrestler, he tossed the females away from the center stage window and pressed his fat nose against the glass hoping to get some reaction. When that didn't work, Ivack started banging and barking up a storm. I was surprised he didn't have a New York attitude and give us the flipper. I guess he knew they were kids present.

Finally, the kids turned around and faced the glass. Ivack started rubbing his head against the glass trying to feel the kids' hands through osmosis.

Satisfied, he went up for a breather. Then he came back down for more attention. I swear, if you'd have handed him a remote control he could have almost passed for a male of our species.

After the walrus encounter, we passed by a tank filled with bright pink coral. Susan stopped. She explained that this was the home of the ghost fish. "We keep records on every fish in the aquarium; where we get them from, the weight of the fish, etc., a file that would make a detective proud. There's a record for every fish except one. On two occasions in the past five years, there has been a purple and pink polka-dotted fish that makes a mysterious appearance in this coral-filled tank. No one knows where he or she came from, and no one knows where he or she disappears to. All we know is that some have seen the phantom fish."

All I spotted was two clown fish playing with a miniature Ouija board.

It was time to head back to the classroom for some hot chocolate, chocolate chip cookies, and mini-pizzas. After the snack, Susan and the kids sat down for a short learning session.

Susan explained that the reason beluga whales are white is because their color acts as a camouflage in their arctic environment. She also said their flukes power up and down (instead of side to side like most fish) to propel them up to the surface, and she said that a newborn whale can measure twenty-five feet long. That's one heck of a baby!

She talked about how the aquarium acquired some exhibits from items confiscated at the airport—items that were illegally brought in, and how other things were donated to the aquarium when people realized they were illegal. Can you imagine not knowing you've got something illegal? "Oh I didn't know I couldn't have this ... doesn't fit in my submarine anyway ... here's the masthead of the *Titanic*. Who needs it anyway, it's rusted."

Susan also told how sharks get a bum rap. "More people get bit by dolphins in one year than sharks in ten years." That's probably because people swim like torpedoes in the opposite direction when they see a shark.

At 9:30,. it was craft time. We had about a half hour to make four crafts. I felt like I was in a game show. "Okay, here are your items: pillowcases, clay, sticks, and buttons. Your object is to decorate each item as nice as you can in seven minutes, then rotate to the next craft station."

I headed toward my favorite substance, clay. I made a seahorse that looked more like brass knuckles. You never know when you'll

Adrenaline Adventures

need a ceramic item to double as a weapon. Spencer made a turtle. Then we went on over to the button-making session where we painted our buttons and had them pressed.

Next, Spencer went to paint the Inuit sticks. (Inuit is the politically correct for Eskimo.) He had to draw pictures that represented a story and later retell the story for the group. I decided to head straight for the pillowcases.

Marine-shaped animal sponges could be dipped in a variety of colors and pressed onto your pillowcase. The grownups were really getting into this. I was anxious to create my Picasso pillowcase, but there was no room at the table, so I did my masterpiece on a chair. I got a bit carried away, because I saw afterward that some of my artwork had made its way onto the wooden seat. I quickly wiped up the paint.

"Time's up!" they called. Wait, I wasn't finished creating! "Pencils down." I was having flashbacks to the SAT tests.

Then they said it was time for bed. Bed? I usually stayed up until two. Did the adults have to sleep, too? We gathered our stuff from the hallway, took the sleeping bags back to the DC room, and sprawled out around the various fish tanks.

Now for the final evening entertainment—the movie, *Andre the Seal*. It was a true story about a seal who adopted a family. The other evening entertainment was creating a fire path so people could walk to the bathroom without stepping on people in the sleeping bags.

Spencer and I stayed up. Others nodded out during *Andre*. The lights were out, but Spencer and I whispered from our sleeping bags until three in the morning. It was cool seeing the fish swimming around all night. The sounds of the tanks finally lulled us to sleep.

At seven the next morning, the lights were turned on slowly as if to simulate a sunrise. After everyone did their morning routine, the sleeping bags were returned to the hallway. We had a nice continental breakfast, painted our sculptures from the night before (nothing like an early morning craft to get you going), did a group hula hoop game, and by 8:45 we were out into the cold January air, with the added bonus of freshly fallen snow.

Our first stop was at the black-footed penguins. These well-dressed guys have a habit of braying. It's their way of saying hello or expressing anger ... Jeez, you better know which is which. Since they sound like donkeys when they bray, they are also called "the jackass penguins." There's a name you want your species carrying around.

As I was copying down the jackass information, I lost sight of the group. They apparently slid through a "do not enter" door. I spent five minutes trying to relocate them. Now who felt like the jackass?

We went over to the main attraction, the reason we were here ... to see the beluga whales. We walked past pipes, an engine room, and up the back staircase leading to the tanks reserved for the privileged trainers and insiders. We had to disinfect the soles of our shoes by putting them in a green substance.

Kristin, one of the trainers, introduced us to the whales. It was a regular

estrogen festival ... only female whales. "Let's see, we have Kathy, who's thirty; Natasha, who's twenty; Marina, who's eighteen; and Maris, who's six."

Maris was darker in color than the adult belugas because, at birth, belugas migrate to warm murky waters. Maris would have blended in perfectly there. We were told that these behemoths eat three to four times a day ... a diet of herring and squid. They also don't have a dorsal fin, because it would get caught in the ice in their natural habitat. They have a dorsal ridge that breaks a layer of ice so they can breathe; after all, they are mammals.

Kristin explained that they are taught husbandry behaviors (and that's not like taking out the garbage!) so they can help the trainer take care of them. Things like opening their mouths so their teeth can be checked. They are taught behaviors, not tricks.

After the brief intro, the four trainers went to the four whales. I watched Natasha, since she was closest to me. Natasha was brought to the aquarium from Church Hill River, Canada, in 1984. She apparently had some kind of eye infection, since she was getting eye drops. Good thing they didn't have to pull out an eye chart.

By 9:20, we were headed over to the dolphins who, we were told, enjoyed mental stimulation. Since chess pieces are too small, Kristin explained they enjoy the husbandry behaviors taught to them. She had the dolphins demonstrate some of their body language such as tail bobbing or slapping, which means the dolphin is under pressure;

Adrenaline Adventures

since he's not going to head to the local bar for an after-work drink, he slaps his tail instead. Kristin explained how all the behaviors were taught via a step-by-step process with rewards given every step of the way. She also noted that their dorsal fin is like a fingerprint.

After watching a few more amusing behaviors, we headed over to another secret passageway that led to the area *above* the fish tanks—the part people don't see at the aquarium but know is there. Otherwise, how would you feed the fish?

We fed the fish. We smelt like fish. It was time to leave the fish.

We headed back to the classroom and did a wish circle where we all wished

for peace and harmony for all living creatures. Then we said goodbye to one another, packed our bags, and took our crafts home.

As we drove out of the parking lot, Spencer and I once again saw the Cyclone. We thought about all the cool animal behaviors we'd seen and the new friends we'd made. But more importantly, especially in New York, we left knowing that one can sleep with the fish and live to tell about it … but only at the aquarium.

Fran Capo

Chapter 47
Adventure at a Glance - Dare to Do it   Mild to Wild Scale: 1
Title: Sleeping at an Aquarium
Children allowed: Yes
Age requirement: Six to twelve years old
Length of trip: Two days
Where to try this adventure:
New York Aquarium
Surf Avenue & West 8th Street
Brooklyn, NY 11224.
Phone 718-265-3448 or 718-265-FISH
Email: mzampella@wcs.org
Website: www.nyaquarium.com
Best time of year: The sleepover is only offered a few times a year. Call the aquarium for more information.
Approximate cost: $130 per person for one adult, one child
Reservations necessary: Yes
Fitness requirements: None
Personal gear required: Sleeping bag, change of clothes, toothbrush, flat shoes.
What NOT to bring: Extra baggage.
Photo opportunities: Yes

Notes: The New York Aquarium has other family and educational programs, as do most aquariums around the country. The Oregon Coast Aquarium and Baltimore's National Aquarium also offer sleepovers. Check aquariums in your state for similar programs.

Cool trivia: On December 10th, 1896, the New York Aquarium opened its doors for the first time in lower Manhattan in what is now known as Battery Park, making it the oldest continually operating aquarium in the United States. After World War II, it moved to its new location in Coney Island, Brooklyn.

"Never give up on your dreams, they are the fulfillment of your heart's desire."
—Fran Capo

Chapter 48
"Becoming a Polar Bear"
Doing the Polar Bear Plunge

I've tried to analyze myself and figure out why the second I hear certain things I am drawn to them instantly. Take, for example, the Polar Bear Plunge. I was driving home from a gig. It was about one in the morning. I was trying to keep myself awake as I drove, and all of a sudden I heard this announcement, "The Tenth Annual Polar Bear Plunge is happening Sunday, February 23 (2003) in Point Pleasant Beach, New Jersey. All monies raised go to the Special Olympics of New Jersey."

The date was just nine days away. I grabbed a pen and jotted down the number as I was driving. At that moment, I knew I was going to do it.

Now, why I would have the desire to jump into the freezing ocean in the middle of the winter—let me correct that—in the middle of the worst winter we've had in more than eighty years, I do not know. But

Adrenaline Adventures

something about challenging myself and doing it for a good cause to boot just woke me right up. As I was driving, my adrenaline started pumping just at the idea of looking forward to another adventure.

I started thinking of Anne Bancroft, the first woman to transverse Antarctica on skis, and how she was exposed to cold weather for months. Then I started thinking about this woman I had seen on the Discovery Channel a few nights previous. This woman swam in the Arctic Ocean for half an hour in just a bathing suit! Scientists were trying to figure out how she was able to do it without getting hypothermia. Then I started thinking about those poor people on the *Titanic* and how the freezing water took their lives in just minutes. The more I thought about all these experiences, the more I wanted to experience something like them for myself. To get a glimpse of how they felt and push my body into one more odd situation.

I got home around 2:30 and immediately went to the Polar Bear Plunge Website to see what the requirements were.

The site gave a brief history: "The plunge began ten years ago with eighty-five plungers and has grown to be the largest in the world. In 2002, three thousand individuals participated and helped raise over $692,000 in one day."

Then I read farther down. "Special Olympics New Jersey is a nonprofit organization that provides year-round sports training and athletic competition in twenty-three Olympic-type sports for more than 13,500 children and adults with mental retardation or other closely related disabilities, completely free of charge."

That did it. Knowing what a rush I get out of being athletic, I felt I had to do my part and let these kids and adults be able to feel the same sense of achievement. I tried to download the application, but for some reason, my Mac wouldn't let me get the PDF file. I tried for a good hour. Finally I had to say, "Capo, you can do it in the morning. I'm sure the forms will still be there." I went to bed wondering who I could convince to do this adventure with me. My first two choices were my fiancé, Steve, and my son, Spencer. Of course, I decided that I would ask a few other friends, as well, to see who was game. All night long I dreamt of penguins.

The next morning I had to stop myself from calling Steve at sunrise.

I called him at nine. "Hi, sweetie."

Right away he knew something was up.

"Okay, what do you want?"

"I was just wondering if we were getting together on Sunday?"

He was suspicious. "Why? What do you have in mind, Capo?"

I laughed. It's not good when your fiancé knows you so well. I figured I'd go in for the kill. "Well, I thought maybe we could go to New Jersey and jump in the water."

He just laughed. "Yeah right." Then I told him the details. The silence on the other end was not a good sign. "Well?" I said.

After another long, dramatic pause he said, "I've already done it."

"Oh, really, when was this?"

He told me he'd done a plunge years ago in Coney Island and that it hurt like hell. He swore he would never do it again. Knowing an immovable force when I see it, I decided I needed to go around that iceberg and onto another subject. I had others to convince.

I called my friend Heidi. She said, "Not me, girlfriend, but I'll video tape it for you." Okay, so I didn't have a partner yet, but at least I had a cameraperson.

I asked a few other friends, who all happened to be busy that day. I turned my efforts to my own flesh and blood ... my dear son, Spencer, who has been with me on many previous adventures.

As soon as I picked Spencer up from school, I asked him. He just looked at me and said, "Mom. Do you know how cold it is?"

I nodded and laughed.

He continued, "Okay, I'll tell you what, when we go home let's fill up the bathtub with ice and stick our hands in it. If you think it feels okay, I'll go."

I knew if we did this, I'd lose the battle. I said, "Spencer, this is not something we want to practice at home. This needs to be the real deal. Besides, just think of how cool it would be. Okay, wrong choice of words ... just think that we can be helping kids that can't even do something like this."

"What about safety, Mom? I don't want to get hypothermia."

"You won't. All we have to do is go in at least chest deep, stay for a few seconds, and then come right out."

Adrenaline Adventures

He rolled his eyes. "You really want me to do this?" I nodded enthusiastically. He smirked. "Only you, Mom, come up with these things. Okay, I'll do it. But I'm telling you right now, I'm never doing it again."

"Okay, that's fine with me. I just want you to try it once. It will be a good mother and son bonding thing."

"Yeah, we'll be stuck together like glue."

We both smiled.

Now that I had my partner, I called the Polar Plunge Hotline and got them to fax me two applications. I filled them out and sent in the registration fees of twenty-five dollars each. Now all I had to do was raise an additional $150, so each of us would have the $100 minimum on our pledge sheets. I figured, in the worse case scenario, if I didn't raise the money, I could always pay it myself. Since there were only eight days left, I sent out a mass e-mail telling my friends about my latest venture. I mentioned that if people wanted to, they could send in five dollars and that I would front the money since there was no way to get it by Sunday.

The response was overwhelming. Almost everyone was willing to pledge some money. Some sent it right away. Steve was the first to put in some cash, and then more money slowly came in. I felt like I was doing a telethon.

The really cool thing was I found out that many of my friends already regularly donated to or were involved with Special Olympics. One friend of mine, Bill, said he was a hugger. I had no clue what that was. He explained that every year he volunteers to stand at the finish line of the Special Olympic races and hug the kids as they run over the line, to congratulate them. I didn't even know they had such a position. I thought that was fantastic.

Over the next few days it was exciting to see all the pledges waiting in my e-mail box. Of course some of my male friends commented that if they'd known it would only have taken five dollars for me to take my clothes off, they would have done it long ago.

Others wanted to see pictures, proof of my endeavor. Great, now not only did I have to jump into the freezing water, I'd have to go on a diet too. I mentioned this to Steve, who found it very amusing. "Can't let your fans down!"

Fran Capo

I told Spencer about the sponsorship money. He shook his head. "Well, I guess we really have to do it now."

Steve laughed. "Better you than me."

Meanwhile, I was counting down the days like a kid waiting for Christmas.

I was so excited. And then the news report came. "We are expecting another major snowstorm, and it's gonna be a big one with as much as twenty-four inches of snow in some regions". Unfortunately, I happened to be in one of those regions.

On the Sunday before the event was supposed to take place, we had our worst snowstorm of the season and whiteout conditions. Spencer shoveled for seven hours and wound up building a two-story igloo in front of our house.

The behemoth snowstorm made me a tad concerned. I didn't mind plunging into the freezing water but running through the snow in a bathing suit to get to it seemed a little beyond the call of duty. I started imagining how I would have to leap over snowdrifts to get to the freezing ocean.

Three days before the event, as the snow was melting, a phone call came from the plunge people saying that the plunge was postponed until March 16 because there was still too much snow.

"Too much snow on the beach? I asked.

" No, we are not worried about the snow on the beach. There is too much snow in the parking lot for the spectators and plungers to park their cars."

"Oh. You mean if the parking lots were cleared, we would have ran through the snow get to the water?"

"Yup. It's been done before. We even have plunges in Alaska where people cut holes through the ice and jump in."

" Really? Good thing there's not many icebergs here in New York to cut through. How cold do you think the water will be in March?"

"Don't worry, honey, it will still be around thirty-two degrees," she said.

"Ah, just what I wanted to hear."

I related the information to Spencer. He was a bit relieved. "At least they have some sense ... Just curious, Mom, would you have made us run through the snow?"

Adrenaline Adventures

I laughed. "Hey Spencer, I do want to live to do another adventure you know ... then again, maybe I might have."

Actually, the way I figured it, this was a good thing since it gave me more time to raise money for a good cause. In the meantime, well-meaning friends were giving me "safety" tips. One friend told me to put Vaseline on my legs to insulate them and prevent ourselves from going into shock. "You know your body is ninety-eight degrees, and the water is thirty-two degrees. Your body could go into shock from the drop in temperature. Put Vaseline on, Olympic swimmers do it."

Yeah, but they are swimming, I'm just plunging in. I felt it was cheating. Yet the thought of going into shock wasn't a pleasant one. And Steve did say it had hurt like hell when he'd done it. I discussed it with Spencer, and we decided we would put Vaseline on one leg and conduct a science experiment.

But just to make sure it wasn't cheating, I called the plunge lady back.

"Are we allowed to wear Vaseline on our bodies?" I asked.

"I've never heard of anyone doing it. You are only in for a minute. The rules are you have to be in bathing suits only. No shirts for the men, and no diving suits at all. Says nothing about Vaseline. But this is a Polar Bear Plunge."

Well, since polar bears don't wear Vaseline, I guess we had our answer; just a bathing suit and raw skin it would be.

By the time March 16 rolled around, we had raised $583. Two friends, Gary and Todd, each made a generous donations of one hundred dollars. We were now ready for plunge.

The night before, I had a gig two hundred miles away in Pennsylvania. Steve drove so I could sleep in the car and get some rest. We got home at one in the morning. I packed our gear for the next day, including bathing suits, towels, a garbage bag for wet clothes, a big towel to change behind to get out of our wet clothes (since we were told there were no changing areas), clothes to wear over the wet bathing suits, and a set of clothes to get into once we got out of our wet bathing suits, and finally a camera and videotape.

Steve decided not to come. He said he didn't want to watch me freeze. My mom came to act as the still photographer and person in charge of worrying. Heidi and her friend met us there to act as videographers.

It was about a two-hour ride to Jenkinson's Boardwalk in Point Pleasant Beach. We left at eight to give us enough time to check in at the late registration desk at ten.

The place was crowded. We lucked out; it was a gorgeous day—fifty-six degrees.

There were several large white tents set up; two for registration, one for the free lunch after the dip, and one for souvenirs to raise extra money.

Since we had raised over five hundred dollars, we got two free polar fleece shirts and a duffel bag. We were given orange armbands to identify us as plungers. Since we were each allowed to bring a guest, we got a pass for my mom for lunch.

The plunge was going to happen at noon. We walked over to the water's edge and plopped down our belongings. There was a huge roped-off area where the plungers would stand when the time came.

Slowly, people began to file in. Not everyone was dressed in your normal, run-of-the-mill bathing suit. One guy was dressed as Elvis. One lady was dressed as a horned opera singer, and another person wore a big Dr. Seuss hat. There was even a guy wearing a boat with a sail that said "Polar Bear Plunge." I asked someone why these people were dressed like this. Apparently when the plunge started years ago they had a costume contest first, but then, as the event got too large, they stopped the contest. But tradition dies hard.

Around 11:30, we hooked up with Heidi. Friends and families of plungers were jockeying for photo op positions. We kept moving our gear closer to the water.

Spencer went over to test the water and came back shaking his head. "Mom, it's cold." Then the radio DJ announced, "Good afternoon, folks, it's a great day for a plunge. The temperature is fifty-six degrees, and the water temperature is thirty-nine degrees. We will be starting the plunge in a half-hour."

I told Spencer to look at the bright side; at least it wasn't freezing.

As we looked around, we noticed divers and safety patrol boats getting closer to shore. The divers went in the water to be close at hand. The police and coast guard were there just in case someone went into shock, even though I was told it had never happened.

At about 11:50, people started getting undressed and lining up. Spencer and I just looked at each other and shrugged our shoulders. "It's now or never, kid," I said.

We undressed and put our clothes in such a way that we could easily get back into them. Heidi tested the camera. My mom was ready with hers.

Spencer and I stood at the very front of the line, next to the horned opera singer. She said, "You'll love it. It's a fabulous feeling. It'll shock you but just keep on running and dive in if you can."

She had done the plunge twice before. Next to her was a virgin plunger like us. The virgin was still wearing her fleece jacket. "I'm keeping this on until the last minute. I hate the cold, but I figured I'd try it."

Spencer and I had made up signs, "Iceberg Ahead" and "Wish you were here, really!" My mom snapped a few pictures of us. I had a disposable camera with me so I could snap pictures of Spencer in the water just in case it became a mad house and Heidi and my mom couldn't get pictures of us. After all, we weren't going to stand there and pose.

The line stretched for blocks; 2,165 other nuts like us were ready to dive in. I looked around. There were people of every color and of all age groups. The youngest kids that year were a pair of fraternal twins, a boy and girl age eight. The horned lady said, "One year there was a man sixty-three years old doing it."

I looked at Spencer as if to say, "See?"

He just said, "Well, I'm doing it now, so I don't have to do it at sixty-three."

It was now 11:59, and a man in a bright orange jacket was standing in front of the lines and giving us a countdown. As he neared the final ten, the crowd started to join in "… three … two … one!" A whistle blew and thousands of plungers broke through the rope and made a mad dash toward the ocean.

Fran Capo

Spencer was right beside me. As my feet touched the water, I felt a shock go through my body. I mentally cheered myself on, "Keep on running, Capo. You have to go at least chest deep." All of a sudden I saw Spencer dive in headfirst. I tried to snap a picture of him. But before I could, he stood up with a look of pure shock on his face and started running toward shore. I yelled, "Wait! I didn't get a picture."

He said, "Sorry, Mom. I'm outta here."

Upset I didn't get the picture, I kept running in, looking for some Kodak moment. I noticed people were already going back to shore. As if awakened from a fog, I said, "What am I, nuts? I gotta get out of here!" By the time I touched the sand, my feet were numb. I looked down and my legs were bright red. Spencer was already toweling off.

I dried off, invigorated but happy it was over. And then we heard the dreaded words—words we hoped would never be uttered. Both my mom and Heidi in unison said, "There were too many people! You have guys have go back in; we couldn't snap a picture! All we got was flying arms and legs."

"What?! You've kidding, right?" I yelled. They shook their heads no.

I looked at Spencer. "Oh brother," he said. "Well, we came this far, Mom."

We both rolled our eyes and ran into the freezing water for a second time. I turned back and yelled, "Please! Make it quick!"

Heidi and mom came over as fast as they could and then asked us to pose. Pose?! It's was cold ... I wanted to be a polar bear, not be buried with one.

Then, just as they snapped the picture, someone ran by and blocked the shot. So, for a third time, we had to trek back in. This was starting to feel like a bad candid camera episode.

When Spencer and I finally came out for good, our feet were numb. It took a good two minutes for them to feel normal again. We put our clothes over our wet bathing suits and walked back to the car so we could change our clothes in the backseat. Spencer, feeling a little awkward doing that, opted to stay in his wet bathing suit. My mom, of course, was worried that he'd catch pneumonia, so she made

Adrenaline Adventures

sure she dried him off as much as possible. Just what every teenager wants, his grandmother towel drying him in a public parking lot.

Heidi and her friend had to leave now that the adventure was over. We thanked them for coming.

Now it was just the three Musketeers left. We went back to the tents and joined the other plungers in the hot lunch that they were serving. I asked Spencer in between bites if he'd liked the plunge. He nodded. "It was a good experience."

Then my curiosity got the best of me. "For someone who really didn't want to go, why did you decide to dive in headfirst?"

"Well, I figured if I was here I might as well go for the full experience. Isn't that what you always teach me? To experience life to the fullest?"

I smiled. "Wow, you listened. I'm really proud of you, Spence. I love you."

He nodded. "Yeah, but I'm still not doing it again."

We both laughed.

With our stomachs full and our feet dry, we drove home in silence thinking about our latest adventure. I was still trying to analyze why I get such a rush out of these things. But then I looked back at Spencer, who was sleeping peacefully with a big smile on his face, and then it hit me. This is what life is about. I feel so alive when I do these things, and very satisfied afterward. Our life clock ticks with each beat of our heart. I want mine to beat with enthusiasm. I don't want to waste a minute of it. I want to live life to the fullest, and if in doing so I can do good things and inspire others to push beyond their fears and do great things too, then that is a rich life. And if one of the people I happen to inspire most is my son, and if I pass on the love of life to him … well, that is worth its weight in gold, and it will always make me look for my next great adventure.

*Special thanks to all my friends and family who pledged money for our plunge. Spencer, I, and the Special Olympics appreciate it.

Fran Capo

Chapter 48
<u>**Adventure at a Glance - Dare to Do**</u>   <u>**Mild to Wild Scale: 4**</u>
Title: Doing the Polar Bear Plunge
Children allowed: Yes, with parental consent
Age requirement: Five and up
Length of trip: The actual plunge only takes one minute, but plan to stay for about half a day.
Where to try this adventure: Special Olympics New Jersey Jenkinson's Boardwalk, 3 Broadway Pt. Pleasant Beach, New Jersey or 3 Princess Road, Lawrenceville, NJ 08648
732-892-0844 or 800-650-SONJ
Web site: www.sonj.org
Best time of year: The last Sunday in February for this particular plunge. New Year's Day for most Polar Bear clubs.
Approximate cost: Each plunger has to raise a minimum of $100 to participate; incentive awards given for raising more.
Reservations necessary: Yes
Fitness requirements: None
Personal gear required: Bathing suit
What NOT to bring: Wetsuit, Vaseline
Photo opportunities: Yes

Notes: "Submerged head" is now part of the requirement. The famous Coney Island Polar Bear Club Plunge takes place every year on New Year's Day, as do many other polar bear club plunges around the country and world.

Cool trivia: Swimming in freezing, ice-cold water has been a tradition of the Polar Bear Club since 1920. There is scientific evidence that plunging into freezing water helps people with cardiovascular disease, asthma, arthritis, and eczema. People also claim it gives your skin a healthy glow and sheds wrinkles. It is also said that if you swim regularly in cold water, you don't tend to get the flu or other contagious diseases.

"Sometimes the seeds of happiness are sown in the darkness."
—Author Unknown

Chapter 49
"An Inward Adrenaline Rush" Floatation Tank

Since most of the adventures that I do have an overt outward adrenaline rush, I thought it might be nice to challenge myself to do what most people are frightened to do the most: face themselves – naked and in pure darkness, devoid of light and sound. To do this, I chose to try a floatation tank, also known as a sensory deprivation tank. In this tank you have nothing but your thoughts, and they say that in the stillness of the dark you learn your true self.

About fifteen years ago, a friend of mine, Keith, told me about floatation tanks, and I immediately wanted to try one. On that adventure, my sister, Sharon, chose to join us. Keith located a tank somewhere in Manhattan in some guy's apartment. The experience lasted forty-five minutes each. Since there was only one tank, we took turns waiting in the guy's living room for each other to finish. While in the tank, I remember feeling very strange at first, testing the limits of the tank and knowing my friends were out there waiting, but within minutes, I drifted off into a peaceful state. I came out feeling I could join some Ashram or Buddhist monk camp. I felt very one with the world and myself.

Fast forward a decade and change. My fiancé, Steve, called me from his office. "Fran, someone here has something to tell you." On a conference call I heard the voice of our mutual friend, Joe. Joe is Steve's ex-wife's new husband. We are all friends, and in fact, his name isn't Joe at all, its Steven. But the first time I saw him, he was playing the lead in an off-Broadway show and the character's name was Joe, so it stuck as a nickname. Joe is very animated. He got on the phone. "Fran, I thought of the greatest adventure for you. You always want to challenge yourself right?" I agreed. "Well, lots of people are claustrophobic and are scared to be in pure darkness. Well, imagine if you, the world's fastest talker, had to keep quiet, in total darkness, with no one to talk to but yourself. Now that would be an awesome challenge for you."

Adrenaline Adventures

I smiled. "Joe, I've already tried it. But I'll tell you what, I'll look into it again. All four of us can go, you, me, Steve, and your wife, Val."

There was a silence. "Wow … hmmm. Okay, I think I'm game."

"Great!" I said. After hanging up, I thought, how funny would it be to have an adventure that all the ex's could go on? It would be great for the family scrapbook.

I spent the next hour trying to locate the number of the place I had gone to years ago. It no longer existed. I did a search on the Web, and after a couple of leads found that although there were a few places that sold tanks, there was only one place left in New York that allows you to rent a tank by the hour. It was a place called Blue Light Floatation. It was run by a man named Sam Zieger. The price was very reasonable. Excited, I e-mailed the ex-gang about my discovery.

To my surprise, there were no takers. My Steve felt funny because the tank was in a guy's apartment. Joe said he was a bit claustrophobic, and Valerie saw no pleasure in it at all.

Now, of course, I was on a mission. I was curious to see if fifteen years later I would experience the same thing. How would time change my perception? Who could I ask to share in this adventure? I called Keith, who I knew would do it in a heartbeat, but he was out of the country.

Then I thought of the perfect candidate, a young, innocent mind, my son, Spencer. I approached Spencer with the idea. He just looked at me and laughed. "Mom, are you ever going to suggest something normal like the movies?"

"Yes, on a rainy day when I'm dead tired."

He agreed to go as long as he could keep his bathing suit on in the tank. "I'm not getting naked in some guy's apartment. How do I know he doesn't have a peephole or something?"

"Spencer, even if he did, you are going to be in total darkness."

"Well, what if he has some night vision lens set up?"

Leave it to a teen to think of all the James Bond stuff. "Spencer, keep your pants on then. I'm going to check this guy out anyway."

With that settled, I remembered that one of my best friends, Janette, had mentioned that she had done many floatations. I called and asked her who she used. Turned out it was the same guy. She raved about him, said she had gone to him for years and gave me the history of the place. Blue Light Floatation is a home-based office located on in the Chelsea district at 148 W 23rd Street in Sam's apartment. It has been in existence since 1985, making it the longest operating floatation service in the New York City. . It's been featured on *Live at Five, Eye on New York*, and the *Evening News*. It has been written about in *The Village Voice, New York Magazine, The New Yorker,* and *GQ Magazine.* I felt totally safe bringing Spencer there.

I called Blue Light Floatation and spoke to Sam. We made an appointment for the following Friday. Sam instructed us to eat light; not drink coffee, tea, or soda prior to coming, not to shave (as the salt in the tank would burn the skin), and to bring a towel and bathing suit, if we liked. Spencer smirked at that idea.

That Friday, on the way into Manhattan, we hit heavy traffic (imagine that, traffic in New York on a Friday) that caused us to be late for our appointment. This adventure was supposed to relax us, and already I felt myself getting stressed. I called Sam to let him know what was happening.

Since there is only one tank, Spencer and I were the only clients scheduled. The sessions are one hour long so it would be uncomfortable for others to be waiting. Sam schedules people with sufficient blocks of time, with room for relaxation afterward. We could keep our appointment.

After our apologies for being late, we took off our shoes and entered the apartment. The first thing I noticed was a soft smell of lavender in the air. In aromatherapy, lavender relaxes and is a stress reliever. I was sniffing hard.

Sam then showed us the flotation tank. It was inside another room. You entered one door, then closed it behind you to keep the heat in. The tank itself was like a giant bathtub except completely closed off by a sliding door. It was seven feet high, eight feet long, and four feet wide. Sam explained that the high ceiling allows the heat inside to be less humid. He showed us the two push- button control panels on the side. One button controls the light inside the tub, the other the sound from within the tank, which connects to an underground stereo system for those who want music or learning

Adrenaline Adventures

tapes instead of silence. Then he showed us the private shower area that we were to use before and after the tank.

After our brief tour, Sam brought us to his pristine office, which was surrounded with gorgeous pencil portraits. I later found out Sam had drawn them himself.

We sat on the leather couch, and Sam gave us a thorough introduction, "Even though floatation is a relatively new concept to our culture, the idea of trying to gain inner peace has been around for centuries with people who engage in yoga and mediation. Without having to learn any type of mantra, the floatation tank gives you that same experience. There is nothing you have to learn today; there is nothing you have to do. You just need to go inside and relax. The first thing I want you to do is to take a shower and use the special natural cleansing soap I have in there. I also need you to wash your hair to get rid of any chemical mildew you have from other shampoo. Once you do that, you simply go to the floatation room, open the door, and I close it quickly behind you to keep the heat in."

"How hot is the water?" I asked.

"The water is maintained at skin temperature of ninety-four degrees Fahrenheit, not internal body temperature of ninety-eight degrees or you would feel too hot. You will notice your skin will feel very soft and silky."

I joked, "Just what every teenage boy wants – soft and silky skin."

Spencer smirked. "Thanks, Ma."

We laughed. "Sorry, Sam, please continue."

"Well, there's not much more as far as what you have to do. Then you get in the tub and lie down on your back. The water is only ten inches deep, but you will float like a cork because of the high concentration of Epsom salt. Just relax and you will see you will not sink. Your ears will submerge in the water, but your head will stay afloat, which is the hardest part for people to feel comfortable with. Trust me, your head will not sink. Then, when you are ready, you turn off the lights and enjoy the experience."

"What if my head goes into the water by mistake and I get salt water in my eye?"

"Glad you asked, Spencer. At the front of the tub there is a squeeze bottle of fresh water. Just run it over your eyes. Remember, you have the buttons, at anytime you can turn the light back on. Also, if you are worried your head is going to go under, float with your hands behind your head and rest on them. Experiment to see which position is the most comfortable for you. At the end of

the hour, I will play music to let you know the session is over. Then take as much time as you like and get out. Once you are out, please rinse off in the shower to get the salt off your body. When you are finished, I will have a glass of herbal tea waiting for you. The tea helps you to stay hydrated and keeps you in the relaxed state."

Spencer chimed in, "Just out of curiosity, I mean, you keep your office clean and all, how clean is the tank with so many people going in it?"

"The floatation tank that you are going to go into today was completely renovated in 2001. It is designed for comfort and safety. Dissolved in the tank is one thousand pounds of Epson salts. The salt maintains a bacteria-free environment, which acts as a natural disinfectant. No organism of any kind can survive in it, bacteria, virus, yeast, mold, etc. But in addition, the entire volume of tank water is filtered and injected with ozone at the end of each session. I am proud to say I have one of the cleanest tanks in existence."

After hearing that description, I urgently felt the need to run home and clean my tub.

Spencer asked, "You clean with ozone? I thought ozone was bad for you?"

"Ozone (O3 to those chemists out there) is active oxygen, one of nature's basic elements. Spencer, you know how after a thunderstorm the air smells fresh? That's ozone. It's one of the safest, most effective water purifiers available. It makes the water soft and clean. And after the ozone cleans, it reverts to oxygen in about ten minutes. So it's better than any harmful cleaning chemicals."

"I feel like I'm taking a science class." Spencer smiled.

Sam continued, "You think *that's* science, listen to this. A lot of the clients that come here come because they are stressed from work. Stress produces harmful chemicals in the body, including excessive cotisol adrenaline and ACTH, which, by the way, is secreted forty times more in a Type A personality like your mother's, than in a Type B personality like yours. Anyway, these chemicals weaken the immune system. The floatation tank allows you to reach a deep state of relaxation, which reduces the buildup."

"So you mean by floating you are actually strengthening the immune system?" I asked.

"That's it in a nutshell."

"Pretty cool. But I'm not really stressed," Spencer said.

Sam continued, "Spencer, you're lucky. You know, you are actually my youngest floater at fourteen. Even though floatation is for anybody of any age, usually people come as stressed out adults. But a lot of times, I get clients who want to rehabilitate overworked muscles or who just want to improve their ability to concentrate. It also lowers blood pressure, cleanses the lactic acid and other body wastes, speeds healing, relieves pain from injury, creates brain wave patterns that slow the mind to learn information faster, if, like, let's say you put in learning tapes during your session. And the great thing is you will feel these effects right after and for about a week afterwards."

"Boy, that's a lot of stuff for one tank of water! Surprised more people don't use it," I said.

"Well, it's very popular in Great Britain, Australia, and New Zealand. And some of your comic buddies like Robin Williams use it. In fact, George Carlin owns his own tank. He calls it, Our Lady of Salt."

"That's cool to know, since Carlin is one of Spencer's and my favorite comics."

Sam smiled. "Who's going to go first?"

"Spencer, you do the honors." I motioned. Spencer nodded and went to the shower. We could hear the door of the tank opening. Then I saw a tiny light in a console go on. Sam saw me looking. "That's so I know if the light is off or on in the tank. Then he turned on a monitor. We could hear Spencer splashing inside. After a few minutes, the light went out and the water went still. Sam then turned off the monitor. He has relaxed now. It took him awhile.

But then, a few minutes later, we saw the light on again, then off, then on.

Fran Capo

Later I found out Spencer had gotten some salt in his eyes.

While Spencer was in the tank, Sam showed me his pencil drawings. They were fantastic. So much detail and so lifelike. Sam checked on Spencer by turning on the monitor. He was splashing around at times. When the hour was up, Sam played the music and signaled Spencer to come out. Spencer rinsed the salt off in the shower, but I could still see dried salt in his ears.

Sam gave him the herbal tea, and Spencer laid on the couch listening to some peaceful music.

Now it was my turn. I showered, feeling a bit awkward. Then I went into the tank room. I lay on my back, turned off the lights, and began to float. I noticed I felt extremely tense. I tried to do deep breathing exercises, but the stress remained. I gently pushed myself so I floated around the tub until I felt the walls. Then I would push myself off again. I liked the slow floating motion, but I still felt tense. I was tense about not relaxing.

I tried again to analyze myself. I wasn't scared of the dark. The water was the perfect temperature and felt silky on my skin. I wasn't scared of drowning. So what was the problem? Too much thinking, I thought. My mind would just not quiet itself. Thousands of thoughts kept racing through my head. I had taken meditation before, how come I couldn't relax? Maybe I was worried my head would sink. I tried holding my head up. That wasn't very comfortable. I thought of rolling on my stomach, but somehow, being face down in heavy salt water didn't seem like a bright idea.

So, I decided to start again. I turned on the light and sat up. I took a deep breath and then gently laid back. I just stared into the darkness. The thoughts slowly crept in again, and started to build up speed. I wanted to know what Spencer was thinking. I wanted to know how long I had been in. I wanted to know why I couldn't drift off into relaxation. Could it be that fifteen more years of life had made my mind a runaway train? I know in meditation they say to let your thoughts flow like in a river, don't fight them, just go with them. But there were too many. Had I lost the ability to just be? Maybe Joe was right, this would be a hard challenge for me. How do people make it in solitary confinement? I didn't feel the need to talk, but I did feel the need to yell "SHUT UP!" to my brain.

Adrenaline Adventures

Then I decided not to be so hard on myself. This was my experience and whatever it was was fine. Once I stopped judging myself, somewhere in all that

mental chatter, I drifted off. Time is distorted with no sensory references. I remember feeling as peaceful as if I had fallen asleep, but I knew I hadn't. When I gave up the fight with myself, it all fell into place. But I became my own worst enemy; once I realized I had relaxed, I was trying to figure out how I'd done it. And so the thoughts began again, but this time I had an added challenge. It started as a light sensation, but then the pressure built up. I had to go to the bathroom—badly. Great! Do I get out and interrupt the session. Do I see how long I can hold it? Do I pee in the tub? (Don't worry I didn't – it was just a thought.)

The last ten minutes became a battle between my bladder and relaxation. I was hoping the music would come on so I could sprint to the bathroom. Somehow that challenged me. Testing to see if I could make it to the bell. Well, I did and I barely made it to the bathroom.

After the shower, I came out feeling crystal clean. My hair squeaked. Spencer was sleeping with a smile on his face. He looked extremely relaxed. As for me, I was relieved to be out of the tank – it was too intense. Yet I found the whole experience fascinating in that it showed me myself. I talked to Sam about the experience. He said, "Sometimes it just takes time to trust yourself again and let go."

It's strange how we as humans just live our lives and don't realize how much stress we carry around until you have the stillness to amplify it. It was a great learning experience.

Sam reminded us to drink lots of water all day long since the floatation tank tends to dehydrate you. He also told us to watch how we see the world differently.

We just nodded, thinking this was some kind of grandiose claim. But sure enough as Spencer and I walked out onto the busy city streets, the city seemed dirtier, the colors more intense, the noise louder. Every action was more perceptible. Yet we felt we were in slow motion and were more peaceful. It was as if we were floating and everyone else was just rushing and walking around us. It was like the windshield wipers of our eyes had been cleared.

Fran Capo

It wasn't my typical adventure, but it was worth doing. Adventure is defined as an unusual, stirring experience. The tank gave me that. In slowing my body down I was able to see my mind race ahead. Sometimes the challenges in life come not in how high you jump or how fast you go, but how deep you are willing to dive into yourself to find the truth. I dove, but I had kept sight of the shore. Next time I will go deeper. This is an adventure that I know I will keep exploring for all the days of my life.

Adrenaline Adventures

Chapter 49
Adventure at a Glance - Dare to Do it   Mild to Wild Scale: 1
Title: Floatation Tank
Children allowed: Yes, with parental consent
Age requirement: None. At fourteen, Spencer was the youngest person to have used this tank.
Length of trip: One hour
Where to try this adventure: Blue Light Floatation - Sam Zeiger (212) 989-6061
e-mail: Zottoman@aol.com
www.bluelightfloatation.com
Best time of year: All year round, Monday through Saturday
Approximate cost: $60 for one hour/$150 for a three-sessions
Reservations necessary: Yes
Fitness requirements: None
Personal gear required: eat light; do not drink coffee, tea, or soda prior to coming; do not shave (as the salt in the tank would burn the skin), and bring a towel and bathing suit.
What NOT to bring: Tight clothes
Photo opportunities: No

Notes: You need to go on a day when you have plenty of time so you are not stressed about getting somewhere afterward. The tank is the perfect solution if you need to unwind but don't have the cash to fly to an exotic island for a few days.

Cool trivia: There are over one hundred universities and medical research facilities, several dozen sports science units, and at least two national sports institutes working with floatation REST.

The effects of floating have been scientifically researched and documented since the first tank was built - as a research tool - more than forty years ago. Floatation REST even played a part in NASA astronaut training programs. Some studies have even shown that floatation tanks are instrumental in eliminating addictive behavior.

"Stress is not an event, but a reaction based upon our perception of the event."
—Fran Capo

Chapter 50
"This Ain't Coney Island!"
Two World Record Rides

Growing up in New York, the big thrill was being able to ride the Cyclone roller coaster in Coney Island, over and over again. The wooden slats on the coaster made you feel that at any moment that baby could become skybound and jerk you right into space. But you always survived and lived to ride another day.

I thought it fitting for the last chapter in *Adrenaline Adventures* to do two things: end with a story about me and my good friend, Viv, who this book started out with in the first place and talk about two awesome high-adrenaline rides that I rode on within a week of each other, and which, for thrill seekers, are a must.

Adrenaline Adventures

The first ride is The Big Shot, which sits on top of the Stratosphere Hotel and Casino in Las Vegas, Nevada. This modern wonder opened on Monday, April 29, 1996, after two years of setbacks and ridicule. On that grand opening night, ten thousand special guests came to experience the ride of their lives, plus free food and drinks.

To give you an idea of how high up this ride is, let's first look at the place on which it sits. The Stratosphere has the tallest observation tower in the U.S. and looms high over the Las Vegas skyline at 921 feet, which is higher than the Eiffel Tower. You can see the entire Vegas Strip from the top of the Stratosphere, including a replica of the Cyclone at the New York, New York Hotel.

Add on top of that observation tower height another 160 feet and you have the ride called The Big Shot. The Big Shot's claim to fame is that it shoots you up in the air at forty-five miles per hour, taking you from the 921-foot level of the top of the Stratosphere to 1,081 above the earth in 2.5 seconds. My kind of ride!

And get this, the tower was originally supposed to be considerably higher. But the FAA (Federal Aviation Administration) nixed that. They determined that building the tower any higher would put it directly in the path of one of the alternate flight routes for planes at McCarran Airport, which is only a couple of miles from there.

Can you imagine having a ride so tall that the riders would interfere with air traffic? Imagine being some poor business-class passenger minding your own business and the next thing you know someone comes crashing into the bottom of your Boeing 747. Not a good idea. With their first plan foiled, the Stratosphere Corporation decided to keep the height of the tower to a mere 135 stories and build the current attractions at the top instead, still making it the tallest building west of the Mississippi.

So naturally, while my mom, Rose; my son, Spencer; my fiancé, Steve; and I were in Vegas, I thought it would be fun for all of us to experience The Big Shot ride first hand. Steve had a ruptured disc so he had an excuse not to ride. My mom hates heights but was willing to go to the observation tower with Spencer and me. She figured she would be closer to God up there and so her prayers of our safe return would be heard faster from inside the Stratosphere gift shop. She stayed inside the gift shop, mind you, because the view out the glass observation deck was too dizzying for her. I told her she was much higher when she rode in the blimp, but she didn't care.

Spencer and I kissed her and told her we'd be fine. Then we giggled and ran to buy our tickets. With tickets in hand, we took the elevator up to The Big Shot. It wasn't until we stepped out onto the platform where the ride was that we realized how high up we really were. We were far above anything else. Just that alone was awesome and added to our anticipation. We both love high-adrenaline rides, and this was one of the ultimate.

The wait was short, which is always good for rides like this since it gives the person less chance to back out. In the time we waited, we were able to read the short info blurb about the ride on a nearby sign. "The Big Shot is a zero-gravity simulator consisting of a 192-foot steel tower. It seats sixteen riders, four per side. The riders are strapped in and then anxiously wait to be catapulted into the sky. It zooms 160 feet to the top and then free-falls back to the launch pad at the bottom. The rider will hit 4 G's on the way up and then 0 G's as they float out of their seats on the way down."

I turned to Spencer. "Four G's, that's more than in my air combat flight!"

Spencer laughed. "Hey, you wanted a ride, Ma, and now you're gonna get it! Are you scared?"

I shook my head no, but that wasn't exactly the truth.

"Are you scared?" I asked.

Spencer smiled. "Nope. I get my nerves from you."

Before we could play more mind games, it was our turn. We were instructed to choose a seat. The ride wasn't full, so Spencer and I sat on a side by ourselves. The ride operator came around and made sure we were strapped in securely and that the shoulder harnesses were on tight. I pushed the harnesses down farther on both Spencer and myself, just to make sure we were bolted in place.

Then we heard a giant swish sound—the sound the engine makes right before it's ready to blast off. My stomach felt nervous, and Spencer and I quickly smiled at each other. Then, before we could turn our heads back, we were jetted toward the abyss … far above EVERYTHING else in Vegas. I saw blurs of birds below us. My face was stretched back like a woman with too many face lifts. Then, just

Adrenaline Adventures

as I thought we were going to break the machine and be launched into space, the ride plummeted downward and we were lifted out of our seats. We zoomed up again, and then down again. In less than a minute it was all over. The view, what I saw of it, was awesome. We survived the highest thrill ride in the world. We got off smiling.

Before we could exit the ride, we were offered the option to either ride The Big Shot again or to try their other sky ride, The High Roller, but this time at a fraction of the cost. Since we were already up there, we sprang for the extra bucks; most people do. It's all sales psychology, and we happily played along.

We decided to give the other roller coaster a try. It seemed pretty tame compared to The Big Shot. The High Roller carries thirty-six riders at a time in nine cars and makes three clockwise rotations while banking sharply at a thirty-two-degree angle. Okay, it is hanging off the edge of the Stratosphere, which does add to the excitement, but, really, how could a mere circle around the perimeter of the building be that scary? Imagine our surprise when we found out the coaster made some dips and that the angle at which the ride was pitched made you feel like you would be spilled out, which is always a nice added touch when there is no ground below you for one thousand feet.

After having our thrills, we came downstairs with our souvenir pictures in hand. Since we had stayed up there a little longer than anticipated, we had to lift my mom off the floor of the gift store and tell her to put her rosary beads away. She kissed us, looked at the pictures, and said, "You're nuts!" With everyone in tact we went on to explore the rest of Vegas.

A week later, my son and I drove twelve hours to Toledo, Ohio, to visit my friend Viv (the scientist) and her family, which consisted of her husband, Bill, (another scientist) and their eleven-year-old twins, Rachel and Mark.

Every year since we were kids, we've tried to plan a fun adventure for our birthdays together. My birthday is on July 29, and Viv's (and the twins') is on July 30. It's been difficult to find the time to get together lately, and for four years in a row, we didn't do it. We were determined to make it happen this year. We planned it for months. So even though my transmission blew on my car, we didn't let it stop us. I rented a car, and Viv graciously offered to split the cost. With a reliable set of wheels, Spencer and I drove out to Ohio.

Our plan was to go to Cedar Point in Sandusky, Ohio, to ride the world's tallest and fastest roller coaster. Hey, if we were going to celebrate, we wanted to do it in style.

Cedar Point is known as the roller coaster capital of the world, having the largest amount of roller coasters on the planet, sixteen to be exact, four of which are over two hundred feet tall. It has been voted Best Amusement Theme Park in the world five years in a row by *Amusement Today*.

As soon as we entered the park, we headed over to the park's latest edition, The Dragster—a twenty-five million dollar ride that is shaped like a giant inverted letter U.

The racing-car-like seats have red and white steel around them. Each Dragster sits sixteen thrill-seekers comfortably in a tiered seating—this way everyone can have a good view as the Dragster hurls its victims 420 feet straight up at 120 miles per hour in less than four seconds. That's a height equivalent to forty-two stories in less that four seconds!

Once you have reached the pinnacle of the tower's height, you go over the top, and then you bank, do a 270-degree spiral, and hit near free-fall as you plummet to the earth at a ninety-degree angle. The magnetic braking system brings you to a halt so you can catch your heart just before it leaps out of your mouth.

Just the thought of it was making my adrenaline flow. It's the first roller coaster ever to drop four hundred feet, the first one to reach speeds of 120 miles per hour, and the first "strata-coaster" built on the planet—three world records!

Spencer mentioned that he didn't want to ride on the Dragster with me because I never scream and never get scared. He's right—I don't scream. I brace myself, take a deep breath, feel my nerves, and inwardly yell my head off. I am scared, but on the outside, I look calm. It's a good poker trick. Besides, my philosophy has always been fear nothing, but if you do, do it anyway.

Spencer, on the other hand, gets a kick out of watching people freak out on the rides; to him, that's half the fun. So he decided he would ride it with Mark, a younger version of Spencer. The two of them figured they would try to scare each other.

Bill wasn't about to ride the Dragster, Rachel was out, and Viv gave me all the scientific reasons that we shouldn't do it. "Fran, you know the G's involved are intense. And the fact is, even if you don't admit your age, we are older than we were when we did our first adventure. I mean, we could have a stroke. Not to mention the fact that the ride was out of commission most of June and the Swiss engineer who built it was being called back to find out why sometimes the ride didn't make it over the hump."

"Viv, I think the answer is simple. I think the ride not making it over the top depends on the weight of the people on the ride. If you have some fat ass in the back, you're going to get stuck. I mean, there are signs up front telling you that guests of exceptional size may have difficulty on this ride. In fact, I remember seeing a Discovery show about a roller coaster ride in Japan where the people are weighed in while on the roaster coaster before it takes off so the computer can make adjustments to the pressure applied for the ride to take off. Makes sense. And as for the age thing … I don't know what you're talking about … I'm the same age I always was. I can't help it if people around me keep getting older."

Viv smirked. "Okay, together we could write a dissertation. I'll think about it."

"Well at least that's a good start."

We were at the beast. We all looked up at the Dragster. Looking at something in pictures is one thing, while seeing it up front is quite another. Unfortunately, there was one problem. The Dragster wasn't working. We questioned a nearby ride attendant and were told it would open later in the day, that they were making some "adjustments."

Viv looked at me as if to say, "See, I told you so."

I looked around for the Swiss engineer, but the closest thing I saw was someone drinking Swiss Miss Hot Chocolate. So we busied ourselves going on a bunch of other rides.

It was a cloudy day, so there weren't many people at Cedar Point, which made the wait to get on the rides extremely short. On some rides, there wasn't even a line. It was amusement park paradise.

Fran Capo

After a few hours, the Dragster still had not opened and the skies started looking ominous. We decided to go on the world's third largest roller coaster, The Millennium Force. It was the largest roller coaster in the world until the year 2000, when the Japanese built one higher. Now the Millennium Force is the second largest and fastest roller coaster in the Northern Hemisphere, and the third largest in the world, still not a bad claim to fame.

The Millennium Force is another twenty-five-million-dollar investment, which seems to be the going rate for building these coasters. It's a 310-foot-tall mountain of steel. It set an incredible ten world records when it opened as the fourteenth coaster in the park. One of its records was for being the first roller coaster anywhere in the world to break the three-hundred-foot barrier. It also was the first coaster to use an elevator lift system to take riders up a forty-degree angle to the top of the imposing structure. Once at the top, the Millennium plummets down ninety-three miles per hour at an eighty-degree angle, which is almost straight down.

Then it takes riders along 6,595 feet of track that winds through the center of the park, crosses a lagoon, and dives onto an island. This coaster sounded right up my alley.

Viv, Spencer, Mark, and I waited on line. Bill and Rachel went off to play elsewhere. It was only about a twenty-minute wait, which is almost a world record itself in a amusement park of this size. But then again, most people don't like to ride fast metal objects in the rain. Even though it wasn't raining yet, it was about to at any moment. We just hoped we could get on this ride in time.

Since this was the first time any of us had ridden this ride, we were all anxious. Spencer and Mark had been riding rides together all day long. Viv and I were going to do this one together. As we got closer, the metal beast looked awesome. The cool part about this coaster is that the ride lasts two minutes and twenty seconds, so you really get your money's worth. There's nothing more aggravating than waiting three hours for a ten-second ride!

On line we talked to other people who had ridden the Millennium. They all said it was one of the best coasters they've ridden in their lives. Which is a pretty big claim, considering they were roller coaster aficionados.

Adrenaline Adventures

As we inched closer, I could feel my stomach getting a little antsy. Then a strange thing happened. All of a sudden all eyes turned to the next ride over—the Dragster. The Capo di Tutti of coasters started running. We heard the screams of the people on board. Viv and I just looked at each other. Spencer and Mark high-fived each other.

Now all my fears about the Millennium were gone. I was going to have to ride the Dragster after all. I had no excuse not to. Spencer and I looked at each other, both thinking the same thing.

Viv observed the ride for a few minutes then uttered, "Uh un, no way I'm riding that."

Mark was ready to jump off the line and run to the Dragster. We were all trying to decide if we should leave the line and head over to the Dragster before the rain clouds broke. A moment of decision was at hand. Ride the world's largest coaster, which was just opening up, or stay on this line and ride a proven fantastic coaster.

As we were about to make a break for the Dragster, Viv stopped us. "Look!"

She pointed. We had no clue what she was pointing at. "Look, guys, there are no passengers on that ride."

We all squinted to get a better look. Sure enough, no one was on the Dragster. Then we heard screams again and realized that what we thought was screaming coming from the Dragster was actually coming from the Millennium. As we watched, the Dragster got stuck at the top of the tower; it stayed at the pinnacle for a moment and then rolled backward to the starting gate. Then the ride stopped altogether. I could feel my heart stop and I wasn't even on the ride.

We all breathed a sigh of both relief and disappointment. Our thoughts shifted again to the coaster at hand.

We were up next. Spencer decided at the last minute that he wanted to ride with me. So much for my not screaming.

All day long Spencer had waited until he was strapped in a ride and then yelled out, "Wait! I've changed my mind. Please ... I have a heart condition." He just wanted to see people's reaction. He looked at me and I must have looked scared because he said, "Maybe I better not scream out loud."

Viv and Mark were strapped into the car in back of us. Viv screamed, "Fran, I'm going to kill you. I can't believe we are doing this!"

Mark laughed.

I said, "If it's any consolation, Viv, I'm scared too."

"What? You've skydived from thirteen thousand feet!"

"Yeah, but each adventure brings a new fear to overcome!"

Before I could say anything else, we were launched up a 310-foot hill. To my left was Lake Erie. We kept going up and up. Going up is the scariest part, because you know what's coming next. My heart was beating fast, and I dug my feet into the floor. The unsettling part was there were no sides of the ride to grab onto. No support. There weren't even shoulder straps, just a lap bar and seat belts. I braced myself. Spencer and I quickly glanced at each other. The next thing I knew we peaked over the top and were heading toward the earth at ninety-three miles per hour.

I heard Spencer and Mark scream, and all I heard from Viv was, "FRANNNNNNNNN!"

In an instant, we were zooming along the smooth tubular tracks. What a rush! There was no jolting, no jarring, no feeling like your head was going to get a concussion from banging on the sides of the ride ... just a pure adrenaline rush.

As we recovered from the first hill, we were sent up another 169-foot hill, then a third hill of 182 feet.

On the curves, we were extremely banked, not to the point of inversion, but to the point where I thought I might just fall out. We dove down more hills and sped through tunnels and continued on a wild journey over thirteen acres of the park's land. Two minutes and twenty seconds later, we came to a stop.

It was the coolest, fastest, tallest, and longest roller coaster ride I had ever been on in my entire life! We immediately wanted to do it again. But the second, and I mean the second, we got off the ride, we saw lighting. By the time we walked down the steps off of the ride, rain was pouring down. Talk about just making it.

Because of the thunder and lighting, they closed all the rides. We met up with Bill and Rachel in the arcade and hung out for a while, but after riding the Millennium, everything else was anticlimactic. The rain didn't let up, so we left the park shortly after.

We talked about how exciting the ride was. Bill said he was proud of Viv for going on the ride. Rachel was still not convinced. Mark and Spencer joked about who was more scared. Viv and I hugged each other and said, "Definitely a birthday to remember."

When our two-day trip was over, Viv and I vowed to meet again the next year.

I told her that I definitely wanted to come back, not only to ride the Millennium again, but next time to try the Dragster.

Viv gave me a look and I immediately followed that up with, "Of course, they have to have the kinks worked out by then."

Viv smiled. "We have a whole year to plan it."

"I know, Viv, but just think about it."

"Fran, with you I always do."

We hugged, knowing that our friendship, as always, would be one adventure after another, and what was really cool was that we were passing the adventure spirit onto our kids.

Fran Capo

Chapter 50- Two World Record Rides - RIDE ONE
Adventure at a Glance - Dare to Do it   Mild to Wild Scale: 5

Title: The Big Shot
Children allowed: Yes
Age requirement: You must be at least 48 inches tall to ride.
Length of trip: One minute
Where to try this adventure: Big Shot at the Stratosphere
2000 S. Las Vegas Blvd., Las Vegas, NV 89104
(702) 380-7777 or (800) 99-TOWER
Best time of year: All year round
Approximate cost: $15 (includes admission to Stratosphere Tower). Tickets to ride both The Big Shot and X Scream are $19. An all-day ride pass is available for $24.95.
Reservations necessary: No
Fitness requirements: Must be in good health, with no back or heart problems, and not pregnant.
Personal gear required: None
What NOT to bring: Loose items
Photo opportunities: Yes, they offer a photo for purchase.

Notes: If you are scared of heights, this is NOT the ride for you.

Cool trivia: The indoor deck of the Stratosphere is referred to as a "pod" because it stands on three legs. Because of the three legs, the glass angles outward, so you can really look down on the city. The indoor deck is also the loading area for the riders. Those afraid of heights are better off on the outdoor deck, where they can watch the riders scream and snap some pictures.

Those not trying the rides will get a kick out of the elevators. They travel 1,800 feet a minute. The total time from the ground level to the pod is thirty seconds.

The tower also features the revolving Top of the World Restaurant and Lounge, which rotates 360 degrees in an hour.

Adrenaline Adventures

Chapter 50- Two World Record Rides – RIDE TWO
<u>**Adventure at a Glance - Dare to Do it   Mild to Wild Scale: 5**</u>
Title: Millennium Force
Children allowed: Yes
Age requirement: You must be at least 48 inches tall to ride.
Length of trip: Two minutes and twenty seconds
Where to try this adventure: Cedar Point Park
One Cedar Point Dr., Sandusky, OH 44870-5259
Call (419)-627-2350 or visit Web site: www.cedarpoint.com
Best time of year: Summer, spring, fall
Approximate cost: General admission to the park is $43.95 for age 3 and older, 48 inches and taller. There are many discount packages.
Reservations necessary: No
Fitness requirements: Riders must be at least 48 inches tall, in good health, with no back, neck, or heart problems, and not pregnant. Also, guests who exceed 6'2", or those who exceed 250 pounds, or who have more than a 46" waistline or 54" chest may experience difficulty on this and some other Cedar Point rides.
Personal gear required: None
What NOT to bring: Loose items
Photo opportunities: Yes, they offer you a picture for sale.

Notes: Not for the faint of heart.

Cool trivia: Cedar Point first opened in 1870 on the banks of Lake Erie. This historic park is the second oldest continually operated amusement park in North America. The early Cedar Point had a massive structure called the Grand Pavilion, which was the center of resort activities for many years. Then, in 1892, they built the granddaddy of today's roller coasters near the Grand Pavilion. The Switchback Railway coaster was a whooping twenty-five feet tall. Riders would accelerate to the then-unbelievable speed of ten miles per hour. Since there was no chain lift, the cars had to be manually hauled to the top with nothing other than muscle power. Now those are people who really wanted a ride!

FINAL NOTE

Well, that's it, folks—fifty personal adventures packed into one book. I stopped there not because I ran out of adventures—in fact I already have ten more that I will write about in my new book—but because I wanted to give you a breather, a chance to get out there and try some of these adventures. Hey, try all of them!

I once read a saying by Charles Schwabb, "The ability to arouse enthusiasm among people is one of the greatest assets to possess, and the way to develop the best in a person is by appreciation and encouragement."

If anything, I hope I have made you laugh and encouraged you to try something new. In life, it doesn't matter if you fear something, it matters that you feared it but did it anyway.

Fear may knock at your door, but if you let faith answer it, you will find no one is there. Go with faith, go with fun, go with adventure in your heart, and live a life full of passion.

And remember, if you have a dream, no matter how crazy it seems to others ... please do everything you can to achieve it. This is your life, and you write the script.

I hope to see you on my next adventure.

Check out Fran Capo's other books

To order, simply circle the amount and put a checkmark next to the item(s) you want.

How to Get Publicity Without a Publicist: (An easy step by step guide to getting yourself in the newspapers, on radio and TV)
$20.00 U.S. / $23.00 Can   Check here to order ___

From building a dynamite press kit to developing a catchy hook, from the differences between how to do a radio interview as opposed to a TV interview, this book will guide you and prepare you to deal with reporters and all aspects of the media to get the highest exposure possible for you or your business.

The Humor Approach: A Guide to Humor in Speaking.
$20.00 U.S. / $23.00 Can   Check here to order ___

Learn the tricks that the professionals use to add punch to your presentations. This book will show you the pitfalls to avoid when using humor, tips on how to make a joke funnier, delivery techniques, when to use humor, and how to select the appropriate humor for each occasion. Whether you're a teacher, a corporate executive, a lawyer, a fundraiser, or a salesman, this book will help you add sparkle to your speech.

How to Break into Voiceovers: An Itty Bitty Guide to Big Business
$20.00 U.S. / $23.00 Can   Check here to order ___

Learn how to: get a dynamite demo tape, audition, get an agent, get your first job, and look professional your first time out. Complete with interviews from agents, producers, and editors.

It Happened in New York (published by TwoDot Books, an imprint of Falcon Publishing)
ISBN I-56044-899-7
$9.95 U.S. / $12.00 Can   Check here to order ___

Thirty true, fascinating events that helped make New York what it is today, told with a comedic yet dramatic flair. Read about the purchase of Manhattan from the wrong set of Indians; how Woodstock started as a sitcom idea; the world's greatest hoax; how they turned off Niagara Falls; and much more! Also includes a trivia section!

It Happened in New Jersey (published by The Globe Pequot Press)
ISBN 0-7627-2358-0
 $9.95 U.S. / $12.00 Can   Check here to order ___

It Happened in New Jersey details thirty true, fascinating events that shaped the state of New Jersey. Learn about the ghosts that swindled money out of Morristown residents, the first terrorist attack on the United States, the fight of the century, and much more. Plus a special trivia section.

Audio Tapes Available:
Fran's Fast Fractured Fairy Tales
$10.00 U.S. / $12.00 Can   Check here to order ___

A collection of modern day, humorous, sarcastic bedtime stories told at the speed of light by The World's Fastest Talking Female.

Look for Fran's upcoming books

Hopeville—The City of Light
(Due out August 2004)
An enchanting story about four people who change a city in the most unusual way. It is powerful in its simplicity, and inspiring in its wisdom.

It Happened in Pennsylvania (published by The Globe Pequot Press)
(Due out March 2005)
The third book in the *It Happened in* series by this author. Thirty true tales of events that made Pennsylvania what it is today. Find out the real story of how Pennsylvania got its land, the story of a million dollar baby, and the story of the worst pollution disaster in history. Also includes a special trivia section.

Adrenaline Adventures II: Dream it, Read it. Do it!
(Due out April 2006)
Fran's follow-up book to *Adrenaline Adventures*. Featuring twenty-five more high adrenaline stories, from a climb of Kilimanjaro to hang-gliding, dirt biking, and much more. These stories will inform, entertain, and motivate readers to enjoy life and follow their dreams!

You can order any of these items online through www.francapo.com.
Or copy this page, check off the items you want, and send a check or money order to:
Fran Capo, P.O. Box 272
Flushing, NY 11358
To learn about and see a video of Fran Capo's corporate events, lectures, articles, stand-up, cybersitcom, and booking information go to www.francapo.com or e-mail Fran at FranCNY@aol.com

Name_____ Quantity _____ Total cost $_____
Address_____ Add $2 S& H for each item_____
City and Zip_____
E-mail address _____
If you would like to be put on Fran's e-mailing list, check here ____
Autograph the book(s) to: (write clearly please)
_____
Books will be mailed out the same day the order is received. Allow 1-2 weeks for delivery.

About the Author

Fran Capo is a stand-up comic, actress, voiceover artist, motivational speaker, freelance writer, adventurer, hypnotherapist, seven-time author, and co-creator of the award winning cybersitcom **The Estrogen Files: Money, Men and Motherhood** at www.TheEstrogenFiles.Net.

She is also the Guinness Book of World Record's Fastest Talking Female as seen on *Ripley's Believe it or Not*, *Larry King Live* and The Discovery Channel, Fox and Family and *Last Call with Carson Daly*. This Queens College graduate has been on over 1,000 radio shows, 250 television shows, and featured in numerous books, Fran is the proud mother of Spencer Patterson (the world's youngest comic). To learn more about Fran Capo go to www.francapo.com.

Printed in the United Kingdom
by Lightning Source UK Ltd.
101304UKS00003B/1-21